Tribal India

Other Published Books of The Author

- Sociology of Marginalised Communities and Weaker Sections of India, 2021
- Shia Muslims of India, 2021
- Handbook of Sociology, 2020
- Indian Society: Themes and Social Issues, 2019
- The Other Lucknow: Ethnographic Portrait of a City of Undying Memories and Nostalgia, 2016
  (Also available in Hindi)
- India's Current Social Problems (co-authored), 2014
  (Also available in Hindi)
- Contested Identities in the Globalised world (co-edited), 2013
- Anthropology in India (co-edited), 2010
- A Study of Women's Problematic (co-edited), 2009
- Towards Empowering Indian Women (co-edited), 2007
- The Indian State and Womens' Problematics (co-edited)
- Beyond Textual Islam, 2007
- Aspects of Islam and Muslim Societies, 2006
- Islam and Muslim Communities of South Asia, 2005
- OBC's in the Process of Change (co-edited), 2005
- Indian Society and Culture: Continuity and Change, 2004
  (Also available in Hindi)
- Introducing Social and Cultural Anthropology (cd-authored), 2004
  (Also available in Hindi)
- Indian Anthropology, 1998
  (Also available in Hindi and Telegu)
- General Anthropology, 1997
  (Also available in Hindi)
- Bonded for Ever, 1982
  (Also available in Hindi)

Tribal India

Nadeem Hasnain

Former Professor of Social Anthropology
Department of Anthropology
University of Lucknow,
Lucknow

PALAKA PRAKASHAN
palakaprakashan@gmail.com

₹ 360/-

ISBN 9788185799766

1st Edition	:	1991
6th Edition	:	2001
7th Revised, Expanded & Updated Edition	:	2019
9th Reprint (7th edition)	:	2020
8th Revised, Expanded & Updated Edition	:	2022
Reprint (8th edition) Jan	:	2023

Editor (Social & Biological Series)
N.K. VAID
Director, Vaid's ICS
Delhi

PALAKA PRAKASHAN

AC-177B, Shalimar Bagh, Delhi - 110088
1244A/84, Shanti Nagar, Tri Nagar, Delhi - 110035
Ph. : +91 - 8744884844 /9873921850
palakaprakashan@gmail.com **www.palakaprakashan.com**

Printed at Sanjay Printer, Delhi.

Dedicated
to
Mangroo
(a Kolta from Jounsar Bawar)

This world may be worth living only when you and your children would be treated as equals and walk under the sun with heads high.

PREFACE TO THE PRESENT EDITION

I write these lines for the Eighth revised and expanded edition with pleasure as well as sadness. As the author I feel so happy to share with you that Tribal India and Indian Anthropology have been enjoying popularity and trust of the readers for more than 30 years with eight editions and dozens of reprints and during this period no other book on the same topic could replace these books. Obviously, it is a matter of great pride and happiness for any author. The sadness has also crept into my mind as the dishonest and unscrupulous elements, taking advantage of the new technology, are not only spreading the iliegal pdf version of the text but also producing and selling it in the print format causing financial losses to the publisher of the book. Obviously, if this is not checked no publisher will be publishing such useful books bearing losses and the authors shall not be writing and revising the text. **It is the responsibility of the readers/buyers not to buy such pirated versions.**

The readers shall find several new things in this edition. **Latest data and analysis have been added wherever required along with new laws/regulations. Beside these, some new chapters have been added in the light of questions asked during recent years. These are Tribal Movements, Tribal Women, Indigenous Knowledge System of the tribal communities and its preservation, Summary of Xaxa Committee Report** and some other relevant items.

This is my earnest hope that you would find this revised and expanded edition more useful. I would continue to welcome your feedback and suggestions for making the book more helpful and useful for you. I shall also expect you to spread the word against buying illegal and pirated editions and tell your friends and others in your circle not to do this for the sake of saving some money at the cost of the author and the publisher.

Happy reading

January, 2022
Lucknow

Nadeem Hasnain
(nadeemhasnain@gmail.com)

PREFACE

INDIA has always been described as a 'melting pot' of races and cultures. The colourful and the amazingly heterogenous mosaid of human affairs that the Indian society is, also dotted with ugly spots of lack of tolerance, harassment, erosion in rights and privileges and outright exploitation of many of its segment. "Tribal India" is the most glaring example of this exploitation indifference and lack of appreciation for our divergent minority groups.

THE present book is a humble attempt to study the tribal life in India in all it's dimensions. The tremendous popularity Tribal India has enjoyed during the last seven years of it's publication among the students of Anthropology, Sociology, Geography, Economics and other disciplines, the trust it has enjoyed among the aspirants of Civil Services opting anthropology, the way development administrators, voluntary agencies, etc. have been using it as a reference book should be taken as a compliment and tribute to the growing popularity of anthropology on the one hand and icreasing conciousness about a relatively lesser known segment of Indian society. The author is overwhelmed by this tremendous response and it has given him inspiration to take up similar academic ventures.

ACKNOWLEDGEMENTS

WHENEVER Tribal India Today is referred to as one of the most popular and largest selling books in anthropology during the last 4-5 decades, my thoughts immediately go back to the early eighties and to a person called *Zamir Ansari* (*Ansari Saheb*), a highly respected name in Indian book trade, who is instrumental in helping my academic ventures achieve a sound take off. I have learnt a lot from him. My cousin and friend Suhail Abidi has always been a constant source of encouragement and help in various ways. My friend and associate Mr. N.K. Vaid (Director, Vaid's ICS Regd.) has helped in it's present format. My wife Nishat, son Aseem and daughter

Samta have contributed through providing me with congenial atmosphere and taking off a number of domestic worries. Mr. Kamal Kishore Gupta the publisher has always been appreciative of the problems and cooperative to the utmost.

15 August, 1991
Lucknow

Nadeem Hasnain
(nadeemhasnain@gmail.com)

SUMMARY OF THE CONTENT

V — SOME OTHER FACETS

VI — Constitution, Administration and Tribal Development

Contents in Detail

V — Constitution, Administration and Tribal Development

ANNEXURES

TRIBAL INDIA

We exist to help tribal peoples protect their rights: the simplest, unarguable rights of all people ... And, moreover to support their right to determine, themselves, their own future and that of their children — tribal self determination.

— Cory (1979) for Survival International

PROLOGUE

I

Mankind is proceeding towards greater and greater homogeneity- racially, culturally and linguistically. This march encompasses a variety of dimensions and some agonising implications. Oldest cultures are either dying or are being exterminated. In such a broad category comes a great segment of **primitive, tribal, indigenous, aboriginal, native** and so on. Some major characteristics of these groups have been : simple premachine economy, unsophisticated rituals and social customs, lack of a script for their speech which itself is not developed, small local community organization and homogeneity.

The 'primitive' of yesterday have come into contact with their more 'civilized' neighbours and are coming to lose their 'primitive' character. "Industrial civilization is now completing its destruction of technologically simple tribal cultures. According to the viewpoint of many authorities ties within industrial civilization, this disappearance or drastic modification of these cultures is considered necessary for the 'progress' of civilization and is thought to be inevitable, natural, and, in the long run, beneficial for the peoples involved" (John H. Bodley, 1982). Before such an ethnocentric assertion could be converted into an established an undisputed premise, the reckless industrialization started demanding its price. Now, the human race, or for that matter the very life on earth is threatened with extinction. Bodley goes on to remark that it becoming increasingly apparent that civilization's "progress" is destroy the environment as well as other peoples and cultures, and that modern civilization may become victim of its won progress. In view this we might well question the wisdom of endorsing and encouraging the final disappearance of peoples who reject our 'advances' and instead find satisfaction in a technologically simple life in close harmony its environment. To brand the tribal economic system, in an ethnocentric fury, as backward and wasteful, customs and traditions as crude and tribal people steeped in primitive ignorance, is one thing and to prove it is altogether another.

II

In India, for thousands of years, primitive tribes persisted in forests and hills without having more than casual contacts with the populations of the open plains and the centres of civilization.

According to Haimendorf (1977), co-existence was possible because there was, on the whole, no pressure of population, and the advanced communities did not feel any urge to impose their own values on people placed patently outside the orbit of Hindu civilization.

NOT until the British appeared on the stage of Indian history and consolidated their position in the country, was any stir felt and experienced in the midst of these people. Such stir was slowly and steadily brought about by several factors, in accordance with the colonial needs and aspirations of the British rulers. The colonial rulers, for obvious reasons, had to 'open up' the entire country to be able to rule effectively and intensively. They were left with no other option but to evolve eventually an effective and extensive communication system including postal, telegraphic, roadways and railway services. Niharranjan Ray (1972) pushes the argument forward by stating that effective and intensive rule called also for a common administrative system that aimed at drawing, as much as possible, the entire country within its orbit, obliging the administration to send its officers, police and army to the farthest and deepest depths of the land, Also, for long, at least upto 1887, there remained primary obligation of British mercantile colonialism, to make the military conquest as complete as possible from one end of country to the other. This called for, internally, a political and military policy that demanded maintenance of a strong thrust into all the resistance areas including the forest depths and hill sides and hill tops.

S.C. Dube (1972) supports this assertion by saying that in respect of law and order the British rulers had maintained a stern posture throughout their sojourn in India, and even in tribal areas they enforced them with an iron hand. Their attitude to the tribes otherwise was paternalistic and protective. But the compulsion of the situation forced them to send their engineers and contractors, and civil and military officials of all ranks and their provision suppliers, the traders and shopkeepers into all these inaccessible regions of the interior and frontiers. Thus, a money economy was introduced among the tribal communities. This was not terrifying in itself but what came to disturb the tribals most was the land hunger of the non-British vested interests. "Taking advantage of their vantage position they started acquiring lands and introducing cash-cropping through means foul rather than fair lands that belonged to and were used by local communities. Ultimately this land hunger affected not only their agriculture but also their hunting and fishing rights" (Niharranjan

Ray, ibid). Still, the friction between the tribals and the non-tribals was limited to a restricted scale due to the British policy of exclusion or partial exclusion of tribal areas which kept the economic competition between the tribals and the non-tribals to minimum. Indirectly, it also helped the tribes to pursue their distinctive lifestyles relatively undisturbed. Though, Christian missionaries of various shades were allowed access to these areas yet their influence was restricted to the north-eastern region and some areas of Central India. S.C. Dube summarises the situation in a realistic way by commenting that culture change did come about but in driblets. Unsupported by dynamic and purposeful social action, this policy resulted in perpetuation of primitiveness. The tribes, thus, were precluded from having a foretaste or even a vision of things that go into raising the standards of living and in adding to material comfort and well-being. Their isolation from the main currents of Indian life helped the tribes in preserving their traditions, but at the same time it also hindered the growth of competence in them to face growing competition in a wider society and to meet some of the challenges of the contemporary world. They could not cope with the modern economic system and were trapped in the vicious circle of exploitation at the 'hands of the land hungry peasantry and the blood sucking moneylenders. The rapidly increasing interference and exploitation resulted in clashes and bloody uprisings (discussed in the chapter on Discontent and Rebellion) that still continue, though in different forms.

This narration will be incomplete without a word or two about the contribution of the earliest ethnographers. For the British rulers, or for that matter any ruler, administering these areas involved detailed and objective knowledge of these tribal communities. It was imperative to know their social and religious life, their political and economic organizations, their behavior patterns and so on. Thus, was initiated a series of studies undertaken by Dalton, Risley, Thurston, Enthoven, Crooke, Russell and others which led to the foundation of what today we call Indian anthropology. The ethnographers mentioned above were all administrators and their investigations involved deep probing into the lives and societies of these people which led eventually to the formulation of policies meant to guide the administration of these tribal communities.

Despite numerous uprisings, social movements and participation in the freedom struggle, though on a restricted scale, the tribal people remained at the periphery of consciousness of the average Indian masses. They were hardly ever taken note of by our social and political thinkers and leaders of even the late nineteenth century and early twentieth century. Thus, we see that our thinkers and leaders like Surendranath Banerjee, Aurobindo Ghosh, Bipin Chandra Pal, Mahadev Govind Ranade, Gopal Krishna Gokhle, Bal Gangadhar Tilak and host of others were unaware and unconcerned with their tribal fellow countrymen. Niharranjan Ray (1972) remarks that the attention of the Indian National Congress was never drawn to this growing socio-political problem, though the question of the lower and depressed orders and the untouchables of Hindu society had started receiving attention from about the 1880's. Not until Gandhiji entered, the scene was this matter looked at as a national issue. His concern for the Adivasi or Adimjati gave a new awakening to our national leadership.

After Gandhiji, among our modern national leadership, Jawahar Lal Nehru was a vociferous champion of the tribals. He has been most outspoken in condemning the imposition of the Hindu way of living on tribal communities reared in other traditions but he could not restrain the so-called reformers from their chosen task of civilizing' the tribal people. Logically, as long as Muslims, Christians and Parsis are free to follow their traditional ways of life, the tribal communities should also enjoy their natural right to follow their social system howsoever distinct it might be from that of the majority community. Nobody has got the right to convert the tribal people into carbon copies of any model.

III

The independence of India has changed the whole scenario. The Constitution of free India is committed to the welfare and development of the tribal people in a special way. The tribal people have awakened from their centuries old slumber. In the words of Verrier Elwin, "roads are everywhere urging their way into places which have hitherto been virtually inaccessible. Education, as it spread, is revolutionising the social and economic conditions of the tribal villages and is creating new demands as it generates new skills". The most important fact that we have to face is the effect of changes of every kind that are sweeping across the hills and forests in India-changes initiated by people, government and by the tribes themselves. The tribal people today are faced by an unprecedented evolutionary crisis in their history.

The most heartening feature of the present tribal situation in India is that a great segment of the tribal population has awakened to the need of finding a solution to their problems and is responding. But they rightly demand that the 'progress' and 'advancement' should not disturb the essential harmony of their life. They like to be assisted largely through their own institutions. A tribal's home and family is the precious and fundamental basis on which the future edifice of his welfare is to be built. "A freedom that does not guarantee him the freedom to decide how he will mould his destiny, official programmes that do not give him the choice of how he will organise his own development and to what end, will be sad imposition on him" (Elwin, 1963).

A Very crucial issue in contemporary tribal situation in India confronting us is the harmonization of national and tribal interests. Such harmonization cannot be attained easily. The issues implicit in the problem touch extremely sensitive areas and even the slightest mishandling is likely to evoke violent reactions. S.C. Dube has struck a note of realism when he says that the tribes have to find for themselves a place in Indian society consistent with their conception of honour, but this must be done without detriment to the integrity or the strength of India as a nation. Tribal competence has to be developed to enable them to face the growing competition of a developing society and to meet the challenges of an uncertain future.

We stand at the threshold of a new era. The tribal people have made an entry into that era with other members of the Indian society but they are not prepared to allow anybody to shatter the harmony of their life. They deserve a better appreciation of their life, mores, and problems from planners, administrators and general masses.

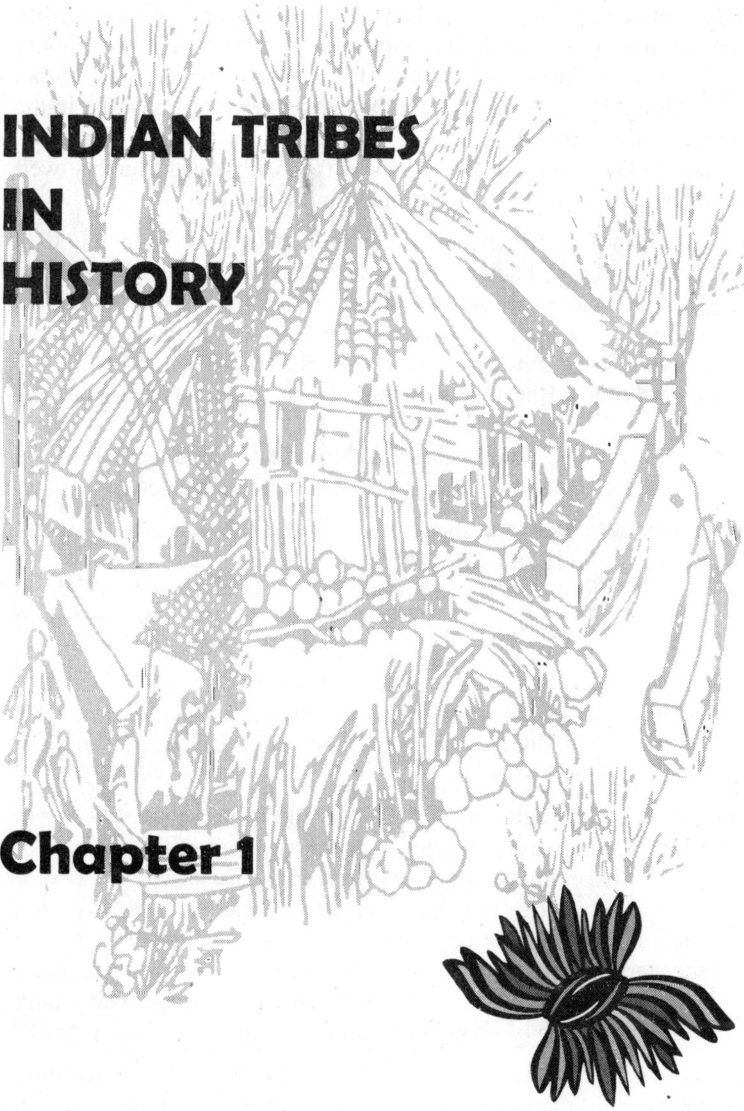

INDIAN TRIBES IN HISTORY

Chapter 1

India has been popularl described as a 'melting pot' of races, tribes and cultures. Considering the enormity, magnitude and complexity of the problem, it is really a very difficult task for the prehistorian and anthropologist to arrange the people and cultures of India in the chronological sequence of their appearance on this sub-continent. Fuchs (1973) rightly states that even their subsequent history well up to the Aryan invasion is shrouded in obscurity.

Though stone implements of prehistoric man have been found in various sites dating back to the Lower Palaeolithic period, so far no skeletal finds have been made of these earlier times. And the human fossil finds of later periods are too few and insignificant to enable us to draw any definite conclusion as to the racial history of India in prehistoric times. But it has now become an established fact that the aboriginal tribes in India are, in most cases, survivals from the later prehistoric groups. Some tribes may even have degenerated from a higher technological level due to adverse circumstances.

It is now pretty clear that the aborigines of the Indian sub-continent do not form a uniform race. Entering India from various directions and from various regions of Asia, they also belong to different races. It has not yet been possible to arrange the aboriginal tribes of India into definite racial groups. Attempts were made by Risley, Guha, Majumdar, etc., but so far they have not been very convincing. Hence, more anthropological research is necessary before racial and cultural history of Indian aboriginal population can be presented in a definite perspective.

Though our knowledge is vague about the origin and subsequent history of the numerous aboriginal tribes of India in the absence of sufficient archaeological and palaeaontological data, yet a story of their glory and decline may be arranged as far as the historic period is concerned. The historical data do shed some light on their life and we start picking up threads of reliable proof instead of clinging to the conjectural schemes of things. This has become possible only due to the invention of script and commencement of written records.

Let us first brief review the rise and fall of Indus valley civilization and advent of Aryans on the Indian soil as background to ascertain the role of earliest known aboriginal tribes of India. The Indus valley civilization is most probably a genuine gradual growth on Indian soil, not an importation by immigrant foreigners establishing a colony in India. The sudden, almost explosive rise of this civilization and its spontaneous growth may have several causes. One of them was the highly favourable ecological situation of the Indus valley. The great fertility of the soil caused the population to increase rapidly. Though, initially, the population of the Indus valley civilization may have been a uniform race, it did not remain so, for the skeletons found in the cemeteries of the sites show a mixed racial composition. The reasons for its decline and final disappearance cannot yet be definitely stated. One cause might have been a disastrous alteration of the course of the Indus river resulting in destructive flooding of settlements and silting of fields. "Since the chronology has been revised and the end of the civilization fixed at about 1750 B.C., the old hypothesis has been revised that the Aryan invaders, the early forerunners of the Rigvedic Aryans-might have destroyed the centres of Harrapan civilization and killed or dispersed its population. The discovery of unburied skeletons on the steps of a building in Mohenjodaro to support such an assumption" (Fuchs, 1973).

The racial immigration that took place in the last phase of prehistoric times and caused the most profound change in shaping the cultures and history of India was that of the Aryans, somewhere in the second millennium B.C. When exactly the first Aryans appeared on the border of India is still unknown. Prehistoric evidence for the early phase of Aryan immigration and conquest is very scanty and some important questions still demand convincing answers. Were the conquered peoples those of the Indus valley civilization? Did they speak Dravidian languages?

The Rigvedic period (2000 to 1000 B.C.) witnessed wild Aryan tribes pouring into the north-western parts of the country, fighting not only among themselves but waging a was unto death against non-Aryan tribes. Indra, the thunder-wielder armed with his bolt, is invoked to shatter the forts of Dasas, cast his dart on Dasyus and increase the Aryan's might and glory. He slays both Dasyus and Samyus. Saraswati kills the Parvatas, a hostile tribe who dwelt on the banks of the Parushni; Vishnu conquers in his battles the bull-jawed Dasyus and together with Indra destroys Sambara's castles. The Asuras who captured an Aryan sage Dabhiti's city, were defeated by Indra and dispossessed of their booty. K.S. Singh (1996) comments that "Indian tribes have not lain 'torpid' on the fringe of civilization but have responded to 'static and dynamic' rhythms of history. Their role is limited not merely to references to such of them as Saoras, Kinnaras and Kiratas (historical Nagas) in ancient texts; it is part of the process of the fusion of races and cultures in the sub-continent, of the growth if Hinduism and its amorphous mass of myths and legends, magic and religion, traditions and customs. Tribal contents in Indian life may be compared to an ice-berg in an ocean and these can be identified as much as the Aryan or the Dravidian. The erosion of tribal mass, ethnic and cultural, and its absorption in the dominant society is a process working even today." The thread of this story is to be carefully picked through ancient literary texts, archaeological and epigraphic evidence, medieval historical works and British records and documents.

The process of fusion of Aryan and non-Aryan tribes continued. The later Vedic period (1000 to 600 B.C.) is marked by further working of the twin processes of emerging Hinduism, Aryanisation of the tribals and the tribalisation of the Aryans. The two great epics, the Ramayan and the Mahabharat, whatever their historical value, refer to tribals such as the Sudras, Abhiras, Dravidas, Pulindas and Sabaras or Saoras. Of these "Sabaras are the most familiar and they are probably the only tribe existing today whose earliest references could be traced to Aittareya Brahman". Sabari, who offered fruits to Rama, has become, in Verrier Elwin's words, "a symbol of the contributions that tribes can and will make to the life of India." Most of the then known tribes claimed to have participated in the Mahabharat and its innumerable episodes. Eklavya, a Bhil, has gone down in legends as an ideal disciple who offered his thumb to Dronacharya. Munda and Naga claimed to have fought on the side of the Kurus against the five brothers. Bhima's son Ghatotkacha who performs prodigies of valour in the war, is born of his tribal wife, Arjuna marries Chitrangada, Naga princess.

The Nagas deserve comprehensive study in view of their significant contribution and participation in the Indian mainstream of earliest historical period. The historical or mythical Nagas have been absorbed so completely into the Hindu society that no trace of theirs is left today. Significantly, the Nagas of Nagaland have no relation with their celebrated namesakes. The extent of the Naga influence may be measured by the observance of Nag panchami, the influence of the snake-cult on the Vishnu creed (Vishnu's snake bed) and Shaivism, Naga motifs in sculptures at Mahabalipuram and Rajgriha and such place names as Takshila, Anant Nag, Nalanda, Nagpur and Chhota Nagpur. The Mahabharat is, in a way, an essentially Nag-story. Buddha converted a few nagas. Naga cult survived in the Kashmir valley and Nag power in central India till second century A.D. The abundance of names with a Naga prefix-Nagdatta, Nagsena, Nagdeva, etc., further testifies to their influence.

During the earliest phase of historical period, small tribal pockets were subjugated by invaders or indigenous imperial power. Ajatshatru destroyed the tribal republic of Vaisali. Alexander wiped out tribal pockets on the north-western border. The Arthasastra refer to Atvikas who are looked upon as potential trouble shooters. Asoka threatens north-western tribes with dire consequences if they rise in revolt, while assuring forest tribes, in his dominion, of his compassion.

Sharma (1961) dwells at length about the social structure of this period. He states the Dhamasutra (600 to 300 BC) and the Manusmriti (200 BC to 200 AD) continued the old process of fusion and assimilation. The concept of mixed castes is only a fanciful and convenient Brahminical way of explaining this trend. These so-called mixed castes were the supposed progeny of male of one begotten on the woman of another caste. A few of these, probably Brahmanised tribes, labelled as mixed castes were Nishadas who lost during this period their earlier position and lived by hunting; Medas, Andhras, Madgas and Chenchus hunted wild animals; Ksahlas and Pukkasas who caught animals and birds; Ayogavas worked in wood; Dhigvana and Karauras in leather; Pandusopake in cane; Margavas were boatmen; Veras played on drums and Sarendhas acted as servants and skilled dressers. The Chandalas, a tribe, were absorbed in Hindu society and assigned the task of removing dead bodies of animals and human beings as also whipping and chopping off the limbs of criminals. Thus, the process of downgrading of tribals continued.

That the tribes were not leading an isolated and alienated existence is borne out by the fact that many of them participated in the sub-Puranic and epic traditions of myths and folk lores. The impact of epic heroes like Rama, Sita, Lakshmana, Ravana, Bhima, etc., on some of the tribes in central India is evident from their treasures of myths and lores. Gonds call themselves children of Ravana. Manu is another Puranic figure who has deeply exercised the tribes, and Mundas call themselves Manoako after him.

Ancient Sanskrit literature is replete with their descriptions. Panchatantra and Kathasarit Sagar present them in a romantic and friendly perspective. Vishnu Puran describes them as "dwarfish with flat nose." In Kadmbari and Harsha-Charita, Bana presented detailed description of the Saora chief.

The feudal period (400-1000 AD) saw a greater opening of tribal areas and Hinduisation of tribal chiefs. The Brahmin priests prepared suitable puranic geneologies for them and the ruling Brahmin class spearheaded the process of Sanskritisation or Brahminisation of tribals. Subsequently in the wake of Muslim invasion in the 11th and 12th centuries, there followed the influx of Rajputs (who did not submit) into the tribal areas and the destruction of tribal pockets. Thus, Parmar Rajputs expelled Cheros from Shahabad and the Chandels replaced Bhuinya in South Monghyr district of Bihar.

The Muslim rule (12th to 18th century) witnessed a new phenomenon the Turko-Afghan and Mughal rulers mostly secured a mere formal allegiance of tribal chiefs or of Hindu rulers in tribal areas of Central India and Bihar. In 1585 and 1616 A.D., Muslim armies marched into Chotanagpur and subjugated the Raja of Khukra. Similarly, the tribal areas of Assam were also subjugated by another Muslim General.

One Daud Khan subjugated the Cheros of Palamau around 1661 A.D. During this period the conversion of tribals in the north-west frontier region to Islam took place. Some Muslim saints worked and preached on the fringes of tribal areas, like Pir Syed Shah Kamal who worked among the Nats and Pir Syed Mohammed who worked among the Kols.

Some streams of Hinduism like Bhakti movement also affected the tribals such as Munda, Oraon, etc. Chaitanya Mahaprabhu passed through Jharkhand and Vaishnava preachers like Binand Das working in Munda area converted many tribals. The Bhuinyas were completely Hinduised and lost all their tribal traits. "The roots of subsequent Bhagat movements among the tribals could be traced to the Vaishnava influence. Nothing illustrates more eloquently than the conversion of the Ahoms in Assam" (K.S. Singh, 1964).

Now appear the British colonialists with their modern technology, new approach and vested interests. The advent of British rule meant opening up of tribal areas along the sea coast and in Bihar and Bengal. The construction of Grand Trunk Road through tribal pockets accelerated the influx of aliens such as merchants, moneylenders and land grabbers. Furthermore, the pressure of growing population and the ruthless exploitation and oppression by Zamindars facilitated migration of peasants and artisans to inaccessible tribal areas. The Christian missions also got their pound of flesh.

The monumental endurance and patience of the tribals exhausted in the wake of the breakdown of tribal order in tribal areas in the 18th century, Munda uprising (1789-1901), the Santhal insurrection (1855-56), the Bhil rebellion (1879-80), Bastar uprising (1910-11) and Gond rebellion (1940) are some of the examples of the new awakening among the tribals of India.

Anoher very significant point to be noted in this historical journey of the Indian tribals is the status of the three major religions of India. While Hinduism and Islam had stopped short at the fringes (in most of the cases), Christianity penetrated deep into the tribal areas under the patronage of British rulers. This led to revitalisation movements among the tribals like Kherwar movement (1871-80), Sardari movement (1881-95), Birsa movement (1895-1901), Tana Bhagat movement (1920-35), and a host of others. The agrarian-cum-cultural movement threw up politico-religious leaders of stature who deeply influenced the tribals' thinking for decades to come.

With the departure of British colonialists and rise of independent India, the tribal citizens of the country were promised a fair deal-in some case privileged to become partners in progress. Upliftment of the tribals was an article of faith for our Constitution makers. Could we realise this dream? The coming chapters shall be reviewing the tribal situation in a multi-dimensional perspective to find the answer.

CONCEPT AND DEFINITION OF 'TRIBE'

Chapter 2

What is a tribe? What exactly are the criteria for considering a human group, a tribe? What are the indices of the tribal life ?

Interestingly but sadly the anthropologists, sociologists, social workers, administrators and such people who have been involved with the tribes and their problems either on theoretical plane or on practical grounds are still not on the same wave length regarding the concept and the definition of their subject matter. Arthur Wilke, et al (1979) puts the problem in proper perspective by stating that for years ambiguity has stalked India's official portrait of tribal people. From 1917 through the 1931 Census, for instance, the nomenclature referring to tribes under-went successive modifications, involving primarily changes in descriptive adjectives such as "aboriginal" or "depressed classes". By the 1941 Census, these qualifying adjectives were dropped, a practice continued after independence with the adoption of the notion of scheduled tribes or as they are commonly called, Adivasi. Such standardization did not, however, remove all ambiguity.

No Doubt with the passage of time, the differences on the concept and definition of a tribe have certainly narrowed down to an appreciable extent, but a theoretical discussion seems imperative to understand this problem in its proper perspective.

Here are a few definitions of tribe' being used as the basis of discussion in the present chapter :

A Tribe is a collection of families bearing a common name, speaking a common dialect, occupying or professing to occupy a common territory and is not usually endogamous, though originally it might have been so.

–Imperial Gazetteer of India

A Tribe is a group of people in a primitive or barbarous stage of development acknowledging the authority of a chief and usually regarding themselves as having a common ancestor.

–Oxford Dictionary

In its simplest form the tribe is a group of bands occupying a contiguous territory or territories and having a feeling of unity deriving from numberous similarities in culture, frequent contacts, and a certain community of interest. –Ralph Linton

A Tribe is an independent political division of a population with a common culture. –Lucy Mair

A Tribe is a group united by a common name in which the members take a pride by a common language, by a common territory, and by a feeling that all who do not share this name are outsiders, 'enemies' in fact.

–G.W.B. Huntingford

A Tribe is a social group with territorial affiliation, endogamous, with no specialization of functions, ruled by tribal officers, hereditary or otherwise, united in language or dialect, recognizing social distance with other tribes or castes, without any social obloquy attaching to them, as it does in the caste structure, following tribal traditions, beliefs and customs, illiberal of naturalization of ideas from alien sources, above all conscious of homogeneity of ethnic and territorial integration. –D.N. Majumdar

Ideally, tribal societies are small in scale, are restricted in the spatial and temporal range of their social, legal, and political relations, and possess a morality, a religion, and world-view of corresponding dimensions. Characteristically too, tribal languages are unwritten, and hence, the extent of communication both in time and space is inevitably narrow. At the same time, tribal societies exhibit a remarkable economy of design and have a compactness and self-sufficiency lacking in modern society. –I. M. Lewis

Majumdar & Madan (1967) rightly comment that when one looks into the definitions given by various anthropologists, one is bound to be impressed by the dissimilarity of their views as regards what constitutes a tribe. Kinship ties, common territory, one language; joint ownership, _ one political organization, absence of internecine strife have all been referred to as the main characteristics of a tribe. Some anthropologists have not only accepted some of the characteristics, but have also stoutly I denied some of them to be characteristics of a tribe. Thus, Rivers did not mention habitation in a common territory as a vital feature of tribal organization, although others like Perry have insisted on it, saying that even nomadic tribes roam about within a definite region. Radicliffe Brown has given instances of one section of a tribe fighting another from his Australian data. The only conclusion one can draw from such diversity of learned opinion is that the views of each anthropologist arise from the type of data with which he is most familiar. One may, therefore, make a list of universal characteristics, some of which would define a tribe anywhere. Thus, Majumdar claims universal applicability of his definition given on the preceding page.

A major hurdle of defining a tribe is that related with the problem of distinguishing the tribe from peasantry. "It is no doubt possible to use the labels 'tribal' and 'peasant' for this type of social organization and to characterise one by contrasting it with the other. But in spite of all the effort invested by anthropologists in the study of primitive societies, there really is no satisfactory way of defining a tribal society. What this amounts to in the Indian context is that anthropologists have tried to characterise a somewhat nebulous sociological type, by contrasting it with another which is almost equally nebulous. Earlier anthropologists had not paid sufficient attention to define tribal society, but tacitly assumed that what they were studying in Australia, Melanesia and Africa were various forms of tribal society. The tribe was somewhat vaguely assumed to be a more or less homogeneous society having a common government, a common dialect and a common culture" (Andre Beitelle, 1973). Though not everybody will agree with the assumption of Beitelle but his statement maybe cited as one of the many schools of thought grappling with the problem.

Most of the above mentioned definitions present a static definition of tribe. B.K. Roy Burman (1994) presents a refreshingly new idea of defining and identifying 'tribe'. He is of the view that a tribe should be understood in in terms of a stage in the techno-economic-cultural evolution and relationship of man with nature. Once a group of people goes beyond this stage, it ceases tobe a 'tribe' though it may continue to retain its ethnic or 'tribal' identity. Even this approach may be debatable because those who wish to identify or define tribe in these terms may be accused of imposing their model of techno-economic development.

The above discussion shows that it is not easy to define a tribe or a tribal society conclusively and any standardization in this regard is very difficult to obtain. Hence, it will be better to shy away from international or universal plane keeping in view the regional connotation of the concept of tribe and focus attention on gaining standardization within the Indian universe to solve our own problems. This seems to be quite sensible in the situation when definitions of universal applicability are either very broad and loose or very narrow and restricted. In this context, Andre Beitelle (ibid) aptly remarks that Bailey is perhaps the only anthropologist working in the Indian field who has tried to characterize tribes in terms of segmentary principles, but the contrast in which he is interested is not between 'tribe' and 'peasant' but between 'tribe' and 'caste'. Further, unlike Bailey, the majority of Indian anthropologists have not given much serious thought to the problem of creating a definition of tribal society which will be appropriate to the Indian context.

Now let us examine the problem specifically in the India context. T. B. Naik (1960) raises the problem in proper perspective by talking of the Criteria and indices of the tribal life in specifically Indian setting. What should be the criteria and indices of tribal life? Living in forest? The Dublas of Surat and a host of others do not live in forests. They live in fertile plains, nevertheless they are included in the Schedule. Primitive religion ? But you do not know what primitive religion is in India, there being a continuance from the most abstruse philosophy to the tribal gods and superstitious beliefs in the religion of most of the advanced communities of India". This index being very fluid and not exact will not do. Geographical isolation? There are hundreds of tribal groups who are not living an isolated life. Primitive economic system? There are many peasant groups who are living by equally primitive economic system. Thus, Naik goes on to present his own criteria for a tribe which are as follows :

1. A tribe to be a 'tribe' should have the least functional interdependence within the community (the Hindu caste system is an example of high interdependence).
2. It should be economically backward, which means :

   (i) the full import of monetary economics should not be understood by its members;

   (ii) primitive means of exploiting natural resources should be used;

   (iii) the tribe's economy should be at an underdeveloped stage; and

   (iv) it should have multifarious economic pursuits.
3. There should be a comparative geographic isolation of its people from others.
4. Culturally, members of a tribe should have a common dialect which may be subject to regional variations.
5. A tribe should be politically organized and its community Panchayat should be an influential institution.

6. The tribe's members should have the least desire to change. They should have a sort of psychological conservatism making them stick to their old customs.
7. A tribe should have customary laws and its members might have to suffer in a law court because of these laws.

Naik further elaborates that a community to be a 'tribe' must have all these attributes. It might be undergoing acculturation, but the degree of acculturation will have to be determined in the context of its customs, gods, language, etc. a very high degree of acculturation will automatically debar it from being a tribe.

Ehrenfels elaborates some of the points already discussed by saying :

1. A community, however small it may be, may remain in isolation from the other communities within a geographical region. This applies to a caste as well as to a tribe. The members of a true tribe, however, are generally not included into the traditional Hindu caste hierarchy and frequently speak also a common dialect, entertain common beliefs, follow common occupational practices and (most important) consider themselves as members of a small but semi-national unit.
2. I would delete in the above definition the words "economically backward", "primitive means" and "underdeveloped stage" and substitute them by the words "self—sufficient" (of Khasi, Gond, Bhil, Agaria and others who are in part more specialized economically, even much more than their non-tribal neighbours). Yet each individual of a tribe may work for his family group and thus may remain functionally dependent of solidarity with the tribe as a whole, rather than as a co-partner in the caste hierarchy of non-tribal Hindus.
3. I agree with the definition of geographical isolation though not every tribe is an isolated unit of people (e.g., Bhil, Santhals, Irula, etc.). But if a tribe has its own system of economy, its solidarity will no doubt be more stable.
4. Common dialects or languages are typical for tribes in Assam and the Central areas, but not in the Southern and Western States of India. Community of language stresses that, but is not imperative for building up tribal consciousness. The original religious concepts of most tribes in preacculturation days were different from their Hindu, Buddhist, Muslim or Christian neighbours, but are not always so now.

5. A tribe need not always be politically organized nor have a community panchayat. It may, or may not, have a single chief or a few elders who may wield more or less power within the community.
6. I would delete the relevant para of the above and substitute it with the words, "The members of a tribe have a feeling of belonging to a group the existence of which is valuable."
7. Almost all tribes have customary laws and practices, more or less different from their non-tribal neighbours. Very often they are indeed made to suffer on this account in law courts and in other contact situations with non-tribals.

The Tata Institute of Social Sciences in its report on the Indian tribes has also joined those who have been criticising the anthropologist's approach of the problem. It says that the (anthropological) criteria apply to ideal typical tribal communities as conceived by the anthropologists for theoretical purpose. These do not appear to be empirically related to communities that have been included in the list of the scheduled tribes. The logical implication seems to be, that communities which do not satisfy the above criteria should not be considered as tribes even though they are included in the list of the scheduled tribes. Arthur Wilke et al (1979) too, like some others, opine that some measure, if not a substantial measure, of the difficulty is inherent in the intellectual legacy of the discipline of anthropology. Aiyappan, provoked by such statements remarks rather skeptically, reminding us of the well-known definition given by Tate Regan of 'species'. Adopting the definition he (Aiyappan) said that a tribe is a group which a competent anthropologist considers to be a tribe. If the administrator wants a clear-cut definition which he can apply blindly and get along with, he says, we should tell him that we don't have it, just as the zoologist is not in a position to give a clear-cut all-purpose definition of 'species'.

Despite such rhetoric and academic polemics on the problem of definition of 'tribe' quite a substantial measure of standardization has been accomplished in designating which people are or are not entitled to particular protection and privilege. This could become possible only due to vigorous academic efforts of the much maligned and misunderstood anthropologists who, with the help of rigorous and painstaking empirical research, ultimately came out with definite and empirically verifiable ethnographic data to clear the cobwebs of misgivings regarding Indian tribes. Majumdar and Madan (1967) demonstrate this new mood by emphatically stating the following facts :

1. In tribal India, a tribe is definitely a territorial group; a tribe has a traditional territory, and emigrants always refer to it as their home. The Santhals working in the Assam tea gardens refer to particular regions of Bihar or Bangal as their home.
2. All members of a tribe are not kin of each other, but within every Indian tribe kinship operates as a stong, associative regulative and integrating principle. The consequence is tribal endogamy and the division of a tribe into clans and sub-clans and so on. These clans, etc., being kin groups, are exogamous.
3. Members of an Indian tribe speak one common language, their own or/ and that of their neighbours. Intra-tribal conflict on a group scale is not a feature of Indian tribes. Joint ownership of property, wherever present, as for instance among the Hos, is not exclusive. Politically, Indian tribes are under the control of the State governments, but within a tribe there may be a number of Panchayats corresponding to the heterogeneity, racial and cultural, of the constituent population in a village or in adjacent villages.
4. There are other distinguishing features of Indian tribes. Thus, there are their dormitory institutions; the absence of institutional schooling for boys and girls; distinctive customs regarding birth, marriage, and death; a moral code different from that of Hindus and Muslims; peculiarities of religious beliefs and rituals which may distinguish tribesmen even from he low caste Hindus.

It may also be important to have a look at the toxonomical exercise of anthropologists primarily focusing on the cultural process. B.K. Royburman (1970) classified the Indian tribes in terms of their Orientation towards the Hindu society :

(a) Those incorporated in the Hindu Social Order
In this category he includes tribes like Bhil, Bhumij etc. who have accepted the ethos of the caste structure and can hardly be differentiated from the neighbouring Hindu peasantry.

(b) *Positively Oriented towards the Hindu Social Order*
He includes tribes like the Santhal, Oraon, Munda, Gond etc. under this who alongwith a number of other tribal communities of Central India are positively oriented towards the Hindu social order.

(c) *Negatively oriented towards the Hindu Social Order*
Tribal Communities like the Mizo and the Naga may be considered to be negatively oriented towards the Hindu Social Order. They definitely reject caste as framework for social organization.

(d) *Indifferent towards the Hindu Social Order*
Most of the tribal communities in Arunachal Pradesh can be considered to be indifferent to Hindu Social Order. They are hardly aware of the tenets of Hinduism. Many of them traditionally eat beef and their moral constraints and systems of pollution and purity do not appear to bear any significant degree of resemblance to those of the Hindus. This classification too is vulnerable on several counts.

To wind up this discussion, it seems to be quite apt to refer to Arthur Wilke *et al* (1979) who opine that even the constraints of bureaucratic decision-making and administration reign supreme, there is a tendency to gloss over the rich and at times puzzling mosaic of human affairs. What accounts for indetermination in the concept of tribe is likely that the dictates of bureaucratic procedures and the unceasing acculturation going on throughout India and particularly among many identified tribal people make it difficult to apply an idea which is in many respects, ideal type formulation.

CLASSIFICATION OF TRIBAL COMMUNITIES

Chapter 3

Due to multiplicity of factors and complexity of problems involved, it is not very easy to classify the Indian tribes into different groups. However, the Commissioner for Scheduled Castes and Scheduled Tribes took up the task and investigated the possibility of adopting classification criteria. Keeping this aim in view the state governments were asked to suggest the characteristics which seemed to them most suitable in distinguishing the so-called "aboriginal" groups from the rest of the population.

The Assam Government suggested descent from Mongoloid stock, affiliation with Tibeto-Burman linguistic groups and the existence of a social organization of the village clan type as the major characteristics. The erstwhile Bombay government considered residence in forest areas as the basic criterion while for the Madhya Pradesh government tribal origin, speaking tribal language and residence in forest areas, were important criteria. Similarly, the governments of Madras, Orissa, Andhra, Mysore, Travancore, etc., suggested various linguistic, geographical, economic and social factors as indicators.

Taking the above mentioned characteristics into consideration the tribes of India may be classified on the bais of their (a) territorial distribution, (b) linguistic affiliation, (c) physical and racial characteristics, (d) occupation or economy, (e) cultural contact and (f) religious beliefs.

Geographical Classification

Looking at the physical map of India and the distribution of tribal population, we find that both geography as well as tribal demography permit a regional grouping and a zonal classification. B.S. Guha has classified Indian tribes into three zones.

(i) The north and north-eastern zone

(ii) The central or the middle zone

(iii) The southern zone

(i) *The North and North-Eastern Zone*

The northern and north-eastern zone consists of the sub-Himalayan region and the mountain valleys of the eastern frontiers of India. The tribal people of Assam, Manipur and Tripura may be included in the eastern part of this geographical zone while in the northern part are included the tribals of eastern Kashmir, eastern Punjab, Himachal Pradesh and northern Uttar Pradesh.

Some of the important tribes living between Assam and Tibet are Aka, Dafla, Miri, Gurung and the Apatanion the west of the Subangiri river. The Mishmi tribes live in the high ranges between the Debong and Lohit rivers. Further east are found the Khamti and the Singpho and beyond them are the different Naga tribes. South of the Naga hills running through the states of Manipur, Tripura and the Chittagong hill tracts live the Kuki, the Lushai, the Khasi and the Garo (now the inhabitants of the newly carved Meghalaya state). In the sub-Himalayan region of the Sikkim and the northern portions of Darjeeling, there are a number of primitive tribes, Lepcha being the best known of them. The Himalayan region of Uttar Pradesh also contains some important tribes like Tharu, Bhoksa, Jounsari (Khasa), Bhotia, Raji, etc.

The entire geographical zone, though quite large in area, does not contain dense population. As a result of geographical similarities most of the tribes of this zone are engaged in either terrace cultivation or Jhum (shifting) cultivation and are steeped in poverty and economic backwardness.

(ii) *The Central or the Middle Zone*

This zone consists of plateaus and mountainous belt between the Indo-Gangetic plain to the north and roughly the Krishna river to the south and this is separated from the north-eastern zone by the gap between the Garo hills and the Rajmahal hills. In this zone, we have another massing of tribal peoples in Madhya Pradesh with extensions in Uttar Pradesh, Madhya Bharat, southern Rajasthan, northern Maharashtra, Bihar and Orissa. Northern Rajasthan, southern Maharashtra and Bastar form the peripheral areas of the zone. The important tribes inhabiting this zone are the Savara, Gadaba and Borido of the Ganjam district; the Juang, Kharia, Khond Bhumij and the Bhiya of the Orissa hills. In the plateau of Chotanagpur live Munda, Santhal, Oraon, Ho and Birhor. Further west along Vindhya ranges live the Katkari, Kol and the Bhil, the Gond forms the largest group and occupy what is known as the 'Gondwan land'. On both sides of the Satpuras and around the Maikal hills are found similar tribes like Koraku, Agaria, Pardhan and Baiga. In the hills of Bastar live some of the most colourful of these tribes like Muria, the Hill Muriya of the Abhujmar hills and Bison-horn Maria of the Indravati valley. Most of the tribes of this zone practise shifting cultivation as means of their livelihood but the Oraon, Santhal, Munda and Gond have learnt plough cultivation as a result of their cultural contact with neighbouring rural populations.

(iii) *The Southern Zone*

This zone consists of that part of southern India which falls south of the river Krishna stretching from Wynaad to Cape Camorin. Andhra Pradesh, Karnataka, Coorg, Travancore, Cochin, Tamil Nadu, etc., are included in this zone. Beginning from the north-east of this zone, the Chenchu occupy the area of the Nallaimallais hills across the Krishna and into the erstwhile Hyderabad state. Along the Western Ghats from the Loraga of South Kanara, the Yeruva and the Toda live on the lower slopes of Coorg hills while the Irula, Paniyan and the Kurumba inhabit Wynaad area. The most primitive of Indian aboriginals such as Kadar, Kanikkar, Malvadan, Malakuravan, etc., inhabit the dense forest along the ranges of Cochin and Travancore. They are also included among some of the most economically backward communities of the world. Except Toda, Badaga and Kota who live in Nilgiri hills most of the tribal groups of this zone depend upon hunting and fishing for food gathering.

Although Guha has not included the inhabitants of Andaman and Nicobar Islands in any of these zones and has skipped their description, yet these tribal people may be said to constitute a fourth zone. The main tribes living in this zone are the Jarwa, Onge, North Sentinelese, Andamanese and Nicobari. Thus separated from the main body of India's primitive tribes, they are ethnically close to the south Indian tribes.

Linguistic Classification

At present people of India may be divided into four speech families viz. the Indo-European (Aryan), the Dravidian, the Austric (Kolar Munda) and the Tibeto-Chinese (Sino-Tibetan), D. N. Majumdar (1955) opines that "so far as the tribal people are concerned the Aryan speech comes into the picture only as a consequence of cultural contact since almost all of our tribal people have pre-Aryan or non-Aryan racial affinities and origins." Most of the scholars, therefore, are of the view that the tribal people of India may be classified chiefly into three speech families: (1) Dravidian, (2) Austric, and (3) Tibeto-Chinese.

The tribal people speaking the language falling under Dravidian v, speech family inhabit the middle and southern India. The most developed languages of Dravidian family are Tamil, Telegu, Kannada and Malayalam. Gonds occupy the chief place among the tribal speeches derived from Dravidian family and it is spoken widely by the Gond tribals who are scattered from Madhya Pradesh to Andhra Pradesh. It has no literature but considering the numerical strength of its speakers, it has been assigned a very important place in the realm of tribal languages. Another important language of this group is Koi which is spoken by the Kandh of Orissa, Oraon of Chotanagpur and Malto of Rajmahal hills. The speeches of Toda, Paliya, Chenchu, Irula and Kadar are also included in the Dravidian family.

The Austric family of speeches is also know as Munda speech family. Max Muller was the first scholar who distinguished it from Dravidian speech and it is he who assinged the term Munda speech family to this group. Speeches of this family are spoken mainly by the tribals of Chotanagapur area but these are also in vogue, to a lesser extent, in some parts of Madhya Pradesh, Orissa, West Bengal, Madras and Terai region of Himalayas stretching from Bihar to Simla hills. The Santhali speech of Bengal, Bihar and Orissa, Mundari, Ho Kharia, Bhumij and some other speeches of Bihar are also included in this family.

Tibeto-Chincsc speeches are spoken most by the tribals of Mongol racial stock. This family is divided into two branches (i) Tibeto-Burman, and (ii) Siamese-Chinese. The tribals of Assam, Meghalaya and other parts of the north-east India speak one or the other speech of this family.

Ethnic / Racial Classification

D. N. Majumdar (1955) has very rightly described the complexity of the problem of classifying the tribal people of India on the basis of racial affinities when he says that fixing the racial origins or affinities of the tribal communities of India is one of the most complicated tasks that has had to be faced by the Indian anthropologists. There is practically no direct evidence of those ethnic stocks who inhabited different parts of India in prehistoric times. The available knowledge about the racial composition of India in historic times is equally scanty. Therefore, all historical reconstructions regarding the racial history of India have to be based on conjecture.

The first scientific racial classification of India was attempted by Sir Herbert Risely. He published his findings in 1915 in the book The Peoples of India. He classifies the entire Indian population into seven racial types:

(i) Turko-Iranian,
(ii) Indo-Aryan,
(iii) Scytho-Dravidian,
(iv) Aryo-Dravidian,
(v) Mongolo-Dravidian,
(vi) Monogoloid
(vi) Dravidian.

These seven types may be reduced to three basic types viz., the Dravidian, the Mongolian and the Indo-Aryan. Significantly, he gave no separate classificatory scheme for the 'aboriginals' of India.

The latest attempts at racial classification of Indian people are those made by 'Hutton, Guha and Majumdar. Guha lists six main races, with nine sub-types:

1. The Negrito
2. The Proto-Australoid
3. The Mongoloid:
   (i) Palaeo-Mongoloids
      (a) long headed
      (b) broad headed
   (ii) Tibeto-Mongoloids
4. The Mediterranean
   (i) Paaelo-Mediterranean
   (ii) Mediterranean
   (iii) Oriental type
5. The Werstern Brachycephals
   (i) Alpinoid
   (ii) Dinaric
   (iii) Armenoid
6. The Nordic

The ancestry of the present tribal population of India is traced chiefly to the first three types : Negrito, Proto-Australoid and Mongoloid.

The tribals of the hills of Cochin and Travancore such as Kadar, Irula, Paliyan, etc., Angami Naga of Assam and the tribals of Rajmahal hills of eastern Bihar are included in Negrito racial type which exhibits short stature, black skin colour, black woolly hair, thin lips and broad nose.

The Proto-Australoid racial type exhibits short to medium stature, long and high head, broad and small face and small flattened nose. Most of the middle or central Indian tribals come within this racial type but some south Indian tribes like Chenchu, Bhill, etc., also exhibit the racial characteristics of this type.

As far as the Mongoloid racial stock is concerned, most of the tribes of north-east India are included in this racial type and exhibit yellowish skin colour, straight and dark hair, flat nose, prominent cheek bones and almond shaped eyes with epicanthic fold. The Naga, Chakma, Lepcha, etc., are some of the important tribes of this racial group.

Despite the above mentioned scheme of racial classification, racially the tribes of India cannot be put strictly under any particular type or category, India having been the "melting pot of races" (Majumdar ibid). The generalized types, referred to above, do not account for all the tribes. Thus, the Todas of Nilgiri Hills, for just an example, are without a racial label as yet. Serological and linguistic researches are being conducted but these have yet to reveal any new aspect of the racial composition of tribal India.

Economic Classification

The classical classification of Adam Smith and the more recent classifications of Thurnwald and Herskovits have been applied throughout the world in classifying tribes on the basis of their economic life. The scheme presented by Thurnwald is taken as most acceptable in the Indian context and is as follows:

1. Homogeneous communities of men as hunters and trappers, women as collectors — the Kadar, the Chenchu, the Kharia, and the Korwa are some of the Indian tribes falling into this category.
2. Homogeneous communities of hunters, trappers and agriculturists —the Kamar, the Baiga and the Birhor are examples of this type from tribal India.

3. Graded society of hunters, trappers, agriculturists and artisans - most of the Indian tribes fall under this category. The Chero and the Agariya, among so may others, are famous artisans.
4. The herdsmen— the Toda and some sections of the great Bhil tribe furnish classic examples in India.
5. Homogeneous hunters and herdsmen — this category is not represented among Indian tribes. The Todas do not hunt, nor do they catch fish or birds.
6. Ethnically stratified cattle breeders and traders — the Bhotiyas of the sub-Himalayan region of Uttar Pradesh breed yaks and are itinerant traders.
7. Socially graded herdsmen with hunting, agricultural and artisan population.

Majumdar opines that such a classification, though useful, does not help much because the purpose herein, in attempting a classification, is mainly to indicate the nature of economic difficulties experienced by the tribal communities.

Taking mainly technological achievements into consideration, a more lucid and clear-cut classification on the bais of the conditions of economic life may be attempted as follows.

1. Tribes hunting in forests.
2. Tribes engaged in hilly cultivation (shifting or slash-and burn cultivation).
3. Tribes engaged in cultivation on levelled (plain) land.
4. Simple artisan tribes.
5. Pastoral tribes.
6. Tribes living as folk artists.
7. Agricultural and non-agricultural labour oriented tribes.
8. Tribes engaged in service and trade.

Those tribes who live by hunting in forests earn their livelihood through collection of edible roots and fruits, hunting and fishing. This class of tribes is found mostly in southern India. The Chenchu and Chandi of Andhra Pradesh, Kadar, Malapatram and Kurumba from Kerala and Paliyan of Tamil Nadu and Onge, Jarwa, Sentenelese and Nicobarese of Andaman and Nicobar Islands are some of the important tribes living in southern zone. The Raji of Uttar Pradesh, Hill Garo of Meghalya, Birhor, Korwa and Hill Kharia of Chotanagpur and Juang of Orissa are also some of the notable examples of this class. Although some groups of these tribes are slowly learning cultivation yet their cultural ethos are still basically of a hunting-gathering type.

A vast chunk of Indian tribes is engaged in shifting cultivation on hilly or mountainous tracts of north-eastern and central India. This mode of cultivation is different from the conventional settled cultivation. Under this system bushes and trees are slashed and burnt. Thereafter seeds are scattered on the ashes and the rest is left to nature. (Details of this mode of cultivation are given in the Chapter on problems of Indian tribes).

Almost all the tribes of Assam, Meghalaya, Arunachal Pradesh, Mizoram, Manipur and Tripura produce their crops through this mode of cultivation. Some tribes of Orissa and Gond and Baiga of Madhya Pradesh are also engaged in this mode of cultivation

Due to intimate contacts with the civilized groups, most of the Indian tribes have taken to settled agriculture on plain land as means of their livelihood. Their technique and mode of cultivation are the same as those of other peasant groups and they also use bullocks, plough and other common implements of agriculture, but most of their land is unirrigated and hence they are often seen to be victims of vagaries of nature. Beside their total dependence on rains, they have to rest content with low and meagre yield because of absence of other agricultural inputs like fertilizers, high yielding varieties of food grains,, pesticides, etc. Among the numerically big tribes Oraon, Munda, Ho and Santhals are successful cultivators.

Some of the Indian tribes earn their livelihood through cottage industries. They are engaged in basket and mat making, weaving, blacksmithy, etc., and supplement the needs of their neighbouring tribal and non-tribal societies. The Gujjar of Kashmir, and Kinnauri of Himachal Pradesh work on wood. Asur of Bihar and Agariya of Madhya Pradesh are proficient in iron smelting, the Kolam of Maharashtra are traditional mat weavers and the Irula of Tamil Nadu make beautiful mats and baskets on bamboo.

Totally pastoral tribes are few in number but Toda of Nilgiri hills, Gaddi and Bakrawal of Himachal Pradesh, Nageshia of Madhya Pradesh, Maldhan of Gujarat and some other tribes of northern and southern India are notable examples of this class of tribes. It is also worth mentioning that not all the pastoral tribes trade in milk. Some of them rear the cattle like sheep and goat for selling them in the market.

Another class of tribes earn their livelihood by performing dances, acrobatics, snake charming, etc., and hence they may be termed as 'folk artist'. The Nut and Sapera of Uttar Pradesh are good examples of this category. The Mundupptu of Orissa are expert acrobats, the Kota of Tamil Nadu are snake charmers, some groups of Gonds of Madhya Pradesh are tattooers and dancers and some other tribes of eastern India and southern India may also be put in this category.

Among the tribes engaged in agricultural labour are those which are traditionally agriculturists but due to their landlessness they work as agricultural labour on others' land. According to a conservative estimate about one-fifth of the total tribal population is engaged in agriculture as wage earners. Non-agricultural tribal labour force includes those tribals who are working in local factories and mines of Bihar, Orissa and Bengal and tea plantations of Assam and neighbouring areas.

A comparatively small number of tribal people are engaged in government and semi-government jobs as a result of the application of Constitutional provisions. Among such tribes are those of Meghalaya, Mizoram and Nagaland on the north-eastern fringe of the country and mainly Christian tribals of Chotanagpur.

Classification According to Culture Contact

Indian tribes can also be classified according to their cultural distance from the rural-urban groups. Majumdar (1976) opines that this comparative approach is the most useful in evolving a plan of rehabilitation because it focuses our attention on those problems of tribal India which are the outcome of haphazard contact with, or the isolation of these tribes from the rural-urban groups.

IN The fifties Varrier Elwin floated a well demarcated classification. He described four type of aboriginals:

(i) those who are most primitive, lives a joint communal life and cultivate with axes;

(ii) those who, though equally attached to their solitude and ancient traditions, are more individualistic, less occupied with axe cultivation, more used to outside life and generally less simple and honest than the first category;

(iii) those, the most numerous, who under external influence are already on the way out by the loss of their tribal culture, religion, and social organization; and

(iv) the tribes like the Bhil and the Naga who are said to be representatives of the old aristocracy of the country, who retain much of their original tribal life and who have won the battle of cultural contact.

Majumdar has aptly termed Elwin's classification as a 'crusader's manifesto'. He further maintains that though Elwin's classification helps in presenting the contemporary picture of the culture crisis in tribal India but as a basis for a programme of rehabilitation, it is unacceptable. He moves on to present his own scheme of classification. According to him, the tribal cultures fall into three groups:

(i) those who are culturally most distant from the rural-urban groups; that is, more or less out of contact;

(ii) those who are under the influence of the culture of rural-urban groups and have developed discomforts and problems consequently;

(iii) those who, though in contact with rural-urban groups, have not suffered thereof, or have turned the corner and do not suffer any more, though they may have in the past, because they have now got acculturated into rural or urban culture Majumdar disagrees with Elwin that every contact with civilized world brings misery to the tribals. He takes the stand that our goal should be to take ahead all these three types of tribal communities and establish, under planned conditions, healthy and creative contacts between them and the rural-urban groups."

The Indian Conference of Social Work (1952) appointed a Tribal Welfare Committee that suggested the following classification :

(i) Tribal communities,
(ii) Semi-tribal communities,
(iii) Acculturated tribal communities, and,
(iv) Totally assimilated tribes

Classification Based on Religious Beliefs

The major religions of India have variably influenced various tribal religions and pantheons and only those tribal communities still maintain their native religious beliefs with purity who are leading an almost isolated social existence in dense forests. On the basis of the latest Census data of, the tribes may be classified into followers of following religions:

(i) Hinduism,
(ii) Christianity,

(iii) Buddhism,
(iv) Islam
(v) Jainism,
(vi) Other religions

Among the above mentioned religions, the influence of Hindu religion on the tribes is tremendous and almost 90 percent tribals follow Hindu religion in one form or the other. Those who have embraced Christianity are also quite considerable in number and about six percent are under the 'shadow of the cross' but those following Buddhism, Islam or Jainism are negligible in number. One important point which is to be kept in mind in this context is that even those tribes who have embraced any of the above mentioned major religions have not necessarily shed their local tribal beliefs and rituals and many of them are found to be practicing their traditional faith alongwith their acquired faith.

When we view this situation in the geographical perspective we see that barring the tribes inhabiting the islands falling under Bay of Bengal and Arabian Sea, most of the tribes of South India alongwith the tribes of western India and central India are more or less Hindu in faith. Christianity has made tremendous headway among most of the tribals of north-eastern India and more than 90 percent of the population of Nagaland and Mizoram follows Christianity. In central India, some major tribes of Chotanagpur also follow Christianity and notable among these are Oraon, Munda and Ho. The tribes following Islam are mostly scattered in Lakshadeep, Himachal Pradesh, West Bengal, Maharashtra and Jammu and Kashmir. Among such tribes about 98 percent of the total tribal population of Lakshadeep, Minicoy and Amindivi Islands are followers of Islam. Buddhsim among Indian tribes is represented mainly by some tribal groups of Arunachal Pradesh. The impact of Buddhism, however, is visible in my other Himalayan and Maharashtrian tribes also.

Angami Naga

A Gond memorial Pillar (Maharashtra)

Women of Bhumij tribal Society, Jharkhand

A 'Sasandiri' where the Munda bury their relatives

Dimasa Kachari

Zemi Naga

Young Boys and Girls from Munda Tribe of Jharkhand

Jarwa - Andaman Nicobar

Postal Stamps related with Tribal India

Postal Stamps related with Tribal India

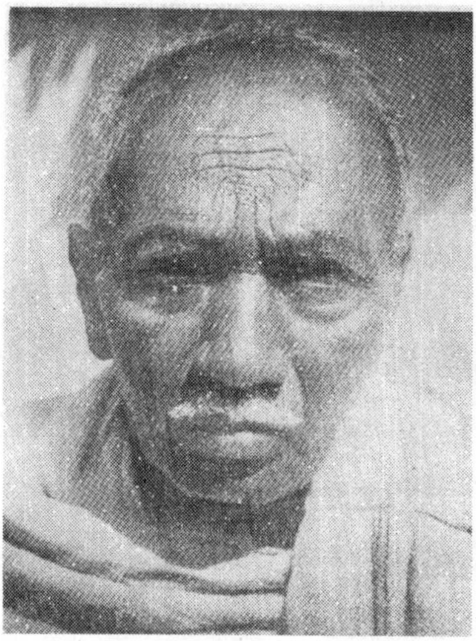

An Aged Munda

A Kolam of Yeotmal district (Maharashatr)

A Old Toda couple, Nilgiri Hills

A Typical Baiga

A Kharia Group

An Kharia from Gumla
(Jharkhand)

An Oran from Gumla
(Jharkhand)

An Oran with his daughter

TRIBAL INDIA:
Glimpses of society and culture

> In a vast country like India there are naturally vast minorities presenting immense problems. But what is disconcerting is the general unawareness-- the vast ignorance-- that people in general show about these minorities...
>
> Majumdar and Madan (1967)

MATRIMONIAL ALLIANCES :
Marriage Types

Chapter 4

The institution of marriage is another point on which the tribal people throughout the world have been much maligned. Wild and baseless charges were hurled at them, fantastic insinuations were formulated and many pseudo-scholars, claiming to have an intimate knowledge of the tribal world, let their imagination run riot for the benefit of a receptive readership. Some degree of laxity regarding sexual laision was taken to mean 'promiscuity' or free sex under which, according to such people, the institution of marriage could not exist. Such spicy phrases like 'sexual communism' were coined to describe a non-existant social situation. 'Interestingly' no ethnographic data collected from any part of the world support this hypothesis. In India too the simplest and the rudest of tribal cultures we know, e.g. the Andamanese, the Kadar, the Paliyan, the Malapanthram, the Chenchu, the Birhor and others do not furnish us any evidence of promiscuity.

Indian tribes like tribes of other parts of the world practise several forms of marriage as a matter of convenience and social acclimatization in their respective cultural-ecological settings.

Monogamy

Monogamy is a form of marriage in which no man may be married to more than one woman at a time. Majority of the Indian tribes practise monogamy. Just to refute the allegation that among the most backward and primitive tribes no clear-cut scheme of marriage exists, the example of the Kamar, a very backward tribe of Madhya Pradesh may be cited. This tribe is monogamous.

Polygamy

Polygamy that is, marriage to more than one person, is fairly widespread all over the world. Among Indian tribes, there are many who are following this type of matrimonial alliance. Polygamy has two aspect: (i) polygamy, (ii) Polyandry. While polygamy is the marriage of one man to several women, polyandry means the marriage of one woman to several men. Both types of marriages are referred to as polygamy in common parlance.

Polygyny is found among the Naga tribes, the Gond, the Baiga, the Toda, the Lushai and most of the Proto-Australoid tribes of middle India. In most cases such form of marriage comes into existence as a result of disequilibrium in sex ratio. Obviously, in a society where the sex ratio is normal, such type of marriage may force many of the male members to remain bachelor. Hence, normally such a practice develops in a society where the number of females is quite larger than the males. In an otherwise normal situation it is the privilege of the powerful and rich who keep more than one wife as a symbol of prestige and status. Among the Indian tribes like Gond, Baiga and Lushai, this type of marriage is resorted, to facilitate a better division of labour.

Polyandry is, comparatively, much restricted in distribution. This type of matrimonial alliance is found in the Himalayan tract stretching from Kashmir to Assam and is popular among the Indo-Aryan and Mongoloid tribes. In its classical form it is prevalent among the Tiyan, the Toda, the Kota, the Khasa (Jounsari) and the Ladakhi Bota. It is also popular among the Tibetans.

Among the Indian tribes, two types of polyandry are in vogue. When several brothers share the same wife, as among the Khasa and the Toda, we have fraternal polyandry. Majumdar and Madan (1967) opine that in the general type, also found among the Toda of Nilgiri Hills, there need not be any close relationship between the husbands, and the wife goes to spend some time with each husband. So long as a woman lives with one of her husbands, the others have no claim over her. Nayar polyandry was of this type. Polyandry is not everywhere explicable with reference to a preponderance of men over women. In Ladakh, it was actually the women who were more in number. Among the Toda, property considerations and sex-disparity explain this institution. Polyandry is found to lead to fewer children to every woman, more male children, and a high incidence of sterility among women.

The Khasa of Jounsar-bawar have evolved a very practical mode of polyandrous matrimony. Among them, when the eldest brother marries a girl, she automatically becomes the common wife of the rest of the brothers. If a brother is minor, he may, on becoming adult, marry another girl to match his age. Hence, this leads to a situation where a number of brothers have more than one wife which is not the classical mode of polyandry. Observing polygamy polyandry mixed up, Majumdar (ibid) coined an interesting phrase, Polygynandry, to describe this situation.

Till some time back the Todas of Nilgiri Hills used to observe an interesting ceremony called bow and arrow ceremony to declare the paternity socially. In this ceremony, all brothers and the common wife assemble amidst the rest of the villagers in the fourth or fifth month of pregnancy of the wife and as a result of consensus one of the brothers presents a set of bow and arrow to the wife. This is taken as declaration that this particular brother will be accepted as father of the coming child. In this way 'sociological fatherhood' overrides the "biological fatherhood' in the bewildering mosaic of human affairs.

Besides demographic factors, an economic factor called bride wealth is also responsible for the prevalence of polyandry among Indian tribes. Under the system of bride wealth the husband/ husbands are obliged to give an agreed amount of cash/kind to the parents of the bride as price which usually varies according to the physical beauty and utility of the bride. With the passage of time the bride wealth continued to soar and a stage came when it became almost impossible to arrange the bride wealth individually. Furthermore, the agricultural holdings in mountains are quite uneconomic and the pursuit of cultivation too hard to be borne by a single individual. Hence, to avoid further fragmentation of holdings and sharing the enormous labour, such a mode of marriage might have come into existence.

Another mode of polygamy, which may be called "bigamy', is also in vogue, though on a very restricted scale. Under bigamy a man is allowed to marry two sisters at one time. This type of polygamy has been reported from the Holiya and Medara tribes of Mysore.

Preferential Marriage and Prohibitions

It is observed that, on the one hand, the society prohibits sexual liaison or matrimonial alliances between particular kins or in the same clan or gotra but on the other hand, it encourages matrimonial alliances between certain other kins. In such cases there is a prescription, or only a preference, expressed for marriage to a particular kin. The following are some of the popular types of 'preferential' marriages prevalent among the Indian tribes.

(1) Cousin marriage
- (a) cross-cousin marriage
- (b) parallel-cousin marriage

(2) Levirate

(3) Sororate

Both types of cousin marriage, viz., cross-cousin marriage and parallel-cousin marriage are quite popular among the Indian tribes. The Gond, Kharia, Khasi and Kadar are some of the important Indian tribes practising cousin marriage. Anthropologically speaking, when the children of a brother and a sister marry, it is a cross-cousin marriage while it is parallel-cousin marriage when the children of two sisters or two brothers get married. A Gond is supposed to marry his or her cross-cousin, and if one likes to have this prescription waived in one's case, a compensation has to be paid to the losing party. Gross-cousin marriage, as observed by Majumdar, is often explained to be a device for avoiding payment of a high bride price, and also for maintaining property in the household. The Gonds of Madhya Pradesh call this form of marriage doodh lautawa (return of milk). The implication is that the bride price paid by 'A' for his wife would be returned to his family when the daughter of 'A' marries her mother's brother's son. Claude Levi Strauss has said that preferential marriage has, for its main purpose, the strengthening of solidarity within tribe.

Levtrate and sororate are two other types of preferential marriages which are also said to promote 'inter-familial cordiality' by making certain linkages imperative. When a woman marries her deceased husband's brother this is called levirate. It may be split into two types : (a) junior levirate (b) senior levirate. When the woman marries her husband's younger brother, it is junior levirate while marriage with the elder brother is called senior levirate. When levirate occurs in non-polyandrous societies, it is of paramount importance because in the event of her husband's death, the widow finds a guardian, husband and partron while the children get a man as their father who has been loving them earlier too. Among some tribal groups, a degree of laxity is allowed in the matter of intimate social relations and sexual liaison between a woman and her husband's brothers as a prelude to the coming event. This situation may be termed as 'anticipatory levirate'.

When a man marries his wife's sister/sisters, it is sororate. It may occur after the death of his wife or even in her life. The death of a spouse is compensated by giving a new spouse, generally a younger sister of the deceased. Levirate and sororate emphasise the acceptance of inter-familial obligations and the recognition of marriage as a tie between two families, and not only between two individuals.

Ways of Acquiring Mates

Nine important ways of acquiring a mate have been found to be popular among the Indian tribes :

1. Marriage by capture
2. Marriage by exchange
3. Marriage by purchase
4. Marriage by elopement
5. Marriage by service
6. Marriage by intrusion
7. Marriage by trial
8. Marriage by mutual consent
9. Marriage by probation

When a man forcibly snatched away a woman from her village and marries her, it is called marriage by 'capture'. Many tribal societies give social sanction to this type of marriage which symbolises valour and chivalry. Marriage by capture has been most popular among the Naga tribes of north-eastern region where Naga tribals of one village used to invade the enemy's village and capture grown up girls. This led to female infanticide. However, with the widening application of the Indian Penal Code and growing social consciousness as a result of culture contacts this practice is fast vanishing into oblivion. Cases of capture have also been reported from the Ho, who call it **Oportipi** and the Gond who call it **Posiothur.**

Among some other tribes like Bhumij, Kharia, Munda, Santhal, etc., this practice has given place to mock capture as a 'survival' of the old practice in which after finishing the marriage the parents of the girl request the groom to come to an agreed place and 'capture' their daughter. In a mock gesture, the girl (bride) also puts on symbolic resistance. Among some tribes like Ho, it is the exorbitant rate of bride price that often leads to marriage by capture.

Majumdar reports that in Assam, physical captures take place during raids by one village on another. In middle India, the method is more peaceful, capture being effected on festival days at inter-village meets when there is much revelry, drinking and intoxication. Such captures are given social sanction by requiring the gallant, who has made the capture, to pay a compensation and/or give a feast to the tribal brotherhood.

Marriage by exchange has primarily been evolved as a means of avoiding the payment of high bride price. Under such a marriage two households exchange women with each other and thus avoid the payment of bride price. This practice is found, in varying degrees, all over India in which a man gives his sister or any other woman of his household in exchange of his wife. Interestingly, Khasi tribals of Meghalaya do not permit it.

Marriage by 'purchase' is highly prevalent mode of matrimony throughout India. Bride price is the central theme in this type of marriage. This is paid either in cash or in kind or partly in cash and partly in kind. Lowie has emphasised that although the economic nature of this transaction cannot be minimised, it nevertheless would be wrong to regard the payment of a bride price as indicating sale and purchase. It may be only symbolic of the utility of women, and by way of compensation to her parent's family. Among the major tribes, marriage by payment of bride price is prevalent among the Munda, Oraon, Ho, Santhal, Rengma Naga, etc. The worst consequences of bride price are probably seen among the Ho tribals of Chotanagpur, Bihar. Their poor economic condition has been made worst by the ever increasing amount of bride price. The amount is so high, and to accept a lower amount being against one's status and prestige, that many young men and women remain unmarried. These unfortunate youngmen often resort to marriage by capture and the spinsters have often to undergo further injustice by being identified with witchcraft and sorcery. In many cases their natural desire to marry leads them into the clutches of the cunning moneylenders and the consequent bondedness.

Marriage by elopement is also a peculiar feature of tribal India. As is well-known, child marriage is a new phenomenon is tribal India. They started adopting it as a result of culture contact with their Hindu neighbourhood. Previously, only adults entered into married life, and therefore, almost everywhere, marriage by mutual consent with parents' approval was the general rule. But with the changing times boys and girls started shedding their traditional submissiveness. In case the parents' consent is not forthcoming, elopement is generally the way out. Of course, the indulgent elders receive back the over-fond couple. This practice is often resorted to in the face of high bride price. The tribes of Chotanagpur are famous for one type of elopement or the other.

Marriage by 'service' is another way of avoiding the payment of bride price altogether or minimising it considerably through service rendered by the prospective groom at bride's residence. Thus, if a Gond or Baiga finds himself not in a position to pay the bride price, he goes to serve in his would-be father-in-law's house as a suitor servant and marries the desired girl after a lapse of some years. Purum of Manipur recognise it as the only traditionally genuine mode of matrimony. They have to work in the bride's household for three years and have to fulfill all the responsibilities of a son. The boarding and lodging arrangements are taken care of by the would be-in-laws during the entire period of stay. Among the Birhor, the father-in-law often lends money, which is returned in installments to enable the son-in-law to pay the bride price. Till such time as the loan is repaid, the sone-in-law is compelled to stay at his father-in-law's household.

The opposite of 'marriage by capture' is also found among the Indian tribes and is known as 'marriage by instrusion'. This is the case of a girl desirous of marrying an unwilling youngman. In such a case the girl thrusts herself on the unwilling groom and his parents. She tries to serve the would be man in his life and his parents but is humiliated and tortured in return. If she persists in her intentions and her endurance lasts for a considerable period she is finally accepted as daughter-in-law of the household. The Birhor and the Ho of Chotanagpur are some of the major tribes who practice it. Ho call it, very appropriately, anadar meaning humiliation or disrespect.

Marriage by 'trial' is another way of acquiring mate among some of the Indian tribes. It is the recognition of personal courage and bravery as highly desirable traits in a youngman. The prospective groom has to prove his prowness before he can claim the hand of the desired girl. It is most popular among the Bhil. During the Holi festival yongmen and women perform a folk dance round a pole or a tree to the top of which a coconut and gur are tied. All the youngmen and women are free to participate in the dance, locally c & Wed gol gadedho. The girls make an inner ring of dancers round the tree. When a youngman attempts to break through the cordon to climb the tree to eat the gur and break open coconut, the girls resist his attempt with their full force. The aspirant may incur even severe injuries but it is taken in good faith. If in spite of these obstacles, a daring man succeeds in this drama, he has the right to demand any of the surrounding girls as his wife.

Marriage by 'mutual consent' is the result of the tribals' contact with Hindus. This practice is similar to that prevalent among the Muslims, Hindus, Christians, etc., in which all the formalities of marriage are arranged by the parties concerned through the process of mutual consultation and consent.

Probationary marriage can be called as primitive version of modern practice of courtship before marriage. Under this practice the prospective husband and wife are permitted to live together for some time in bride's house. If they like each other and decide to marry, elders arrange their early marriage. In case the couple do not find each other's temperament to be suitable and compatible they separate and the man has to pay cash compensation to the girl's parents. Such a practice is widely prevalent among the Kuki of Arunachal Pradesh. Some tribal groups of Chotanagpur also approve of this practice and call it Raazi-Khushi.

Pre-Marital and Extra-Marital Sex Relations

This is another area of tribal life which has been shamelessly exploited by many authors and journalists who have tried to enter into overnight fame by unthoughtful and exaggerated versions of the tribals' pre-marital sex life. When the imagination of others run riot, it is to the anthropologist's credit who skillfully avoids these pitfalls and makes a serious and objective study of all the aspects of tribal life, including his sex life.

Pre-marital sex relations, in varying degrees, are seen to be permissible all over tribal India, as with the tribal people of other parts of the world. Obviously, the conception of virginity or chastity in a society plays the crucial role in this context.

Among the tribes of middle India, pre-marital sex relations are overlooked unless of course they lead to pregnancy which is regarded as shameful for the girl's parents. Also for a girl to become pregnant is regarded as an extreme family disgrace. She is asked to name the child's father and he is forced to marry her. In this case the amount of bride price is either reduced considerably or it is waived altogether. Among the Konyak Naga, the girl continues to live in her parent's house even after marriage where her conduct is overlooked by the parents and other village people. Usually after the birth of her first child, she moves to her husband's household. Among the Muria Gond of Bastar, young boys and girls are traditionally allowed a degree of permissiveness within the four walls of the youth dormitory. All the stages of courtship are gone through and they get married with the blessings and approval of their parents. Ao Naga, too, do not attach undue importance to the so-called virginity of the girls.

Extra-marital sex relations are not as common or permissible as pre-marital liaison. It has been reported that among the Maria, the main cause of high incidence of murder and suicide has been marital infidelity. But the Tharu tribe of Uttar Pradesh presents an interesting spectacle. The Tharu men are said to be so much overwhelmed and ' overawed by the beauty of their wives that they play only second fiddle to them. The wife may indulge in extra-marital sexual liaison and get away with it.

The Khasa of Uttar Pradesh have evolved a different value system regarding the extra-marital sex relations. Since most of the girls are married off at an early age, there is hardly any possibility of pre-marital liaison. Hence, their main worry is about extra-marital relations. In her parental house, the wife is called dhanti, while in her husband's house she is called rhanti. These two seemingly ordinary words of native dialect carry a very significant connotation. When she is dhanti, a woman enjoys all sorts of freedom. She is a free bird. She can meet anybody, allow anybody to take liberties with her. But the same woman is like a chained slave while she is rhanti. In her husband's house she has to work hard in the fields and in house, she is generally frustrated and her conduct and movement always remain under the strict control of her husband/husbands and other affinal relations. For a little respite, she comes to her parents' house generally during local fairs and festivals. The strains which these women suffer by being wife to several men, who are mentally and physically unlike each other, are relieved by the unfettered life which she can lead in her parents' village.

This sort of dual role prompted some anthropologists and sociologists like Majumdar (1962) and Saxena (1964) to term it as "dual morality" which is quite a misnomer when viewed by an outsider who tries to measure the moral fabric of these simple folk with his own yardstick of puritan hypocracy and so-called morality.

Divorce

Unlike Hindus, marriage is not a religious sacrament among the tribes of India. Hence, divorce or dissolution of marriage is not only possible but widely practised. It may easily be obtained if the parties no longer wish to live in wedlock.

The ground for divorce, however, varies from tribe to tribe. The Khasis permit divorce for reasons of adultry, barrenness and incompatibility of temperament. In some cases, the party desiring the dissolution may have to pay compensation to the other party and remarriage between such people is not possible. The divorce, like marriage, has to be a public ceremony where the mother gets the custody of the children. The Lushai, however, allow marriage between those once divorced. The Gond, Kharia and others also allow divorce freely on grounds of marital irfidelity, sterility, laziness, etc.

Despite contacts with the Hindus, widow remarriage is still practised among almost all the tribes of India and there is little likelihood of its discontinuation. Since widow remarriage carries no stigma among the Indian tribes, the plight of a young woman falling widow is far from miserable.

NETWORK OF SOCIAL RELATIONS : Family and Kinship

Chapter 5

Man has the gift of a highly developed brain which enables him to engage in organized behaviour to exploit and harness nature. The groupings thus come into existence may have for their immediate cause and binding force several principles of integration: the simplest and most obvious of these is the principle of kinship, that is, relationship between different members of family based on marriage and on descent. "This relationship is of a three fold nature: that between husband and wife, that between parents and children; and that between children of the same parents "(Majumdar and Madan, 1967).

Family

Tribal India exhibits a colourful diversity of families because of varied rules and customs among different tribes. Two types of families may be distinguished on the basis of the number of family members:

(i) simple or nuclear family, (ii) extended and joint family.

The first type represents the basic grouping of the mates and their children. Such families have very limited number of members. Many Indian tribes like the Birhor, Pariya, Korwa, etc., maintain this type of family. If this nucleus is extended by the addition of other closely related kins, then it is called an extended family. If this is still further extended by the principle of kinship, then we get a family like the Hindu joint family. The Nairs of Kerala are taken as a classic example of this type of family and the Nair's Tharawad is an important institution in itself.

A Variety of families may also be distinguished on the basis of the number of marriage partners. Although most of the tribes have monogamous families, i.e., families consisting of a husband, a wife and children but polygamous families are also not very uncommon. Such families come into existence on the basis of two forms of polygamy viz., polygyny and polyandry.

A Polygynous family consists of a husband, two or more wives and their children. This is a condition of marital arrangement common all over the tribal India. Then there are polyandrous families in which the husbands are more than one, as for instance among the Todas of Nilgiri Hills of Tamil Nadu and the Khasas (Jounsari) of Jounsar-bawar in U.P. where several brothers marry one wife without any exclusive right of cohabitation for any one spouse. The shortage of women was formerly due to the custom of female infanticide which tilted the sex ratio heavily towards the abundance of males. This does not imply, however, that sexual relations are promiscuous. Actually, strict rules are observed by the parties concerned; and when a child is born, its paternity is established by means of a social ceremony instead of biological considerations.

Several other forms of family are also found among the tribes in India or the basis of authority of father and mother. Who is more important in the family, father or mother? This determines the patriarchal and matriarchal nature of the family. This situation further leads to two more sets of situations: patrilineal/matrilineal and patrilocal/ matrilocal. Most of the Indian tribes acknowledge the authority of father in family affairs and hence they have partriarchal families where descent is also traced from father, i.e., patrilineal and the wife leaves her parents' home and comes to reside with her husband, i.e., patrilocal. However the Khasis of Meghalaya and the Nairs of Kerala are the classic examples of the rare matrilineal, matriarchal and matrilocal family. The Khasis live in the Khasi and Jaintia Hills of Meghalaya.

They are famous all over the world as the best example of a society which is nearest to being matriarchal. They trace their desent from mythical female ancestresses. Their family consists of mother, her unmarried children, male and female, her husband, her married daughters and their husbands. Majumdar aptly remarks that whereas the Khasi family grows round a nucleus of blood-related females who are surrounded by fringe of males-unmarried brothers and sons, fathers and husbands and whereas property, authority, religion, residence are all in the hands of women, menfolk also are respected and even exercise some authority. The all powerful Khasi woman addresses her husband as her lord. The above description is the traditional situation and the Khasis are also changing with times.

Kinship

People in all parts of the world and in all the societies, irrespective of their technological level, are bound together in groups by various kinds of bonds. The most universal and the most basic of these bonds is that which is based on reproduction, an inherent human drive, and is called kinship. But social recognition is seen to override biological fact in the affairs of kinship, especially among the primitive societies all over the world.

The tribes of India are divided into lineages. While most of the tribes are divided into patrilineages, Khasi and Garo of Meghalaya have matrilineages.

Like other people of India, the tribal population too recognizes both types of kinship viz., consanguinous kinship and affinal kinship. While consanguinous kinship includes all the kins related through blood or biological ties, affinal kins consist of those recognized through marriage. But an interesting and significant fact, as mentioned earlier, is that the consanguinous kinship among them does not include only biological ties. The case of Todas of Nilgiri Hills following fraternal polyandry may be cited as an instance where paternity is established through 'bow and arrow ceremony'. Until another brother makes the ceremonial presentation, all children born to her of several brothers are regarded as the children of the brother who last performed the ceremony.

The most profound impact of kinship ties on the social life may be felt, through kinship usages found in every society. Kinship usages among the tribes of India present very interesting and significant spectacle. Such types of behaviour pattern, verbal and non-verbal, explain many complex intricacies of kinship system.

It has been found among many tribes that many sets of kins avoid each other. The avoidance between daughter-in-law and parents-in-law is quite common. Likewise, though less universally and also less rigorously, a son-in-law's relations with his parents-in-law are found to be cramped by certain restrictions. Among the tribes of Andaman and Nicobar Islands, the elder brother does not talk with his younger brother's wife. Radcliffe-Brown has given one of the most plausible of contemporary explanations. He points out that avoidance is a social fact and must, therefore, have a social explanation. He says that whenever people come in contact with each other the possibilities of cooperation as well as conflict are always equally present. But there are certain kinds of kinship where hostility is regarded as against social norms. The best way to prevent such hostility from becoming manifest is to put restrictions on the growth of intimacy; and hence the kinship usages of avoidance. Freud's psycho-analytical explanation is based on sexual attraction and the need to prevent sexual intimacy between various kinds of relatives.

Another kinship usage which is reverse of the avoidance relationship is an extreme degree of familiarity expressed through joking relationships. Such joking may amount even to exchange of abuse, obscene and vulgar references to sex, ridicule and so no. Apart from joking relationship between sister-in-law and brother-in-law and between a wife and her husband's brothers, such relationships have also been reported between grandparents and grandchildren among the Oraons and the Baigas. The Ho tribe of Chotanagpur also indulge in a variety of joking relationships. Majumdar opines that joking relationships may be indicative of equality and mutual reciprocity. They may also be indicative of a potential sexual relationship. Thus, is explained the joking relationship between a man and his wife's younger sister or elder brother's wife. In each case the two may be potential mates. A joking relationship, when not mutual, assumes the role of social control. It becomes indicative of correction through ridicule.

Avunculate and amitate, as known in anthropological parlance, are two other kinship usages prevalent among the Indian tribes. Among the Khasis, Garos, Nairs, and a couple of other societies the maternal uncle enjoys a pre-eminent place in the life and affection of his nephews and nieces as a matter of convention. He has special obligations towards them which exceed those of their father and transmits his property to his nephew. The kinship usage is called avunculate. Obviously, this is a common usage among matrilineal societies. A special role, similar to that outlined in case of the maternal uncle, for one's father's sister is designated as amitate. This is explicable in patrilineal tribes.

Among Khasi, Toda, Ho, Oraon, and a host of other tribes, a queer practice has been reported, called couvade, on the basis of a similar practice known among the Trobriand Islanders by the same name in their local dialect. The practice consists in "making a husband lead the life of an invalid alongwith his wife whenever she gives birth to a child. He refrains from active life, goes on sick diet and observes certain taboos" (Majumdar and Madan, 1967). Thus, the Khasi husband, like his wife cannot cross a stream or wash clothes until the spirits connected with child-birth are propitiated. Sometimes, among some other tribes, this practice is extended to the extent of putting up the poor husband in an adjacent hut to his wife and made to ape the actions of his wife. Malinowski believed couvade to be a cementing bond of married life and a social mechanism designed to secure paternal affection. Other anthropologists have sought to give a psycho-analytical explanation. They have attributed this usage to the husband's desire to lighten the wife's discomforts, in the absence or lack of proper modern medical care, by a process of participation through identification. Some scholars have attributed this practice to the matriarchal and matrilineal mode of social organization but the prevalence of this practice, till recent past, among some patriarchal and patrilineal societies like the Ho, Oraon, etc., negates this assertion.

ECONOMIC ORGANIZATION

Chapter 6

The economic organization of Indian tribes is not different from the primitive economic organizations of other parts of the world. Basically, their economy is geared to the satisfaction of basic subsistence needs and hence they fall into the broad category of production-consumption economies. Contrasting this system with the more advanced one, Majumdar (1967) comments that with the accumulation of an economic surplus, human attention is increasingly devoted not only to various material needs other than food, sex and shelter but also to the refinement of the manner in which these three primary, and other derived and secondary, needs are satisfied. These latter types of economies are called the production-consumption-distribution type.

Another very remarkable characteristic of contemporary primitive economies is that they used to be run in the absence of currency and other modern economic phenomena before their contacts with the modern world. Primitive societies living in isolation are still managing without these monetary instruments.

Before taking up the economic organizations of Indian tribes, it seems imperative to make a brief overview of various types of economies man evolved as a result of cultural adaptation in different situations. Adam Smith was the first scholar who tried to present a classification of economic organization. He talked of hunters, pastoralists and agriculturists and later the categories of handicrafts and industrial pursuits were added to make it more comprehensive. Ernest Grosse, with the help of evolutionary perspective, put forward the following stages of development:

(i) Collectional economy,
(ii) Cultural nomadic economy,
(iii) Settled village economy,
(iv) Town economy,
(v) Metropolitan economy.

Similarly, Ehrenfels has put forward the four economic types among the early human societies of South Asia:

(i) Food gatherers,
(ii) Higher hunters,
(iii) Plant cultivators,
(iv) Nomadic herdsmen.

Most of the tribal people of India fall under the first and the third of these categories.

Daryll forde (1950) does not agree with the idea of economic stages because he does not believe that people live at economic stages and finds no single exclusive economy but combinations of economies; the growth of cultures. Gordon Childe holds more or less the similar opinion with regard to prehistoric economies. Ford agrees with Herskovits' (1952) five-fold division of economies:

(i) Collection,
(ii) Hunting,
(iii) Fishing,
(iv) Cultivation,
(v) stock raising.

Also, both agree that a people need not abandon one economy to adopt another.

Thurnwald has presented a scheme of various types of economic life, some of which concern us directly:

(1) Homogeneous communities of men as hunters and trappers, women as collectors. The Kadar, the Chenchu, the Kharia, the Korwa are some of the Indian tribes falling into this category.

(2) Homegeneous communities of hunters, trappers and agriculturists. The Kamar, the Baiga and the Birhor are examples of this type rom tribal India.

(3) Graded society of hunters, trappers, agriculturists and artisans. Most of the Indian tribes fall under this category.

(4) The herdmen, The Toda and some sections of the great Bhil tribe furnish classic examples in India.

(5) Homogeneous hunters and herdmen. This category is not represented among Indian tribes. The Todas do not hunt nor do they catch fish or birds.

(6) Ethnically stratified cattle breeders and traders. The Bhotiyas of the sub-Himalayan region of Uttar Pradesh breed yaks and

jibus (cross between yak and cow) and are itinerant traders; they come down to the plains in winter and go over the hills right upto Tibet in summer.

(7) Socially graded herdmen with hunting, agricultural and artisan population.

These are some of the important classifications encompassing various facts of economic life as lived in different corners of the world. But it does not seem possible to study the economic organization of Indian tribes on the basis of any single classification given above. Every tribe lives by a variety of economic activities. A certain type of activity may be playing a dominant role in the economic organization but some others are also there to supplement. However, the tribes of India may be divided into following broad categories on the basis of dominant economic activities in the respective economies:

(i) Food gatherer and hunter
(ii) Shifting cultivator
(iii) Cultivator
(iv) Pastoralist
(v) Artisan
(vi) Industrial labour

Food Gatherers and Hunters

This is a fast vanishing category of tribes which persist in deep forests and mountain ranges. Due to fast expanding means of communication and consequently increasing culture contacts with the people possessing advanced technology, they are turning into cultivators. However, there are some tribes who still depend upon collection and hunting unaware of the techniques of cultivation.

This category includes those who earn their livelihood through collection of edible roots, fruits and honey and hunt small animals for food. They also go for fishing if the avenues are there. Some such tribes also collect wax, gum tusks, etc., for the purpose of barter or exchange. In this way they are able to fulfill their essential needs even in the absence of cultivation of foodgrains.

The dependence of gathering and hunting people on nature is so pronounced that they appear to be a part of the nature exhibiting excellent mode of cultural adaptability. Most of such tribes are found in southern India and prominent among them are the Kadar inhabiting the forests of Cochin; Malapatram, Paliyan, Irula, and Kurumba of Tamil Nadu and the Chenchu dwelling in the Annamalai mountain ranges of Andhra Pradesh. Besides, the Birhor and the Kharia of Bihar, Kamar, Baiga and Abhujmaria of Madhya Pradesh, Yenadi of Andhra Pradesh, Koya and Kontareddi of Tamil Nadu and Katkari of Maharashtra may also be included in this category. The Onge, Jarwa, etc., of Andaman Islands also fall in this category. Though most of the above mentioned tribes are also engaged in some other subsidiary economic pursuits, yet the dominant mode of economic organization still remains food gathering and hunting.

Most of the characteristics of primitive economic organization are present in the economies of food gathering and hunting tribes of India, foremost of which is the lack of resources, tools and implements. Mostly, they live by their physical prowness and competence amidst the aweful lack of technological alternatives which is quite natural at this stage of technological development. The very notion of 'surplus' is absent in their economies because neither they are in a position to generate surplus nor they are equipped to preserve the surplus commodities of everyday life. Furthermore, their nomadic existence also prohibits the development of techniques of preservation and conservation among them. Since their entire physical existence is spent in procuring food, there is hardly any scope for rapid development in any other sphere of life.

Shifting Cultivators

A Conservative estimate suggests that more than 90 percent of the total population in India practise one type of agriculture or the other. Most of the Indian tribes who depend upon agriculture follow this pursuit in two ways viz, primitive and traditional mode of slash and burn known as shifting cultivation and settled or plough cultivation with the help of various types of agricultural tools and implements. Since the problem of shifting cultivation among the Indian tribes has been dealt with in detail in a separate chapter on 'Shifting Cultivation' a brief account shall suffice in the present chapter.

Shifting cultivation is an age-old institution among the Indian tribes. This, in principle, means the cultivation of a plot of land for a temporary period and then leave it fallow. It consists of clearing the forest slopes, burning the fallen trees and bushes, and broadcasting the seed in the ash covered soil. The rest is left to nature. The sowing on the plot may be done for one or more seasons but not beyond this. After that, fertility of the soil is exhausted and then another plot of land is cleared and the agricultural operations are transferred to it.

In India this mode of cultivation existed in remote hill areas of north-eastern region, Orissa, Madhya Pradesh, Bihar and to a lesser extent in several other parts of the country. Although, it has been declared unlawful in most of the areas, it still exists on a lesser scale.

Shifting cultivation is known by different regional names in India. It is called Jhum among the tribes of Assam, Meghalaya, Tripura, Mizoram and Arunachal Pradesh; Bewar or Dahya in Madhya Pradesh; Podu in Andhra Pradesh; and Roman or Bringal in north Orissa. The major tribes practising it are Lohta, Angami Naga, Khasi and Kuki of north eastern region, Asura of Bihar, Saora and Juang of Orissa, Baiga and Gond of Madhya Pradesh and Korwa of Uttar Pradesh.

An Interesting aspect of shifting cultivators is that they themselves inhabit permanent villages in a more or less settled way but keep on changing the plot of land for the purpose of procuring foodgrains.

Till recently, the shifting cultivators confined their agricultural pursuit to producing only foodgrains and cereals. Now some of them have started growing even cash crops clinging to their age-old mode of cultivation. The shifting cultivators of Assam, Meghalaya and Nagaland grow cotton as cash crop while maize, vegetables, etc., are grown for domestic consumption. The Juangs of Orissa produce oil seeds as cash crop and paddy for themselves.

Since this mode of cultivation is highly uneconomic due to extremely low yield, most of the shifting cultivators spend their days in poverty and misery. It has been pointed out that if shifting cultivation is not stopped it will tie down the tribes practising it to an underdeveloped and low socio-economic level. However, it must be recognized that a change over from shifting to permanent plough cultivation cannot take place suddenly as the economic life of a people is woven inextricably with all the other aspects of their life.

Cultivators

Most of the Indian tribes have adopted the popular mode of cultivation, i.e., permanent plough cultivation like the rest of the peasantry of India. Such tribal cultivators have their own plots of land for agriculture and they employ various animals and agricultural implements in their agricultural pursuits. Adoption of this mode of agriculture has been either due to highly uneconomic and unproductive nature of shifting cultivation or due to culture contacts with the neighbouring peasantry.

The Mizos of Mizoram and the Apatanis of Apatani valley in Arunachal Pradesh are two such examples of shifting cultivators emerging as expert cultivators. The Mizos grow various varieties of rice which is their staple food. The Apatanis are also expert cultivators of rice. Both men and women work together with dedication in the field and despite their lack of knowledge of modern agricultural implements and manures, get enough yield. They grow crops either on the meshy lands of lower plains or the terraces prepared on the mountains. Terrace cultivation which is another type of permanent plough cultivation provides a classic example of cultural and ecological adaptability of these people. The streams of upper forests are tapped in such a ways as to provide each terrace sufficient quantity of water and, if need be, extra water may be siphoned out. Though quite labour consuming, it exhibits the extreme dedication of the cultivator.

Among the tribals of India who have emerged as expert cultivators are the Santhal, Oraon and Ho of Bihar (including Jharkhand) and Bengal, Tharu and Korwa of Uttar Pradesh (including Uttrakhand), Gond, Bhil and Bhilala of Madhya Pradesh (including Chhatisgarh). Saora of Orissa and Badaga of Nilgiri Hills in Tamil Nadu.

The Tharus and Korwas of Uttar Pradesh have adopted settled cultivation to such an extent that they are aware of all the means of agriculture. Cowdung manure is used extensively, and dams are harnessed for irrigation and, above all, they grow Rabi and Kharif crops with the precision of the neighbouring peasantry.

It is also commonly observed that the tribes who have embraced Christianity are highly advanced in agriculture as compared to other tribes. This may be due to the fact that missionaries working in these areas have not only preached the gospel of Christianity but have also equipped their followers to grasp the modern means of economic pursuits and take advantage of various developmental schemes floated by government and other developmental agencies. In this connection, the educational institutions run by missionaries are playing important role in shaping the destiny of the concerned tribal people.

Pastoralists

Pastoral economy is another aspect of economic organization of the tribes of India. Most of the Indian tribes rear cattle for a variety of purposes but when a people breed and rear cattle for commercial purposes and make it their source of livelihood, they may be said to be living under pastoral economy. The Indian pastoralists usually lead a settled life and become wanderers and nomads only under the pressure of changing weather. The pastoral tribes who inhabit mountainous regions migrate to the plains alongwith their cattle during severe winters but go back to their permanent abode at the advent of summer. Hence, they may be termed more or less as 'settled pastoralists'. Probably, this is a response to the urge of entering settled life from the food gathering-hunting nomadic life of bygone ages.

Among the Indian tribes the famous Toda, inhabiting Nilgiri Hills of Tamil Nadu, furnish a classic example of pastoral economy, their social and economic organization being built around their buffaloes. The Toda, in the words of Majumdar, "obtain their living by drawing directly upon milk and milk products and by exchanging the same with neighbouring people to acquire other necessities of life. The buffaloes are ubiquitous, figuring in all aspects of their life. They form the economic base of Toda culture. They or their milk, play the prominent part in the socio-religious life of the tribe. The daily life of the Toda men is mainly devoted to the maintenance and care of their buffaloes and dairies"

The Gujjars of Himachal Pradesh are also prominent pastoralist and they rear cows, buffaloes and sheep for commercial purposes. The Bhotia of Uttarakhand division of Uttar Pradesh are cattle breeders and traders at the same time. They breed yak and jibus and weave woollen pullovers, shawls and blankets and sell them in the cities of the plains. In this way, they are itinerant traders who come down to the plains in winter and traditionally go over the hills right upto Tibet in summar. But after the outbreak of war with China in 1962, their trade with Tibet has been ruined and now they depend mainly on the rearing of sheep and goat for milk, meat, and wool. These animals are also used as beasts of burden. Under the increasing pressure of fast changing economic life they are also adopting agriculture as one of the means of livelihood.

Artisans

Artisans practising various handicrafts are found in all tribal zones of India. But there are very few tribal communities who live by their handicrafts alone. Many tribal communities take it as their subsidiary occupation often pursued in leisure to supplement their income. The Maria Gonds distil spirit from forest produce. The Saoras devote themselves to metal working, weaving, can working, pottery and so on. The Korwas and the Agarias are traditionally well-known iron smelters, producing tools for local use only, their techniques being very crude. The Ghasis make gut from the fibre tissues of animals. The Tharus make furniture, household utensils, baskets, musical instruments, weapons, rope and mats. The Irulas make bamboo mats and baskets, and plough-shares and wheels for local use only.

The Apatanis are expert makers of knives and swords and manufacture them for commercial purposes. The Kotas of Nilgiri Hills are efficient blacksmiths, carpenters and potters. The Mizos, Riangs, Nagas and Apatanis of north eastern region and the Saoras of Orissa are expert weavers of cloth which they sell in the nearby markets. The Marias and Muria Gonds of Bastar are famous for their toys and icons made of clay and metal which are marketed by various handicraft emporia in the country. The Bhils and Bhilalas of Jhabua district weave beautiful durris and cushions out of old clothes and cotton fibres.

Industrial Labour

Industrial labour is a comparatively new phenomenon in the economic organization of tribes of India. It encompasses very serious and significant implications. The problems of tribals as 'industrial labour' have been dealt with in a separate chapter on 'Industrialization' in tribal areas in view of the serious nature of this problem. Indian tribal people have come into contact with industrial life in two ways. Either they have migrated to industrial areas or industries have sprung up in the areas they inhabit. Large numbers of Santhals, Konds and Gonds have migrated to Assam and taken up various jobs in tea plantations. The other manner of contact with industrial life is more important in view of its far reaching consequences. Certain tribal areas in middle India have been found rich in natural ores; coal, iron and steel, and other industries have sprung up in these areas. This has happened particularly in West Bengal, Bihar, Orissa and Madhya Pradesh. "Thus industrialization of these peoples' life has taken place, establishing a kind of tribal-urban continuum" (Majumdar).

The situation described above distinguishes two categories of tribes. The Santhal, Oraon, Munda, Kharia, Gond and some others may be lumped together in the first category. In view of growing economic hardships, they migrate to Assam and the adjoining areas to work as tea plantation workers, while some members of the family migrate to other cities and towns to work as unskilled labour. The other category includes Santhals, Hos and others who are working in the mines and mills situated in their area. The steel complexes of Jamshedpur, Ranchi, Rourkela, Bhilai and Bailadila employ tribals in large numbers.

Industrialization of these areas has certainly presented millions of tribal people new and permanent source of livelihood, but at a enormous and aweful cost. Industrialization and urbanisation have damaged their social fabric substantially. Decay and disintegration in their traditional social institutions have set in. Industrial values have distorted their own value system. Liquor addiction, gambling and prostitution are eating the vitals of their social organization. These 'victims' of industrialization have been pushed into an alien milieu without equipping them to face the hazards of a strange world.

Division of Labour

Compulsion of physiological factors like sex, infancy or old age and physical disability provide the only basis for specialization in pre-urban societies. Majumdar opines that besides this basic recognition of physiological differences and their implications which are reflected in the division of labour in primitive societies, there have been extentions of this basic fact which have resulted in further compulsive factors decreeing a sexual division of labour. The inability to understand the variety of physiological processes connected with healthy life of a woman, like menstruation and childbirth, has given rise to strange norms. The pampered and well-treated Toda women, for example, have been barred from touching the sacred buffalo or stepping into the dairy.

The association of women with infants has also imposed checks on them, preventing their full participation in the tasks of men. They have to take care of the infants and of cooking which naturally force them to stay longer at home. Among most of the Indian tribes, men never cook such food in which milk and milk products are used, obviously on ritualistic ground. Women do undertake most of the tasks generally done by men. Women among Indian tribes gather food; engage in cultivation (sowing and harvesting); go fishing; make baskets, cloth and pottery and so on. But they never go for hunting big game, nor for felling trees, nor do they become blacksmiths or carpenters.

The tribal women of hilly and mountainous regions are most hardworking, their menfolk being examples of laziness. The Khasa women of Jounsar-bawar in Uttar Pradesh are a glaring example of this situation. Here the women do all sorts of work from dawn to dusk, from collection of wood to carrying water from the mouth of steep slopes and from sowing and harvesting to taking care of the cattle, whereas the menfolk relax in tea stalls sipping tea, gossiping and smoking, discussing factional politics and scandals. The impact of industrialization, however, has affected both men and women. In such areas as affected by industrialization, men work in iron and steel factories, coal mines and tea gardens while women workers are engaged in mica and coal mines, in tea gardens, in quarries and so on. Engaging menial labourers is unknown in tribal India except among a couple of tribes like the Jounsari of Uttar Pradesh where Kolta, the traditionally landless and ritually untouchable section of the tribe, are kept as slaves, bonded forever by the higher caste Rajput-Brahmin landlords. Thus, except for a couple of such examples, division of labour into master and slave is unknown in tribal India.

Property, Ownership and Succession

The conception of property varies from one form of society to the other and hence modern conception of property cannot be applied to primitive societies. Among the tribes of India, all the commodities controlled and regulated by social values may be termed as property. Misra and Tiwari (1975) while elaborating this point in the Indian context express the view that even among the food gathering and hunting tribes, forests and means or implements of food gathering and hunting constitute property. Though the members of the society are entitled to use and consume forest produce and fauna in independent ways, yet their use is subject to certain social rules and values. Among the pastoral tribes, pastures, cattles, cattle-sheds, dwellings, clothes, objects obtained from animals, etc., are different forms of property. Similarly land, agricultural implements, house, clothing, etc., are forms of property among the agricultural tribes while sources of raw material, tools and implements, finished goods, clothing, houses, etc., constitute property among the artisan tribes.

Among the Indian tribes both types of ownership, viz., collective as well as individual, are fairly known. In whichever form property may be recognised, its recognition entails the existence of some rules of inheritance. Inheritance acquires particular importance when individuals possess property by themselves. In communal inheritance the group as a whole never ceases to exist suddenly as individual does, and is replenished through fresh recruitment from time to time. Though the emphasis nowadays is on individual ownership, there are instances like the Nagas who traditionally own the lands of the village collectively. Since the individual property is quite meagre, it is a custom among many tribes to burn the items of individual use alongwith the deceased.

The laws of inheritance may be patrilineal or matrilineal or some kind of a combination of both depending upon the social structure of a particular society. The daughters inherit the property among the matrilineal tribes, like the Khasi of Meghalaya, and the sons among the vast number of patrilineal tribes. In some cases the eldest daughter or son inherits the entire property. Among the Toda tribe of Nilgiri Hills the eldest and the youngest son get an extra animal. The Badaga of the neighbouring region practise a different set of rules. Among these people the eldest son leaves home the moment he get married. It is the youngest son who remains in the house with his parents and he only inherits the property of his father and becomes his lawful successor.

Market

Except with some food gathering and hunting tribes, the institution of market is seen to be present in one form or the other among almost all the tribes of India. However, regular markets are still a rarity among them. In most of the cases people assemble in an assigned place and on an appointed time and exchange their commodities with each other. Such markets are usually weekly or fortnightly. The markets held in tribal regions usually trade in commodities of local use like vegetables, cereals, meat, spices, salt, utensils, agricultural tools and implements, clothing, cosmetics, etc. Non-tribal traders are also seen to be interested in some of these markets which are visited by them in search of local produce at cheaper rates. Their transaction becomes easier when they lure the simple tribals with urban products and get away with the local produce at throw away prices.

The tribal markets usually run for a few hours and during the day time. Some markets are held once a year and they continue for days. In the Bastar region of Madhya Pradesh such markets are known as Marai. These are held usually after harvest and people visit these markets alongwith their families to buy necessary commodities for the year. Such markets present festive look where people sing and dance and engage in all sorts of merrymaking. They serve manifold purpose. Distant relatives meet each other, marriages are arranged, local politics is discussed and thus these annual markets carry a lot of social and cultural significance. To be more precise, the markets not only fulfil certain needs of the buyers and sellers but also act as agents of culture change.

POLITICAL ORGANIZATION

Chapter 7

Political organization is generally taken as that aspect of total organization which is concerned with the control and regulation of the use of physical force and regulation of relations between groups or members of different groups within the society at large. The tribes of India exhibit a variety of forms of political organization due to their varied technological and ecological conditions. On the one hand we find the nomadic gathering-hunting tribes of South India like the Kadar, Irula, Chenchu, etc., who are still living on a very low technological level, while on the other there are tribes like Khasi and Garo Hills of Meghalaya and the Apatanis of Arunachal Pradesh who are leading quite a comfortable life with the help of their highly developed mode of agriculture and horticulture. We may also distinguish the tribes on the basis of their intimate contacts with Hindus and Christians. On the one hand there are highly Hinduised tribes of Chhotanagpur region and Madhya Pradesh while on the other hand there are tribes of Meghalaya, Assam, Nagaland, and Mizoram who are highly advanced Christians. These examples are meant to emphasise the point that the tribes of India are no more a solid, monolithic mass but a collection of socially, economically and culturally diverse groups living under different, socio-cultural and ecological conditions. As a result of this bewildering diversity, these tribes have developed a wide ranges of political organizations. Thus, we find a highly decentralized political organization existing side by side with an automatic and centralized authority. Now let us examine the political organization of the tribes of India divided into three geographical zones.

Political Organization among the North-Eastern Tribes

This geographical zone consists of Assam, Arunachal Pradesh, Meghalaya, Nagaland, Mizoram, Manipur and Tripura. The Khasi, Garo, Lushai, Jaintia, Mizo, Apatani and a variety of Naga tribes are the prominent tribal groups inhabiting this highly picturesque region of India.

The tribes of Assam maintain a democratic political organization. Most of these tribes recognize collective ownership of land giving scant respect to individual rights over land. People of one village are free to do cultivation anywhere they like. Though economic status of different families in a village varies, yet this variation could not develop social stratification on any sharp lines.

While most of the tribes are divided into exogamous clans, others live in village communities without a clan system, each under its ruler, independent of the rest of villages. Among the Khasis, the dignity of a chief is inherited by the eldest son of the eldest sister, after his death by his eldest brother or by the maternal grand nephew. If male heirs are absent, the eldest sister (or eldest sister's daughter) has the right to succession. Politically, the Khasi area was, in the past, divided into twenty five Khasi states which were independent. Though headed by a chief known as siem, administration was on democratic lines. A Khasi chief had no power over land or forests. He could not impose taxes or promulgate new laws or any policy independently. Decisions were taken on the basis of general consensus in a congregation which was an open door assembly in which all the male adults of the state took part. Attendance was compulsory in such congregations.

Similarly, though the chieftain of Lushai tribe commands more dominance than the Khasi siem, yet it is similarly difficult for him to ignore the opinion or advice of the seniors of the village. Though these offices are hereditary, the administration is run on thoroughly democratic lines.

Among the tribes of North Cachar district, the principle of heredity and election go side by side. Tribal issues are resolved in the presence of all males of the village in an open court. Any decision taken with regard to an offender is deemed to be a collective decision of all the villagers. The elders of the village form an informal council and discuss the problems facing the village or the cluster of villages.

The political organization of the Garo tribe is also run on democratic lines. In fact, the Garos have no chiefs. A headman is only a nominal head while the important affairs are decided by village councils consisting of elders or heads of families. Stephen Fuchs (1973) describes the political organization of the Mikirs as having a three-fold village administration, the lowest office of which is filled by the Achom Asar, usually an old, influential man well versed in Mikir customs. He is appointed by a Habe, the next higher authority, the headman of a village whose jurisdiction does not go beyond the limits of the village. The Habe is, in turn, appointed by a Pinpo, in the past appointed by the Jaintia ruler as his representative for the administration of the Mikir hills. There are now nine houses of

Pinpo, and their office is hereditary. Each Pinpo is selected from the clan to which his predecessor belonged.

The political organization of the Naga tribes is marked by great diversity. Some of the Naga tribes subject to chiefs who rule almost autocratically while other tribes form democratic village communities in which the headman has only a nominal authority. Most of the Naga tribes have been labelled as blood thirsty, savage and war loving but no sweeping generalization is fair to describe the situation. Though, it is correct that most of the Naga tribes have always been at war with each other and vendetta is the rule but this should be viewed in the socio-historical perspective. Many of the people wonder how stable administration can exist under such conditions of anarchy and lawlessness where every individual is law in himself. But even within these limitations and under such conditions political organization of flexible type has always existed. The Konyak Naga are subject to a chief who is sacrosanct and tabooed and rules often several villages with much authority. "He is regarded as the repository of tribal fortune, virtue, or its life principle" (Fuchs). In some villages, he was so heavily tabooed that he was not permitted to touch the ground and on a journey had to be carried.

Among the Angami Nagas, the basic unit of the tribe is not the village but an exogamous sub-division of the population thus concentrated, called Khel or Tepfu, and said to be derived from a single ancestor. Factional fights and blood shed between these bodies are frequent.

The political organization of the Naga tribes has always been in need of security protection against supernatural and natural hazards. Haimendorf (1976) opines that the institution of the sacred chiefs who were believed to have leased in support of the supernatural through their birth in the right families and who could mobilize the coercive and productive powers of the society, was an insurance against the hazards.

Central Indian Tribes

The tribes of Bihar, Madhya Pradesh and Orissa constitute the largest tribal belt of India. These tribes share certain traits of political organization based on clan solidarity. The village headman assisted by a council of elders oversees the administration of the village. The decision of this council is reached either through consensus or majority verdict and the headman has no power to overrule the majority verdict.

THE Oraons, Gonds and Bhils are three numerically most important tribes of this zone. The Oraons have developed Parha organization which is a confederacy of a number of neighbouring villages with a central organization known as the Parha Panch. Each Oraon Parha consists of a number of villages-one of the villages is called the Raha (king) village, another the Dewan (prime minister) village, a third the Panrey (clerk of the crown) village, a fourth the Kotwal (bailiff) village, and so on. Such of the villages as have got no such denominations are known as Praja (subject) villages. Raja village is the head village of the Parha. Although, every functionary of the Parha no longer possesses a distinctive badge of office, every village of the Parha has its own distinctive flag and other badges which may not be used by any other village. Maintenance of law and order and the settlement of disputes between villages is also the function of the Parha council. T.B. Naik (1964) tells us that the different villages of the Parha hunt together, fight together and on stated occasions meet together in dancing trysts, social feasts, and deliberative and judicial committees.

The lowest political authority among the Santhals and the Malers is the village headman called Manjhi. He and the village elders meet and talk over the village affairs. The headman is entitled to certain gifts at weddings and other feasts and he holds rent free land. The Manjhi is both a civil and moral authority. In his civic functions he is assisted by a sub-headman, the Paranik.

Among the Mundas the village headman is known by the same, i.e., Munda while his religious counterpart is called Pahan. About twelve villages constitute a Patti or Parha and the man who heads it is known as Manki who is usually the most influential of the village headmen forming a group. The Munda and the Pahan are hereditary offices.

The basis political unit of the Gonds is the village community. The village headman is called Patel, Mandal or Bhoi. He is assisted by some elders of the village in settling the village affairs. Though the king of Bastar, Hindu, does not command any political authority over the Gonds, yet he has been the centre of spiritual veneration of all the groups of the Gonds. An interesting aspect of political organization among the Bison Horn Maria is that the priest responsible for religious rituals and ceremonies and the medicine-man are more influential than the village headman.

South Indian Tribes

This tribal zone is very important in view of the fact that this is the abode of some of the economically and technologically most backward tribes of the world. Most of the tribes of this zone live in small groups dispersed in forests or on the outskirts of villages of the cultivators. Usually they live a life of their own and try to avoid contacts with and interference from outsiders. They want to be left alone.

The tribes of Andaman and Nicobar Islands are still living in gathering-hunting stage of economic development. Though most of them are nomadic groups yet they roam about within a definite geographical zone. Every local group consists of 5-10 families and every group has its own headmen. These local groups live and act independently. However, during special hunting sprees or certain festivals they may unite temporarily. The headmen of the local groups take care of the affairs of their respective local groups.

Among some other nomadic tribes there is no such institution as a headman of a settlement. The heads of the single families simply come together and settle the affairs of the group whenever problems arise and decisions have to be taken. Thus, the Allars and Aranadars have no headman. Affairs of the community are discussed at a gathering of elders whose decision is binding. Those who disagree simply leave the group and join another one. Among the Kadars, another food gathering tribe, the hereditary institution of the headman has ceased to exist.

Among the Adiyars of Kerala, the office of the headman is hereditary. If a son is unsuitable for the office a nephew may inherit it. The headman has a special title but he is not an autocratic ruler; he only presides over the meetings of the elders at which affairs of the community are discussed. His sanction is required, however, for any important undertaking, a marriage or divorce, and he presides at funeral ceremonies.

RELIGION — The Wonder World

Chapter 8

Religion is said to be the human response to the apprehension of something, or power, which is supernatural and supra-sensory. It had been regarded as a product of civilization until Tylor convincingly proved that "primitive" societies have their own versions of religious activity, not very different from that of civilized societies. Ever since Tylor's views were published in the late nineteenth century, no ethnographer has reported any primitive society without religious beliefs and practices.

Tribals India presents a colourful panorama of religious faiths and practices which is the manifestation of adjustments with their cultural, ecological conditions. Till late forties, tribal religions in India were termed as animism in various Census reports and literatures. "By animism was implied that exceedingly crude form of religion in which magic is the predominent element. It conceives of man as passing through a life surrounded by the ghostly company of powers and elements, mostly impersonal in their character. Some of these are regarded as presiding forces' over various 'departments' of life, each 'force' having its sphere of influence. Thus, there may be a spirit presiding over various diseases, spirits dwelling in rocks, rivers and waterfalls and so on. These are diligently propitiated to ward off the dangers associated with their influence" (Majumdar and Madan, 1967).

Spirits dwell everywhere and men have to be at peace with them to enjoy freedom from illness and a long life. If anybody falls ill the general belief is that some relationship has been violated. The men and women skilled in the art of magic and sorcery decide what should be done for the sufferer. Among more sophisticated communities, certain places, probably enclosed by a wall and covered by a roof, are marked off as specially sacred. But among the animistic tribes all places are holy as they are the seats of spirits.

Among the Korwas there is a spirit presiding over crops, one over rainfall, one over cattle. Besides, there are several spirits which dictate the attitude of the Korwas towards their neighbours, priests, headmen, etc. Animism carries with it a belief in benevolent as well as malevolent spirits which are supposed to influence the destiny of man. The benevolent ones generally go unattended, as no one is afraid of them. Thus, for instance, the great sun god, Singbonga, of the Munda tribe is seldom worshipped as he is benign and does not harm anyone. This is a typical hallmark of primitive religions; they are more concerned with all forces, fears and frustrations. But it will not be fair to accuse those people of living in perpetual fear of ghosts and spirits. All men have their hopes and fears and to single out a few elements of tribal religions and say that the latter are born only of fear is doing injustice to them.

The tribes of Chhotanagpur like Munda, Oraon and Ho believe in a supernatural power known in their local dialect as bonga. Among the Ho the bonga are vaguely understood as powers indefinite and impersonal and they do not seem to have any objective appearance or existence. "The overall supremacy of the bonga over Munda life shows only the extent of anthropomorphism. The impersonal bonga uses the medium of dreams to foretell, day dreams being used for fore-warning about bad things. Bonga is the manifestation of a vague supernatural power, one that is the cause of all energy. The bicycle has, of late, become a bonga, the powerful steam engine is a bonga, and the aeroplane is a greater bonga than any of the above" (Majumdar). Differences of power, prestige and so on among individuals are regarded to be due to the degree of the bonga power possessed by a person.

There is hardly any tribe in India which does not believe in the conversion of soul of the deceased into a potential spiritual force. It is believed that these souls continue to remain in contact with the intimate relatives. Ancestor worship among them seems to be the logical result of such beliefs. The Todas of Nilgiri Hills and the Hos of Chhotanagpur perform two types of ceremonies after cremation. The second one is meant to make it sure that the departure of the soul from the body is final and forever. The Todas, while returning from the second such ceremony, scatter thorns so that the malevolent soul may not enter their village.

Most of the tribes of India believe that life does not end with death, and that it continues to be present in one form or the other. Propitiation and worship of the souls of ancestors seems to be the result of such beliefs. The tribes of middle India believe that the souls of their ancestors come to their rescue in diseases to ward off other evil spirits. The tribal people of Chhattisgarh invoke the spirits of their ancestors through special ceremonies.

It is also believed by many tribes that certain objects are 'possessed' by some spiritual powers and thus a sort of festishism appears to be the guiding principle among such tribes. Worship of such objects contains an element of magic which is further extended to the beliefs and practices of religio-magical nature. The Bondas of Orissa worship a particular sword in the belief that is connects them with the mightly Rajput warriors of yesteryears. On a special occasion Bondo people assemble near a banyan tree and the sword is hidden in the thick foliage. After performing certain rituals, the priest climbs up the tree and comes down holding the sword in his right hand. Now a goat and a cock are sacrificed with this sword and the blood is thoroughly smeared on the sword. The frenzied devotees compete with one another to obtain some blood dropping from the sword. Those who obtain the blood smear it on the forehead. The priest, amidst chant of hymns, invokes the spirit to work for the devotees. Afterwards the sword is hidden in the foliage of the tree till further ceremonies. The Murias of Bastar possess a big drum in each village and believe that this is the abode of their chief deity lingopan who takes care of their well-being.

Hinduism, Christianity and the Tribal Gods

Reviewing the relationship between tribal religions and the wider Hinduism, Majumdar very rightly comments that though "it is true that the association of tribal religions in India with animism exists, it is not the whole truth. It was left to Hutton to reclaim these religions from the 'wastepaper baskets' of animism. He found it difficult, on the basis of evidence from all over India, to draw a sharp line of distinction between Hinduism and tribal religions. Not that the two were not regarded as different by him but that he found that the two fuse and grade into each other. He is the author of the aptly famous statement to the effect that the tribal religions represent a kind of surplus material which has not yet been built into the temple of Hinduism. He finds this material very similar to the material already used in building up post-Vedic Hinduism."

Elwin also has, in his various monographs, pointed out the futility of distinguishing between tribal religions and Hinduism. He further points out that tribal people are always willing to worship a few more gods if by doing so they can enjoy some material or social advantages. This is evident from their contacts with Hindus and Christian missionaries.

Contact with non-tribals has been proved instrumental in changing the religious beliefs of many a tribal group. In certain cases these contacts have given a fresh lease of life to a tribal group by providing it with better tools of adaptation. As N. K. Bose (1971) points out, Christianity has undoubtedly brought the message of a richer life, a wider companionship and a new sense of dignity to converts. But it is interesting that the Christian religion has always been attended by the belief of modern western civilization. And this was particularly so during the British rule when the converts felt closer to the British rulers than to their 'benighted' countrymen. It is only after independence that allegiance to one's native culture is being encouraged. It is now gaining acceptance that there can be a Christian religion which does not necessarily draw men and women away from their own culture and civilization. Yet, upto now, the principal agent of westernization, often regarded as modernization, among the tribal folks has been Christian missionary enterprise.

The tribes of Chhotanagpur and Jharkhand region stretching upto Orissa and West Bengal, and of the north eastern region are the best examples of the result of contacts with Hinduism and Christianity. The relation of tribal folk to Hinduism or Christianity has been different because Hinduism has not been a proselytizing religion and secondly most of the tribes of India except those in north-eastern region have been profoundly affected by Hinduism. While Hinduism has been unobstrusively making an impact on tribal life and culture, Christianity began making deep dents in it from the nineteenth century. Contacts with the Hindus led to the gradual adoption of popular Hindus deities, festivals and religious beliefs. This did not involve any significant break with the past. The tribals adopted these without giving up their own deities and gods. As mentioned earlier in this chapter the tribals willingly adopted and worshipped a few more gods. But this was not so in the case of Christianity. It meant total break with the past. The Christian priests and missionaries assured them that their (tribals) gods were blasphemous and obscene. Sometimes, it led to disintegration of stheir lives.

As a result of culture contacts with the Hindus, the worship of Mahadeo in various forms is found not only among the Oraons but also among Gonds. Worship of Kali and Lakshmi is also common among many tribes. The growth of Bhagat cults such as Vishnu Bhagat, Tana Bhagat, etc., among the tribes of Chhotanagpur is also directly related to cultural contacts with the Hindus. It is also interesting that many tribes tend to give up or atleast claim to give up such practices as are not acceptable to their Hindu neighbours so as to raise themselves in their esteem.

The impact of the Christian mission, however, is different. Acknowledging its impact, Sachidanand (1964) says that all over the world, the Church has been one of the most important agencies of social change. The religion of any primitive people inevitably reflects the social structure of the community in which it develops. Same is the case with Indian tribes and here lies the basic contradiction. Christianity reflects another type of social system in which geneological relationship is not so important. The Church asserts universality. A basis is provided for broadening the concept of brotherhood in which not only kith and kin but strangers are included as co-religionists. Christianity introduces a new kind of leadership and a new principle of social control. The priest becomes the all-round leader—the path finder, the friend, philosopher and guide. The importance of the traditional leader at once goes down. The concept of sin and the fear of retribution become powerful instruments of social control. This is accompanied by changes in material culture, outlook on life, worldview, etc. There is a change in dress, increased devotion to education, acceptance of the new system of medicine as well as loss of faith in magic and witchcraft. For political affiliation, the converts turn to the priest for guidance. Change of this nature may easily be discerned in Meghalaya, Mizoram, Arunachal Pradesh and Nagaland. It is also of immense importance that the impact of the mission is felt not only among the converts but also on those who come in contact with the Christians and are influenced by them by education, precept or example.

HEAD HUNTING

The very mention of 'head hunting' induces many in India to think of Naga tribes of north-eastern region. However, it is a fact that the practice of head hunting has been widespread in many regions of the world. 'Head hunting' refers to the practice of severing or slashing a head and keeping it as souvenir for a variety of purposes. Till the last century this practice has been prevalent among many primitive societies of the world including some of the Naga tribes of the north-eastern region of India. However, with the advent of the present century especially during the last fifty years or so, head hunting has become a thing of the past with the erstwhile 'heau hunters' resorting to it in exceptional circumstances.

The head hunters believed that the soul and all the extra ordinary powers of the hunted person become subordinate of the hunter and he becomes more powerful. It also served as a means of status elevation in the society. It was also believed that head hunting brought good fortune, fertility and increased productivity in crops. Beside serving as a marker of muscular powers, head hunting was also believed to contribute for more reproductive power. Among the Nagas expertise in head hunting was considered an added qualification for an eligible bachelor. Displaying the severed heads on bamboo poles as talisman, especially of the aged women, was the usual practice among the primitive Melanesians for obtaining better crops. Among all the head hunting groups the usual modus operandi has been to ambush the victim, usually of enemy groups, with utmost expertise. Heads of women were always more coveted because they were more guarded and hence their head hunting signified more valour on the part of the hunter. As far as the Naga tribes are concerned head hunting is no more prevalent. The British rulers dealt with it with iron hands and later on the government of independent India too made a multipronged attack on this custom through various socio-political and administrative means. The result of all these efforts is that except in very rare circumstances head hunting has become a thing of the past.

SHAMANISM

Shamanism and Shaman are widely distributed phenomena among the tribal and non-tribal peasant communities in the world. Shamanism include those rituals and beliefs which are based on the principle that certain spirits enter into certain men who become 'possessed' and in turn are dictated by those spirits in performing various types of acts and rituals. Such people as the ones described above are popularly known as 'shaman'. Terms like 'Ojha' are also quite prevalent among a number of communities in India. Shamans are endowed by superhuman powers. They may be both benevolent as well as malevolent but more frequently they exist in benevolence.

Among most of the societies maintaining the Institution of Shamanism, the Shamans act as 'faith healers' or Yolk doctors'. However, they may also engage themselves in sorcery and witchcraft. In the former role they perform rituals and prescribe folk medicine to the affected people. If the practitioners of folk medicine are not able to deliver good, the Shaman steps in, communicate with the spirits and suggests propitiation of spirits as remedial measure.

THIS may include **havan, sacrifice of animals** or any strange or 'bizarre' rituals. Many tribes of Bihar, Madhya Pradesh, Orissa and West Bengal have a strong Institution of Shamanism. The tribal communities specially primitive tribal communities feel very insecured because of uncertainties of the world around them. The fear of epidemic, natural disasters, inter group warfare, sorcery and witchcraft sustain Shamanism.

BIRDS IN TREES :
Youth Dormitory

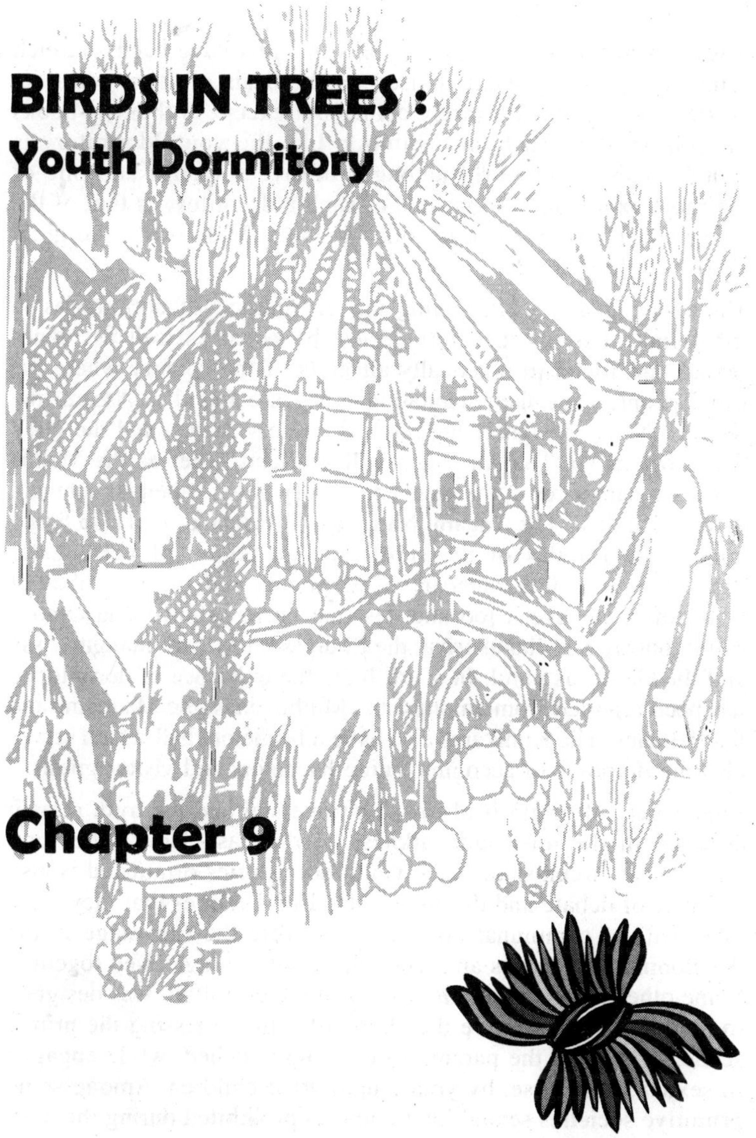

Chapter 9

Youth dormitories among the tribals of India have been so much romanticised and sensationalised on the basis of their romantic, erotic aspect that truth rarely comes out except in the text-books of anthropology, such an institution like the youth dormitory is found all over the world among primitive societies and one of the most exquisite descriptions of such a dormitory is that of the Trobriand Islander's bukumatula given by Malinowki, the great British anthropologist.

Majumdar (1967) while giving the distribution of dormitories in tribal India tells us that dormitories, bi-sexual as well as mono-sexual, are found in practically all parts of the country where the tribal people have their habitation. They are found in Assam; the Konyak Nagas designate the boy's dormitory as ban and the girl's dormitory as yo. The Ao Nagas call it arichu, whereas the Memis have two names for it, the men's dormitory being called **ikhuchi** and women's **iloichi**. The Angami Nagas call it **Kitchuki**. It is also found among the Bhotias of the sub-Himalyan region of north Uttar Pradesh, who call it rangbang. The Munda and the Ho tribes of Chhotanagpur have it too and designate it as **gitiora**. The Oraons call it **jonkerpa** or **dhumkuriya**; the Bhuiyas know it as **dhangarbassa** and the Gonds as **gotul**. In south India the existence of dormitories has been reported from amongst the Muthuvenas, the Mannams and the Paliyans. The Kunikaras also have a bachelors hall which serves also the purposes of accommodating bachelors and visitor guests.

The subject of origin is always controversial and the truth remain dropped in the mist and darkness of the past. How, when and under what circumstances the youth dormitories originated is also a matter of debate and discussion. Hodson believes that they are a 'survival' of communal houses which were the first stage in the development of homes and when the whole village lived together. Some other scholars hold the view that the dormitory was designed to prevent incest, to save the children from witnessing the primal scene, or to save the parents from being watched, while engaged in sexual intercourse, by young unmarried children. Among some primitive societies sexual intercourse is prohibited during the busy agricultural season, and therefore, a man's house has to be separately provided for. During such times, the lonely women would also have to keep together among themselves. Besides, menstruating women have often to be segregated. Among the Marias and the Murias, husbands are not allowed to sleep within the house with their wives so long as the naval chord of the new born child does not fall. Also, many tribes do not permit sexual relationship between men and women till child is weaned. Further, Grigson reports about the Hill Marias that, generally speaking, they do not regard the home as the proper place for sexual intercourse. Some or all of the above mentioned reasons may have led to having a common dormitory house for both the sexes.

Two types of youth dormitories are found among the tribes of India. Some may be common, i.e., shared by both boys and girls as is the case with the Muria gotul or they may be confined to one sex only, as are the Konyak morung and yo.

Mostly, the dormitories are built on the outskirts of the village so that their members may maintain secrecy and carry on their activities without any disturbance. The dormitory is generally housed in a specially built building, which may be simple and bleak, like the one doored, low roofed dhumkuriya of the Oraon, or elaborate with carved wooden doors like that of Naga morung.

Though the life lived inside dormitories appears to be of a light-hearted type on the surface, however, as Majumdar puts it, underlying these semblances are deep socio-economic and educative motives. Youths collect in the dormitories by the evening to dance, sing, play, tell each other folktales and folklore and later to sleep for the night. It's members may be divided into two sections - the seniors and the juniors. It is the seniors who being well versed in tribal lore and tradition, pass on what they have learnt and experienced to the juniors, who in their turn, one day assume the role of seniors. The officers who are supposed to manage the affairs of the dormitory are chosen from amongst the seniors. They are also supposed to control the activities within the dormitory and maintain discipline.

Where there is a dormitory, it is obligatory on the part of the boys and girls to become its members. Though the age at the time of entry into dormitory varies from tribe to tribe yet the common average age seems to be around ten years and the membership continues till the member gets married.

Besides the recreational activities, its members led by the 'officer' assist in several collective endeavours like doing work at marriage, house-building or harvesting. Its members stay with their house people during the day but after taking the evening meal they proceed towards their respective dormitories.

The members are supposed to maintain strict secrecy as regards the activities inside the dormitory. Majumdar states that this happens particularly in view of the fact that amorous affairs are freely carried on inside the dormitories, although sexual intercourse is not, generally speaking, permitted within their four walls. In the Muria gotul, senior girls often train younger boys in the sexual act, and no permission is needed from the leaders for sexual intercourse. An interesting, but inadequately investigated, aspect of dormitory life is the comparative infertility of the numerous sexual liaisons established inside or outside the dormitory during one's membership days. There is also evidence of the use of the rhythm method of birth control. So far as the Murias themselves are concerned, they give many supernatural explanations, such as that of the gotul being protected by Lingo, its patron god. Sexual congress taking place inside the gotul would not lead to pregnancy, since such a thing happening would bring disgrace to Lingo himself. They offer sacrifices and prayers to prevent impregnation which is not however regarded as much of social stigma. It only complicates the economic aspect of marriage due to the presence of a child who after his mother's marriage to her child's father or someone else, is accepted as a fullfleged member of the wife's husband's household.

The social and sexual training imparted in dormitories proves very crucial in the coming married life of the members and cannot be dismissed as unimportant or unhealthy. Interestingly, even the most advanced societies of the world lack such a training in an institutionalized manner.

S.C. Roy, the famous ethnographer who has done pioneering work among several major Indian tribes, provides a three-fold purpose for the dormitory of Oraons of Chhotanagpur. Firstly, it is said to serve as an effective economic organization for purposes of the food quest; secondly, as a useful seminary for training young men in their social and other duties; and thirdly, as a place for the performance of magico-religious ceremonies designed to bring about success in hunting and to augment the procreative powers of youngmen. Inderjit Singh while talking about the Gonds mentions participation in joint economic pursuits, training in social and sexual behaviour and provision of accommodation as important functions of the gotul.

Decline

Culture contacts with the Hindus and spread of Christianity in the tribal areas are two major causes for the decay of the dormitory institution. Majumdar is of the view that culture contacts with the non-tribals have proved disastrous for the institution of dormitory. Frequent and deeper contacts with the urban ways of living have resulted in the loss of love for, and confidence in, their own typical ways of living. Attempts are made to rise in the estimation of the neighbouring non-tribal people, and in this process indigenous institutions are often sacrificed.

Thus, boys going to schools not only disown going to dormitories but actually stop going there. It has been found that the Ho tribe, with their deep contacts with urban agencies, have constantly denied the existence of giitora, their dormitory institution, reported by earlier investigations.

The spread of Christianity has also played its part. All the tribals, in middle India or in north-eastern region, who have been converted to Christianity, have been brainwashed by the missionaries to dismantle the very institution of dormitory. These tribal folks are not allowed to go to the dormitory. The result of such a sustained and systematic effort is that the youth dormitories have disappeared from the villages of the Christian tribals.

The decay of once virile, colourful, and useful institution of dormitory among the tribes of India is a study in melancholy. Sachidananda's various studies of the tribal life in Chhotanagpur region bring forth the present condition of dormitory. While making a study of Ratu, Mandar and Chiri tribal villages of Chhotanagpur, he remarks that the present condition of dhumkuriya is much different than it was 40-50 years ago. It seems that this institution is breathing its last. In several villages the only thing left in the name of dhumkuriya is a dilapidated and neglected house standing as a memorial to a great social institution of the tribal folks.

ETHNOGRAPHIC PROFILES OF SELECT INDIAN TRIBES

The Toda (Pastoralists)
The Chenchu (Food gatherer-hunters)
The Khasi (Matrilineal & Matriarchal)
The Oraon (Agriculturists)

ETHNOGRAPHIC PROFILES OF SELECT INDIAN TRIBES

Chapter 10

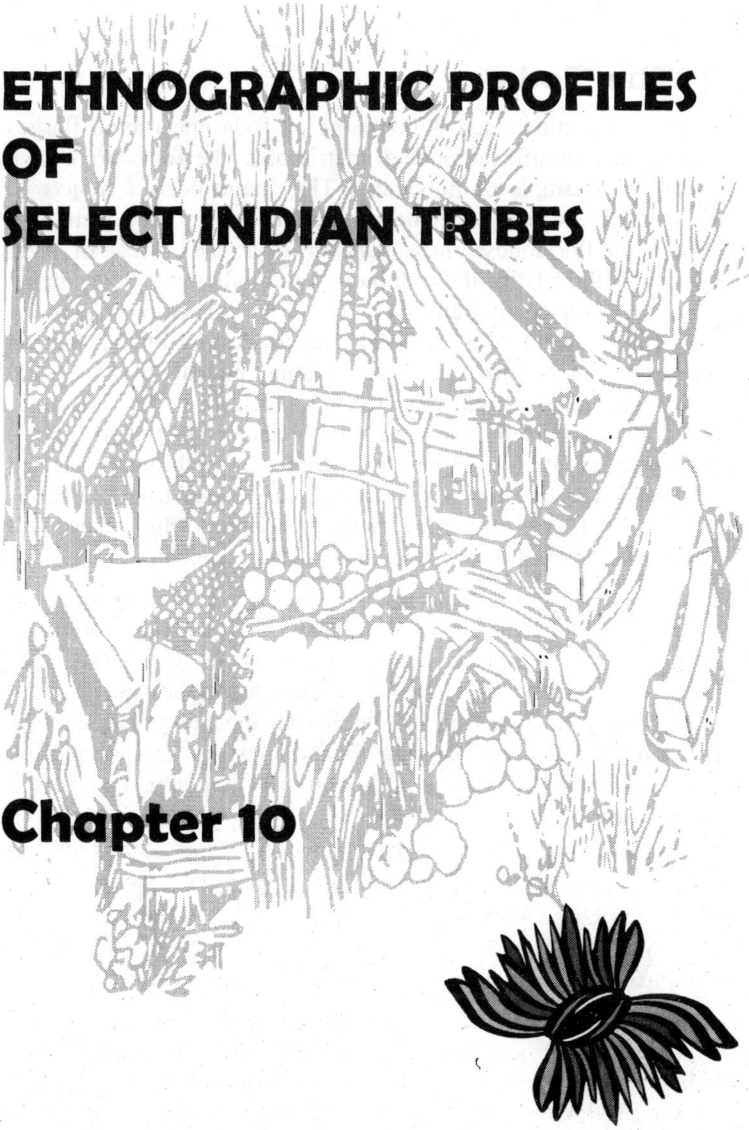

(a) The Toda

Whenever one comes across the name of Toda one's mind flashes back to a very significant mode of matrimony. The Todas are known as a classic example of polyandry. They have been a subject of interest since the early seventeenth century when they were first visited by a Portuguese missionary in 1602 A.D. Most of them inhabit the Nilgiri Hills of South India which fall under Ootacamund and Kunoor districts of Tamil Nadu while the remaining inhabit the contagious Kollegal taluk of South Kanara district of the State of Karnataka. The Nilgiris are an undulating plateau of about 478 square miles in area and 3000 to 8000 feet above the mean sea level. The Todas are probably the most extensively studied tribe of India which has been engaging the attention of anthropologists and other social scientists for more than a century. Apart from polyandry they are also famous for their pastoral economy which they have raised to the level of a cult-the-cult of buffalo worshipping.

They call themselves as Tora and are known to their neighbours as the same. Among their closest neighbours are four other primitive tribes the Badaga, the Kota, the Kurumba and the Irula. According to the local social hierarchy the Todas share the highest social status with the Badagas followed by the Kotas, the Kurumbas and the Irulas. These four tribes play significant roles in the economic life of the Todas who maintain a high degree of interaction especially with the Badagas and the Kotas.

The Nilgiris - their principal area of habitation are very rich in flora and fauna. The important wild animals include elephant, tiger, leopard, sambhur, bison, pigs and wild dogs. It's forests are also replete with white cedar, satinwood, rose wood, ebony, silver oak, eucalyptus and a host of other varieties of important trees.

The Todas have their dialect but no script of their own. It exhibits similarities with Tamil language but the presence of some archaic words in it suggest some sort of previous connection of the Todas with the Brahuis of Baluchistan. The word Toda has possibly been derived from the word tudra which is the sacred tree of the

Todas. To their neighbouring Badagas a Toda is he who worships the tode tree.

Their light skinned complexion, tall stature, high and narrow nose, brown eyes, long beards and abundant body hair put them on a separate pedestal-strangers and misfits amidst the surrounding dark skinned Dravidian population. The males bear an athletic and robust physique while the females sport quite pretty and dignified appearance. Their racial affinities are still a matter of debate among the anthropologists and others. Some hold the view that they are a group of proto-Aryans who share a series of similar physical characteristics with the Ainus of Japan while others believe that they are Indo-Afghans or Nordics. The bewildering variety of opinions is enough to indicate the confusion regarding their racial composition and affinities and same is the case with their origin which is still shrouded in mystery.

Settlement Pattern and Housing: A Toda village usually consists of about six huts meant for individual families. It is mostly located at a slight elevation near a wood and a stream. A typical Toda hut is semi-barrel in shape with the barrel being split longitudinally. It usually consists of a big room with provision of several beds. Bamboo and thatch are the basic material used in the construction of these huts. The entrance of these huts is usually so low and narrow that one has to literally crawl while entering. A strict division is seen in the huts where the place meant for preparing milk produce is strictly earmarked from the rest of the place.

Social Organization: The Todas are strictly divided into two divisions or moieties called *Taratharal* and *Teivaliol,* thus possessing a dual organization. These moieties are strictly endogamous meaning they marry in their respective moieties like the castes but some irregular unions are allowed. Interestingly all the sacred herds and dairies are owned by the *Tarthar* while the Teivali only tend the herds, so the *Tarthar* occupy a higher status in the social hierarchy. These two moieties are further divided into several clans. The clans are endogamous. Each clan is territorial in nature and possesses a number of villages and is named after the chief of these villages. All the villages of a clan are usually located in the same part of the hill. Members of a clan are free to move over from one village to another in search of greener pastures or to perform certain ceremonial obligations. Thus, clans among the Todas have some social arid ritual significance.

These clans are divided into families locally known as *Kudupeli.* Since fraternal polyandry is the most popular mode of marriage among the Todas, a typical Toda family consists of brothers, their common wife or wives and their married and unmarried sons and unmarried daughters. The authority lies with the eldest male of the family. The division of labour in the family is not evenly balanced. While the adult male members do the herding, milking, churning, fuel gathering, cooking, trading and a host of other tasks the females perform minor domestic chores like fetching water, embriodering clothes, pounding and sifting grains, sweeping the floor, cleaning utensils and some other less significant tasks. The above disparity being not enough, the males also control all the political, religious and ceremonial activities thus further enhancing their role in the life of the tribe. Such a set up has given rise to a situation where women have been assigned an inferior status as compared to males.

The females have been made to believe that their inferior status is directly proportional to their negligible role in the economy of the tribe. However, they are not treated with contempt or cruelty. But honestly speaking it is just the over-simplification of the situation. It certainly goes back to the days when female infanticide was in vogue. Fortunately enough, this nefarious and cruel practice has almost stopped and the status of women is also climbing up the ladder of respectability.

Although they are still not allowed to meddle in the preparation of any milk produce but in many cases they have taken up the responsibility of cooking other food. The very notion of ritual pollution imposed upon women is also loosening and the long suppressed 'untouchables' of the Toda society are gradually gaining respectability and acceptance in a variety of socio-economic spheres. The most popular form of marriage among the Todas is still fraternal polyandry though monogamy and polygamy are also not uncommon. They have adopted polyandry in such a way that there is hardly any jealousy among the husbands on the issue of the common wife. Significantly, it is the eldest brother who actually marries and the rest become husbands by the force of custom. If the brothers decide to marry another girl the actual bridegroom still remains the same. However, when the husbands are not brothers (that is, in case of non-fraternal polyandry which is also permitted) but clan brothers even then the eldest of them marries the girl and the common wife adopting the role of 'visiting wife' keeps on visiting every husband. Such visits usually stretch to a month or so.

Unlike the majority of Indian tribes, the Todas practice child marriage. Sometimes, their marriage is performed at the age of two or three. In these circumstances, the parents of the nascent bride and bridegroom settle the marriage and the bride remains at her parents' house till she attains puberty. A custom reported by earlier researchers but not easily verifiable today is quite important in this context especially when we analyse the status of women in the Toda society. It pertains to the initiation of the bride into sex life before she actually attains puberty and sent to her husband's house. It has been reported that just before the bride attains puberty a ceremony is held in which a young man of some other clan is invited to violate the 'chastity' of the bride. Now sometime later her groom comes with clothes and jewellary and takes away the bride to his house. Such practices may be taken as a strong testimony to the fact that through such customs women are made to believe that they are nothing but merely a chattel or commodity which can be used by its owner in any manner he likes. The custom of transferring wife from one man to another, with or without her consent, may be yet another proof in support of this statement. Under such circumstances of sexual permissiveness, extra-marital sex relations are also permitted. Moreover, the sacred dairymen have socially sanctioned right to enjoy sex with any woman they desire. Provoked by such a permissive attitude some scholars have remarked that the Todas live in a condition of 'promiscuity' or free sex and their world view is devoid of any notion of chastity or adultery.

The Todas trace their descent through father but biological fatherhood does not carry much significance among them because of polyandry where it is almost impossible to know the actual father. Thus, they have evolved a ceremony known as 'bow and arrow ceremony' through which sociological fatherhood is ushered. During the seventh month of pregnancy any of the common husbands with common consent presents the wife with a bow and arrow in an elaborate ceremony and it is this husband who is regarded as father of not only the expected child but all children to come until some other husband, of course with common consent, presents another bow and arrow in the same way. Significantly the Toda children are considered children of the whole clan and not of a particular man. Also significant is the fact that all the husbands, who are not necessarily brothers, treat the children with the same affection and care and nobody bothers himself with the mystery of biological fatherhood. The bow and arrow ceremony still carries so much social and ritual force that it is shameful for a women to deliver a baby without undergoing this ceremony.

Divorce is freely permitted among the Todas and it does not carry any stigma. The ground of divorce is usually laziness or foolishness and not barrenness or adultery like many other tribes. If a man divorces his wife he has to pay a fine of one buffalo to his wife's parents and is entitled to get in return any number of buffaloes he has given as funeral contributions from time to time.

The Todas system of reckoning kins is of classificatory type. For example the term 'father' includes not only ones' physiological or legal fathers but also ones' paternal uncles, husbands of ones' maternal aunts and all other males of fathers' clan and generation. Similar is the case with the mother. Such a kinship system is well reflected during several eventualities like death when all such kins are supposed to contribute towards funeral of the deceased. It is prohibited among the Todas to pronounce the names of father-in-law and mother-in-law and it is customary for everyone to pay respect to father-in-law and other males of his status in a particular way. One has to prostrate and touch the feet of such male kins.

The Todas have elaborate rules of property and inheritance. They recognize individual ownership as well as family and clan ownership of different kinds of property. Such movable items as dress, ornaments, household utensils and a host of other minor things belong to individuals. Ordinary and some of the sacred buffaloes are owned by individuals or families but the most sacred ones called '*ti*' belong to clans only. Among the immovable items, house and smaller villages are owned by the families while the land and the chief villages including the dairies are owned by the clans. The inheritance of property is followed along patrilineal lines which means that only sons inherit their fathers' property. The legal or 'sociological sons' of a man either share their fathers' property in common or equally divide it among themselves. In such cases an extra buffaloes is given to the eldest and the youngest ones. When a man dies in debt, his liabilities are also distributed in the same way.

Their political organization is devoid of any tribal chief. Instead, the people are governed by a council of five elders locally known as '***naim***'. It has an interesting composition. Three of its members traditionally come from the *Tarthar* clans, one is taken from *Teivali* clans and the fifth one comes from the Badagas, the neighbouring tribe which has no independent existence of its own in isolation from the Todas. This representative from the Badagas usually sits in cases involving the relations between the two tribes. Significantly the council enjoys hardly any power in criminal cases and it exercises its authority in civil disputes between individuals, families and clans. But interestingly it is not strong enough to assert itself fully even in its limited jurisdiction. It frequently succumbs to individual pressures and may be subdued with the help of bribery or intimidation. Besides this council the clans possess informal heads and each family has a head who is responsible for the collection of its share in clan's expenses.

Though some Todas have converted to Christianity, the majority still adhers to their tribal religion which is marked by polytheism. They believe in an indefinitely large number of spirits, gods and godesses.

Two of their most important deities are *Teikirzi* and *On.* The former being the supreme goddess rules the people on the earth. The latter is her younger brother who rules over the world of the dead. The remaining important deities are associated with different hill tops. There are also two river deities associated with the two chief rivers of the area. On the whole the dominant Toda religion is marked by elaborate rituals. The dairies are like temples for the Todas and the dairymen are like priests. But all the dairies are not equal in their veneration and their ritual importance varies. They also believe in divination and sorcery. They cremate their dead with elaborate rituals and fanfare in which offerings are made and buffaloes are sacrificed. Interestingly the flesh is not eaten but given away to others.

ECO-System and Economy: The Todas have not been quick to adapt themselves to their changing environment of predatory competition and exploitation by the new comers to the Nilgiris. Their whole economic life rotates round buffalo and they have remained static or developed along their own line of social evolution embracing the all important buffalo. They practice neither agriculture, nor horticulture nor any craft. They also do not make use of such food gathering pursuits as hunting and fishing which are important pre-requisites of collectional economy. Interestingly they are vegetarian in their food habits and a little bit of food gathering which they occasionally indulge into is related to collection of some edible roots, fruits, and tubers as a supplement to their predominant milk diet.

Before taking up the salient features of their pastoral economy let us take a look into another significant aspect of their life viz. their intimate economic relationship with their neighbouring tribes. Apart from the Todas, the Badagas, the Kota, the Kurumba and the Irula are the other four tribes inhabiting the plateau. It is difficult to find any other tribal belt in the whole of India where a cluster of different tribes with such interdependence. Among all these tribes, the Kotas are one who live in a kind of symbiosis with the Todas. Traditionally, they are blacksmiths and musicians inhabiting seven villages interpersed among the Toda settlements and several Badaga villages. Although the Kotas have a definite vocational specialization yet interestingly their main source of livelihood is agriculture. They speak a dialect of their own which, however, is understood by the Todas. They traditionally serve the Todas, the Badagas and the Kurumbas. They supply iron tools and implements, wooden utentils and other articles of use. They also play music in rituals and ceremonies. In partial payment they receive the carcasses of the cattle and their flesh whenever they are sacrificed along with butter. They pay respect to the Todas and donate some grain to their pastoral neighbours as tribute. On ritual grounds they are not allowed to enter a Toda or Badaga house. The Todas consider their mere touch as polluting and a bath is required in such an eventuality. The Badaga are agriculturists and are mainly potato growers. They have been largely Hinduised and are highly ambitious and prosperous people. The Kurumba serve the Badaga as agricultural labour due to their inferior status in the local hierarchy. The Irula fall on the periphery of their social and economic life and hence do not play any significant role in this socio-economic symbiosis.

The buffaloes constitute the economic as well as social backbone of the Todas. They have raised buffalo herding to the level of a cult. They subsist on the products of their buffaloes. On an average each household possesses eight to twelve buffaloes that belong to a finer variety than the common buffalo of India. Each buffalo is given a separate name and their pedigrees are carefully remembered. But all are not equal in sanctity. The ordinary buffaloes are taken care of by the boys and ordinary men and all the dairy operations as churning of milk etc. are performed in the house. But the sacred buffaloes are kept in sanctified yards treated as sacred dairies and all the diary operations including preparation of various produce are performed in the dairy itself with elaborate rituals. The ritual status of diarymen varies with the sanctity of buffaloes they tend to and take care of.

As already stated the dairy operations fall in 'all male domain' because females are considered by them as ritually impure, due to menstruation and other reasons, and are not supposed to touch the buffaloes. In some cases the women are not allowed even to tread on the path used by the sacred buffaloes. Thus, the males completely dominate all the spheres of economic activities leaving the women high and dry with their inferior status. The dairymen have been elevated to the position of priests and they are admitted to this office only after an elaborate ordination.

They begin their day with the grazing of the buffaloes who are escorted by young males to the pastures. Just before dusk they are escorted back to their sacred quarters for milking operation. On the whole it may be said that they live buffalo, think buffalo and act buffalo which is omnipresent in all the spheres of their life.

The elaborately made milk products are sold to the people of the plains usually through the Badagas who act as efficient middlemen. After retaining a part for personal consumption the rest is exchanged with neighbouring tribes for other articles of everyday life.

Milk products, vegetables and food grain constitute the staple diet of the Todas. Though, they are allowed to eat deer's flesh they usually avoid any non-vegetarian food including fish. Significantly, unlike many other Indian tribes who are addicted to alcohol, opium or other narcotics, the Todas have remained relatively free from such habits. If at all they are addicted to anything, they are certainly addicted to whey.

Problems and Prospects : The Todas have not been quick to adapt themselves to changing conditions. They have remained almost static or developed on their own line of the Badagas who came and settled in the Nilgiris much later advanced economically to the deteriment of the Todas. But the foremost problem of the Todas is their steadily declining population. Partly on account of diseases, chiefly veneral diseases and partly on account of female infanticide coupled with their miserable economic condition. Veneral diseases are certainly the gift from the early European and Indian tourists who had converted a great part of the Nilgiris into a summar health resort to escape the scorching sun. The Todas came across all sorts of tourists for the first time only during the British rule. Thanks to the dedicated work of certain medical agencies the rot has stopped and they can certainly look forward for a better tomorrow at least on their population front.

The Todas have traditionally been the lord of the land in the Wenlock Downs near Ootacamund. This area comprised of about 18000 acres of land and it is reported that in 1822, the collector if Ootacamund had to purchase land from the Todas for building the first bunglows. When European settlers started coming in increasing numbers and the vicious process of land alienation began, the government had to formulate what was called the 'Todapatta Land Policy' under which land was reserved for the Todas for pastoral purposes. With the advent of modern times when the land came under forest department, the Todas had a taste of the coming days of their diminishing authority over land. However, they were statutarily allowed to use the forest produce and agriculture. The Todas having different frame of mind could not be weaned away from their buffaloes. Thus, the lands were leased to the Badagas while Todas became absentee landlords. The Todas continued to be given Patta (agricultural rights), renewable every year for cultivation but they did not fall in line. The demand of the Todas, however, is that they should be alloted these lands permanently. By virtue of their psychological attachment and deep rooted religious beliefs, the Todas would not like to leave the Wenlock Downs-their traditional abode and migrate to other areas. If they cannot be weaned away from cattle hearding to some other profitable ventures, the cattle herding itself may be made profitable and rewarding to these people with imaginative planning and purposeful assistance.

(b) THE CHENCHU

The Chenchus represent that segment of tribal population of India whose economy does not seem to have changed in any significant manner for the last few thousand years. Concentrated in a small pocket situated in the heart of Andhra Pradesh, the Chenchus live on either side of the famous river Krishna with the Nallamalai forests on the southern side and the rugged and densely wooded plateau on the northern side. District wise, the majority of Chenchus are scattered in Mehboobnagar, Kurnool and Prakasham.

They are one of the largest food gathering tribes belonging to the pre-agricultural level of living depending upon wild roots, tubers, fruits, honey, yarn and small game. Carrying digging stick and bow and arrow they are clinging desperately to the outmoded food gathering economy. It is said that when the food gathering economy of southern India gave way to the food producing economy and tribal groups were transformed into village settlements. The majority of Chenchus faithfully resisted this change and finding themselves helpless against the onslaught of settled life, withdrew themselves from the mainstream of technological innovations and hid into the depths of the forests. The remaining ones settled in peripheral villages and hence are distinctly different. They are mostly settled cultivators who have adopted the cultural pattern and economic pursuits of the neighbouring plains people.

The Chenchus are medium statured and their complexion varies from wheatish to light brown. On the basis of their physical characteristics most of the anthropologists prefer to put them in the australoid racial stock but at the same time agree that they also contain some negrito strains. Though looking shy and fragile they demonstrate a high degree of physical endurance. They speak a corrupt dialect of Dravidian origin.

Settlement Pattern and Housing : Till recently the Chenchus had been leading a wholly nomadic life. They still carry the fond memories of those bygone days and this is reflected in their folklore. Under certain economic compulsions they have given up their wholly nomadic life to a great extent and have started living in semi-permanent thatched huts. But this hardly means that they have downed the shutters of the past. They still keep on shifting their settlements after every couple of years. They make small conical thatched huts with the leaves touching the ground. These huts have such a small entrance that one has to stoop very low to enter it. Most of the Chenchu settlements contain two to fifteen houses with individual families occupying them. For a new settlement they prefer hill slopes or high ridges so that the enemies may be sighted from some distance and they have ample time to escape. Invariably, these settlements are located away from the water source to avoid wild animals who will also be coming to drink water from the same source. Their in-built defence mechanism has taught them to avoid the ferocious animals who cannot be tackled with a mere bow and arrow.

Social Organization : They are divided into exogamous clans with animal totems whose killing or eating are taboo for the members of the clan. Nuclear family containing the husband, wife and the unmarried children, is the most popular mode of family among them. In the mundane affairs of life husband and wife enjoy equal rights but in the scheme of ownership, except items of individual use, usually the husband owns all the property. This implies that authority and succession are patriarchal. Though, residence is partrilocal, matrilocal residence for a specified period is also not uncommon, especially immediately after marriage.

Like most of the other tribes child marriage is not popular among the Chenchus. In most of the cases the spouse is sought from outside one's own clan but among some selected ones life partner is usually selected from mother's clan and preference is given to mother's brother's daughter. This mode of matrimony is prevalent to such an extent that they have the same kinship term for maternal uncle and father-in-law. Though, marriage is an arranged affair among them yet care is taken to ascertain the wishes of the bride and groom before finalising; girls are also allowed to express their views freely on matrimonial affairs. The highly liberal attitude of the Chenchu towards their womenfolk is further reflected in the liberties the girls enjoy even before marriage. They are not captive birds. They freely mix up with the boys of those clans which may provide them life partner. In other words, courtship is quite popular especially during festive seasons when everybody enjoys life till the lease. But such affairs are not carried out publicly and a curtain of privacy is required in order not to hurt the feelings of the elders who may not react favourably if such affairs become public. Such relationship may result into sexual intimacy but every care is taken to camoflague it lest it should invite wrath from the elders. They maintain a 'reserved' posture in the matters of sex and avoid any discussion on sexual affairs and problems.

Usually the groom's side takes initiative in finalising marriage but the bride's side may also take first step. After it has been finalised, the biggest problem for the groom is to arrange a *Saari* and *Choli* for the bride and a *Choli* for his mother-in-law. Next comes the communal feast. These arrangements are enough to burden the groom economically to a considerable extent.

Fragility of conjugal bonds presents lot of worries to the married couple. Family among them is unstable due to frequent divorce. A woman is free to choose her life partner with whom she lives at her will while the husband also enjoys these and frequently uses his customary right to send her wife back to her parents if he does not carry on well with her. In case the wife breaks the wedlock the husband may demand the amount of money back which he incurred on marriage. Traditionally, a divorced woman is not allowed to remarry another man in the life time of her former husband but interestingly she may live with any person of her choice without a formal marriage. Though the Chenchus are permitted to be polygynous yet the popular mode of martimony is still monogamy.

A very interesting and important feature of their kinship system is the deeply rooted suspicion of blood relatives especially brothers.

This is amply reflected during hunting expeditions or honey collection when they maintain a distance from their brothers and other blood relatives and tend to be closer to their affinal kins like brother-in-law and prefer them for lending one a helping hand.

The Chenchus have also evolved the institution of elderman. Every settlement has a traditional leader known as *Peddamanshi* but his hold on the community is quite loose and he cannot govern with a firm hand. He represents his village before the outsiders, settles minor disputes with the help of other elderly people, acts as priest and blesses the couple at the time of marriage. Though, his office is hereditary yet any elderly, knowledgeble and respected male may be unanimously appointed to this office.

Under the Chenchu social organization only movable property may be owned individually. The immovable property like land, forests, trees etc. come under comunal ownership and every member of the community enjoys equal right over them. With the enactment of forest laws the complexion of the situation has considerably changed and now everybody has to follow them.

Like their simple economic life they have evolved a simple system of religious beliefs and practices. Although due to growing cultural contacts with the neighbouring Hindus of the plans, their religion, too, is undergoing changes, yet some of its features may still be distinguished. *Bhairov* is their most popular local deity to whom a small part of the hunted animal is offered but godess *Garelamaisama* still reigns supreme among that segment of Chenchus which still totally depends upon hunting and gathering for subsistence. She gives them strength and skill for success in hunting expeditions. On the whole, their religion is conspicuous by the absence of festivals and elaborate rituals.

Traditionally the Chenchus bury their dead but to growing Hindu influence those who reside amidst plains' Hindus have started cremating their departed ones.

ECO-system and Economy: The Chenchus depend mostly on what nature provides them. Their economic system is essentially that of a tribe of hunters and foodgatherers. On the top of it they have developed a psyche in which saving for future is alien to them and this has led to a carefree and hand-to-mouth existence.

The changing seasons witness quick changes in a Chenchu's life. In one part of the year they go on digging out edible roots, in another collection of edible fruits is resorted to while in yet another all the emphasis is laid on hunting and their life all the year round rotates round gathering and hunting.

As a matter of routine a Chenchu wakes up in the morning with almost no food in the house and proceeds leisurely with his spouse to the forest to collect roots and fruits and consuming it at the same time. After a couple of years when the warmth of conjugal ties cools down a little bit, males and females resort to segregation and now males and females in small groups of 3-6 persons go out separately.

All available fruits and tamarind, *mahua* etc. constitute the staple vegetarian diet. With the onset of summer the bushes and leaves dry up and it becomes very difficult for them to trace the edible roots and tubers. Now they resort to hunting. Though their surrounding forests are quite rich in fauna where all sorts of small and big games are present but they are not good hunters. Hence, it becomes quite an uphill task for them to hunt according to their needs and requirements. They go out with their bows and arrows to hunt the birds, small games like hare, squirrel, black monkey etc. and when they spot their target like squirrel or monkey they chase it into the open by hurling sticks and stones until it comes within range of their arrows. When the animal has been hunted down a fire is made in the forest and after roasting the animal it is consumed right there with its skin on. It is rarely that some part is saved and brought home. They also use sharp pieces of stone, with amazing competence, as an important hunting weapon. Using them as missiles birds and squirrels are hunted down with much ease. The Indian monitor locally known as *Udumu* is also one of their favourite games who comes out of its hole usually in the rainy season in large numbers only to fall prey to the waiting Chenchus who break its back with sticks and relish it as a delicacy.

Some Chenchu groups who have developed a knack for domesticating a couple of animals also use dog in hunting. Their dependence on the mercy of nature may be gauged from the fact that they have no hesitation in eating even stale and highly decomposed flesh of animals found as left overs of wild dogs especially during days of scarcity. Some Chenchus have also started domestication of cattle like cow, buffalo and goat but they rarely stay with them for any long time due to their economic vulnerability. They are sold away for subsistence.

Fishing is also one of their modes of subsistence but it is restricted to a very small extent because only very few of their villages are situated near rivers and streams. The traditional method of fishing is through poisoning and poisoning substance is prepared out of a powder produced from a local tree mixing it with sand and moth. But nowadays the Chenchus have started employing hook and rod techniques of fishing wherever possible.

Honey constitutes an important item of their diet. They are very deft in handling honey combs hanging from trees and cliffs. When they get a honey comb they eat it entirely including the wax and the nascent bees. They have attained such an expertise in procuring honey that they do not have to search for the combs; they know where, when and how to find it.

The budding season of Mahua brings such a gusto, happiness and ecstacy in their lives that they wait for it. Its flower dropping down are gathered eagerly all the year round. A great amount of it is eaten after boiling it and the remaining is used in brewing liquor. The much yearned and sought after mahua liquor tranforms their drab and monotonous existence into an orgy of marrymaking. This is the only time when they forget their miseries and hard struggle for existence and spend, much of their time in dancing and making love.

Despite a variety of food items their diet is nutritionally inadequate. It is ill balanced and lacks several essential nutrients. Infact only the intake of cereals during the summers and leaves during the rains is satisfactory to an extent. However, the consumption of oil, sugar, jaggery, vegetable and milk products is neglible. The net result of this ill balanced diet is that they are always deficient of Vitamin A and Calcium. Hence malnutrition is a rule rather than an exception.

Problems and Prospectus: They are yet to grow out of their food gathering stage and with the passage of time they are no more completely isolated and insulated either geographically or culturally. And this is the crux of the problem. Now the situation prevailing among them is that they can neither obtain their food completely from the forest due to depletion of forest resources and stringent laws, increase in the density of population, competition from the non-tribals, commercialisation of forests and unscruplous role of forest officials nor can completely switch over to the food of the neighbouring peasantry by taking up agriculture, animal husbandry or cottage industries. They are caught in a dilemma and are 'misfit' in a fast changing society.

With the adoption of clothing arid growing requirement of better tools and implements for food gathering and hunting the economic pressure is mounting. Since they do not have cash they have to give something in exchange. Initially they offered such forest produce as honey, mahua, etc. With the growing demand they had to part with their cattle. Even this was not the end. Further growing demand and unscruplous dealing on the part of non-tribal traders pushed them into a situation when they were forced to offer their labour and quite a considerable number of Chenchus have forefeited their freedom and are working as beasts of burden for the contractors. Unfortunately, the psychic make up of the Chenchus is also responsible for this sorry state of affairs to a considerable extent. Their worldview is devoid of any vision of tomorrow. Curiously they always preferred a carefree and hand to mouth existence which was fully exploited by the technologically more advanced and unscruplous neighbours. Lack of cooperation is another factor responsible for their present state of affairs. Except taking care of an ailing relative or in construction of huts they seldom demonstrate a semblance of cooperation. They venture out in the forests for collection in groups but do the actual work individually and everybody prefers to fill up his own basket rather than doing the work collectively and dividing the fruits of labour on equal basis. Even during hunting expeditions they avoid taking each other's help. Such an attitude in the face of fast changing economic scenario only helped the impending disaster sooner and more severely than expected.

With the advent of independence a variety of programmes of tribal welfare and development have been initiated but nothing considerable could be done for the poor Chenchus. In view of the small size of population and scattered nature of their settlements no tribal development block could be started in their midst. After their identification as a primitive tribe new development schemes have been taken up. They have yet to show concrete results.

Even forest cooperative societies in their area did not survive for a longer period though a society named Chenchu Cooperative Society managed by the forest department still exists at least in name. As far back as 1940s attempts were made to lure them to settled life, agriculture, animal husbandry and cottage industries but the Chenchu lost almost all the lands through alienation and they returned back to forests. This shows that a more careful and imaginative planning is needed from the grassroot level, keeping firmly in mind their cultural ethos, world view and value system. It seems that their only hope lies in taking to agriculture for which they have not yet demonstrated any real taste or zeal.

(c) THE KHASI

The Khasi tribe holds the distinction of being one of the few remaining matriarchal tribes of the world. They are one of the most advanced tribal communities in India having an economy now diversified with substantial commerce, industry and urbanization. Educationally they are far a head of many non-tribal communities and they enjoy substantial representation in the higher All India Services. The erstwhile districts of the United Khasi and Jaintia Hills of Assam - the traditional homeland of the Khasi - now falls under the nascent state of Meghalaya which became a full fleged state in 1972. Now an overwhelming majority of the state of Meghalaya consists of the Khasis, Garos and some minor tribes the Khasis being the numerically largest and politically dominating tribal community in the state.

Socially the Khasis are divided into four main sub groups, viz., Khynrian Khasis or upland Khasis of the Shillong plateau of the Khasi hills, the Pnar of the Jaintia Hills - the War of the Western and Southern slopes of the district and the Bhoi of the lowlands. Besides these four divisions two other groups-the Hadem of Jaintia Hills and the Lynngam of the Khasi hills, have been recently recognised as Khasis. Since each of the above divisions of the Khasis observed territorial endogamy in the past they may be designated as sub-tribes.

The erstwhile district of the United Khasi and Jaintia Hills - the homeland of the Khasi is 5541 sq. miles in area. It is bounded on the north by Brahmaputra Valley (Kamrup and Nowgong districts of Assam), on the east by the United Mikir and North Cachar Hill districts, on the south by Sylhet (now part of Bangladesh) and Cachar and on the west by the Garo Hills. The land of the Khasi consists of four plateaus rising abruptly above the low plains of Sylhet to a height of about 4000 feet above the mean sea level at Cherrapunji, the highest rainfall centre on the earth. Further towards the north at a higher level there is another plateau at Mawphlang where some of the villages are situated at an elevation of about 6000 feet above mean sea level. This happens to be the highest tract within the district. Shillong, the State Capital, is situated in this part.

The whole area is characterised by the breath taking natural beauty. Some to the finest orchards in the whole of Assam where orange, pineapple and banana of an excellent quality are cultivated, are to be found here. The most striking natural feature of the Khasi area is provided by the large number of rivers and rivulets coupled by some wavering waterfalls and picturesque surroundings. The climate of the whole area is very salubrious and Shillong has developed into a fashionable and popular health resort. This hill tract is richly covered with forests of sal, oak, pine and host of other woods while bamboo flourishes on the low hills of the north and the west. The fauna largely consists of bees, fowls, pigs, monkeys elephants, tigers, deer, wild dogs, etc.

Racially the Khasis are sharply differentiated from the Indo-Mongoloid tribes surrounding them. According to the majority opinion they are an off-shoot of the Mon people of further India and they exhibit a fairly close proximity to the Malay type. Linguistically, they belong to the Mon-Khmer family because they speak a dialect that belongs to the Mon-Khmer branch of Austric family. They are, probably the only known representative of this family in India. Under the influence of the Christian missionaries they have adopted the Roman script, though in some places they still follow Bengali script.

The term Khasi has particular significance. *Kha* means born of and *Si* refers to an ancient mother. It assumes a great degree of significance when one tries to go into their social origin because apparently the name Khasi is itself indicative of their matrilieal system of reckoning descent.

Presently, a majority of the Khasis (about 55%) have embraced Christianity with some choosing Islam or Hinduism and the remaining still adhering to their original faith.

Settlement Pattern and Housing: The Khasi villages are usually situated a little below the hill tops, generally in small depressions unlike those of their neighbouring Naga and the Kuki tribes who prefer the summit of the hills. Since their economic life is intimately connected with their permanent fields for cultivation, they seldom change their village sites. Moreover, they have sentimental attachment with the memorial stones of their dead.

A traditional Khasi house is made largely of wood, bamboo and stones. It is oval shaped with low roof and a small entrance. The house is generally erected on a plinth some two to three feet above the ground. An ordinary Khasi house, consists of three portions, viz, a porch, a centre room and a retiring room. The hearth is generally situated in the retiring room with inadequate provision for the smoke to melt out of the room. With the growing prosperity and trends of modernization the traditional pattern is giving wayo modern designs.

Nowadays the houses are rectangular and corrugated iron sheets and tin sheets are being used for walls and roofs and economically sound Khasis have bunglows of modern style with iron roof, chimneys, glass windows and beautiful doors.

Social Organization: As already mentioned the Khasis include a number of sub-tribes each inhabiting a particular tract, speaking little varying dialects but sharing a common socio-cultural tradition. Each of these groups or sub-tribes is divided into a number of clans locally known as *Kur.* These clans are strictly exogamous and their member are not allowed to marry within their clans. Infact it is considered the greatest sin for a Khasi to marry within his clan. The members of these clans trace their descent from a common ancestress locally called *Ka iawbei tynrai* which means mother-progenitor. They attach great reverence to such mother ancestress and erect memorial stones as a mark of respect.

Significantly some of these clans are named after certain animals and trees which is indicative of totemic practices but they are no more revered. The Khasi clans are characterised by a system of matrilineal descent which means that the descent is carried through female line downwards. The foremost function of a clan is to regulate marriage and the relationship between the clansmen is well exhibited on a ceremonial occasion when uncalcinated bones of a deceased member are transferred temporarily before their final disposal in the clan ossuary. The social bond is further characterised by the performance of common religious ceremonies, worship of common deities and spirits and the observance of mourning for a fellow clansman. Common ownership of land exhibits economic ties between members of clan. The clan is further subdivided into sub-clans locally known as *Kpoh.* It is composed of the descendants of one great grandmother.

Family or household is the smallest social unit of a sub-clan. It is denoted by a terming and it carries far reaching significance. A family generally consists of the grandmother, her daughters, their husbands and children. The grandmother is recognized as the head of the family as long as she survives. The permanent members of a family are the daughters who after their marriage, settle in their mother's family alongwith their husbands. The son after his marriage goes to live in his wife's family thus giving the matrilineal Khasi family a vertically extended structure. In a classical matrilineal family the youngest daughter holds the most prominent place because only she is entitled to live in the main house while the remaining ones have to establish new homes either in the compound or in the adjacent quarters. Although the mother is always regarded as owner of the house but the actual authority lies with the father. This contradicts any such notion that in matriarchal-matrilineal society males have to contend with a subordinate status. In the scheme of division of labour males are expected to carry on agricultural chores, house construction, hunting and fishing and the females perform household chores alongwith the occasional work on the orchards.

A Khasi is supposed to marry within his sub tribe but they are not strongly rigid on this issue. They are strictly monogamous; polyandry is unknown to them and polygyny having little chance to be accepted in a matriarchal society. Like the majority of Indian tribes they are clan exogamous which implies that they have to marry outside their clan. The job of selection of spouse is fairly simple. A young man gets attracted to a girl or develops a liking for her and convey it to his parents. The rest is taken care of by the elders and the marriage is performed with elaborate ceremonies and much fanfare. Significantly, the range from which one has to select one's spouse is quite narrow because marriage is not unconditional. Traditionally a man can marry his mother's brother's daughter only after the death of his mother's brother. Same is the case with his father's sister's daughter. Also, a man can marry his Tribal Education deceased wife's younger sister but he cannot marry his wife's sister even after divorce as long as the divorced wife is alive. They do not practice child marriage.

In Conformity with the norms of a matriarchal-matrilineal society the mother's brother holds an important position. He manages the mother's ancestral property and looks after important social ceremonies. Thus, lack of importance and authority of a man is compensated through his predominantly significant status in the affairs of her sister's family.

House and all movable property is owned by the wife and though the husband is regarded as the executive head of the family he enjoys no property rights. Even the self acquired property of a man before his marriage cannot be retained by him and goes to the common family fund of his maternal grandmother or mother. A part of the property acquired by the man after his marriage is given to the members of his clan and the rest goes to his wife and children. All moveable property and the house of the family are inherited by the youngest daughter. The landed property in the absence of any will goes to the youngest daughter. If the deceased mother wished to distribute it among tall the daughters, the youngest one gets the greater share. It is by virtue of her position as the youngest daughter locally known as *iing Khaduh,* that she is enjoined to perform all the religious rights and ceremonies of the family especially those related with its ancestress and that is why she is duly rewarded for shouldering this responsibility. With the spread of modern education and growing influence of Christianity the complexion of the situation is undergoing rapid changes among the Christian Khasis where the youngest daughter or for that matter any member of the family does not have to perform all those religious rites and ceremonies due to change of religion and all the daughters are supposed to be equal. But in many cases the youngest daughter does not reconcile to this situation and demands the status of sole heiress of all the property and thus complicates the matter further.

The traditional Khasi political organization still prevails in the land, though the advent of the British rule and the promulgation of the Constitution of India have modified it to a certain extent. It is characterised by an elaborate system of State, its chief and a council of ministers. The Khasi 'state' is formed by the voluntary association of villages or groups of villages. The head of the state or chief is called *siem* but his authority is very limited. The *siem* cannot perform any important business independently and he has to depend upon his *durbar* (court) which is an executive, council having judicial powers. He manages his state through the council of ministers. He exercises his judicial powers with the help and concurrence of the jury. In the absence of any system of land revenue the income of the Khasi state is quite meagre. Apart from the judicial fines, the most important source of state income is the collection of tolls that are charged on the commodities sold in the market. As the executive head of the state he is responsible for such work as the maintenance of the village paths, overseeing the safety of the orchards, maintenance of the markets, collection of toll and a host of other minor responsibilities. Originally the siem used to be a hereditary office and he was always succeeded by the eldest son of the his eldest sister and it was controlled by a small electoral body constituted by the heads of certain priestly clans. At present he is elected through adult franchise.

The traditional Khasi religion is characterised by theistic and animistic beliefs where propitiation of spirits constitutes the important segment of religious rites. *Ka lawbei* is the most popular and revered ancestress and a large number of megaliths are testimony to her predominant position in the Khasi pantheon. Besides her there are also some other ancestral spirits. Natural phenomena exercise tremendous influence upon them and each of their villages has its own quota of sacred groves. Under the impact of Christianity and Hinduism their religion is undergoing important changes. Even among the non converted the traditional concepts have much beed affected especially by western education and exposure to newer populations and ideas. The non converts cremate their dead but after retaining the dead body in the home for some time.

ECO-System and Economy: The natural environment has inevitably made a deep imprint on the people and has provided materials towards moulding and shaping the pattern of Khasi life and culture. Although a growing number of them are now employed in government offices or are working as teachers, physicians, nurses, magistrates, administrators, merchants and businessmen the majority of them is still attached with the exploitation of land. The extent of their adaptation in the local physical environment may be gauged from the fact that even those who no more depend upon the exploitation of land and are engaged in other occupations have no qualms or hesitation in taking to hoe in their spare time. Even such people still love a day out in the woods hunting and fishing.

The Khasis are living in a food producing economy. Cultivation of land, horticulture and domestication of animals form the principal occupation of the large majority of the Khasis. A monograph dealing with their economic aspects of life has rightly observed that no other among the hill tribes can compete with the Khasis in the value of their staples or the enlighted character of their agriculture.

Due to its rugged and irregular nature a substantial portion of land always remains under water or quite wet while the rest remain dry. In order to cope with this situation they have developed two types of cultivation viz, dry and wet cultivation. The dry cultivation is done in clayey soil. The procedure being followed is that in winter the soils are turned up with the hoe and are left to dry for about two months or so. Then the grasses are collected and burnt and the ashes are strewn over the field. Now the seeds of paddy, millet and other crops are sown. Bottoms of the valleys and depressions between two hills are considered as ideal places for wet cultivation. The land so obtained is divided into numerous blocks with high embankments. After this an irrigation channel is made to pass through these embankments in such a way that each block receives only the desired quantity of water. For sowing, the soil is prepared by hoeing and ploughing the muddy land. When the crop is ready for harvest the ripened corns are collected. Significantly the reaping is done by hands under the force of custom.

Besides the above mentioned modes of cultivation another method is also resorted to, generally on forest land, which is known as *Jhum* cultivation. This is simply a version of shifting cultivation. This is an age old institution among the hill tribes of India. This method involves the cultivation of a plot of land for a temporary period and then leaving it fallow. It consists of clearing the forest slopes by burning the fallen trees and bushes, and broadcasting the seed in the ash covered soil. The rest is left to nature. Maize and other coarse grains are main crops for *Jhum* cultivation. This method of cultivation is partly responsible for the fast pace of deforestation and attempts are being made to wean the *Jhum* cultivators away to settled mode of cultivation like the rest of the Khasi cultivators. Besides rice which is their principal crop, various kinds of millet, maize, potato, orange, beetelnut, paan (betel), pineapple, pulses and vegetables are also grown. Potato and orange are their cash crops and fetch them money.

The Khasis also practice hunting and fishing and supplement their food with rich meat. As a matter of fact they resort to occasional hunting and fishing as a sport and pastime rather than as an economic activity. Bows, arrows and spears are the chief weapons of hunting and sometimes trained dogs also lend a helping hand. Big games are hunted by way of pitfalls, traps etc. while small ones and birds are taken care of with the help of bow and arrow. Communal hunting is still very much cherished by them specially in killing tigers. With the enactment of statutory ban on killing tigers this practice has almost been given up but a brief description of it shall interest the readers. At first the trained dogs get the scent of the tigers and the bush is encircled. Now the group is divided with hunting dogs and some men on one side and the drum beaters and shouters on the other side. When the scared tiger comes out the expert hunters with their dogs chase the tiger to a freshly dug out pit. When the prey falls into the pit it is covered with dried leaves and logs, a fire is put on and the tiger is burnt. As far as the fishing is concerned, poisoning of stream is the traditional and most popular way. With the introduction of nets, small fishes are now caught with its help. Like communal hunting, communal fishing is also cherished by them.

SIGNIFICANTLY, although they have completely come out of the food gathering economy, it does not stand in the way of following their traditional mode of gathering forest produce like roots, tubers, fruits, firewood etc. It goes a long way in providing them some much needed nutrients and at the same time helps them maintain their ties with their erstwhile abode.

They have also taken to rearing of animals and their livestock consists mostly of pigs, cows, sheep and goats. When the cattle reach maturity they are sold to the traders in plains. They also rear bees on a substantial scale and after consuming some honey fondly, sell the surplus away.

Sericulture, weaving, spinning and dying are some such crafts where the Khasis feel quite at ease though the mill made clothes are fast catching up. They also make earthen pottery and are quite deft in using the black clay for making a variety of earthen vessels. They also practice bamboo work and make mats, baskets and other items of everyday life. Bamboo pipes used as water containers are the proof of the local genius. They are aware of iron smelting and are expert blacksmiths.

The staple diet of Khasis is rice followed by potato which is also consumed in large quantities. They are very fond of taking meat of different animals and relish beef, mutton, chicken and pork. Hinduised Khasis however, avoid beef. Fresh fish is also taken as a delicacy among them. Formerly they did not like milk and almost abhorred it but with the spread of Christianity the consumption of milk has picked up. They are hard drinkers and consume large quantities of locally brewed liquor of rice and millet.

The Khasis are inveterate chewers of pan leaf and beetelnut. Many of them irrespective of age and sex, indulge in this. Their addiction to the beetelnut may be gauged by the fact that in the interior parts of their lands the distance is often measured by the number of beetelnuts that are usually chewed on a journey. This addiction touches the fringe of obsession and many Khasis fancy of heaven as a huge betel nut garden.

Problems and Prospects : The problems facing the Khasis are not much different from the problems of hill people of India and in the context they practically do not have any economic problems exclusively their own. They do have some political and socio-political problems of their own but they chose not to go Naga or Mizo way of obtaining their objectives. Implicitly and explicity there has always been a realization among the Khasis that they are a part of the Indian nation. Significantly, inspite of the influence of foreign missionaries like the case with Mizos and Nagas, the Khasis never believed in the philosophy of separation from the rest of India.

Their aspirations have largely been motivated by the desire for safeguarding their economic interests from the economically more advanced neighbouring communities and maintaining their cultural identity in the vast sea of India, or to be more precise Hinduism.

The birth of Meghalaya in 1970, an autonomous state within Assam, was the culmination of the political movement started by the people of the United Khasi and Jaintia Hills and the Garo hills. Then Meghalaya became a full fledged state in 1972 and they attained their aspired goal. This has certainly diffused as potentially explosive situation.

Another problem faced by the Khasis is related with readjustment in a changing socio-cultural milieu. They have been trying to make as smooth a readjustment as possible in the face of cross currents of contacts with Christianity, Hinduism and to a lesser extent Islam. Surprisingly the basic structure of their society remained largely intact inspite of the centrifugal pull of a variety of cultural contacts. However, the matriarchal structure of the Khasi society has been considerably weakened.

Their first contact with Christianity dates back to the early years of the nineteenth century but organised efforts to spread Christianity were made for the first time only around 1950 by the Welsh Mission and, from then on, there was no looking back. Now around 60% of the Khasi population has embraced Christianity.

Although their contacts with the Hindus are quite, older than with Christians or Christianity but in the absence of any organised efforts of proselytisation, Hinduism could not make much of a head way. But many elements of Hinduism did creep in very smoothly which do not interfere with their social structure. Many Khasi **siems** formally embraced Hinduism followed by their subjects. The writings of some eminent Khasi authors also indicate that they have been influenced, to a certain extent, by the Hindu literary traditions. Now we find a substantial number of Hinduised Khasis who have adopted a different cultural ethos; for example such Khasis have stopped eating beef.

The contact of the Khasis with Islam is also a significant development in the traditional structure of the Khasi society. Unlike Christianity, there has never been an organised attempt to spread Islam and convert the Khasi. It was simply due to the presence of a small groups of Muslims who married Khasi women and thus started a gradual process of 'Muslimisation' or 'Islamistation'. Muslims of as far away place as Uttar Pradesh, Kashmir, Kerala and Punjab had been visiting the Khasi land as traders and wanderers. Some of them settled there and married local Khasi women. Significantly these Muslim Khasis, though negligible in number, have been instrumental in bringing in a variety of changes in the local social structure. Initially they shared all the local social traits, except religion, with their non-muslim brethren. With the passage of time they started providing themselves as a harbinger of Important changes. The weakening of the pre-eminent position of the youngest daughter and then the growing decline of the very matriarchal system maybe ascribed to the presence of Muslim elements in the Khasi society. Interestingly most of the Muslim Khasis declare that their religion has nothing to do with their tribal identity. Their claim alongwith such claims of Christian and Hindu Khasis may be taken as true. But the opening up of the Khasi land coupled with the cross currents of Hinduism, Christianity, Islam and tribalism are changing the simple tribal society of the Khasis to a sort of complex society. The Khasis are in for a bewildering variety of pressures and pulls hitherto unknown to them.

(d) THE ORAON

The Oraon, one of the major tribes of India, represent the agriculturist segment of tribal population. They are distributed over a large tract of eastern India. They are concentrated mostly in the plateau of Chotanagpur and occupy large areas of Ranchi, Palamau, adjoining districts Bihar and the neighbouring states of Orissa and Madhya Pradesh. Due to loss of land, population pressure and atrocities a large number of them have left their traditional habitat and have settled down as labourers in the tea gardens of Assam and West Bengal.

The traditional abode of the Oraon i.e. Chotanagpur contains rich flora and fauna. Here one sees a rich growth of *sal* and *mahua* trees. Bamboo also grows in abundance. The fauna consists of tiger, leopard, bear, sambhar, antelope, spotted **dee**, hare, different varieties of snake, etc. Several types of birds also inhabit this region.

Most of the Oraons speak a language of their own which belongs to the Dravidian family. It carries influence of those languages that are spoken in the vicinity wherever the Oraons live. That is why the influence of Oriya, Bengali and Hindi most discernable. Racially, the Oraons are put in the Pre-Dravidian or Proto-Autraloid category. Physically, they are characterised by dark brown complexion, black hair, black eyes and medium stature.

Settlement Pattern and Housing: The settlement pattern of the Oraon shows a marked preference for high altitude. Most of the Oraon villages are traditionally situated on the higher level of usually cultivable wasteland. The houses are generally huddled together in disorderly fashion. The houses are mud built with tiled roofs. The relatively affluent ones maintain kitchen-garden in the rear for domestic consumption.

Social Organization : The popular mode of family among the Oraons is nuclear family which consists of husband, wife and their unmarried children. The bride comes to reside in her husband's house after marriage, but the husband residing with his in-laws is also not uncommon. Being a partriarchal and patrilocal tribe the authority in the family lies with the eldest male member. In the local scheme of division of labour adult males work on the fields and the females assist them and also do the whole of the domestic chores. Grown-up children also contribute to family economy.

The Oraons recognise both types of kinship bonds viz. consanguineal and affinal. The rule of descent is patrilineal and the clan name descends from father to son. The Oraons are divided into exogamous clans. Their clan names are taken from their respective totems. Hence these are derived from birds, fish, vegetables, plants, minerals or whatever totem they followed. For example *Tirki* clan name has been derived from young mice, *Lakra* from tiger, *Bek* from salt and so on. Like most of the totem following tribal groups, Oraons too do not eat or destroy their totem and consider it as a sacred heritage. Though the totems are neither ritually worshipped nor it is believed by them that they have descended from it yet these are revered and sometimes their replica is exhibited.

As Regards marriage, monogamy is the most popular mode of matrimony. In exceptional cases one is allowed to go for more than one wife but polyandry is not permitted. The force of tribal endogamy is still very strong and those marrying outside the tribe are usually ex-communicated. Due to the concept of common ancestry they do not marry within the lineage or clan. Further, they also do not prefer the marriage of a boy with a girl of the same village. Like the majority of the Indian tribes Oraons, too, do not like child marriage. By force of tradition 'marriage by service' is also allowed in which the prospective groom serves the family of his prospective groom serves the family of his prospective bride for some time, but such a way of acquiring mate has almost faded away from a number of

Oraon villages. Due to changing values marriage by mutual consent or elopment seems to be the most prevalent way of marriage.

They are quite liberal vis-a-vis widow re-marriage and 'Junior Levirate' is resorted to which means that the widow is supposed to marry his diseased husband's younger brother. In case the younger brother cannot marry her then only she is free to marry anyone. Now-a-days a widow may also refuse to marry her diseased husband's younger brother. Divorce is also allowed and it is not infrequent. It is permissible on various grounds. Fugitiveness, laziness, adultery, barrenness, impotence, lunacy etc. may be valid grounds for seeking divorce. If the wife is found guilty, her parents are supposed to return the 'bride price' paid by the husband at the time of marriage and only then she can marry another man.

Due to patrilineal nature of society the rule of inheritance is that when the head of the family dies the property is divided among all his surviving sons. As regards land, the eldest gets a small plot in excess of his usual share. When the sons are born of different mothers, the sons by the first wife get larger share. And ex-communicated son is not entitled to any share unless he is re-admitted to the social fold. A widow does not inherit but she is provided reasonable share for her proper maintenance, and an unmarried daughter, too, is entitled to a suitable maintenance until her marriage. All heirs of her deceased father are supposed to share the marriage expenses of their sister.

The traditional political organization of the Oraons is based on the authority of the regional council called *Parha-Panchayat.* A parha (region) is a territorial unit consisting of a number of contigous villages which may vary from five to thirty. Each *parha* defends its agricultural land, village sites, forest tracts, grazing lands, water supply, fishing pools, etc. One of the villages in a parha is called the raja village, another the *dewan* (prime minister) village, third *the panrey* (clerk), a fourth the *Kotwar* (orderly) village, and the remaining villages are the *praja* (subject) villages. The headman or *mahato* of the *raja* village acts as chairman. The village community is, in fact, administered by the authority of the *pahan* (village priest) and the *mahato* (secular head). Both these offices are usually hereditary. All the villages in the *parha* hunt together, fight together, and dance together at festivals. Although, the *pahan* and *mahato* exercise considerable authority, neither of them has economic or jural authority without the concurrence of the village panchayat.

The religious beliefs of the Oraons are based on animism. *Dharmesh*, a spirit, is their supreme deity who is equated with sun for perpetuating light and life. They also have a strong belief in witchcraft and sorcery. The Oraon cremate their dead.

The Oraons have been one of the tribes famous for their colourful youth dormitories locally called *Dhumkuria*. Though, under the impact of Christianity and outside influence this institution has almost faded away but wherever it still survives it fulfils a variety of functions. The Oraon *dhumkuria* caters mainly to the boys who are admitted to its membership at about eight years of age. A male supervisor known as *dhangar mahato* and a lady supervisor called *barki dhangrin* instruct the boys and girls in their social and religious duties. The *dhumkuria* boys and girls also serve as scouts. They cook at wedding, provide labour in house construction, run as errands, extend helping hands in the face of natural calamities, etc. If they receive cash in lieu of their services it is spent on *dhumkuria;* either musical instruments are purchased or it is spent on the upkeep and maintenance of *dhumkuria*. The boys and girls dance together and enjoy each other's company. It also provides opportunities to come together and freely mix with each other. This free mixing between boys and girls is, to a great extent, responsible for the negligible incidence of crimes against women. The advance of the so-called 'new civilization' has hit hard on this beautiful institution that has been serving the tribals of the region in a variety of ways. In several villages, the only thing left in the name of *dhumkuria* are dilapidated and neglected houses standing as memorial to a great social institution of the tribal folks.

Eco-System and Economy : Like the other major tribes of Chotanagpur, Oraons are also agriculturists. Hunting-gathering, fishing, cattle rearing and handicrafts are no more their primary occupation, but activities in leisure or any eventuality. In some cases these may be taken as their subsidiary occupation. Many of them who have become landless' or have land of uneconomic nature provide labour in road construction and other activities. A large number of them are also engaged in mines and tea gardens. They grow coarse rice, millet, pulses and oilseeds. Since most of their fields are unirrigated, they have to depend entirely on nature's generosity. As far as the food gathering is concerned it is confined mainly to roots, tubers, fruits and flowers. They also collect honey from honey combs whenever they find one.

The livestock play an important role in their overall family economy. They rear such animals as cows, buffaloes, goats, pigs, sheep and fowl. Goats and sheep supply them with meat and also serve as sacrificial animals. They also relish pork and it is usually consumed during festival season. Among the birds, they rear ducks which is a steady source of ' supply of meat and egg. They do not seem to be very fond of milk which is used mainly in preparing tea or for ailing children. Their staple food is rice and pulse and their vegetarian requirements are fulfilled by wild plants, leaves, roots and tubers. They are also fond of smoking and chewing tobacco.

Problems and Prospects : Since some ground has already been covered in other chapters, even a brief overview will do. Most of the tribal areas of Bihar, including Oraon's habitats, have never been entirely isolated from the rest of the State. Non-tribal Hindu and Muslim communities have been living in the midst of the tribes for several centuries. There is hardly any tribal village in which a few Hindu caste families do not reside. They provide certain essential services for the tribals and speak the tribal languages. In many ways they have also been a source of destabilization of the tribal social organization and also their exploitation. At the same time they have also been a source of culture change.

One of their most glaring problems is land alienation. As Sachchidanand (1972) rightly points out, most of the land in tribal areas has been reclaimed from the forest and made fit for cultivation by them and their forefathers. As they are predominantly agriculturalists, they are deeply attached to land. Land is not just a means of subsistence for them, it is a spiritual bond between them and their ancestors. As such any loss of land is deeply resented by them. The process of land alienation has been in operation for a long time. The recurrent needs of cash, frequent famines and the habit of drinking have forced the tribals into the clutches of moneylenders who are mainly responsible for grabbing their land. Land acquired in the wake of industrialization (see Chapter on "Problems') has also been a source of land alienation.

In the matter of planned development they feel that they have always been neglected. Obviously agriculture in tribal areas cannot look up unless a big boost is given in providing irrigation facilities. They have, by and large, not benefitted even from industrialization. Despite a plethora of schemes their claims have been skipped over even for unskilled jobs and no concrete scheme ever implemented for their industrial training.

Since education has made impressive headway in the whole of the tribal region the Oraon's level of aspirations has also risen.

Unemployment among the educated Oraons is also mounting which further pushes them into frustration.

As the majority of the tribal agriculturists of this region are not able to produce enough for their subsistence, they have been in the practice of going out to seek employment in the four month's lean agricultural season. Hence, migration has also been one of their problems; they go to the tea gardens of Assam and North Bengal, to the jute mills and brick kilns round about Calcutta and, of course lately, to Punjab and Haryana as agricultural labour.

As Rightly pointed out by Jyotisen (1972) apart from the Christian Missions, there seems to be no voluntary organization which takes intelligent and effective interest in welfare of the tribals. There is none to give them proper guidance in matters relating to proper utilization of the official benefits meant for them.

They have become part of the larger *Jharkhand* movement. The maladies that gave rise to this popular movement are economic, administrative, sociopsychological and political (for details please see the chapter on "Regionalism"). Official apathy and indifference have been allowing the situation to drift more and more. Let those responsible for the present state of affairs understand that these tribal people are also normal, thinking human beings and their patience, too, cannot be stretched beyond a certain limit. The problems cry for solution.

TRIBAL COMMUNITIES IN SOME STATES

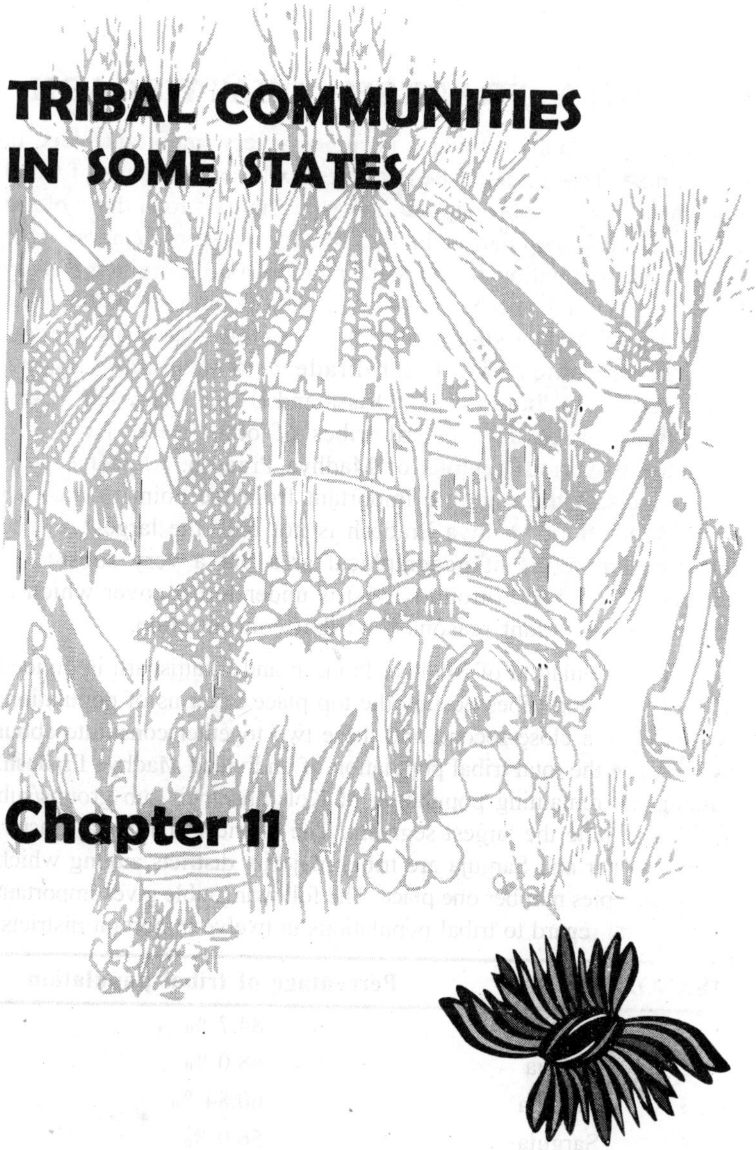

Chapter 11

MADHYA PRADESH – CHATTISGARH

The State of Madhya Pradesh occupies a very important place in tribal India. Though the state occupies sixth rank in terms of tribal percentage to the total population of the state, it tops the table in terms of tribal population in the country in absolute terms; the total tribal population in the state is about one crore and twenty lakh but does not exceed 23% of the total population of the state (1981 Census). The state of Madhya Pradesh shares its borders with seven states viz. Uttar Pradesh, Rajasthan, Gujarat, Maharashtra, Andhra Pradesh, Orissa and Bihar. The result of this contagiousness is that several tribes of other states have also extended to various regions of Madhya Pradesh. Almost half of the districts of the state are important from the point of view of tribal population. Madhya Pradesh is not only the largest among the states in terms of geographical area but a very substantial segment of the state (around 33%) is under forest cover which is one of the important reasons for tribal concentration.

The tribal population of Madhya Pradesh and Chattisgarh is divided into 58 large and tribes occupy the top place in terms of population; Bhils follow a close second and these two together constitute about two third of the total tribal population of undivided Madhya Pradesh. Among the remaining population of Kols and their sub groups/sub tribes constitute the largest segment. The districts of Jhabua, Bastar, Mandla, Dhar and Sarguja are tribal majority districts among which Bastar occupies number one place. The following table gives important figures with regard to tribal populations in twelve important districts.

S. NO.	District	Percentage of tribal population
1.	Bastar	84.7 %
2.	Jhabua	68.0 %
3.	Mandla	60.84 %
4.	Sarguja	56.0 %

5.	Dhar	53.38 %
6.	Shahdol	48.23 %
7.	Raigarh	47.2 %
8.	Khargaun	39.55 %
9.	Sivani	37.49 %
10.	Chindwara	35.0%
11.	Sidhi	32.53 %
12.	Betul	30.4%

A comprehensive study of the tribal population of Madhya Pradesh is no easy task; here the tribes are divided into several overlappings causing a lot of confusion. The 1981 Census recognised 48 scheduled tribes in Madhya Pradesh with more than fifty sub tribes of Gonds having been recognised.

List of Scheduled Tribes

Agariya, Aandh, Baiga, Bhains, Maria, Bhumiya, Bhuihar, Bhatra, Bhil, Bhilala, Bhujiya, Biyar, Bijhwar, Birhua, Birhor, Dhanwar, Gadaba, Gonda/Gond, Chalwa, Halvi, Kamma, Karaka, Kama, Charewa, Rathiya, Chatdi, Keet, Khaimar, Kharia, Kol, Kolam, Kodh, Khond, Koraku, Korwa, Majhi, Mahawar, Mawasi, Meena, Mongiya, Munda, Nagesia, Nat, Navdigar, Sapera, Kubuttar, Nihal, Oraon, Dhanka (including Dhangar), Panika, Pao, Pardhan/Pathari/Sarouti, Pardhi, Parja, Sahariya, Sauta, Saur, Savar/Saura, Sehariya, Sauj.

In this special supplement on Madhya Pradesh an ethnographic account of two of the most important tribes is given below.

THE BHILS

The Bhils are considered as the largest tribe in India. They constitute (together with their all sub groups) about six million souls. The Bhils inhabit substantial area of Madhya Pradesh, Maharashtra, Rajasthan and Gujarat. They also occupy some of the border areas of Karnataka and Andhra Pradesh. They are about fifteen lakhs in Madhya Pradesh alone.

From the point of view of their economic life they should be considered as settled cultivators although they are traditionally known as excelled archers. Geographically speaking, their traditional habitat has been the hills of Aravalli, Vindhyas, Satpura and Rewakantha plateau. It is believed that the word Bhil has been derived from the word Bil from Dravidian language which mean bow; hence, the people with bow are Bhils.

The skin colour of the Bhils is brownish dark, head hair a bit wavy with scant body hair. Most of the scholars consider them as Dravida while Guha included them among the proto-australoid. Bhils speak a variety of dialects resembling each other but with the respective regional tinge. Collectively speaking all these dialects may be put under the linguistic category of Bhilli, this collection of dialects contains substantial number of Mundari and Dravidian words but due to regional variations the impact of Gujarati, Marathi, and Marwari may also be seen. Among the traditional neighbours of Bhils who have influenced them are the Gonds, Bhuiya and Kolar tribes.

The Bhils prefer to make their settlements on the small hillocks and live in huts. Most of their houses are built from wooden poles and wooden logs with the traditional Khaprail or clay slabs providing the ceiling. These houses lack the provision of windows, which is a striking feature of their settlement pattern.

Social Organization

The Bhils are divided into two exogamous moieties. These moieties in turn, are divided into numerous exogamous clans or gotras which are further divided into lineages composed of several families. The lineage may go back to 5-6 generations. The traditional family unit of Bhil is called as Vasilu. A family consists of male, his life and their unmarried children. With addition of some other kins it becomes an extended family. The head of the family is usually the eldest male member and all the earning members deposit their incomes in the common pool managed by the head of the family. They have a strong patriarchal setup and the eldest males authority is unassailable.

The Bhils are strictly endogamous and those marrying outside the tribe may be excommunicated or penalised heavily or undergo both. They are largely monogamous but a few of them may have more than one wife. However, polyandry is not practised at all. They practice cousin marriage as 'preferential marriages'. Widow remarriage is common and usually the widow marries her deceased husband's younger brother. If she wishes to marry anybody else, she is free to choose her life partner again. Likewise a widower usually marries his deceased wife's younger sister. Thus levirate and sororate both are prevalent. Divorce is also common and in case of dissolution of marriage the children usually remain with their father.

The rules of succession are such that the eldest son of the deceased gets the largest share and the youngest smallest with property being distributed proportionately according to age. The liabilities left by the deceased are also distributed in the same order. The daughters do not have any claim over the father's property.

Generally speaking they cremate their dead while the children and those dying of unnatural causes are buried. The religious beliefs of the Bhils are largely based on animism or animatisim. They also believe in spirits and ancestor worship is also popular among them. After coming into contact with the Hindu society they have started observing festivals like Holi, Diwali, Dussehra, etc. but they continue to observe their traditional festivals. The ojhas or sorcerers occupy a special place in their society.

Economy and Ecosystem

The economy of the present Bhil society is based on agriculture though the outsiders tend to view them in their traditional image—the nomads with exceptional hunting expertise. Earlier they used to do shifting cultivation but now they have switched over to settled cultivation. Their staple diet is maize while cotton is grown as cash crop. Besides these they also grow paddy, pulses, sugarcane, oilseed and wheat. The spirit of cooperation they display in various agricultural chores is been to be believed. The mutual cooperation at the time of harvest in known as helma.

The occupations related with forests are an important aspect of the Bhils' economy. By being basically forest dweller they are expert hunters and they, are able to hunt even ferocious animals through very ordinary weapons. Perhaps that is why, they still carry an image of a tribe of expert archers. They are also woodcutters. They have no parallel in extracting honey, procuring the edible roots and fruits and gathering mahua. They also do fishing and practice poultry farming. They donot weave their cloths but purchase it from the market.

The pressure of population, land grabbing and alienation of their land by the neighbouring peasantry, harassment and exploitation by the lower level forest officials, contractors and moneylenders have made their life miserable. Though certain schemes of tribal development have made some dent, the life is still harsh.

THE GONDS

The Gonds constitute one of the largest segments of tribal India coming immediately after the Bhils. The Gonds consist of a group of tribal communities and they have been known to the people because of their colourful youth dormitories. The Gond tribal community inhabits a contagious geographical belt passing through Madhya Pradesh, Maharashtra, Andhra Pradesh, Bihar, Karnataka, West Bengal, and Gujarat. However, their original place of habitation is considered to be Bastar region of Madhya Pradesh alone. They are divided into more than fifty sub-tribes; and inhabit the plateau region of Madhya Pradesh (Mandla, Sewni, Chindwara and Betul) and Bastar region. They constitute more than half of the population of Mandla district.

One of the important features of this tribe is that they do not introduce themselves as Gonds but through their sub-tribal name or Kotar. The terms Koia, Koitov, or Kotor, in the local dialect stand for 'man of hills or mountains'. Their traditional neighbours are the Baiga, Khond, Agariya, Bhumia and Gadaba tribes.

The Gonds are dark complexioned people whose skin colour varies between chocolate brown to blackish. They have coarse, black and wavy hair with dark black eyes, thick lips and big nose. Guha has included them among Proto Ausatraloid group. They have their own language known as Gondi. Grierson is of the view that the Gonds use a variety of languages and dialects of the Dravidian language family. In several cases they have been observed to be fairly competent in using their neighbours' languages too. Mostly, they are bilingual.

In the settlement of their habitation and villages geographical conditions/factors play important role especially sources of water. In the hilly regions they prefer the top and in the plains river banks are their favourite locations. In the house construction the raw materials being available in the nearby forests are used. They make their huts by logs of wood, bamboo, grass and clay plaster. Traditionally they used to have youth dormitories known as Ghotul in the village or between 2-3 villages. Under the impact of modern civilization the institution of youth dormitories is fast declining (for details see a separate chapter on Youth Dormitory'). Also, every village has a provision of a guest house.

Social Organization

As already mentioned they prefer to introduce themselves by their sub-tribal names. In Bastar they are known as Maria or Muriya. They are divided into several clans (gotra) consisting of a number of families each. Family is the basic unit of their social organization. Generally the families are quite small but in some cases they may have large extended families. The eldest male member enjoys atmost authority. In their scheme of division of labour the adult male members do agriculture and hunting while the females perform all the domestic chores.

The Gonds are generally monogamous. Keeping more than one wife may be due to the barrenness of the first wife or merely a way to flaunt one's high economic status. They practice tribal endogamy. The practice of levirate is prevalent among them and if any woman marries any other person except her deceased husbands' brother, he is to be compensated because of the practice of 'bride price'. Sororate is also popular among them. Matrimonial alliances may be established between distant cousins but parallel cousin marriage is forbidden. They do not practice child marriage. Divorce is permissible and this right may be exercised equally by the women folk. Widow remarriage is liked by the society.

Generally speaking, the Gonds cremate their deads but .those dying of diseases or unnatural causes are buried. Their religious beliefs are based on animatism or animism but due to increasing, cultural contact with the Hindu society their pantheon has been undergoing radical changes and they are getting 'Hinduised'.

The land under shifting cultivation is owned communally. Sons inherit their father's property and the daughters do not have property rights. In the division of property the house is generally given to the youngest son while the land is divided equally among all the sons. Among the sons whosoever takes the responsibility of the widowed mother and unmarried sisters gets the largest share in the property. In the absence of sons, all the property-moveable as well as immoveable-is divided among the sons-in-laws.

They live in villages and every village has its' own Panchayat. Besides other members, every Panchayat has two special members-one looks after public works and the second, religious affairs. Tribal issues are resolved through penal fines, etc.

Economy and Ecosystem

Gonds are, by and large, self sufficient in various spheres of economic life. Though the majority of the Gonds have taken to settled cultivation, a section of them is still practicing shifting cultivation known locally as Penda and Dippi. Their chief crops are Kutvi, Kodo, Bajra, Urad and Moong while rice and Kutki are their staple diet. They are also fond of meat, jungle fruits, fish and eggs.

Their main occupation used to be hunting but now it can be carried on only clandestinely and only on restricted scale. They are expert collectors of local and minor forest produce. They have been consuming chironji, honey, golar, mahua, etc. in substantial quantities but these days they are known only as collectors of Tendu leaves. Traditionally, they have been practising cattle rearing for meat consumption and transportation but they have now adopted piggery and poultry as important means of livelihood under various tribal development programmes. They make tools and implements of day to day use, themselves. Of late a substantial number of Gonds have taken to construction labour or mining. Like many other tribes, Gonds too are living under constant exploitation and harassment and this has been at the root of several minor and major tribal uprising in the central Indian tribal belt.

MADHYA PRADESH – CHATTISGADH

The Scheduled Tribe (ST) population of the State of Madhya Pradesh - Chattisgadh is 12,233,474 as per 2001 census. This constitutes 20.3 percent of the total population (60,348,023) of the State. Madhya Pradesh holds 1st rank among all the States/UTs in terms of ST population and 12th rank in respect of the proportion of ST population to total population. The growth of the ST population during 1991-2001 has been 26.4 percent, which is 2.1 percent higher than the overall growth of total population (24.3 percent). The State has a total of forty six (46) Scheduled Tribes, and all of them have been enumerated at 2001 census.

2. The Scheduled Tribe population in the State is overwhelmingly rural, with 93.6 percent residing in rural areas. At district level, STs have returned the highest proportion in Jhabua district (86.8 percent) followed by Barwani (67 percent), Dindori (64,5 percent) and Mandla (57.2 percent) districts.

Bhind district preceded by Morena and Datia has the lowest proportion of STs (0.5 percent).

Population - Size & Distribution

3. Out of forty six (46) STs, Bhil is the most populous tribe having a number of 4,618,068, constituting 37.7 percent of the total ST population. Gond is the second largest tribe, with a population of 4,357,918 constituting 35.6 percent. Four other STs in the descending order are Kol, Korku, Sahariya and Baiga. Along with Bhil and Gond, the six tribes constitute 92.2 percent of the total ST population of the State. Pardhan, Saur and Bharia Bhumia have a population ranging from 105,692 to 152,472; together, they form 3.2 percent. Four tribes, namely, Majhi, Khairwar, Mawasi and Panika having population in the range of 47,806 to 81,335 account for another 2.2 percent of the ST population; remaining thirty three tribes along with the generic tribes constitute the residual 2.5 percent of total ST population. Tribes having below 1000 population are twelve in number. Of them, five tribes, namely, Mina, Andh, Birhul, Parja and Nagesia each have less than 500 population.

4. Bhils have the highest population in Jhabua district followed by Dhar, Barwani and West Nimar districts. Gonds have major concentration in Chhindwara, Mandla, Betul, Seoni and Shahdol districts. Other four major groups Kol, Korku, Sahariya and Baiga have registered the highest population in Rewa, East Nimar, Shivpuri and Shahdol districts respectively.

Sex Ratio

5. The over all sex ratio of the ST population in Madhya Pradesh is 975 females per 1000 males which is lower than the national average of 978 for all STs.

6. At the individual level, Gond and Baiga have over all sex ratio higher than that of the national average. Sahariya have shown the lowest overall sex ratio.

7. The sex ratio among the STs, in the age group 0-6 years (979) is higher than that of all STs at the national level. Except Korku, Kol and Sahariya, the three major tribes have higher child sex ratio than that of the national average.

Statement - 1 ; Sex Ratio

Age group	All STs (India)	All STs (MP)	Gond	Baiga	Bhil	Korku	Kol	Sahariya
All ages	978	975	989	984	975	959	948	938
0 - 6 yrs.	973	979	986	983	977	967	969	969

Literacy & Educational Level

8. The overall literacy rate of the STs has increased from 18.4 percent at 1991 census to 41.2 percent at 2001 census. Despite this increase, the literacy rate among the tribes of Madhya Pradesh is lower if compared with that of all STs at the national level (47.1 percent). Male and female literacy rates among the tribes (53.5 percent & 28.4 percent) are also lower in comparison to those at the national level (59.2 percent & 34.8 percent).

Statement - 2: Literacy Rate

Literacy rate	All STs (State)	Gond	Korku	Kol	Bhil	Baiga	Sahariya
Persons	41.2	50.3	38.8	35.9	34.5	32.3	28.7
Females	28.4	36.4	24.5	22.9	23.0	20.1	15.9

9. Among the major tribes, only Gonds have registered the higher overall literacy as well as female literacy if compared to those of the national average. Sahariya have returned the lowest overall literacy and female literacy both.

10. Among ST literates, 57.3 percent are either without any educational level or have attained education below primary level. The proportion of literates who have attained education up to primary and middle levels constitute 24.8 percent and 9.7 percent respectively. Literates, who are educated up to matric/secondary/higher secondary, constitute 6.6 percent only. Graduates and above are 1.4 percent while non-technical & technical diploma holders constitute a negligible proportion.

Statement-3: Levels of Education among the major Scheduled Tribes

Names of STs	Literate without educational level	Below primary	Educational levels attained				
			Primary	Middle	Matric/Secondary Higher Secondary/ Intermediate	Technical &Non-technical diploma	Graduate and above
All STs	10.8	46.5	24.8	9.7	6.6	0.1	1.4
Bhil	15.5	47.1	21.2	8.2	6.3	0.1	1.6
Gond	8.4	45.0	27.4	10.9	7.0	0.1	1.2
Kol	7.2	47.1	26.9	11.4	6.6	0.0	0.6
Korku	10.1	56.0	22.9	6.8	3.6	0.0	0.5
Sahariya	15.4	62.2	16.1	4.0	1.8	0.1	0.5
Baiga	11.4	50.4	26.0	8.3	3.4	0.0	0.5

11. The data on the education levels attained by all STs show that the drop-out rate is high after primary level. It declines sharply from the middle level onwards. Similar trend has been shown by the major STs in attainment of education.

12. Out of total 35.1 lakh tribal children in the age group 5 -14 years, only 16.1 lakh have been attending school, constituting 46 percent. As many as 18.9 lakh children in the corresponding age group have not been going to school. Among the major tribes, Gonds have more than 57.7 percent of the total children in the corresponding age group attend school; these proportions are below 50 percent among Kol, Korku and Baiga below 40 percent among Bhil and Sahariya.

Statement - 4 : Percentage of school going children in the age group 5-14 yrs.

Age Group	All STs	Bhil	Gond	Kol	Korku	Sahariya	Baiga
5-14 yrs.	46.0	36.3	57.7	49.4	43.3	34.7	42.7

Work Participation Rate (WPR)

13. The Work Participation Rate (WPR) of the ST population is 50.5 percent, which is slightly higher than that of total STs at the national level (49.1 percent). There has been a marginal decline of 1.3 percent in the tribal working population during 1991-2001. Male and female work participation rates among the tribal communities are 53.2 percent and 47.6 percent respectively. Among the total workers, 67.8 percent are main workers and this proportion is at par with the national average recorded for all STs (68.9 percent).

14. Among the major tribes, Bhil, Gond, Korku and Baiga have higher WPR than that of the national average.

Category of Workers

15. 'Cultivators' constitute the highest proportion (46.8 percent) among the total workers, which is higher than that of all STs at the national level (44.7 percent). 'Agricultural Labourers' account for 42.1 percent, which is higher than the national average of 36.9 percent recorded by all STs in this category. 'Cultivators' and 'Agricultural Labourers' together constitute

89 percent of the total workers. 'Other Workers' constitute 10 percent. This proportion is lower than that of the national average (16.3 percent) whereas workers engaged in 'Household Industry' (HHI) constitute 1.1 percent, which is almost half of the national average (2.1 percent).

Statement- 5 : Percentage Distribution of Workers in four Economic Categories

Economic category	All STs	Bhil	Gond	Kol	Korku	Sahariya	Baiga
Cultivators	46.8	60.7	46.8	12.0	38.8	28.2	32.6
Agricultural Labourers	42 1	31 4	42 5	70 4	54 5	56 9	54 7
HHI Workers	1.1	0.3	1.4	1.0	1.5	0.9	1.8
Other Workers	10.0	7.6	9.3	16.6	5.2	14.0	10.9

16. Among the major tribes, Bhil have more than 60 percent workers are 'Cultivators' whereas 70 percent Kol workers are 'Agricultural Labourers'. Sahariya, Baiga and Kol have more than 50 percent of total workers are 'Agricultural Labourers'. In the category of 'Other Workers', Kols hold the first position, followed by Sahariya, Baiga etc.

Marital Status

17. The data show that 51.9 percent of the ST population is 'never married' whereas 'married' persons constitute 43.9 percent. 'Widowed' persons form 3.9 percent while less than half percent are (0.4 percent) 'divorced and separated'.

18. Marriages of girls and boys below the legal age for each are in practice among the tribes of Madhya Pradesh. Married girls below 18 years and married boys below 21 years constitute 2.5 percent and 4.6 percent respectively. These proportions are higher than those recorded for all STs at the national level (2.1 percent and 2.8 percent). The STs namely, Kol, Sahariya and Baiga have registered the proportions of such marriages higher than the State average.

19. The mean number of children ever born per ever married ST woman (45 - 49 yrs.) is 5 which is higher than the total STs at national level (4).

Religion

20. Hinduism is the pre-dominant religion (91.1 percent) of the State. As many as 96.1 percent STs are Hindus. Tribes following 'other religions and persuasions' account for 3.2 percent. Christian and Muslim tribes constitute 0.5 percent and 0.1 percent respectively.

CHHATTISGARH

According to 2001 census, the Scheduled Tribe (ST) population of Chhattisgarh State is 6.616,596 constituting 31.8 percent of the total population of the State. The State holds 8th position among all the States and UTs in term of the proportion of ST population to the total population (20,833,803). The decennial growth of ST population has been 15.7 percent, which is 2.6 percent lower than the overall growth of population (18.3 percent). The State has a total of forty two (42) Scheduled Tribes and all have been enumerated at 2001 census.

2. As many as 94.7 percent of ST population resides in rural areas. At the district level, tribals have their highest concentration in Dantewada (78.5 percent) followed by Bastar (66.3 percent) and Jashpur (63.2 percent) districts. Janjgir-Champa district has the lowest proportion of tribal population (11.6 percent).

Population - Size & Distribution

3. Out of forty two (42) tribes, Gond is the most populous tribe with a population of 3,659,384 constituting 55.3 percent of the total ST population. Four other STs in descending order are Kawar, Oraon, Halba and Bhattra. Along with Gond, the five STs constitute 84.3 percent of total ST population of the State. Binjhwar, Korwa and Sawar have a population ranging from 100,692 to 104,718. Together, they form 4.6 percent. Ten STs, namely, Bharia Bhumia, Nagesia, Baiga ..... to Kharia having population in the range of 88,981 down to 41,901, constitute another 9 percent of total ST population; remaining

twenty four (24) STs along with generic tribes constitute the balance 2 percent of total ST population. Nine tribes have below 1000 population. Of them, five tribes, namely, Sonr, Damor, Karku, Andh and Bhil Mina are very small having population less than 100.

4. At the district level, Gonds have registered their high population in Bastar, Dantewada, Kanker Surguja and Raipur districts. Kawar are mainly concentrated in Surguja, Raigarh and Korba districts. Other three major tribes, Oraon, Halba and Bhattra have the highest concentration in Jashpur, Durg and Bastar districts respectively.

Sex Ratio

5. The over all sex ratio of the ST population in Chhattisgarh is 1013 females per 1000 males, showing the preponderance of females. This is significantly higher than the national average of 978 for the total ST population.

6. At individual level, females outnumber the males among all the five major tribes, having over all sex ratio above 1000.

7. The sex ratio among STs, in the age group 0-6 years (998) is higher than that of the national average. All the major tribes have recorded child sex higher than the national average with Gond and Bhattra having preponderance of female children.

Statement - 1 : Sex Ratio

Age groups	All STs (India)	All STs (State)	Halba	Gond	Bhattra	Kawar	Oraon
All ages	978	1013	1035	1018	1013	1008	1002
0- 6 yrs.	973	998	989	1002	1040	997	978

Literacy & Educational Level

8. The overall literacy rate of the STs is 52.1 percent at 2001 census. This is higher if compared to 26.7 percent recorded at 1991 census. This percentage is also higher than that of all STs at the national level (47.1 percent). The male as well as female literacy rates (65 percent & 39.3 percent) among the STs are also higher than those at the national level (59.2 percent & 34.8 percent).

Statement - 2 : Literacy Rate

Literacy rate	All STs (state)	Halba	Oraon	Kawar	Gond	Bhattra
Persons	52.1	74.1	62.2	61	49.2	38
Females	39.3	63.3	52	45.6	36.6	23.6

9. Among the numerically larger tribes, Halba, Oraon and Kawar have registered overall literacy rate higher than that of all STs at the state level. Bhattra have recorded the lowest overall as well as female literacy rates.

10. The data on different levels of education attained by the tribal literates show that slightly more than half (50.5 percent) of tribal literates are either without any educational level or have attained education below primary level. The proportions of literates who have attained education up to primary and middle levels are 26.3 percent and 12.3 percent respectively. Person's educated up to matric/secondary/higher secondary constitute 8.8 percent only. Percentage of ST literates who are graduates & above is only 1.9 percent. Non-technical & technical diploma holders constitute a negligible proportion.

11. Among the major tribes, Oraon have the highest proportion of matriculates whereas Bhattra have the lowest proportion of matriculates preceded by Gond.

12. The data on education levels attained by all STs show that the proportion of the tribal literates decline sharply after the primary level. Percentage of literates in middle school is less than half of the primary level literates. This proportion further declines to a considerable extent from secondary level onwards.

13. Out of total 17 lakh tribal children in the age group 5 -14 years, 10 lakh attend school, constituting 58.7 percent. As many as 7 lakh (41.3 percent) children in the corresponding age group do not go to school. Gond have 4.2 lakh children do not attend school while among Kawar, 61,385 children do not go to school. On the other hand, Halba and Oraon have more than 70 percent school going children.

Statement-3: Levels of Education among the major Scheduled Tribes

Names of STs	Literate without educational level	Below primary	Educational levels attained				
			Primary	Middle	Matric/Secondary Higher Secondary/ Intermediate etc.	Technical &Non-technical diploma etc.	Graduate and above
All STs	11 .1	39.4	26.3	12.3	8.8	0.2	1.9
Gond	12.2	40.7	26.3	11.5	7.7	0.1	1.5
Kawar	8.9	38.6	28.8	13.3	8.3	0.1	2.0
Oraon	6.3	30.5	24.9	17.0	16.4	0.3	4.6
Halba	9.2	32.6	28.0	15.8	11.5	0.4	2.6
Bhattra	13.9	45.7	22.2	11.5	5.8	0.1	0.7

Statement - 4 : Percentage of school going children in the age group 5 -14 years

Age group	All STs	Gond	Kawar	Oraon	Halba	Bhattra
5-14 yrs.	58.7	55.7	66.5	71.2	77.3	52.6

Work Participation Rate (WPR)

14. The Work Participation Rate (WPR) of the ST population is 53.4 percent which is lower than that of all STs at the national level (49.1 percent). There has been a marginal decennial decline of 0.7 percent in the WPR. Male (56.7 percent) as well as female work participation rate (50.2 percent) among the tribes are higher than the corresponding figures (53.2 percent and 44.8 percent) recorded for all STs at the national level. Among the total workers, 67.4 percent are main workers and this proportion is marginally lower than that of all STs at the national level (68.9 percent).

15. At the individual level, among the major tribal groups, Gonds have WPR (54.2 percent) more than the state average whereas Oraon, Halba and Bhattra have recorded WPR below the state average.

Category of Workers

16. More than half (56.6 percent) of the total tribal workers are 'Cultivators'. This figure is higher than that of the country (44.7 percent). 'Agricultural Labourers' constitute 32.7 percent, which is comparable with the national average of 36.9 percent. 'Cultivators' and 'Agricultural Labourer' together constitute 89 percent of the total tribal workers. 'Other workers' account for 9.7 percent only. This proportion is also considerably lower if compared to the national average of 16.3 percent. Workers engaged in Household Industry (HHI) account for a meagre 1.2 percent, which is lower than that of all STs at the national level (2.1 percent).

Statement - 5 : Percentage Distribution of Workers in four Economic Categories

Economic Category	All STs	Gond	Kawar	Oraon	Halba	Bhattra
Cultivators	56.6	59.6	63.9	61.5	62.1	44.2
Agricultural Labourers	32.7	30.5	27.8	25.4	23.7	45.7
HHI Workers	1.2	0.6	0.4	0.7	0.4	0.4
Other Workers	9.5	9.3	7.9	12.4	13.7	9.7

17. Among the major tribes, Kawar, Oraon, Halba have more than 60 percent workers are 'cultivators' followed by Gond. Bhattra have the highest proportion of 'Agricultural Labourer'.

Marital Status

18. The data on marital status of STs show that the proportion of 'never married' persons is marginally higher (48.9 percent) than the 'married persons' (45 percent). 'Widowed' persons constitute 5.4 percent while half percent (0.6 percent) are 'divorced and separated'.

19. Marriages of girls and boys below the legal age for each are rarely practiced among the tribes of Chhattisgarh. While the proportion of the married girls below 18 years (1.5 percent) is slightly lower than the national average of 2.1 percent, the proportion of married boys below 21 years (2.7 percent) is almost equal to that of all STs at the national level (2.8 percent).

20. The mean number of children even born per ever married ST woman (Age-group 45-49 yrs.) is 4 which is same as that of all STs at the national level.

Religion

21. Hinduism is the predominant religion (93.7 percent) of the tribes of the State. Christian tribes have a share of 4.7 percent. The tribes professing 'Other religion and persuations' and Islam constitute 1.4 percent and 0.1 percent respectively.

UTTAR PRADESH – UTTRAKHAND

Uttar Pradesh has traditionally been centre of diverse castes, tribes, communities, religions and traditions. However, the tribal segment has been occupying the fringes of consciousness of the people living in this state. It is true that the culture of the 'elites' does not fit into the realm of the tribal culture but it is also correct that the so called elite culture has sprung from several of these tribal communities. The cultural evolution, thus, has seen ups and downs.

It may sound strange to many but the fact remains that there were no Scheduled Tribes in Uttar Pradesh before 1967. It was only in this year that five tribes were declared as Scheduled tribes under Article 342 by the President of India. These are

1. Tharu
2. Bhoksa
3. Jounsari (Khasha)
4. Bhotia (Shauka)
5. Raji (Banravat)

The total population of all these five scheduled tribes is 2.88 lakhs which comes to about 0.21% of the total population of Uttar Pradesh. However, the scheduled caste population is about 21.16% of the state's total population. The population growth of the scheduled tribes in the state between 1971-81 was only 17.19% while the average growth rate of the state's population was 25.49% during the same period.

All the five scheduled tribes are concentrated in the state's northern hilly areas and the neighboring Bhabbar and Terai regions. Population wise the Tharus are the largest tribe (1991:1,18558) and the Raji the smallest (1991: 755) tribe.

In terms of district wise population 33% of the state's tribal population lives in Dehradun while another 32% inhabits Nainital. It means that about 65% of the total tribal population is concentrated in only two districts. These two districts are the original home of Tharus, Boksa and the Jounsaris. Among the remaining districts of the state Lakhimpur Kheri, Gonda, Bahraich, Bijnore, Pithoragarh and Chamoli are the home of a substantial number of Tharus, Bhotias and the Rajis.

Apart from these scheduled tribes a substantial population of tribes also exists in the state. They inhabit the southern plateau of the state. Thus Mirzapur, Allahabad, Varanasi, Banda, Jhansi and Lalitpur are such places inhabited by people who are primitive tribes in all respects but they have still not been brought under the protective umbrella of the Constitution by declaring them scheduled tribes while in the neighbouring Madhya Pradesh and Bihar members of the same tribes are scheduled tribes and their condition is definitely better than their counterparts living in Uttar Pradesh. Initially they were recognised as scheduled castes in 1950 but later on they were brought under a special category known as 'Non-Scheduled Tribes'. These tribes are as follows:

1. Agariya
2. Baiga
3. Bhuiya/Bhuiyar
4. Chero
5. Gond (Dhuriya, Nayak, Pathari, Ojha, Rajgond)
6. Khairwar
7. Korwa
8. Kol
9. Majhwar
10. Oraon
11. Parhhathiya
12. Sahariya (Sahariya Rawat)

Except the Sahariya, almost all of these tribes are found in Mirzapur district. Their total population is about 3 lakhs and the Kols are the largest of these tribes, whose population is around sixty thousand only. The first step for their betterment is that they should be declared scheduled tribes immediately so that they begin enjoying all the facilities, and provisions under the Integrated Tribal Development Programmes (ITDP).

In a recent development most of the tribal groups mentioned above and some others in Uttar Pradesh were put under the category of scheduled tribes vide The Scheduled Castes and Scheduled Tribes Order (Amendment), 2002. Most of these tribal groups inhabit Maharajganj, Siddhartha Nagar, Basti, Gorakhpur, Dewaria, Mau, Azamgarh, Jounpur, Balha, Ghazipur, Varanasi, Mirzapur and

Sonbhadra districts of Uttar Pradesh. Thus, the newly listed scheduled tribes are : Gond, Dhuria, Nayak, Ojha, Pathari, Rajgond, Kharwar and Khirwar, Sahariya, Paraihya, Baiga, Pankha and Panika, Angaria, Patari, Cheru, Pahiya and Punhiya.

After the creation of Uttrakhand only the Jharu and a section of Bhoksa remained in Uttar Pradesh. With the inclusion of the newly listed scheduled tribes, Uttar Pradesh has again emerged as an important place on the map of tribal India. There is an immediate need of research on these tribal groups.

THE THARUS

The Tharus are the largest of the five scheduled tribes of the state. They are spread over a vast tract between Nainital and Janakpur. They inhabit Nainital (Khatima and Sitarganj tehsils) Lakhimpur Kheri/ Gonda, Bahraich and Gorakhpur in Uttar Pradesh ; Champaran and Darbhanga districts of Bihar ; Jalpaigudi in Assam and in the region between Bhenchi and Mahakali in Nepal. About four lakh of them live in Nepal alone. According to the 1991 Census their total population was 1,18558 only. They claim their ancestry from Kirata and they are divided into several subgroups.

The Tharus are usually short statured, yellow complexioned, broad faced and plain nosed people showing lot of signs of Mongoloid racial Stock. Some scholars regard them as descendants of the Rajputs while some others trace their origin to the Mongols of Central Asia. Their language seems to be highly influenced by Hindi and Nepali.

They extensively use logs of wood and bamboo for constructing their houses; perhaps this is because of the fact that their areas of habitation are flood prone. Usually their houses are built in north-south direction with doors always opening towards the east.

Social Organization

Marriage among the Tharus is settled usually through some mediator. Traditionally, they used to practice **badla** marriage in which marriage with each other's sisters was the usual mode of matrimonial alliance. Now Tean Tiki is becoming popular in which instead of marrying each other's sister, marriage with any near female relative is finalised. Although they are primarily monogamous, but polygyny may be practised.

The practice of joint family among them is still very strong. The eldest, male member of the family serves as head of the family. They have got an elaborate division of labour and every member of the family follows one's role seriously. The Tharus give more importance to their daughter-in-law than to their daughters. They are strongly patrilineal, patriarchal and patrilbeal.

The kinship system of the Tharus resembles that of the neighboring Hindu society. Sex relations between close kins are prohibited. Joking relationship exists with one's younger brother's wife but avoidance is practiced with ones' wife's elder brother.

They have a biradari panchayat to maintain political organization. These are their rural courts. The deliberations in the panchayat are carried with the locally brewed liquor. Even during arguments the 'Judges' keep on sipping the liquor. Traditionally speaking no appeal can be made against the judicial verdict of their local courts.

The religious beliefs and the pantheon of the Tharus resemble those of the neighboring Hindus. They also believe in witchcraft and sorcery and offer the sacrifices of goat and pig to their deities except to Jagannathi devta who is offered milk only. They believe in about 36 deities. Among their major festivals are Dussehra, Diwali, Maghki Khitchri, Kanhaaiyya Ashtmi and Bajhar. They go on drinking and dancing spree both males and females, during Holi. Bajhar festival falls during rainy season and is celebrated more like a picnic with outdoor cooking and marrymaking.

The Tharus bury their dead and observe daswan (tenth day after death) and Terhin (thirteenth day) rituals. When they return back after burial, they make a small bridge of clay on a crossroad believing that the spirit of the deceased shall be able to cross all the hurdles.

Economy and Ecosystem

The Tharus are basically an agriculturist tribal community. They are also expert in fishing. The Tharus living along forest are also expert hunters. By and large the Tharus are considered to be lazy people lacking the spirit of adventure and dynamism. They have also not taken to modern means of cultivation despite lots of incentives. All transactions, right from sowing to harvest, are practised in traditional ways and new market forces have still not become effective. They live under subsistence economy.

Fishing has a special place in a Tharus' life. Males and females do fishing separately and females usually do not take fish touched by the males. During rainy season they don't get fish because of fast currents and hence they do fishing in village ponds. Most of the Tharus are living in utter poverty and the saving, if any is spent on the consumption of local liquor. Spate of festivals and payment of bride price have further aggravated these conditions. A large number of Tharus remain chronically indebted and the moneylenders have cornered vast chunks of Tharus' land.

The region inhabited by the Tharus is rampant with malaria and it has been taking a heavy tool. Repeated floods make their life more miserable; they become houseless and lose their cattle in large number with diseases erupting all around. Paucity of pure drinking water, lack of transport, communication and electrification and several other factors keep them educationally and economically backward.

The Ministry of Welfare has been carrying on a number of scheme of welfare and development with ITDP being prominent among these. These programmes have started showing results in several areas and the overall situation is not hopeless.

THE BHOTIAS (Shauka)

In the border districts of Uttar Pradesh-Pithoragarh in Kumaon region and Uttarkashi and Chamoli in Garhwal region-live a number of tribal and subtribal communities popularly known as the Bhotia. The term Bhot has been derived from a Sanskrit word that stands for Tibet. The use of the word Bhotia (Tibetan) for the inhabitants of Indo-Nepal and Indo-Tibet border areas is not at all rational. Perhaps, that is why Rahul Sanskritayan has named this tribe as Bhotantik.

The Bhotia is a generic name that includes the Shauka of Munsiari (Pithoragarh), Rang of Dharchula (Pithoragarh), Tolcha and Marchha of Niti and Mana Valleys (Chamoli) and Jaad of Harsil (Uttarkashi). But the fact of the matter is that all these groups prefer to be called-as Shauka. Among the communities which have seen lots of ups and downs, Shaukas may be considered as one of the prominent groups. Those who had been enjoying lot of affluence tili early sixties because of trade and commerce are now forced to lead a miserable existence as a result of India-China War. They have started recovering a bit only after they were declared Scheduled Tribe in 1967.

Their stature varies between short to medium, fair complexion, straight brown hair, high cheekbones, epicanthic fold on the eyes and well built body are their important physical features. All these feature point towards their affinities with mongoloid racial stock. Being inhabitants of higher altitudes their chest region is quiet voluminous. Generally, Shauka languages are included in the category of Sino-Tibetan or Tibeto-Burmese language families. The elderly Shaukas are also conversant with Tibetan, Nepalese, Kumaoni, Garhwali etc. dialects.

Because of economic constraints the Shaukas have generally two houses which they inhabit according to seasonal cycles. During the summer season (May-October) they live in their villages located at the altitudes varying between 8,000 to 12,000 feet while during winters they migrate to lower altitudes. They prefer such places for their settlements as those which are not prone to such natural calamities as floods and glaciers. The traditional Shauka houses have slanting roofs and are usually double or triple storeyed-the ground floor is meant for cattle (goat and Jhebu /jeebu a hybrid of cow and yak) and their fodder, while the second storey is used for residential purposes. The third storey is generally for storage. Traditionally, a Shauka house is made of stone and logs of wood.

There are certain cultural diversities in the five above mentioned Shauka societies. For example the Shauka of Munsiari area are Kumaoni speaking while the remaining groups are having their own dialects; The Shaukas of Chaudans valley in Dharchula do not usually migrate arid live in settled villages; the Jaad Shaukas of Uttarkashi have a Buddhist temple (Gompa) which occupies an important place in their cultural life, while the Marchha of Mana valley are affiliated with the Hindu pilgrimage centre of Badrinath in one way or other.

Each Shauka society on the basis of ritual purity is divided into two endogamous moieties which are known as Bharet and Kunkiya. The primary unit of society is family, the joint family being quiet popular among them. Being a patriarchal society the Shaukas are patrilineal and patrilocal. Generally, they practice village exogamy. They are forbidden to many within their own lineage locally called as Rath. There are several forms of marriage among the Shaukas but by and large the elderly people of the family finalise a marriage proposal. The elderly kins of potential bridegroom visit the to-be-bride's place with the bottle of Chhang (the locally brewed rice beer), a red cloth and a couple of other gifts and initiate negotiations. Traditionally, the bride's father makes a formal refusal and gives his formal consent only after persistent persuasion by accepting the gifts brought by the bridegroom's side. With this marriage preparations are started by both the parties. The practices of marriage by capture and 'marriage by elopement' are rarely found. As a result of increasing culture contact with neighboring Hindu society they have started adopting the evil of dowry. The divorce and remarriage are very common among them. Either of the parties may take initiative in the dissolution of marriage. The divorce proceedings are very simple; A thread is severed in the presence of elderly members of society and divorce is announced. The life is so harsh that a lonely woman cannot survive and hence remarriage of a divorced woman or a widow is quite common. The Shaukas generally follow monogamy but they may also be polygynous. The Jaad Shauka, to some extent, still practice polyandry. Kinship and kinship obligation are very important in the local Shauka society. Chaumasa (May-September) is usually the time of festivals during which the kins living even in distant villages visit each other. Because of the practice of village exogamy, migration and joint family, kinship is not merely a bundle of formal relations but is symbolic of the Shauka society's solidarity. The mutual economic relations are an important aspect of Shauka social organisation. Being a localised society virtually every Shauka is related with each other through consaguineal or affinal ties.

Every Shauka society has its own traditional political organisation on the basis of which all the political, economic, social and ritual quarrels are resolved. Generally, the punishment is in the form of mass feast, local beer or some cash. Every village or a cluster of villages or valley has a headman who supervises a panchayat consisting of the village elders locally known as Sayana. The decision of panchayat is generally impartial, irrevocable and binding on both the parties and anybody not confining to it may be ex-communicated. Till recently they were not carrying their affairs to the formal court of law. But the situation is fast changing.

The Shauka society exhibits the impact of several religions. Traditionally speaking, they believe in animism and animatism but they have also observed some elements of Buddhism and Hinduism. Every lineage has its own deity, every village has its protector deity as will as the deities protecting land and crops. There is a great variety of deities, Gods and Goddesses. Every rock represents one Goddess or the other and numerous trees are the abodes of deities. They also offer the sacrifice of sheep to their deities and meat is consumed as deity's prasad.

Economy and Ecosystem

The traditional Shauka economy conforms to the migratory life. Till 1962 they used to go to the markets of Tibet during summers in connection with trade. They use to carry gur, rice, salt etc. and bring back wool, suhaga, some precious stones and herbs etc. It was based on barter and the Shaukas used to earn heavily. Just before the commencement of Indo-China War the Shaukas had to return from Tibet not as affluent traders but as shattered beggars. Thus began the agonising period of physical and mental tortures from which they have still not recovered, the Shaukas of Chaudans valley of Dharchula were settled cultivators and hence they remained unaffected by these changes.

With the migratory trade coming to an end the condition of the Shaukas became miserable. Education had never made any dent among the Shaukas and they were not conversant with any other trade or occupation. That is why this transitory phase proved to be very agonising for them. Gradually they reconciled with the contemporary realities, grappled with them and started tasting success. The pace of spread of education during the last three decades has been such that now-a-days virtually every Shauka village has a primary school and several degree colleges in the whole of the region. Several Shaukas are today doctors, engineers, teachers and officers. Some of them have established their own permanent shops while some have become contractors. A substantial number of them have also got employment through tourism especially through pilgrimages. Most of them do not prefer military service. The newly acquired status of a Scheduled Tribe has contributed a lot towards their betterment.

UTTAR PRADESH

Data Highlights

The Scheduled Tribe (ST) population of Uttar Pradesh is 107,963 at 2001 census, constituting a meagre 0.1 percent of the total population (166,197,921) of the State. The decennial growth of ST population has been 42 percent, which is 16.2 percent higher than the growth of total population (25.8 percent) during 1991-2001. The State has a total of five (5) Scheduled Tribes and all of them have been enumerated at 2001 census.

2. The tribal population of the State is predominantly rural with 88.8 percent of them residing in villages. District wise distribution of ST population shows that Kheri district has the highest proportion of STs (1.2 percent), followed by Balrampur (1.1 percent), Shrawasti & Bahraich (each 0.4 percent) districts. Nine (9) districts, each having a proportion of 0.1 percent tribal population whereas remaining fifty seven (57) districts have negligible proportion of ST population.

Population - Size & Distribution

3. Out of five STs, Tharu is the most populous tribe, having a population of 83,544; they constitute 77.4 percent of the total tribal population of the State. Buksa IS the second major tribe, having a number of 4,367, followed by Bhotia, Jaunsari and Raji. These four tribes along with generic tribes constitute the balance 22.6 percent of total ST population.
4. At the level of individual tribe, Tharu are primarily concentrated in Kheri. Balrampur and Bahraich districts. Buksa have the highest concentration in Bijnor, followed by Farrukhabad districts. Other three STs, Bhotia, Jaunsari and Raji have returned maximum population in Agra, Kheri and Gorakhpur districts respectively.
5. Among the five STs, Buksa and Raji tribes have been recognized as Primitive Tribes. Together, they constitute 5 percent of the total tribal population of the State.

Sex Ratio

6. The overall sex ratio of the ST population is 934 females per 1000 males which is lower than the national average (978) for all STs.
7. Individually, all the five tribes have recorded an overall sex ratio lower than the national average. While Tharu, Bhotia and Buksa have sex ratio above 900, Raji and Jaunsari have the sex ratio below 900 and 800 respectively.
8. The sex ratio among STs, in the age group 0-6 years (973) is equal to that of all STs at the national level. Tharu have recorded the child sex ratio marginally lower than the national average whereas remaining four tribes have registered child sex ratio above 1000, showing a preponderance of girl children.

Statement - 1 : Sex Ratio

Age group	All STs (India)	All STs (U P)	Tharu	Bhotia	Buksa	Raji	Jaunsari
All ages	978	934	946	939	907	897	732
0- 6 yrs.	973	973	970	1027	1082	1019	1026

Literacy & Educational Level

9. The overall literacy rate of the STs has increased from 20 percent at 1991 census to 35.1 percent at 2001 census. Despite improvement, the literacy rate of STs is considerably lower than the national average of 47.1 percent aggregated for all STs Male and female literacy rates (48.4 percent and 20.7 percent) are also considerably lower in comparison to those recorded for all STs (59.2 percent & 34.8 percent) at the national level.

Statement - 2 : Literacy Rate

Literacy rate	All STs	Jaunsari	Bhotia	Tharu	Raji	Buksa
Persons	35.1	51.1	42.0	34.9	31.3	31.2
Females	20.7	26.1	31.3	20.0	19.1	20.7

10. Among the five STs, only Jaunsari have shown the overall literacy rate (51.1 percent), higher than that of the national average. All the five STs have shown female literacy lower than the national average (34.8 percent).

11. Among tribal literates, 45.2 are either without any educational level or have attained education below primary level. The proportions of literates who have attained education up to primary and middle levels are 25.2 percent and 16 percent respectively. Persons educated up to matric / higher secondary/ Intermediate constitute 10.8 percent. Graduates and above are 2.8 percent.

12. Among all the STs, Raji have the highest proportion of secondary level literates, followed by Bhotia and Jaunsari. Bhotia have shown the highest proportion graduates followed by Raji. The percentage of the tribal literates decline sharply from the secondary level onwards.

Statement - 3 : Levels of education among the Scheduled Tribes

Names of STs	Literate without educational level	Below primary	Educational levels attained				
			Primary	Middle	Matric/Secondaryl Higher Secondaryl Intermediate etc.	Technical & Non-technical diploma etc.	Graduate and above
All STs	8.2	37.0	25.2	16.0	10.8	0.1	2.8
Tharu	8.1	38.8	25.1	16.3	9.7	0.0	2.0
Buksa	8.2	39.9	29.7	11.5	8.0	0.1	2.7
Bhotia	7.6	26.1	21.2	14.1	17.4	0.3	13.3
Jaunsari	3.0	39.4	24.4	14.7	14.2	0.0	4.2
Raji	8.2	26.6	21.3	16.0	20.1	0.0	7.8

Statement - 4 : Percentage of school going children in the age group 5-14 yrs.

Age group	All STs	Tharu	Buksa	Bhotia	Jaunsari	Raji
5-14 yrs.	40.3	40.8	26.8	44.0	58.1	25.1

13. Out of total 31,994 ST children in the age group 5-14 years, 12,889 children have been attending school, constituting 40.3 percent only. As many as 19,105 children in the corresponding age group have not been going to school. Jaunsari have more than half of the total children in the above mentioned age group are school going; this proportion is below 50 percent among Tharu and Buksa.

Work Participation Rate (WPR)

14. The Work Participation Rate (WPR) of the ST population is 40.3 percent which is lower than that of all STs at the national level (49.1 percent). There has been a slight increase of 2.4 percent in the over all WPR of STs during 1991-2001. Male arc female WPR (49.9 percent & 30.1 percent respectively) are lower than those of the national average. Among the total workers, 66.6 percent are main workers and this proportion is marginally lower than the national average (68.9 percent).

15. At thc individual level, Buksa, Jaunsari and Bhotia have overall WPR lower than the State average. Except Raji and Tharu, other three tribes have female WPR lower than that of the State.

Category of Workers

16. 'Cultivators' constitute the highest proportion (44.6 percent) among the total tribal workers, which is equal to that of all STs at the national level (44.7 percent). 'Agricultural Labourers' account for 31.4 percent, which is lower than the national average of 36.9 percent recorded by all STs in this category. 'Other Workers' form 21.6 percent which is higher than the national average of 16.3 percent. Workers engaged in 'Household Industry' (HHI) constitute 2.4 percent which is same as that of the national level (2.1 percent).

17. At the individual level, Tharu have more than fifty percent workers are 'Cultivators'. Buksa have the highest proportion

of 'Agricultural Labourers' (42.3 percent) whereas more than 70 percent of Bhotia workers are 'Other Workers'. Among all tribes, Raji have the highest proportion of 'HHI' workers followed by Bhotia and Buska.

Statement- 5 : Percentage distribution of workers in four Economic Categories

Economic category	All STs	Tharu	Buksa	Bhotia	Jaunsari	Raji
Cultivators	44.6	54.5	18.3	12.2	15.0	8.6
Agricultural Labourers	31.4	32.0	42.3	10.1	31.8	18.1
HHI Workers	2.4	1.3	5.0	5.8	1.8	12.1
Other Workers	21.6	12.3	34.4	72.0	51.4	61.1

Marital Status

18. The data on marital status show that more than half of the ST population is 'never married' (53.6 percent) whereas 'married' persons constitute 43.6 percent. 'Widowed' persons form 2.7 percent while a negligible 0.1 percent is 'divorced and separated' .

19. The proportion of married girls below 18 years (2.9 percent) is slightly higher than that of all STs at the national (2.1 percent) whereas married boys below 21 years constitute 5.4 percent which is considerably higher than the national average of 2.8 percent. Among all tribes, Jaunsari and Bhotia have registered the proportion of married girls below the stipulated age higher than that of the State. On the other hand, Raji and Tharu have shown the proportion of married boys below legal age higher than the State average.

20. The mean number of children ever born per ever married ST woman (45 - 49 yrs.) is 5, which is higher than the all STs at national level (4)..

Religion

21. Hinduism is the predominant religion of the tribes of the State (80.6 percent). The STs professing Hinduism account for 98.5 percent. Muslim tribes constitute 0.9 percent. Tribes

following Christianity (0.3 percent), Sikhism and Buddhism (each 0.1 percent) together constitute half percent only.

UTTRAKHAND

Data Highlights

The total population of Uttarakhand in 2001 Census has been 8,489,349. Of these, 256,129 persons are Scheduled Tribes (STs) which constitutes 3 percent of the total population of the state. The state has registered 20.9 percent decadal growth of ST population in 1991-2001. There are total of five (5) notified STs in the state, and all of them have been enumerated in 2001 Census.

Population: Size & Distribution

2. Tharu is the largest of the five STs of Uttarakhand. They account for 33.4 percent ST population of the state, followed by Jaunsari (32.5 percent), Buksa (18.3 percent), and Bhotia (14.2 percent). Raji is small in number (Statement-I).

Statement -1: Population and Proportion of STs, 2001 Census

SL. No.	Name of the Scheduled Tribe	Total population	Proportion to the total ST population
1.	All Scheduled Tribes	256,129	100
6	Tharu	85,665	33.4
4	Jaunsari	83,262	32.5
3	Buksa	46,771	18.3
2	Bhotia	36,438	14.2
5	Raji	517	0.2

3. The STs in Uttarakhand are predominantly living in rural areas with 93.8 percent rural and only 6.2 percent urban. Bhotia have recorded a high of 25.8 percent urban population among them. Raji with 8.9 percent urban dwellers among them come next. On the other hand Buksa and Tharu are predominantly living in rural areas with only 0.8 percent and 1.9 percent urban population respectively.

4. A majority of the ST population is concentrated in four districts, namely, Udham Singh Nagar (43 percent), Dehradun (38.8 percent), Pithoragarh (7.5 percent), and Chamoli (4.1 percent).

Sex Ratio

5. The overall sex ratio among the STs is 950, which is below the aggregated national figure for STs (978). Bhotia (1049) have registered more females in their population. On the other hand very low sex ratio of 833 has been recorded among Raji.
6. The child sex ratio (0-6 age group) of 955 among the STs is also low as compared to the national average (973) for STs The Raji also have registered low child sex ratio (757).

Literacy & Educational Level

7. Among STs, 63.2 percent of the population has been recorded as literate, which is well above the national average (47.1 percent). The male and female literacy rate of 76.4 percent and 49.4 percent respectively suggest for wider gender gap in literacy. Bhotia with 79.9 percent literacy rate are well ahead of other STs The female literacy rate (69.1 percent) among Bhotia is also the highest among the five STs of the state. Raji have recorded the lowest literacy rate of just 35.8 per cent, statement -2

Statement -2 Literacy Rate

SL. No	Name of the Scheduled Tribe	Literate Rate (7+ years and above)		
		Total	Male	Female
1.	All Scheduled Tribes	63.2	76.4	49.4
2	Bhotia	79.9	91.5	69.1
3	Buksa	49.9	66.0	32.4
4	Jannsari	58.9	71.7	44.8
5	Raji	35.8	47.2	22.5
6	Tharu	67.0	80.4	53.1

8. As per 2001 Census, 76.6 percent of the ST population of age group 5-14 years has been attending educational institutions. Bhotia have recorded the highest percentage (86.4 percent) of school attending population, closely followed by Tharu (82.3 percent). On the other hand Raji have recorded the lowest of 50 percent. The Jannsari (75.1 percent) and Buksa (63.7 percent), the remaining two STs, also have recorded below the state average.
9. Merely 4.3 percent of total literates among STs are having educational level graduate and above. Bhotia with 11.6 percent

of their literate population as graduate or having higher level of education are on the top among STs. On the other hand Buksa have recorded a low of just 0.7 percent.

Work Participation Rate (WPR)

10. In 2001 Census, 41.1 percent of the STs have been recorded as workers, which is below the aggregated national level for STs (49.1 percent). Of the total workers 73.1 percent have been recorded as main workers and 26.9 percent as marginal workers. The female WPR of 31.9 percent is just lower than male (49.9 percent), Statement -3

Statement -3: Distribution of Total, Main & Marginal Workers among STs

T/M/F	Percentage of Workers		
	Total Workers	Main Workers	Marginal Workers
Total	105,300 (41.1)	76,961 (73.1)	28,339 (26.9)
Male	65,502 (49.9)	55,597 (84.9)	9,905 (15.1)
Female	39,798 (31.9)	21,364 (53.7)	18,434 (46.3)

11. Bhotia have recorded the highest WPR of 41.1 percent, while it is lowest among Buksa (34.9 percent).

Category of Workers

12. Industrial category wise of the total ST main workers, a high of 67.9 percent has been recorded as cultivators, 7.7 percent as agricultural laborers, 5.2 percent in the category of household industry, and the remaining 19.2 percent as 'other workers'.

13. Jannsari and Tharu are predominantly cultivators. Of their total main workers. 80.6 percent among Jannsari and 78.5 percent among Tharu have been recorded as cultivators. Buksa have recorded 54.1 percent of their main workers as cultivators. However, a high of 28.3 percent as agricultural labourers among recorded among Buksa speaks for their greater dependency on primary agricultural sector.

Marital Status

14. As regard marital status, 53.8 percent of the ST population is never married, 41.9 percent currently married, 4.1 percent widowed, and 0.2 percent divorced /separated.

15. The child marriage is not common among the STs of Uttarakhand. Merely 1.9 percent of total female population among STs of below 18 years - the minimum legal age for marriage - has been recorded as ever married. Raji have recorded the highest percentage of marriage below the stipulated age (3.9 percent), while the same is the lowest among Buksa (0.8 percent).
16. The ever married males below 21 years - the minimum legal age for marriage - constitute 2.7 percent of the total population. Tharu have recorded the highest 3.4 percent of their population of this stipulated age as ever married, closely followed by Jannsari (3.1 percent).

Religion

17. The STs in Uttarakhand are predominantly Hindus constituting 99.1 percent of the population. Besides, a total of 1,344 persons have been returned as Buddhists.

BIHAR – JHARKHAND

The undivided Bihar occupied a very important place in 'Tribal India'. In Chotanagpur plateau it contains a tribal belt covering some of the largest tribes of the country such as the Oraon, Munda, Ho, Santhals, etc. It also happens to be the nerve centre of the Jharkhand movement.

The tribal population of undivided Bihar was around 8.7 million (1991 census) which comes about 10.06% of the total population of the state. Although, Bihar is placed at twelth position in terms of ranking of states by scheduled tribes percentage but in terms of absolute number it is behind only Madhya Pradesh and Orissa. Of the total scheduled tribe population of the country the tribals living in Bihar constitute about one fifth segment. Most of these tribes inhabit Ranchi, Hazaribagh, Dhanbad, Singbhum, Palamu and Santhal Pargana. Beside these, considerable tribal population is found also in Sahasram, Bhabhua, Bhagalpur, Mungher, Purnia and Champaran. Among the main and relatively known tribes come Munda, Oraon, Ho, Santhal, Kharia, Pahariya and Birhor.

Like the whole of the Tribal India, Bihar is not a monolith. It is the home of heterogenous types of tribes with different linguistic and racial affiliations, living at different levels of economic development.

The Birhor and Hill Kharia are still food gatherer-hunters while the tribes like Asur, Korwa and Mal Pahariya practice shifting cultivation. The large tribes like Munda, Oraon, Ho, Santhal, etc. have transformed themselves into peasant societies. Beside belief in animism, the process of Hinduisation and spread of Christianity present important dimensions of their religious affiliation. Demographically speaking the large tribes show normal, consistent growth of population, among the relatively small tribes the population either stagnates or they are afflicted by depopulation.

List of Scheduled Tribes

Asur, Baiga, Banjara, Bathudi, Bedia, Bhumij, Binjhia, Birhor, Birjia, Chero, Chukbaraika, Gond, Gorait, Ho, Karmali, Kharia, Kharwar, Khond, Kisan, Kora, Korwa, Loharor Lohar, Mahli, Mai Pahariya, Munda, Oraon, Parhaiya, Santhal, Saoria Paharia, Sawar and 'other tribes' (unclassified).

Among the above mentioned tribes the Asur, Birhor, Birjia, Savar, Hill Kharia, Korwa, Mai Pahariya, Pahariya and Sauria Paharia are the tribes living at an extremely under-developed stage and they have been classified as 'Identified Primitive Tribal Groups' for special treatment.

Following are the brief ethnographic profiles of two of the scheduled tribes.

SANTHAL

Santhals are a tribe of settled agriculturists. They are one of the largest tribes of India inhabiting a large tract of land spread over Bihar, Orissa and West Bengal with a total population of around four million people. Although, they are widely distributed in Bihar but their highest concentration is found in Santhal Pargana located in the eastern extremity of Chotanagpur Plateau in Bihar and this region is regarded as their traditional habitat. The whole region is rich in flora and fauna with a thick cover of foliage. Beside Santhal Parganas they also inhabit Bhagalpur, Mungher, Hazaribagh, Ranchi, Singbhum, Dhanbad and Palamu.

The Santhals are believed to come from proto-australoid racial stock. Their skin colour varies between dark to dark brown; they have coarse, black, straight and occasionally curly hair. They have broad head and are usually medium to short statured. They, are found to be highly laborious and enterprising as compared to their neighbouring tribes. They have their own language known as Santhali which belongs to the Munda language family. The Mundari language belongs to the Austro-Asiatic subfamily of languages. Though, Santhali has drawn from several languages but the influence of Bengali is most pronounced. The Santhals live in well settled villages. A Santhals village is usually small in size and it consists often to fifty households. Every village is divided into several '**tolas**' which are headed by a '**mukhiya**'. Most of the houses are very close or adjacent to each other with each of the doors opening in front of the street. The streets of these villages are usually so broad that a couple of bullockcarts may pass through them simultaneously. Most of their houses are made of clay with their ceilings made of wooden slabs and bamboos. Now the landscape may be seen dotted with a number of 'pucca' or brick cement housed. They maintain their houses in extremely neat and clean condition.

Social Organization

The Santhals are divided into twelve patrilineal exogamous clans which are Hansda, Murmu, Kisku, Hemborm, Mandi, Soren, Tudu, Baske, Besra, Pauria, Chore and Bedea. All these clans are considered equals in terms of social status except Besra and Chero which are regarded relatively inferior. Mostly, they maintain nuclear or primary family consisting of husband, wife and their unmarried children. Some times some more kins are added to it such as married sons, wives and their children or married brothers and their wives and children make it some sort of extended type of family. The authority in the family lies with the senior most male member. In their scheme of division of labour the adult males perform the outdoor jobs while the females do household chores but their contribution to family economy is multifarious The children also contribute to the family economy.

The Santhals are usually monogamous. They go for polygyny in extreme conditions like the barrenness of wife or for any other important reason. Sometimes they are seen practicing sororate but cousin marriage is not allowed. The Santhals practice about a dozen ways of acquiring mates. Remarriage of widow and divorced women is not unusual but such marriages are performed without much fanfare and least ceremonial observances. Marriage may be dissolved and both the parties enjoy equal right in the dissolution of marriage. Adultery and practice of witchcraft usually culminate in divorce.

The political organization of the Santhals rests over the village council or panchayat headed by a hereditary chieftain. If the council fails to resolve the problems or crisis the entire village sits over a meeting to sort out the matter. According to Santhal tradition those who clear the forest for village sites and cultivation had the right to the land but the situation has undergone radical changes after the enactment of the second National Forest Policy after independence. All property, movable as well as immovable, is divided equally among the sons on the death of the father. In the absence of the sons, the property goes to the brothers in equal proportions. Women have no right of inheritance.

The pantheon of the Santhals consists of numerous gods, deities and spirits. Rituals and ceremonies are abundant. Their presiding deity is known as Thakur, the creator of the universe. They are staunch believers in magic, sorcery and witchcraft. Sorcery occupies an important place in their cultural life and they believe in curing many diseases through sorcery. Females are regarded experts in this craft. The Santhal religion has undergone considerable changes as a result of persistent cultural contacts with the neighbouring peasanty. The Santhals cremate their dead.

Economy and Eco-system

Santhals are primarily agriculturists who have gradually, over a period of time, transformed themselves into peasanty. They raise sorghum, maize, millet, pulses, cotton and rice depending upon different kinds of land in different seasons of the year. They employ bullocks and buffalo for ploughing. Although, they have developed an artificial system of irrigation through embankments constructed across ravines, hollows, or other natural depressions, they still mainly depend on rainfall. Female workforce is a crucial input in their agricultural operations. As supplementary food or at the time of scarcity certain forest plants—flowers, fruits and young shoots are eaten raw or cooked. Among such plants come sal, mahua, bamboo, etc.

They are also fond of hunting and fishing. They also practice domestication of chickens, pig, goat, cow, buffalo, sheep, etc. which beside their flesh are also considered useful for their bye products, besides rice beer, known as **handia**, they also consume 'hard' liquor distilled from mahua flowers. They also smoke **bidi** made on the locally grown **saal** leaf. BECAUSE of rise of population and land alienation on large scale, Santhals are no more a happy lot. Their existence (except that of 'elite') is characterised by chronic indebtedness, land alienation, migration and harassment by landlords, contractors and moneylenders. A number of Santhals have also taken to work in coal mines. A majority of the migrant Santhals have become unskilled labour.

BIRHOR

Birhors are considered to be one of the most economically backward tribes of largely food gatherers-hunters. They have been included in the special category of primitive tribal groups.' They inhabit the fringes of the south-eastern region of Chotanagpur plateau and Palamu. The whole region is replete with small hills rich in vegetation and forest cover. The Birhors have become a depopulating tribe whose population shows a consistent decline. The result of this phenomenon is that they have been reduced to about five thousand souls divided into around seven hundred households.

The Birhors are put under the category of proto-australoids with some marked negroid features like dark complexion, slightly curly hair, broad nose and medium to short stature. They speak a language from Austaro-Asiatic family but due to their cultural contacts with their neighbouring tribes such as the Santhals, Mundas and Hos they also show familiarity with their languages.

Social Organization

Birhors are mainly divided into two groups viz: **Uthalo** and **Janghi**. The **Uthalo** lead mainly nomadic existence while the **Janghi** have almost adopted a sedentry life. The former keep on changing their abode almost every month except during the rainy season. The popular term for the habitation is **tanda** and each **tanda** consist of about ten huts. Some of them also keep goats and some other cattle. Each **tanda** is headed by a chief known as **Naya** who holds religious and temporal authority. The social distance between these two categories of Birhors is fast widening and they have virtually stopped sharing meals or establishing matrimonial alliances.

The Birhors maintain nuclear family. Parents and the minor children live together in a hut while those above 10-12 years sleep in the dormitory know as **Gatiora**. Boys and girls sleep in separate youth dormitories. Though they practice monogamy but there is no bar on polygyny. They do not practice child marriage. The disputes are resolved by the local panchayat which is usually a council of elders of a temporary nature and may be constituted and reconstituted frequently with every case/dispute.

The Birhors have a large pantheon and **Bora Bonga** is the presiding deity. Virtually every forest, orchard and fountain is the abode of their one deity or the other. Propitiation of various deities through ritual observances is an integral part of their religion.

Economy and Eco-System

Their economic activities rotate around gathering-hunting. They go to jungle in groups and do collection of edible roots-fruits and hunting. The females usually stay back and perform household chores beside looking after the children. They are very fond of eating mahua flowers; they also consume monkey's flesh. Among the fruits they fondly consume mango's, tamarind etc. The Birhors also keep domesticated animals such as chickens and goats; some times they also keep pigs. Dog is their favourite animal and is their best friend and companion who helps them in their hunting expeditions beside performing the role of 'watchman'. They are expert string weavers and makers of wooden items which they dispose off in the nearby markets. Catching monkeys is also one of their chief means of livelihood.

Since the Birhors live by forest economy and forests provide their resource base they have been hit hard by the growing depletion of forests. The subsequent National Forest Policies have been curtailing the rights of the forest dwellers. Their distorted and sometime inhuman interpretation by the forest officials have made the life of the forest dwelling tribes miserable. The Birhors too are no exception to this trend. They seem to have lost the battle.

BIHAR

Data Highlights

The Scheduled Tribe (ST) population in the State of Bihar is 758,351 as per 2001 census, constituting 0.9 percent of the total population (82,998,509) of the State. The decennial growth of ST population has been 32.4 percent which is 3.8 percent higher than the State's total population. The State has a total of twenty nine (29) Scheduled Tribes and all of them have been enumerated at 2001 census.

2. The Scheduled Tribes are overwhelmingly rural as 94.6 percent of them reside in villages. District wise distribution of ST population shows that Katihar district has the highest proportion of STs (5.9 percent) followed by Jamui (4.8 percent), Banka (4.7 percent) and Purnia (4.4 percent). Sheohar district has the lowest proportion of the STs (0.01 percent), preceded by Darbhanga and Khagaria (0.03 percent each).

Population - Size & Distribution

3. Out of twenty nine (29) STs, Santal is the most populous tribe, having a number of 367,612, constituting 48.5 percent of the total ST population of the State. Oraon and Kharwar are the second and third largest tribes, having a number of 120,362 and 100,735 respectively. Two other major tribes in the descending order are Gond and Munda. Along with Santal, Oraon and Kharwar, the five STs constitute 86.8 percent of the total tribal population. Eight tribes, Bedia, Ho, Mahali, ... upto Lohara having population in the range of 2,572 to 13,993 account for another 8.1 percent and the remaining sixteen tribes, along with the generic tribes constitute the residual 5.1 percent of the total tribal population of the State. Twelve tribes have below 1000 population. Of them, eight tribes are less than 500 in number.

4. At district level, more than three fourth tribal population of Banka, Jamui, Kishanganj, Araria and Madhepura are Santal, closely followed by Saharsa (72 percent) and Purnia (65 percent) districts. Though, Oraon are primarily concentrated in Purnia and Katihar districts, they have their highest proportion (70 percent) to total ST population in Supaul district. While Kharwar have their maximum concentration in Bhagalpur district, Gond in Siwan district followed by Bhojpur and Kaimur (Bhabhua) districts. Munda have their highest concentration in Katihar districts but they constitute only 4.3 percent total tribal population of the district.

Sex Ratio

6. The over all sex ratio of the ST population in Bihar is 929 females per 1000 males which is considerably lower than the national average of 978 for the total ST population.

7. At the individual level, all the five major tribes have registered the sex ratio lower than the national average. While Santal, Oraon and Gond have sex ratio above 900, Kharwar and Munda have the sex ratio below 900 and 800 respectively.

8. The sex ratio among STs in the age group 0-6 years (975) is marginally higher than that of the STs at the national level (973). Among the major tribes, Kharwar, Oraon and Santal have the child sex ratio higher than the national average whereas Munda and Gond have child sex ratio lower than the national average.

Statement - 1 : Sex Ratio

Age groups	All STs (India)	All STs (Bihar)	Santal	Oraon	Gond	Kharwar	Munda
All ages	978	929	950	926	922	895	782
0 – 6	973	975	976	980	933	989	956

Literacy & Educational Level

9. The literacy rate among the STs has increased from 18.9 percent registered at 1991 census to 28.2 percent at 2001 census. Despite this increase, the literacy rate among the tribal population is lower, if compared with that of all STs at the national level (47.1 percent). Male and female literacy rates among the tribal (39.8 percent and 15.5 percent) are also low in comparison to those at the national level (59.2 percent & 34.8 percent).

10. Among the numerically larger tribes, Gond and Kharwar have returned over all literacy rate (45.2 percent) which is close to the national average. Oraon, Munda and Santal have the over all literacy rates almost half of the national average for all STs.

Statement - 2 : Literacy Rate

Literacy rate	All STs state	Gond	Kharwar	Oraon	Munda	Santal
Persons	28.2	45.2	42.7	25.1	22.4	23.3
Females	15.5	28.3	26.9	13.4	16.2	11.4

11. Among ST literates, 37 percent are either without any educational level or have attained education below primary

level. The proportion of literates who have attained education up to primary and middle levels are 28.2 percent & 14.4 percent respectively. Persons educated up to matric/secondary/ higher secondary constitute 16.3 percent. This implies that every 6th tribal literate is a matriculate. Graduates and above are 3.8 percent.

12. Among the numerically larger groups, Santal have the lowest proportion of matriculates preceded by Oraon and Gond whereas Kharwar have the highest proportion of matriculates followed by Munda.

13. As discerned from the data, the proportion of tribal literates declines sharply in higher level of education as the percentage of students after matriculation drops down to almost one third in higher secondary level.

14. Out of the total 2.2 lakh tribal children in the age group 5 - 14 years, only 60,153 attend school, constituting 27.4 percent. In other words, 72.6 percent (1.6 lakh) children in the corresponding age group do not go to school. Among the major STs, Kharwar and Gond have 41 - 46 percent school going children whereas Munda, Santal and Oraon have less than 25 percent children attending school.

Statement - 4 : Percentage of school going children in the age group 5 -14 years

Age group	All STs	Santal	Oraon	Kharwar	Gond	Munda
5-14 yrs.	27.4	22.5	24	41.4	46.2	21.4

Work Participation Rate (WPR)

15. The Work Participation Rate (WPR) of the ST population is 45.2 percent which is lower than that of all STs at the national level (49.1 percent). There has been a slight decline in male WPR from 53.6 to 52.9 percent whereas female WPR (36.9 percent) has increased by 5.9 percent during 1991-2001. Among the total workers, 68.7 percent are main workers and

Statement - 3: Educational levels among the major Scheduled Tribes

Names of STs	Literate without educational level	Below Primary	Educational levels attained				
			Primary	Middle	Matric/Secondary Higher secondary/ Intermedlate etc.	Technical & Non-technical diploma etc.	Graduate & above
All STs	5,8	31.3	28,2	14.4	16.3	0.2	3.8
Gond	4,6	29.8	26,7	16.4	17,7	0.2	4.5
Kharwar	3,6	27.7	26,9	15,3	20,9	0.6	4.9
Munda	7,5	29.0	21.6	12,7	19.2	0.4	9.5
Oraon	5.5	34.2	27.6	12.9	15.1	0.2	4.5
Santal	6.3	32.8	30.1	14.4	14.2	0.0	2.1

this proportion is almost equal to that of all STs at the national level (68.9 percent).

16. Among the major tribal groups, Munda have over all WPR (52.8 percent) higher than the national average whereas Santal (48.5 percent) and Oraon (46.9 percent) have recorded WPR close to the national average.

Category of Workers

17. 'Agricultural Labourers' constitute the highest proportion (62.5 percent) among the total tribal workers, which is considerably higher than that of the national average (36.9 percent). 'Cultivators' account for 21.3 percent, which is less than half of that recorded for all STs at the national level (44.7 percent). 'Agricultural Labourers' and 'Cultivators' together constitute 83.8 percent of the total workers. 'Other Workers' form 12.2 percent which is comparable with the national average of 16.3 percent in respect of all STs whereas workers engaged in Household Industry (HHI) constitute 4 percent which is twice that of the national average (2.1 percent).

18. Among the major tribes, Santal and Oraon have more than 60 percent workers are 'Agricultural Labourers' followed by Munda, Gond and Kharwar. Kharwar and Santal have every 4th worker, a 'Cultivator' and Munda have every 3rd worker belong to the category of 'Other Workers'.

Statement- 5 : Percentage Distribution of Workers in four Economic Categories

Economic category	All STs	Santal	Oraon	Kharwar	Gond	Munda
Cultivators	21.3	25.6	13.8	27.9	17.1	7.1
Agricultural Labourers	62.5	64.1	69.1	53.3	54.4	57.1
HHI Workers	4.0	4.1	1.4	2.2	3.6	0.9
Other Workers	12.2	6.3	15.6	16.6	25.0	34.9

Marital Status

19. The data on marital status show that 'never married' persons (52.2 percent) exceed the 'married' persons (43.6 percent) in total ST population. 'Widowed' persons form 3.9 percent while a negligible 0.2 percent has been in the category of 'divorced and separated'.

20. The proportion of married girls below 18 years (2.5 percent) and married boys below 21 years (3 percent) are slightly higher if compared with those at the national level (2.1 percent & 2.8 percent).

21. The mean number of children ever born per ever married ST woman (age-group 45 - 49 yrs.) is 3 which is less than that of all STs at the nationallevel(4).

Religion

22. Hinduism is the predominant religion of the tribes of the State as 89.7 percent STs are Hindus. The tribes professing 'Other Religions and Persuations' account for 6.3 percent. Christian tribes are 3.4 percent and less than half percent (0.4 percent) are Muslims.

JHARKHAND

Data Highlights

The Scheduled Tribe (ST) population of Jharkhand State is as per 2001 census 7,087,068 constituting 26.3 percent of the total population (26,945,829) of the State. Among all Sates and UTs, Jharkhand holds 6th and 10th ranks terms of the ST population and the percentage share of the ST population to the total population of the State respectively. The growth of the ST population has been 17.3 percent which is lower by 6 percent if compared with the growth of the State's total population (23.3 percent) during 1991-2001. The state has a total of thirty (30) Scheduled Tribes and all of them have been enumerated at 2001 census

2. The Scheduled Tribes are primarily rural as 91.7 percent of them reside in villages. District wise distribution of ST population shows that Gumla district has the highest proportion

of STs (68.4 percent). The STs constitute more than half of the total population in Lohardaga and Pashchimi Singhbhum districts whereas Ranchi and Pakaur districts have 41.8 - 44.6 percent tribal population. Kodarma district (0.8 percent) preceded by Chatra (3.8 percent) has the lowest proportion of the STs Population.

Population- Size & Distribution

3. Out of thirty (30) Scheduled Tribes notified for the State, Santhal is the most populous tribe having a population of 2,410,509, constituting 34 percent of the total ST population of the State. Oraon, Munda and Ho, the 2nd, 3rd and 4th largest tribes constitute 19.6, 14.8 and 10.5 percent respectively of the total ST population of the State. Four other major tribes, Kharia, Bhumij, Lohra and Kharwar having population ranging from 164,022 -192,024 along with Santhal, Oraon, Munda and Ho, constitute 89.1 percent of the total tribal population. The tribes namely, Chero, Bedia, Mal Pahariya and Mahli in the population range from 75,540 to 121,174 account for another 5.6 percent; the remaining 18 tribes, along with the generic tribes constitute the balance 5.3 percent of the total ST population.

4. District wise distribution of the individual ST shows that Santhal have the highest population in Dumka district followed by Purbi Singhbhum, Pakaur and Sahibganj districts but they constitute the highest proportion of the total ST population in Giridih (90.8 percent), followed by Dumka (89.7 percent) and Pakaur (85 percent) districts. Oraon have returned the highest population in Ranchi district followed by Gumla. They have the highest percentage share in the total tribal population (81 percent) in Lohardaga district. Other six major tribes, namely Munda, Ho, Kharwar, Lohra, Bhumij and Kharia are concentrated in Ranchi, Pashchimi Singhbhum, Palamu, Ranchi, Purbi Singhbhum and Gumla districts respectively.

Sex Ratio

5. The over all sex ratio of the ST population in Jharkhand is 987 females per 1000 males which is higher than the national average (978) for the total ST population.

6. Among the major tribes, Kharia and Ho have females who outnumber the males in their total population. While Munda,

Oraon, Santhal, Bhumij have their overall sex ratio above national average, Lohra and Kharwar have their over all sex ratio below the national average.

7. The sex ratio among tribes in the age group 0-6 years (979) is marginally higher than that of all STs at the national level (973). At the individual level, except Oraon, other seven major tribes have registered the child sex ratio higher than the national average. (Statement 1 shown on the next page)

Literacy & Educational Level

8. The overall literacy rate among the STs has increased from 27.5 percent at 1991 census to 40.7 percent at 2001 census. Despite this improvement, the literacy rate among the tribes is much below in comparison to that of all STs at the national level (47.1 percent). Like the over all literacy rate among the STs, male and female literacy rates (54 percent and 27.2 percent) are also considerably lower than those at the national level (59.2 percent & 34.8 percent).

9. Among the numerically larger tribes, Oraon and Kharia have more than half of the population in the age of seven (7) years and above are literates while Munda have the literacy rate almost equal to that of all STs at the national level. Remaining five larger tribal groups have shown the over all literacy rates lower than that of the national average. (Statement 2 shown on page 184).

10. Among the total tribal literates, 33.6 percent are either without any educational level or have attained education below primary level. The proportions of literates who have attained education up to primary level and middle level are 28.6 percent & 17.7 percent respectively. Persons educated up to matric/secondary/ higher secondary constitute 16.5 percent. This implies that every 6th tribal literate is a matriculate. Graduates and above are 3.5 percent while non-technical & technical diploma holders constitute a negligible 0.1 percent only.

11. While Kharia, Oraon and Ho have the highest proportion of matriculates i.e. every 5th literates of these tribes are matriculates closely followed by Munda who have every 6th literate a matriculate. Kharwar have the lowest percentage of matriculates, preceded by Bhumij, Lohra and Santhal.

Statement - 1: Sex Ratio

Age groups	All STs (India)	All STs (Jharkhand)	Kharia	Ho	Munda	*Draon*	Santhal	Bhumij	Lohra	Kharwar
All ages	978	987	1026	1010	994	992	985	983	970	944
0-6	973	979	977	986	983	966	980	984	982	991

Statement - 2 : Literacy Rate

Literacy rate	All STs (state)	*Draon*	Kharia	Munda	Bhumij	Ho	Lohra	Santhal	Kharwar
Persons	40.7	52.5	51.0	47.9	41.5	39.2	38.9	33.4	29.6
Females	27.2	40.8	42.2	34.9	24.0	23.9	25.0	19.5	13.9

Statement - 4: Percentage of school going children in the age group 5-14 yrs.

Age group	All STs	Oraon	Kharia	Munda	Bhumij	Lohra	Ho	Santhal	Kharwar
5–14 yrs.	43.1	55.0	53.3	50.1	46.6	44.1	37.6	36.3	28.6

While Oraon and Kharia have the highest percentage of graduates, Bhumij have the lowest proportion of degree holders, preceded by Kharwar, Lohra and Santhal. (Statement 3 shown on page 184).

12. The data show that the proportion of tribal literates decline sharply in higher level of education as the percentage of students after matriculation drops down to almost one third in higher secondary level.

13. Out of the total 19.8 lakh tribal children in the age group 5 -14 years, only 8.5 lakh children have been attending school constituting 43.1 percent. Alarmingly, as many as 11.3 lakh (56.9 percent) children in the corresponding age group have not been going to school. The Statement below shows that among the major STs, Oraon, Kharia and Munda have more than 50 percent school going children whereas Santhal, Ho, Lohra have 36 - 47 percent children attending school. (Statement 4 shown on page 186).

Work Participation Rate (WPR)

14. The Work Participation Rate (WPR) of the ST population is 46.3 percent which is lower than that of all STs at the national level (49.1 percent). While there has been a slight decline in male WPR from 53.4 to 51.9 percent, female WPR has increased from 38.3 percent up to 40.6 percent during 1991-2001. Among the total workers, 59.4 percent are main workers and this proportion is quite below the national average for all STs (68.9 percent).

15. Among the major tribal groups, only Kharia have over all WPR (51.6 percent) higher than the national average whereas other seven major tribal groups have recorded WPR lower than the national average.

Category of Workers

16. 'Cultivators' constitute more than half of the total workers and this figure is significantly higher than the national average of 44.7 percent recorded by all STs in this category. 'Agricultural Labourers' account for 31 percent which is less than that recorded for all STs at the national level (36.9 percent). 'Other Workers' form 13.5 percent which is comparable with the national average of 16.3 percent whereas

Statement - 3: Levels of Education among the major Scheduled Tribes

Names of STs	Literate without educational level	Below Primary	Educational levels attained				
			Primary	Middle	Matricl Secondary Higher Secondary/Intermediate etc.	Technical & Non-technical diploma etc.	Graduate & above
All Scheduled Tribes	3.0	30.6	28.6	17.7	16.5	0.1	3.5
Santhal	3.5	34.3	30.0	17.0	13.2	0.1	2.0
Oraan	2.4	26.9	25.3	18.5	20.8	0.2	5.9
Munda	2.8	27.9	29.6	18.9	17.1	0.1	3.7
Ha	2.4	26.4	28.4	19.9	19.7	0.1	3.1
Kharwar	5.5	38.2	32.3	11.3	10.8	0.1	1.8
Lahra	3.5	35.5	30.5	16.1	12.5	0.1	1.9
Bhumij	2.9	36.1	32.8	15.7	11.1	0.0	1.4
Kharia	2.0	26.0	26.5	18.3	21.4	0.1	5.6

workers engaged in Household Industry (HHI) constitute 3 percent which is marginally higher than that of the national average (2.1 percent).

17. Among the major tribes, Oraon, Munda and Kharia have 62-71 percent workers engaged as 'Cultivators' followed by Kharwar and Santhal. Bhumij and Lohra have recorded the highest proportion of 'Agricultural Labourers' in their total working population. Lohra have also registered the higher percentage of 'Other Workers' as well as 'HHI' workers in comparison to other major tribes. (Statement 5 shown on page 188).

Marital Status

18. The data on marital status show that 'never married' persons with a proportion of 53.2 percent exceed the 'married' persons (41.1 percent) in total ST population. 'Widowed' persons form 5.3 percent while a negligible 0.4 percent is of 'divorced and separated' persons.

19. Marriages of girls and boys below the legal age for each, are not in common practice among the tribal of Jharkhand. Married girls below 18 years and married boys below 21 years constitute 2.1 percent and 2.5 percent respectively. These proportions are almost same as those recorded for the total STs at the national level (2.1 percent & 2.8 percent respectively). Among the larger groups, Kharwar and Santhal have registered higher proportions of married girls and boys below the legal age if compared to those of all STs at the national level.

20. The mean number of children ever born per ever married ST woman (age-group 45 - 49 years) is 4 which is same as that of all STs at the national level (4).

Religion

21. Although, Hinduism is the predominant religion of the State (68.6 percent), the Hindu tribes constitute 39.8 percent only. As many as 45.1 percent of the tribal population follow 'other religions and persuations'. Christian tribes are 14.5 percent and less than half percent (0.4 percent) are Muslims. Among the major tribes, Santhal have more than half of the total population (56.6 percent) professes Hinduism. Oraon and

Statement- 5 : Percentage Distribution of Workers in four Economic Categories

Ecnomic category	All STs	Santhal	Oraon	Munda	Ho	Kharwar	Lohra	Bhumij	Kharia
Cultivators	52.6	48.6	62.1	64.6	49.4	52.5	28.3	35.5	70.5
Agricultural Labourers	31.0	38.4	21.0	21.2	34.1	39.7	33.5	47.3	20.5
HHI Workers	3.0	1.4	1.1	1.3	3.0	1.0	14.7	1.7	1.1
Other Workers	13.5	11.6	15.8	12.8	13.4	6.9	23.5	15.4	7.9

Munda have more than 50 percent of population follow 'other religions and persuasions' followed by Christianity. Ho tribe has the highest proportion (91 percent) of persons professing 'other religions and persuations'.

ANDHRA PRADESH – TELANGANA

Andhra Pradesh has got a fairly large tribal population. Though, in terms of ranking of states by scheduled tribes concentration, it is placed at 13th position, it has the largest concentration of tribal population in south India. This tribal population is of the size of 4.75 millions which comes about 7% of the total population of Andhra Pradesh. The implication of this seemingly ordinary fact is quite important, it means that about seven out of every hundred persons in Andhra Pradesh come from a scheduled tribe.

The demographic scenario of Andhra tribes is also interesting. On the one hand there are such 'major' tribes like Yenadi and Koya which exceed two lakh souls alongwith other tribes like Yerukala, Kondh, Konda Reddi and Gond which exceed a lakh each and on the other hand there are tribes like Rona, Kulia, Kattunayakan and Bhil who are found in hundreds, the Rona being the smallest consisting of just 12 souls.

The tribal world of Andhra Pradesh is not a monolith even in term of their economic development. It consists of tribes living at different levels of technology and pursuing different types of economies. While the tribes like Chenchu and Yenadi are pursuing gathering-hunting economy, Goudu and Sugali are pastoralists; Kammara, Kulia, Thoti, Pradhan and Yerukala are artisan tribes; Konda Dora, Konda Reddi, Kolam, Khond and Saora follow simple/primitive agricultural economy while the tribes like Bagatha, Koya, Gond, etc. have transformed themselves into tribal-peasantry.

List of Scheduled Tribes

Andh, Bagatha, Bhil, Chenchu, Gadaba, Gond, Kammara, Kattunayakan, Kolam, Konda dora, Konda Reddi, Kondh, Kotia, Koya, Kulie, Mali, Manne Dora, Muka Dora, Naikpods, Nayak, Pradhan, Paraya, Reddi Dora, Rona/Rena, Saora, Sugali, Thoti, Valmiki, Yenadi, Yerukala.

The distribution of tribal population in Andhra Pradesh may be understood through two broad categories viz. Agency Areas and the Plains. The Agency Areas are also known as Partially Excluded Areas. These are largely mountaneous areas with dense foliage and some difficult terrain while the Plain Areas are mostly level land. Historically speaking the Agency areas symbolize the retreat of the primitive tribes in the face of invasion of land hungry Hindu peasantry. The Agency Areas are spread across parts of Srikakulam, Vizianagaram, Visakhapatnam, East Godavari, West Godavari, Khammam, Warangal, Adilabad, and Mehbub nagar. Some of the important tribes inhabiting the Agency Areas are the Andh, Bagatha, Khond, Kolam, Konda Dora, Konda. Reddi, Kotiya, Koya, Kulia, Mali, Manne Dora, Muka Dora, Naikpod, Poraja, Pradhan, Reddi Dora, Saora, Thoti and Valmiki. Even these Agency Areas are no more our of bound for the non-tribal population and many such people have started settling down in these exclusive areas. Some of the important tribes of the Plains Areas are Kattunayakan, Rona, Sugali, Yenadi and Yerukala.

As far as the distribution of linguistic elements is concerned the tribal population may be classified into three groups. The largest group of tribes belong to Dravidian language family, followed by those speaking languages from Indo-European and Austric family of languages. Because of growing cultural contacts with different types of people many tribes have become bilingual. As for as the ethnographic profile is concerned the Chenchu have been described in detail in the preceding chapter on the ethnographic profiles of the selected Indian Tribes.

ANDHRA PRADESH

Data Highlights

The total population of Andhra Pradesh, as per the 2001 Census, is 76,210,007. Of which, 5,024,104 (6.6 percent) are Scheduled Tribes (STs). The ST population constitutes 6 percent of the country's ST population. The Scheduled Castes and Scheduled Tribes Orders (Amendment) Act, 1976 have notified 33 STs in the state. Out of the 33 STs, five namely, Goudu, Malis, Nayaks, Thoti and Valmiki have been notified with an area restriction. Goudu, Nayaks and Valmiki have been notified in the Agency tracts area, which comprises Srikakulum, Vizianagaram, Visakhapatnam, East Godavari, West Godavari and Khammam districts. Malis have been notified in the state excluding Adilabad, Hyderabad, Karimnagar, Khammam, Mahbubnagar, Medak, Nalgonda, Nizamabad and Warangal districts. Thoti have been notified in the Adilabad, Hyderabad, Karimnagar, Khammam, Mahbubnagar, Medak, Nalgonda, Nizamabad and Warangal districts.

2. Twelve tribes namely, Bodo Gadaba, Gutob Gadaba, Bondo Poraja, Khond Poraja, Parangiperja, Chenchu, Dongaria Khonds, Kuttiya Kondhs, Kolam, Konda Reddis, Konda Savaras, and Thoti have been recognized as Primitive Tribal Groups (PTGs). Except Kondareddis and Thoti, population on other PTGs are not available separately as these are notified as sub-groups/sections of main communities. The population of Kondareddis and Thoti is 83,096 and 2,074 respectively, as per the 2001 Census.

3. The growth rate of ST population in the decade 1991 -2001 at 19.6 percent has been higher if compared to the overall growth rate of 14.6 percent of the state population as a whole. Among the numerically major STs, highest growth rate of 36 percent has been recorded in the case of Sugalis, followed by Koya (24.4 percent), Gond (18.9 percent), Yenadis (16.8 percent) and Yerukulas (12.8 percent).

Population- Size & Distribution

4. Out of the 33 STs, Sugalis are numerically the largest ST with a population of 2,077,947 constituting 41.4 percent of the state's ST population. They are followed by Koya 568,019 (11.3 percent), Yenadis 462,167 (9.2 percent), Yerukulas 437,459 (8.7 percent) and Gond 252,038 (5 percent). These five (5) STs together account for 76 percent of the ST population of the state.

5. Of the total ST population, 92.5 percent are residing in rural areas. Among the major STs, Gond have the highest (97.6 percent) rural population, followed by Koya (95.5 percent), Sugalis (93.7 percent), Yenadis (86.4 percent) and Yerukulas (77.5 percent). District-wise distribution of ST population

shows that they are mainly concentrated in the districts of Khammam, Visakhapatnam, Warangal, Adilabad and Nalgonda. These five districts constitute 48.9 percent of the total ST population of the state.

Sex ratio

6. The overall sex ratio of the ST population is 972 females per 1000 males, which is marginally lower than 978 reported for the state population as a whole at 2001 Census. The over all sex ratio of the ST population has registered an increase over 960 reported at the 1991 Census. The sex ratio of above 1000 among ST population in the five contiguous districts namely, Srikakulam (1009), Vizianagaram (1025), Visakhapatnam (1003), East Godavari (1011) and West Godavari (1018) have returned higher sex ratio among STs. In the remaining 18 districts it varies between 994 (Nizamabad) and 921 (Nalgonda).

The Statement below shows the sex ratio and child sex ratio (0-6) at the national, state and numerically the largest five STs at 2001 Census:

Age Groups	All STs (India)	All STs (Andhra Pradesh)	Sugalis	Koya	Gond	Yenadis	Yerukulas
All Ages	978	972	939	1006	1013	957	984
0-6	973	972	944	1000	999	950	971

7. As shown in the statement, the child sex ratio (0-6) of ST population of Andhra Pradesh is equal to the child sex ratio of ST population at the national level. Among the numerically major STs, Sugalis and Yenadis have lower sex ratio both in overall and 0-6 age group populations than the state ST population and the other major STs.

Literacy and educational level

8. Literacy and level of education are two basic indicators of the level of development achieved by a group/society. The literacy results in a more awareness besides contributing to the overall improvement of health, hygiene and other social conditions.

According to 2001 Census, percentage of literate persons (those who can read & write with understanding), aged 7 years and above, among ST population of Andhra Pradesh is 37 percent, which is lower than 60.5 percent reported for state population as a whole. The literacy data show that the ST population of the state has made significant improvement in literacy during the decade 1991-2001. The literacy rate, which was 17.1 percent in 1991, has increased by 19.9 percentage points in 2001. But in comparison to other states/ UTs, the position of ST population of Andhra Pradesh is not satisfactory. It is just above Uttar Pradesh (35.1 percent) and Bihar (28.2 percent), which are bottom two states in literacy rate for ST population among all states/UTs. At the district level, the highest literacy rate has been recorded in Hyderabad (55.4 percent) and the lowest in Mahbubnagar (25.8 percent).

9. Among the major STs, Yerukulas have reported the highest literacy rate (45.4 percent), followed by Koya (41.8 percent), Gond (36.4 percent), Yenadis (35.3 percent) and Sugalis (34.3 percent). The female literacy rate of 26.1 percent among the ST population is matter of concern as almost a fourth of ST females are illiterate in the state.

10. Out of total literates, 48.3 percent are literates without any educational level or have attained below Primary level. The literates, who have attained education up to Primary level and Middle level, constitute 28.4 percent and 8.5 percent respectively. 12.3 percent are having educational level up to Matric/Higher Secondary etc. levels, implying that every 8th ST literate is a Matriculate. Literates with educational level of Graduation & above are 1.8 percent. Individually, Yerukulas (3.3 percent) have the highest percentage of Graduate & above educational level.

11. The educational level table also shows that the drop out is conspicuous after the Primary level and again after Matric/ Secondary levels. This pattern is consistent among all the major SCs.

12. Population in the age group 5-14 years are the potential students. Only 60.7 percent of the ST population in this age group has been attending various educational institutions.

Economic activity

Work Participation Rate (WPR)

13. The work participation rate (WPR) is the percentage of workers to the total population. The WPR of the ST population is 53.9 percent at 2001 Census, which is almost equal to 54.3 percent recorded in 1991. The WPR among male 55.7 percent and females 52 percent more than half of male/female have been returned workers among ST at 2001 Census.

14. At the individual caste level by & large consistent pattern is noted in WPR. The highest WPR of 56.5 percent is reported for Yenadis and lowest among Yerukulas (50.5 percent). Yurukulas have also recorded the lowest female WPR of 45.2 percent.

Category of Workers

15. There has been a decline in the main workers from 93.9 percent at 1991 Census to 79.3 percent at 2001 Census. This, in turn, has resulted in corresponding increase in the marginal workers from 6.1 percent in 1991 to 20.7 percent in 2001. Out of total workers, 'agricultural labourers' constitute 49.3 percent, which is significantly higher when compared to 36.9 percent recorded for ST population at the national level. 'Cultivators' accounts for 34.3 percent and 13.5 percent have been returned as 'other workers'. Remaining 3 percent have been workers in 'household industry'.

16. At the individual caste level, among major STs, Yenadis have the maximum 76.2 percent 'agricultural labourers'.

Marital status

17. Marital status is one of the important determinants of fertility and growth of a population. The 2001 Census data on marital status show that 48.7 percent persons among the STs of Andhra Pradesh are 'never married'. The 'currently married' constitute 46.9 percent while 4 percent are 'widowed' and only 0.5 percent are 'divorced and separated'.

18. A majority of girls and boys among STs in Andhra Pradesh are getting married after attaining the legal age of marriage. However, marriages of ST girls below 18 years (3.2 percent) are higher than that recorded among ST population at national

level (2.1 percent). Similarly, the incidence of marriage among boys below 21 years at 3.6 percent is also higher than 2.8 percent aggregated for ST population at the national level.

19. The mean number of children ever born per ever married ST woman of all ages as well as 45-49 years age group are 2.7 and 3.6 respectively, which are lower than corresponding figures of 3.2 and 4.1 for ST population at the national level.

Religion

20. The 2001 Census data show that Hindus constitute 98.9 percent of ST population of Andhra Pradesh, followed by Christians 35,983 (0.7 percent) and Muslims 4,643 (0.1 percent).

PROBLEMS IN TRIBAL INDIA

> We do not conceive of people being forcibly changed by other human beings. We conceive of them as seeing a light and following it freely.
>
> — Mead (1961)

> In aiming at progress...you must let no one suffer by too drastic a measure, nor pay too high a price in upheaval and devastation, for your innovation.
>
> — Maunier (1949)

APPROACHES TO UNDERSTAND TRIBAL PROBLEMS

Chapter 12

For thousands of years primitive tribes persisted in forests arid, hills without having more than casual contacts with the populations of the open plains and the centres of civilization. "Now and then, a military campaign extending for a short spell into the vastness of tribal country would bring the inhabitants temporarily to the notice of princes and chroniclers, but for long periods there was frictionless co-existence between the tribal folks and Hindu caste society in the truest sense of the word" (Haimendorf, 1960). But the physical isolation of most of the aboriginal tribes drew to an end when the modern means of communication like railways and roads were introduced in the nineteenth and early twentieth century coupled with the sudden growth of India's population. This caused land-hungry peasants of the plains to invade the sparsely populated tribal regions of middle and south India. Moreover the extension of law and order to areas which in earlier days had been virtually unadministered, enabled traders, money landers and a host of administrators, social workers, etc. to establish themselves in their villages.

The onslaught of moneylenders and traders from the plains played havoc with the tribals who, as many examples show, lost their economic independence and lot of land within a span of twenty to thirty years of their contact with the cunning and professional people of the plains. The plight of the poor and vulnerable Indian tribals has been surfacing from time to time for about hundred years or so. But after independence they have been considered a 'problem' for government and their more advanced fellow citizens. The administrators, anthropologists, Christian missionaries and social workers have viewed this 'problem' from different angles with different perspectives. For the matter of convenience these views and approaches may be divided into three categories. The discussion that follows this categorization rotates round the three views:

(i) No change Isolationism

(ii) Assimilationism

(iii) Integrationism

Many of the so-called aboriginal peoples or tribals have been pronounced by all those who came into close contact with them as rather simple, truthfully honest, usually jovial, colourful and happy-go-lucky. They had their own peculiar social organization and some of had retained it till their contact with the British. "Even after the British contact, which rendered their contact with the Hindus more rapid and intensive, some of them retained it, especially those who have been governed through their old tribal organization. In the case of others, whether Hinduised or not, the organization itself has not completely disappeared, but has been lacking in that vitality and vigour which are characteristic of true tribal life" (Ghurye, 1963). Let us take a brief view of their social and economic organization and then the resultant problems:

(1) Most of these tribes have been practising a crude type of cultivation called 'shifting cultivation' known by respective vernacular names. It required little labour, care and vital inputs. Under this scheme of cultivation trees and shrubs are felled with axe before the start of monsoon, fired and allowed to burn down into ashes. Now the desired seed is thrown and the nature is left to take care of the yield. To supplement their dietary requirement they collect all kinds of edible roots and fruits and hunt their favourable animals.

(2) Further, most of the tribal people are habituated to drink, formerly to their home brewd liquor of rice, mahua-flower and other varieties and later to all kind of distilled liquor. As a group, Jounsari, Bhil, Gond and numerous other tribes drink and even their children drink liberally. This is due to their local environmental and ecological conditions. Liquor has also been a part of their ritual and religious practices.

(3) Contacts with Christian missionaries especially in Bihar and north-eastern region played havoc with their spiritual world. The faith in their old gods was shaken and everything tribal was called blasphemous.

(4) Different tribes have different customs in regard to marriage and inheritance. The tribal customs were not properly understood and they were punished by the regular courts. It hurt the tribal sentiments.

(5) Tribal people have been, naturally, illiterate. When various schemes were taken up for their educational upliftment, very little care was taken to impart primary education in their respective mother-tongues even in case of informal education.

Commenting on the "life and death struggle of many primitive tribes in India and elsewhere in consequence of adverse economic conditions," D.N. Majumdar (1938) enumerated eleven causes : (1) The excise laws have hit them hard. (2) The displacement of tribal officers by those of the administration has disorganized tribal life in all aspects. (3) Tribal land used for shifting cultivation has been taken away from them. (4) Quarrying in the land owned is not allowed except with the payment of heavy licence fee. (5) Shifting cultivation is prohibited in most areas. The people, thus, have been forced to take to the kind of agriculture unsuited to them or for which they do not know adequate offering and sacrifices which will "please the gods presiding over agriculture". (6) "Marriage by capture' has been treated as an offence under the Indian Penal Code. It was generally resorted to in order to avoid payment of heavy bride wealth, and the substitute has worked smoothly. The recognition of this custom as offence punishable by law will seriously undermine social solidarity and lead to racial disharmony. Already we know that late marriage is customary among the tribal people and there are a large number of men and women in every tribe who cannot afford to marry under normal conditions (7) The fairs and weekly markets which have begun to attract these people are ruining them financially. (8) Education which has been and is being imparted has been more harmful than otherwise. (9) The judicial officers, not been able to give them satisfactory justice. (10) Missionary effort has resulted in creating in their minds a loathing for their own culture and a longing for things which they have no means to obtain. (11) Contact has introduced diseases in tribal peoples for which they possess no efficient indigenous pharmacopoeia. Medical health rendered by the state is meagre.

A.V. Thakkar, popularly known as Thakkar Bapa", one of the most vociferous champions of tribal cause has analysed the situation in the straight manner of a social worker. According to him the "problems of the aborigins may be analysed into (1) poverty; (2) illiteracy; (3) illhealth; (4) inaccessibility of the areas inhabited by tribals; (5) defects in administration; and (6) lack of leadership.

After viewing aft anthropologist's and a social worker's reactions, let us take up Hutton's view, a defender of British policy of tribal affairs. According to Hutton, most cruel tribal customs were put down and warfare was stopped. Modern medicine was applied and infant mortality curtailed. The arts of reading and writing were introduced and easier intercourse and communication placed at their disposal through roads and post offices. However, "the ills to which primitives were exposed to came from two slightly different aspects of British rule.

(1) Introduction of an administrative system which failed to take into account any special needs.

(2) Deliberate measures intended to ameliorate the condition of these tribes.

Three major evils proceeded from these sources: (1) loss of land and supplanting of the tribal village headman by foreigners, particularly by the Hindus from the plains, whether cultivators, moneylenders, traders, or mere land grabbers; (b) loss of means of subsistence and other evils; (c) disintegration of tribal solidarity."

After analysing the plight of the tribal people let us go back to the three major approaches to the tribal problems to assess the impact of these approaches.

Protagonists of the first approach hold the view that all the alien links, responsible for the unregulated and unrestricted contacts with the modern world and the resultant miserable condition of the tribes, should be snapped and the primitive people should be allowed and encouraged to flourish in their own primitive environment.

This approach also includes what is now widely known as 'National Park Theory' credited to Verrier Elwin. He suggested that "the first necessity is the establishment of National Park, in which not only the Baiga but thousands of simple Gonds in their neighbourhood might take refuge. A fairly large area was to be marked out for this purpose. The areas should be under the direct control of a tribe's commissioner who should be an expert standing between them as was resorted to in the case of the Hos and Santhals. viz., through the leaders or headmen of the tribe. The usual other steps like licensing all non-aboriginals, were to be taken to safeguard the aboriginals from being exploited by unscrupulous adventurers. In short, the administration was to be "so adjusted as to allow the tribesmen to live their lives with utmost possible happiness and freedom. No missionaries of any religion were to be allowed to breakup tribal life". This approach has been severely criticised on the ground that in the name of protecting the culture of the tribals, they cannot be kept aloof from the rest of India. They are not domestic cattle or zoo exhibits but equal citizens of free India and thus they should be allowed to contribute towards the advancement of their country and enjoy the resultant fruits of development.

The second approach viz., assimilation has got considerable acceptance when lobbied by social workers. The protagonists of assimilation' advance the view that tribes should be assimilated with their neighbouring non-tribal cultures. The policy of total assimilation has also not been in conformity with the trend of Indian history. Despite thousands of years of cultural contacts and inter-cultural exchanges, the Indian society could not become totally homogeneous. Though some cultural characteristics did take shape that are trully 'national' in character as the by-product of historical development of Indian society, this can not be denied that Indian society has been formed with Santhal, Gond, Oriya, Telegu, Kashmiri and numerous other cultural currents. Under such conditions the policy of total assimilation of tribal culture as the solution of their problems in unfair and futile. Even, the thought of forced assimilation or putting of as fate accompali smacks of 'cultural authoritarianism'.

Jawahar Lal Nehru has been very outspoken in condemning the imposition of the Hindu way of living on tribal populations reared in another tradition. Due to his deep sympathy for the tribal people and keen appreciation of their problems, the approach of the state towards the tribal people is based on the theme of 'integration'.

The approach of integration' of the tribal population with the rest of the Indian population on the basis of equality and mutual respect is propagated by the anthropologists. The principle of cultural autonomy' has been an article of faith with the anthropologists. Integration should be differentiated from forced assimilation. We have got so many linguistic and religious groups who are being integrated to form one Indian nation without anybody making a demand that they should be forced to give up their cultural identity and identify themselves with the majority community. Perhaps, there will be more meaningful and durable 'integration' when every minority group feels secured; when, in this pluralistic society that India is, people can exist as Hindus, Muslims, Christians, Sikhs etc., when one can exist here as Tamil, Oriya, Gujarati, Bengali, Punjabi etc. then why not a person can exist here with respect and dignity as a Santhal, a Gond, a Tharu, a Meena and a Yenadi? Integration can never be achieved under the shadow of threat and no plural society can afford to keep disgruntled, distressed, restless and frustrated minorities in its fold and still aspire for the harmonious development of the country. To ensure integration in this way the non-tribals need education as much as the tribals.

MAJOR PROBLEMS AND RELATED ISSUES

Chapter 13

Indebtedness

The chronic indebtedness has been, and still is, probably the most difficult problem facing almost the entire tribal population of India. Consequently one of the worst forms of exploitation to which the tribal people are exposed is through traditional money lending. Barring certain areas in the north-eastern region which were closed to the middlemen and contractors during British rule, indebtedness is quite widespread and crushing among almost the entire Indian tribes.

The chronic indebtedness of the tribals is certainly due to rampant poverty and deficit economy. Reliable ethnographic evidence prove that the tribal people were certainly not that much handicapped in their struggle for living a carefree life when their places of habitation were isolated and devoid of middlemen and contractors. They were living in self-sufficient economic conditions. Forest wealth was at their disposal to sustain themselves. But unfortunately when their abodes were thrown open as a result of economic development all around, they found themselves completely ill-equipped to enjoy the fruits of development. Outsiders, the so-called civilized people, exploited their vulnerability in the absence of any concerted efforts on the part of administration. With the passage of time, their plight continued to worsen and they have been reduced to the position in which we find them to-day.

Although we have little scientific data about the extent of their indebtedness, it is obvious that the size of the problem is enormous. Indebtedness among them does not have only economic dimensions but social and psychological too. For a large number, happiness and peace desert them, for others it makes the entire system impervious to hope. In many areas it leads to bondedness due to the debt descending from father to son and even to the successive generations.

Among a large number of tribal people indebtedness has become unavoidable and thus normal phenomenon of their existence. Following are some of the important reasons of indebtedness common to almost all the affected groups :

(1) Loss of tribal rights over land and forests;

(2) Poor and primitive mode of agriculture resulting in deficit supply of food grains;

(3) Ignorance;

(4) Expenditure beyond their means due to extravagant spending on marriages, deaths, fairs and festivals;

(5) Fatalist attitude and locally-oriented worldview; and

(6) Adherence to panchayat decisions regarding fines for fear of excommunication.

Due to the above mentioned reasons he is always in need of money and thus becomes an easy victim of exploitation by unscrupulous moneylenders and middlemen. Small amounts borrowed at usurious rates of interest from time to time snowball into a sum beyond his capacity to repay and what little he possesses by way of land is snatched by the moneylender. "No programme of economic development is likely to have any impact on the tribal economy unless vigorous measures are taken to rescue the tribal from the clutches of the moneylender". (Planning Commission's Report of the Study Team on Tribal Development Programmes, 1969).

Apart from borrowing in cash a system of borrowing in kind is also in vogue in many parts of the country, especially in Maharashtra and Tripura. In Maharashtra, this system is known by the name of Palemod. Under this system the needy tribals take seed on loans at the time of sowing and return thrice or even four times the original quantity at the time of harvest. Grain taken for consumption during this period or any time during the year is also returned at this rate. Thus, during the harvesting season a major portion of the crop and sometimes the whole crop is surrendered to the moneylender. Likewise in Tripura, a system called 'dadan' is prevalent. The creditor purchases the crop in advance at very low rates.

Role of Moneylender

It is essential to study the role of traditional moneylenders to understand the failure of various government and semi-government credit agencies to wean away the tribals from their traditional sources of credit.

The modus operandi of the traditional moneylender is very simple and convenient to the tribal debtors. They are the men on the spot and ever present on the scene. Whenever a tribal needs money for whatever reason, he has to walk a few furlong or less to reach the moneylender's house. where he is always welcome-day in and day out. The moneylender provides him money without any condition, sureties, guarantees and guarantors since an average tribal has very little to offer in the way of movable or immovable property, All that he has is his honest desire to fulfil his loan obligations out of his earnings and some land that he may possess. The moneylender recognises these as good security, though at some other places he may demand mortgaging the tribal's land against the loan as prevalent in parts of tribal areas of Madhya Pradesh. By way of any formality the only thing a debtor has to do is to affix his thumb impression on a blank piece of paper or under a draft which he cannot read.

Now compare this procedure with other sources of credit like cooperative credit societies established by various state governments. Most of these are found to be situated at far off places from the tribal's habitat. He has to encounter a number of formalities, cumbersome procedures and documents. Besides, security and guarantor are also needed to fulfil various provisions of credit disbursement. Normally there is a time lag of at least a couple of months between the date of application and date of disbursement of loan. Then unscrupulous officials demand their share. All these hurdles apart, the government sponsored credit societies advance loans for only productive purposes like improvement in cultivation, purchase of implements, soil conservation, etc., but the poor tribal needs loans for consumption and subsistence, to fulfil various social and ritual obligations. The moneylender places no conditions and offers loan for any purpose.

THE personal human contact which the moneylender maintains with his debtor is also significant factor. He speaks the tribal's language, knows the entire family history and background and circumstances leading to the debtor's need of money. Significantly, he accepts the repayment of the loan in any form - in cash or in kind.

Consequences of Indebtedness

Since most of the tribal people are illiterate they have no idea of what is being entered in the account books of the moneylender. They put their thumb impression very submissively wherever desired by the moneylender and that seals their fate forever. In many cases these transactions are oral and they cannot afford to approach a court of law for seeking redress. But even those transactions, which are recorded in the account books, are nothing but legal fiction because of the wrong entries of inflated amounts and the most the poor tribal can do is to call the Village panchayat which usually serves the interest of the moneylender. Studies from various tribal areas bear testimony to the fact that in most cases, indebtedness leads to bondedness and land alienation. The total picture of this state of affairs, however, indicates that one or more of the following are the consequences of indebtedness.

(1) Loss of freedom and the consequent utilization of their labour power by the creditor;

(2) Alienation of land and its acquisition by the creditor;

(3) Sale of girls and prostitution; and

(4) Chronic venereal diseases.

The heavily indebted among them who are 'acquired' by the money-lenders-landlords as their bonded labour are incapable of breaking the vicious circle of indebtedness. They are reconciled to their fate and have virtually no stake in life. The most important values for their independent existence viz., economic values have been lost to them. The Koltas of Jaunsar-Bawar (U.P.) are the classical example of the worst consequences of indebtedness and these unfortunate people are carrying the burden of all the above mentioned curses.

Legislation and Remedial Steps

The Fifth Schedule of the Constitution empowers the Governor of a state to regulate the carrying on of the business as moneylender by persons who lend money to members of Scheduled Tribes in Scheduled Areas. In pursuance of this provision various state governments have promulgated and enacted various Laws and Acts. Following are some of the important Laws from different states to control moneylending, debt redemption and abolition of debt bondage:

(1) The Andhra Pradesh Scheduled Areas Moneylenders Regulation, 1963.

(2) The Agency Debt Bondage Abolition, 1964.

(3) The Assam Moneylenders Regulation, 1968.

(4) The Bihar Moneylenders (Regulation of Transaction) Act, 1939.

(5) The Bombay Agricultural Debtors Relief Act, 1947.

(6) The Kerala Moneylending Act, 1958.

(7) The M.P. Anusuchit Jan Jati Rini Sahayata Act, 1966.

(8) The Madras Indebted Agriculturists (Repayment of Debt) Act, 1955.

(9) The Mysore Pawn Brokers Act, 1961.

(10) The Orissa Money lenders (Application of Certain Provisions) Regulation, 1950.

(11) The Rajasthan Sagri System Abolition Act, 1961.

A comprehensive list has been provided in the annexure.

Enquities by various agencies have revealed that despite regulations the exploitation of tribal people has been continuing unabated. There is a lot of evasion of the regulations and legislation and the moneylenders have taken very little notice of the restrictions imposed on their operation. The Report of the Scheduled Areas and Scheduled Tribes Commission and Planning Commission's Report of the Study Team on Tribal Development Programmes support such findings. This state of affairs continues due to the following reasons :

(a) The state governments have not made adequate use of the protective provisions of the Fifth Schedule to lend protection to the tribals against bonded labour.

(b) The state governments have not been able to make effective use of the penal provisions in their existing legislation against evasion by moneylenders.

(c) Lack of will and commitment, of all reasons, are most responsible for the continued exploitation of tribals by the greedy moneylenders.

Planning Commission's Report of the Study Team on the Tribal Development Programmes has summed up the situation with clarity. It is of the view that the attack on tribal indebtedness should be two-pronged if it is to be effective and enduring. On the one hand, long-term credit should be provided to enable the tribal to free himself from the stranglehold of the usurious moneylenders, and on the other hand his repaying capacity should be raised by improving his economic conditions. Cooperative credit should be forthcoming in an adequate measure and the procedure simplified to attract the tribal to take advantage of the credit facilities provided by the society. But the crux of the problem still remains it needs political will, commitment, honesty and integrity on the part of those who are supposed to be protectors of tribal interests. In the absence of these the coming regulations, provisions and schemes shall continue to be treated as mere pieces of paper.

Land Alienation

According to latest statistics nearly 88 percent of the scheduled tribes are engaged in agriculture. The tribals have great emotional attachment with their lands. Agriculture is the only source of livelihood which most of them have known for centuries. The Report of the Scheduled Areas and Scheduled Tribes Commission, 1961, describes the situation with utmost clarity. It says that 'like his brother in the plains the tribal is land hungry. There are several reasons for it, besides the common desire to posses land. One is that those tribals who practice shifting cultivation are growing in numbers and the Jhum cycle is shortening alarmingly in most places. Similarly, those tribals who have taken to settled cultivation are also increasing in numbers. The heavy pressure on land of an ever growing population is more and more apparent."

On an average a person dependent on agriculture in India has 1,6 acres of land as against 7.5 acres in the U.S.A. and 4.5 acres in the U.S.S.R. However, there are regional variations as shown below :

Northern Region	1.01 Acres
Eastern Region	1.25 Acres
Southern Region	1.17 Acres
Western Region	2.29 Acres
Central Region	2.57 Acres
North-Western Region	2.59 Acres

Due to lack of data it is not possible to make any precise assessment regarding the size of tribal holdings in each area separately but some selected examples from a couple of states may give sufficient idea of the situation. According to the Report of the Scheduled Areas and Scheduled Tribes Commission, 1961, Gujarat Vidyapeeth conducted a socio-economic survey of Khedbrahama Tribal Development Block in the Sabarkantha district of Gujarat in 1959. It shows that out of 459 families surveyed, 12 were landless and each family had on an average of 5.32 acres of land.

The Madhya Pradesh Government conducted an economic survey in selected villages in its tribal development blocks. It shows that average size of the holdings was about 15.59 acres. As a result of the socio-economic surveys, conducted by the Government of Rajasthan, of Dungarpur and Banswara districts, which are Scheduled Areas, it was found that the size of average holdings was 4.40 and 5.95 acres in Dungarpur and Banswara respectively. A similar survey was carried out in Manipur which disclosed that the size of average holdings there was 2.80 acres.

The above examples shows that the land situation is by no means uniform in all the tribal areas but there is a lot of uniformity in the ease that most of the tribal cultivators have uneconomic holdings. Their holdings appears bigger in size as compared with those of non-tribal cultivators but the vastness of size is nullified by the poor quality of soil, poor techniques of cultivation and the ever increasing burden of indebtedness.

It seems appropriate to describe the general situation before coming to the crux of the problem—land alienation. Due to spectacular expansion in the means of communication, almost the entire tribal areas were thrown open and the non-tribal people entered these areas with varying motives. The potential land-grabbers among them proved a nightmare for the tribals.

Causes

Among the major causes for land alienation, chronic shortage of cash has been enemy number one of the poor tribals ever since they came into contact with the civilized world and its monetary institutions. The tribal people are always in need of cash for various purposes like marriages, fairs and festivals, clothing, liquor and a host of needs of everyday life. Due to poor and inadequate yield and uneconomic agriculture they have also to purchase foodgrains from the market. Thus, their chronic indebtedness to the neighbouring shopkeepers and moneylenders becomes the primary factor in land alienation. The omnipresent money-lender posing as godfather and saviour of the tribals is ever ready to advance loan to them without demanding any guarantee and for whatsoever purpose. The only thing a tribal has to do is to affix his thumb impression on a blank paper or against a draft in a language the illiterate tribal is unable to decipher. Sometimes, the loan may be extended on oral commitment, no matter this seemingly innocuous oral commitment may become a commitment to total slavery or forfeiture of land.

Of late many tribals have started approaching the state-sponsored cooperative credit societies but their experience with the societies has been no better. Another factor for their approaching the local moneylender is that the cooperative societies advance only short-term loans for productive purposes while most of the tribals need loans for consumption and subsistence too, which fall short of government policies, But for even those who borrowed from cooperative societies, the experience often has been nerve shattering. They are not prepared to be imprisoned or their belongings be confiscated in case they are unable to repay these loans. Hence, most of them prefer to take loan from the familiar sources even at usurious rates of interest.

Case from M. P. and U. P.

Although the problem of land alienation has been rampant in all the states containing some tribal population but it has happened on such a large scale in these two states that its modus operandi may be taken as representative of this evil.

Korwa tribe of Sarguja district of Madhya Pradesh and Tharu and Bhoksa of Tarai region of Uttar Pradesh have been the worst victim of deceit and plunder of their land. The entire region inhabited by the Korwas is surrounded by Muslim moneylenders locally known as Miyan. They are ever ready to advance loan at the slightest pretext with the only condition that the Korwa has to mortgage some of his land. Under chronic conditions of poverty and scarcity they are unable to repay it and the moneylenders occupy the land. Addiction to locally brewd liquor is also an important Reason for taking loans. Although the tribals are exempted from excise regulation of brewing liquor for personal purposes, yet they are not allowed to make their own liquor by these moneylenders and they have to purchase liquor from the illicit breweries of the moneylenders who are not troubled by the excise officials in carrying on their illegal trade. Thus, once caught in the vicious circle of indebtedness, the Korwa is left with no other option but to surrender and forfeit his land.

The Tharu and Bhoksa tribes of Tarai region of Uttar Pradesh are the victims of Punjabi refugee moneylenders - traders who have grabbed thousands of acres of land reclaimed by the tribals. The climate of this region was always very inhospitable to the non-tribal. Malaria was rampan and the land was marsh with abundance of poisonous insects. Due to these reasons the non-tribals rarely entered these areas. Being acclamatised with such a climate, the Tharu and Bhoksa people cleared the forests, reclaimed thousands of acres of land and made it cultivable. With the first wave of invasion of this region by the uprooted Punjabi refugee from Pakistan the entire scene underwent change. The labourious and enterprising Punjabi refugees settled here in thousands and taking advantage of the ignorance and economic vulnerability of the Tharu and Bhoksa tribals grabbed their land. The new Punjabi settlers adopted the same modus operandi being in vogue in other parts of the country, i.e. advancing loan unconditionally and providing cheap liquor to the tribals.

Other Methods

According to the Report of the Scheduled Areas and Scheduled Tribes Commission, 1961, there are various other methods resorted to by non-tribals to get possession of the tribal land. One is the familiar method of utilizing the machinery of the courts, before which the tribal is more or less powerless. The second is the method of temptation of immediate gain. The tribal under a monetary inducement allows himself to be used by the moneylender or usurper as a witness against himself. The third method is called bazdawa by which the tribal is induced to suffer a decree being passed by a court of law against himself. A fourth is that of the tribal accepting before a court of law that his opponent holds the land by adverse possession. Then there is voluntary surrender. Though those surrenders are usually taken as voluntary, in most cases they are actually engineered by the landlords who take advantage of their victim's ignorance.

The reasons for this state of affairs are obvious. One of the most important is the lack of adequate knowledge of the real conditions in the tribal areas on the part of the authorities. The tribal is at the mercy of unscrupulous moneylenders who mostly come from outside and who have no interest in maintaining the tribal social structure or improving the tribal economy. The second reason is complicated legislation. Formerly, the tribal panchayats settled all disputes, thus avoiding recourse to endless litigation in costly law courts, the proceedings-of which are totally incomprehensible to the tribal. The great reason, is lack of alternative source of credit which keeps him under the thumb of the moneylender.

Remedial Steps

Taking into consideration the three bases of land alienation of tribal people viz., (a) the lacunae in the laws, (b) the ignorance of the tribal people, and (c) the complicated legal procedures to be followed, various state governments have been doing something to help the tribals. But except in the hill districts of Assam, Manipur and Mizoram the resulting benefits have been only nominal.

Before looking into various legislative steps taken to safeguard tribal interest in land, it will be in the fitness of things to study the crucial recommendations of Scheduled Areas and Scheduled Tribes Commission, 1961, on the basis of which various states passed a number of legislations. Its major recommendations are as follows:

(1) "There is need for a detailed scrutiny of all legislation affecting tribals' land. The complicated procedures that have resulted in depriving the tribal of assistance also require to be examined. All existing Acts and Regulations should be examined by a committee in each state and Union Territory with the ultimate object of preventing completely the transfer of tribals' lands to non-tribals for some time to come. It may be necessary to amend the present laws drastically in may cases. If this is likely to take time, we recommend that the governors may, in exercise of the powers conferred on them under the Fifth Schedule, issue the necessary Regulations without delay.

(2) "We also recommend that there should be a general prohibition of all transfer, whether by sale, mortgage, gift or lease under any kind of agreement or contract entered into by tribals in favour of non-tribals without the permission of the Deputy Commissioner or the Collector. The Government should make Rules in consultation with the Tribes Advisory Council governing grant to the permission by the Deputy Commissioner or the Collector, after ascertaining the conditions prevailing in each area.

(3) "There should be a bar against suits or applications against any such order made by a Deputy Commissioner or Collector and courts of law should be precluded from taking cognizance of such transfers by sale, mortgage, gift or lease or any other agreement or contract and from passing decree thereon unless arrangement has been entered into with the previous permission of Deputy Commissioner or the Collector.

(4) "Deputy Commissioner or the Collector should have the powers suo moto or at the instance of the aggrieved tribal land holder within a period of 12 years to institute enquiries and restore possession of the land with or without payment of any compensation to the transferee. This provision should be made applicable to all transfers of land by tribals to non-tribals with retrospective effect from the 26th January, 1950. Adequate machinery should be created to-implement these laws or regulations.

(5) "Finally, we recommend that all surrenders must only be to the state, which should hold the surrendered land as a trustee for the tribals".

THE following legislations were in vogue at the time of the above recommendations and hence either they were amended or changed to make them sharper and more protective :

(i) Andhra Pradesh Scheduled Areas Land Transfer Regulation, 1959.

(ii) The Scheduled Areas Estate (Reduction of Rent Amendment) Regulation, 1951.

(iii) Madhya Pradesh Scheduled Areas (Allotment and Transfer of Land) Regulation, 1954.

(iv) The Madhya Pradesh Land Revenue Code, 1959.

(v) Bombay Tenancy and Agricultural Land Reforms Act, 1948.

(vi) Orissa Scheduled Areas Transfer of Immovable Property (Scheduled Tribes) Regulation, 1956.

(vii) Rajasthan Tenancy Act, 1955.

A comprehensive list has been provided in the annexure part of the book.

Some of the important legislations enumerated above may be divided into two types: One is protective, intended to prevent non-tribals acquiring tribal land, and the other deals with the question of land reforms. Both types of legislation have fallen short of the needs of the situation. The protective legislation could not be of much use as no sufficient arrangement for alternative credit was made. The land reform legislation could not help the tribal to any great extent because it was too intricate for him to follow. But the most important factor in this state of affairs is the lack of will and integrity on the part of administration to ameliorate the suffering of the tribal masses. Hence the vested interests exploiting the tribals have been and still are in a position to carry on their nefarious and criminal activities sometime with the help of indifference of officials and sometime with the active , connivance of officials at lower levels. Due to their growing contacts with radical political elements and sincere pro-peasantry cadres of radial organizations, an explosive situation is fast growing up. The Naxalbari movement or Srikakulum uprising should not be considered as mere occasional happenings because the ferment continues and the long exploited tribals are fast gaining consciousness for their rights.

Shifting Cultivation

Shifting cultivation is an age-old institution among the Indian Tribes. This in principle means cultivating a plot of land for a temporary period and then leaving it fallow. It consists of clearing the forest slopes, burning the fallen trees and bushes, and broadcasting the seed in the ash covered soil. The rest is left to nature. The operation actually starts just before summer season when the trees and bushes are felled and allowed to be dried by the scorching sun during first half of summer. In the second half, they are set on fire and are allowed to burn to ashes. On the ashes produced by the burning of these trees and bushes, seeds are sown at the onset of the rainy season. No other operations are required , and the crop is reaped when it is ripe after rains. The sowing on the plot may be done for one or more seasons but not beyond this. After that, fertility of the soil is exhausted and the plot is allowed to remain fallow. Another plot of land is cleared and the agricultural operations are transferred to it. Meanwhile trees and bushes continue to grow on the original plot and in a few years time it regains part of its original appearance.

The beginning of shifting cultivation goes back to the neolithic times, 8,000-10,000 year ago. The manner of its origin has often been speculated. With the increase of population during the relatively genial post pleistocene climate, the only possible way of procuring more food, which would have occurred to primitive man, would have been a shift from hunting to cultivation. Keeping into consideration the vast stretch of land then available and the nomadic nature of man, the only remedy would have been to spread a handful of seeds, preferably cereals, small millets, paddy or barley on some suitable patch of land, allow it to grow through the rainy season and reap it when it was ready. After repeating the process twice or thrice when the yield became thin, it would nave been wise to shift this process to another patch of land and hence the cycle of shifting cultivation.

Leach (1949) opines that in vast tropical and subtropical regions of Africa, Asia and the new world shifting field cultivation is co-existensive with agriculture.

In india it existed in remote hill areas of Assam Orissa, Madhya Pradesh, Bihar and to a lesser extent in several other parts oil the country. Although it has been declared unlawful in most of the areas, it still exists on a lesser scale.

This type of cultivation is known by different regional names in india. It is called **Jhum** among the tribes of Assam, Meghalaya, Tripura, Mizoram and Arunachal Pradesh; Bewar or Dahya in Madhya Pradesh; **Podu** in Andhra Pradesh; **Koman** or Bringa in north Orissa. The problem of shifting cultivation is acute in the states of Andhra Pradesh, North-Eastern region, Bihar and Orissa.

Though shifting cultivation has been quite widespread in the above mentioned regions and it is a way of life with its practitioners but the only people who have exalted it into a regular cult are the Baigas of Madhya Pradesh and Orissa. According to their mythology, they were ordered by bhagwan to practise this type of cultivation. This legend grew out of the concept of mother earth and the mother earth should not be tortured through the dagger of plough. Since the shifting cultivation does not require any ploughing, the mother earth blesses the Baiga for the respect shown to her. They also believe that adoption of plough cultivation shall bring misery.

Two Views

Shifting cultivation has always been an eyesore to forest department. They are dead against it on the ground that it is ruinous and wasteful, dries up the springs in the hills, causes soil erosions, destroys valuable forest, affects rainfall and deprive the people of the benefits of the forest and forest produce. Report of the Scheduled Areas and Scheduled Tribes Commission quotes Nicholson, one time conservator of forests in Orissa, for his statement before the Partially Excluded Areas Enquiry Committee of Orissa :

"The damage done to the forests by shifting cultivation was serious and only under certain conditions where the area of land available is large and population small, such cultivation does little harm"

M.L. Bor, Botanist of the Forest Research Institute, Dehradun in his presidential address to the Botanical section of the Indian Science Congress in 1942 went so far to say:

"Of all practices initiated by man, the most obnoxious is that of shifting cultivation".

Modern opinion, however, is more liberal and regards this practice as an organic response to certain geophysical conditions. M.D. Chaturvedi, formerly Inspector General of Forests opined :

> "The notion widely held that shifting cultivation is responsible in the main for large scale soil erosion needs to be effectively dispelled. The correct approach to the problem of shifting cultivation lies in accepting it not as a necessary evil, but recognizing it as a way of life; not condemning it as an evil practice but regarding it as an agricultural practice evolved as a reflex to the physiographical character of land. For too long, jhuming has been condemned out of hand as a curse to be ashamed of, a vandalism to be decried. This attitude engenders

an inferiority complex and unhealthy atmosphere for the launching of any development scheme seeking to improve the current practice."

S.H. Howard, another former Inspector General of Forests suggested that instead of discouraging this method of cultivation, a trial should be given by regulating it, which means that if a longer period of rest is given between the fellings, there is little danger of soil erosion. J.P. Mills, with his long experience in the tribal areas of Assam believed that, wisely regulated, the method could probably be carried on indefinitely without causing excessive deterioration.

Factual Situation and Pragmatic Aspect

All things apart, this very fact cannot be ignored or brushed aside easily that nearly ten percent of the Indian tribal population depends on shifting cultivation and they cannot be deprived of their land, their livelihood and their way of life for a theoretical opinion on which not all experts agree.

Theoretically, shifting cultivation is now legally prohibited except in a few pockets of Madhya Pradesh and north-eastern region where it is still practised with the permission of the competent authorities. It is allowed in Madhya Pradesh though grudgingly in the Baiga chak (district Mandala) and Abhujmar (Bastar) and a few other pockets inhibited by Baiga tribals. With the strenuous efforts of Verrier Elwin and support of the late Prime Minister Nehru some parts of north-eastern region were also exempted from this prohibition. In the rest of the erstwhile jhuming areas any violation of the rule is severely dealt with. If the 'culprit' is caught, he is fined and prosecuted, otherwise collective fines are imposed on all the inhabitants of the area.

Everyone agrees that it is not ideal method, and that, wherever possible, terracing or other means of cultivation should be introduced. Even some of the sympathisers of tribal cause hold the view that this system of cultivation promotes laziness and inertia among its practitioners.

The people who practice it have their own version. The Korku, Baiga, Korwa and Maria tribals of Madhya Pradesh and Nagas of Assam and adjoining areas claim that shifting cultivation is done with simple implements like axe, hoe, digging stick, sickle, etc., which they can afford to purchase and repair easily. Whereas plough agriculture needs a number of costly implements, regulation of time, routine work on the field, money and devotion. Also, their traditions suit this system of cultivation due to their sedentary, carefree and routineless life.

Notwithstanding its obvious disadvantages, shifting cultivation cannot be stopped with one stroke an it has become a way of life of the tribals who have been practising it for generations. Over vast areas in the interior, where area suitable for terracing is not available, shifting cultivation has to be tolerated. But every effort should be made to regulate this system of cultivation on scientific lines to minimise its after effects and help in building up of the fertility of the jhumed areas.

Solution of the Problem

The Report of the Scheduled Areas and Scheduled Tribes Commission, 1961, has given some important suggestions for implementation. Some of the major suggestions are as follow :

(1) The total replacement of this system, if it comes at all, will be a long term process. In the meantime the proper course is to regulate it, experiment with it, improve it and try other workable alternatives, Shifting cultivation is tied up with tribal way of life and it is thus much more than a technical problem pertaining only to the improved techniques of farming and agriculture. It is a mixed problem, partly connected with the physical conditions of the land and partly with social customs, traditions and beliefs. Any hurried departure may create complications.

(2) Shifting cultivation may be converted into terraced cultivation Wherever the hill slopes permit and the soil is sufficiently deep, the holds out immense possibilities of improvement, and in many places throughout the tribal areas it has already been taken up with enthusiasm.

(3) Establishment of agricultural colonies may also be an effective solution to wean away tribals from shifting cultivation to settled cultivation. Some agricultural colonies have already been established in parts of Andhra Pradesh, West Bengal and Madhya Pradesh where each tribal family was given some cultivable waste land, financial assistance for the construction of houses and for reclamation of the land, bullocks, agricultural implements and seeds. Facilities for communications, drinking water, irrigation, medical aid etc. were also proposed. But the result has not been much encouraging partly due to mis-man agement of the whole scheme and partly due to refusal of the tribal psyche to adjust in lower plains and alien lands.

Planning Commission's Report of the Study Team on Tribal Development Programme, 1969 straight away suggests that steps should be taken to make agriculture more remunerative by encouraging the tribal agriculturists to take to improved methods of agriculture. The following measures may be undertaken for the purpose:

(a) Setting up of demonstration farms.

(b) Distribution of improved agricultural implements, manures and fertilizers and high yielding varieties of seeds.

(c) Providing credit facilities.

Improved agricultural implements distributed to tribals should be such as would meet their approval.

Poverty

Poverty and exploitation are, now synonymous with the majority of tribal population. 'Chronic' and 'mass' poverty had been embedded in India's colonial history. The effort to solve our economic problems and achieve all round development began with our plans which have transformed the country in numerous ways - substantial industrialization, green revolution leading to surplus food production, improvement in the average lifespan and a fast increasing middle class opulence. It is, however, a paradox of our planning that it has failed to improve the living conditions of India's poor. Persistance of poverty is clearly manifest in the country's low levels of per capita income and the substantial percentage of population living below the poverty line, set at the consumption level of Rs. 3500/- subsequently revised to Rs. 6400/-. The Planning Commission estimated the incidence of poverty at 37.4% in 1983-84 and 29.9% in 1987-88. These percentages are for total population and in the rural population and the Scheduled Castes/Scheduled Tribe populations the incidence is substantially higher. However, the expert group on the estimation of poor, constituted by the Planning Commission, estimated its incidence in 1983-84 at 44.8% and in 1987-88 at 39.3%. The figures for 1993-94 are yet to be released. The per capita income at 1980-81 constant prices was Rs. 2362/- in 1993-94. For the 493 million people below the poverty line, development has been a distant phenomenon, watched from the way side (UNDP, 1993).

The state of poverty is attributed to various facets inherent in our model of planning and also the socio-political structure of the country.

Our plans have laid emphasis on industrial growth, both in manufacturing and also in agriculture. In the latter sector we have encouraged large irrigation projects, chemical fertilizers, etc. which, by and large, benefit the substantial and not subsistence farmers. It was generally assumed that the benefits of industrial expansion and increased production and employment would 'trickledown' by undertaking a modicum of income distribution have proved to be quite inadequate. Analysts have pointed out that the pattern of state intervention through measures like land reforms, redistribution of agricultural incomes and surplus, adoption of educational infrastructure to employment potentials have been half-hearted and dominated by the entreprenuerial and 'capitalist' class which have gradually obtained a stranglehold over the political and economic regime. As a consequence of these trends, the removal of rural poverty through targetting the specific groups emerged as one of the main objects of the IV Plan and thereafter. Besides, the key issue of land reforms emphasis was laid on certain income and employment generation schemes under a package of anti-poverty programmes. These include schemes for generating employment and creation of assets for rural poor and rural areas, IRDP which would help through margin-money and loans to improve agriculture and develop sources for additional income, TRYSEM for creating alternate skills for employment, and programmes to enable rural women to get additional incomes. After the early 80s IRDP expansion and its honing to reach the most disadvantaged has succeeded in making some dent on the situation.

The poverty levels among the Scheduled Tribes are naturally much higher when compared to the others. In 1983-84 the percentage of persons below the poverty line among the Scheduled Tribes was 58.4 in the rural areas (where 94% of them live) and 39.9% among the urban population. The working Group on VIII Plan for the ST estimated that the number of ST families below the poverty line in 1991 was 99.24 lacs. The IRDP has assisted about 42% families upto the end of VIII Plan. However, accurate estimates of families being able to cross the poverty line were not available and IRDP evaluations had placed this percentage at quite a low level. The Group worked out that an investment of Rs. 8000/- per family would be necessary to enable it to cross the poverty line and against this the actual investment had been of Rs. 3481/- per family. Moreover, the investment per ST family was substantially lower than the investment on non-ST families. It has been perceived that the impoverishment and marginalisation of the bulk of tribal communities has been intensified in the context of our macro level goals of national development. The tribal populations have gradually been sucked into a process where their resource base and produce have got hinged to a national and even international economy on the one hand and the appropriation of their traditional community rights and economic bases by the state and commercial interests on the other hand. In the words of Dr. B.D. Sharma, former commissioner for Scheduled Castes and Scheduled Tribes, a "careful review of the present situation clearly brings out five levels of deprivation namely (1) non-recognition of rights over resources and restriction of their use; (2) Alienation of workers from the means of production; (3) Denial of due instalment of labour; (4) Bartering of liberty and finally; (5) Psychological state of accepting deprivation and destitutions and demise of self respect and dignity." In other words, the tribals have lost their traditional rights and access to forests and its produce. They are losing their better quality lands to non-tribal cultivators and Being gradually driven to poorer lands and, further, a very large number of them have become wage earners and even the minimum and fair wage is denied to them, even by the government departments. As a result of emphasis on industrial development and large irrigation projects, which mostly benefit the substantial agriculturists, tribals have been displaced from their lands in large tracts. Our legal process has been such that they have been getting a raw deal by way of compensation and woefully inadequate rehabilitation programmes. A study of 22 districts in A.P. (1990) points out that while the SC and BCs were found to be highly responsive to anti-poverty efforts, among the ST, the responsiveness was not so strong. While perceptible dents could be made on the poverty levels of SC & BC households the efforts of development are to be stretched more through innovative schemes for making inroads into the poverty of ST. In the global march of development the wealth on earth is being appropriated by elites impoverishing the nature as well as the vast human masses who depend on these natural resources over the centuries. Adivasis have constantly fought an unequal battle against outside oppressors (Baviskar 1995).

In the context of this widespread deprivation and even pauperization on the tribal scene, even the large scale intervention by the state through the impact of anti-poverty and rural employment programmes, revamped public distribution system for the tribal areas and other programmes with similar aims in the cooperative and other sectors have not so far proved to be extensive enough.

Employment

Before reviewing the tribal situation vis-a-vis employment, let us have some idea about the occupational patterns of tribal population in India. The overwhelming majority of tribal people (about 75%) works in agricultural sector - cultivators and marginal farmers and agricultural labour. A small segment is engaged in industrial sector as factory labour while further smaller segments like the Todas of Nilgiri Hills, Tamil Nadu, Bhotias of Sub-Himalyan Region, U.P. and Gaddis and Bakrewals of Jammu & Kashmir and some others are cattle herders; some are artisans such as Mahalis of West Bengal, Asur and Agaria of Bihar and M. P. are iron smelters and blacksmiths while about seventy small tribal communities mostly located in southern India are foodgathrer-hunters. Of late, a growing number of tribal people have joined the ranks of migrant agricultural labour and unskilled workers engaged in house construction and brick kilns. In between the total tribal population a microscopic minority of educated tribals are either government employees or professionals such as doctors, entrepreneurs, teachers, etc. Thus, poverty and impoverishment is their lot. The tribal population of north eastern India is a pleasant exception because in this region the model of development has been based upon the axiom of 'education first'.

In the present scenario the National Rural Employment Programme (NREP) funded equally by Central and State Governments' has been under implementation since 1980. The Rural Landless Employment Guarantee Programme (RLEGP) has been under implementation since 1983. Both these programmes are aimed to rural landless labour, many of whom belong to SCs/STs, particularly in the lean period of the year.

Since 1989, both NREP and RLEGP have been merged in to a national rural employment programme named the Jawahar Rozgar Yojna (JRY). This programme is to be funded 80% by the Centre and 20% by the States. The objectives of the JRY are generation of additional gainful employment, creation of productive community assets, and improvement of overall quality of life in rural areas. The special provisions for SCs/ STs in the JRY include preference to SCs/STs for employment, special integrated projects for nomadic tribes and 15% of the resources at both district and Village Panchayat levels for individual beneficiaries scheme for SCs/STs. Further, monitoring of works exclusively for the benefits of ST and employment generated for STs has been prescribed. Besides these The National Scheduled Castes & Scheduled Tribes Finance and Development Corporation has been established in 1989 mainly for identification of trades/ business/professions and other economic activities of importance to SCs and STs and undertaking supportive projects, so as to generate employment and/or raise their income levels (a profile of this organization is given in the chapter dealing with tribal development). However, as the evaluation of tribal development programmes and various official and non-official documents and studies reveal, the employment situation in the tribal areas are replete with exploitation, pilferage of resources, lack of response, callous attitude of the lower level bureaucracy, and a host of other factors.

Health

The normal health of the tribal people cannot be said to be very bad but their condition often becomes chronic after repeated infections. Besides, the fundamental question that arises in this context is that how much of the modem amenities in public health are percolating down to the tribal strata of Indian society. Before taking up this question let us examine the problems of health facing the tribals.

The tribals suffer from many chronic diseases but the most prevalent taking heavy toll of them are water borne. This is mainly due to the very poor drinking water supply. Even when it is available in plenty, it is mostly dirty and contaminated and consequently the tribals are easily susceptible to intestinal and skin diseases. Diarrhoea, dysentery, cholera, guinea worm, tapeworms, etc., are often the results of this situation.

Deficiency of certain minerals and other elements is also one of the reasons for the diseases. In the Himalayan ranges there is goitre, a disease of the thyroid gland due to iodine deficiency. The incidence of venereal diseases is also high among the tribals of certain parts of Himachal Pradesh, Himalayan Uttar Pradesh, Madhya Pradesh, Bihar, Orissa and Andhra. Tuberculosis which is intensified by nutritional deficiency is also common in many tribes. Besides, most of the tribal people have not yet developed an immunity and when they come in contact with new diseases they fall an easy prey to them. According to Dhebar Commission, one of the diseases of which the tribal is mortally afraid is yaws which occurs in the northern region of the Agency Area in Andhra Pradesh, southern

Orissa, Chanda district of Maharashtra and Bastar district of Madhya Pradesh. Hansen's disease, as leprosy is now called, is common throughout India and has not spared the tribal people. It is extremely bad in the Agency Area in Andhra Pradesh, in Kikir Hills in Assam, Bankura and Purulia districts of West Bengal, Santhal Parganas of Bihar, from Mayurbhanj upto Puri in Orissa. Scabies, ringworm, smallpox and anaemia are also common.

Dhebar Commission is of the view that there is no lack of will on the part of the State Governments to do as much as possible in the direction of the health and medical facilities. There are four principal reasons for the shortfall:

(a) the need for a correct approach;

(b) problem of personnel;

(c) inadequacy of communications; and

(d) rules about supply of medicine.

It is often seen that in many interior areas, tribals are reluctant to come forward for medical treatment because they have got their own system of diagnosis and cure. It is a popular belief among many tribes, especially those inhabiting far flung interior and isolated areas, that disease and misfortune are caused by hostile spirits, ghosts of the dead or the breach of some taboo. It leads to the 'logical' conclusion that what is caused spiritually should be cured spiritually and that is why the tribals of interior areas prefer their own witch doctors, sorcerers, shamans, etc. Medical personnel are contacted as a last resort. This state of affairs becomes further agonising when the physician starts considering the local witch doctor-priest as his rival. Dhebar Commission, interestingly comments that "a pious invalid will send for both the priest and the physician. The priest will pray for him, the physician will give him a pill. The theory is that God answers tne priest's prayer by; making the pill more efficacious: the physician is the instrument through which the divine compassion works". The local sentiments, sensitivities and susceptibilities should be well taken care of if the fruits of the modern medicine have to reach this section of the society. Dhebar Commission cites interesting examples from north-eastern tribal areas where the medical staff has been asked to regard the native medicine-man not as his rival but his ally. The doctors have been directed not to be antagonistic to the system of tribal's diagnosis and cure, cease to sneer at it as 'superstitious' and extend to it the sympathy they would feel for any other kind of faith healing and psychological treatment, of which there are ample examples throughout the world. A wise doctor, under such conditions, will make friendship with local priest, invite him to visit his hospital and let him offer prayers and make sacrifices for his patient, exampling that his own way of treatment is supplementary to his. The work of the local priest-doctor has really valuable psychological function is some cases. If the patient thinks that he is ill because a ghost or a demon has attacked him, only priest can remove the fear and restore confidence to his patient. The essential thing for the medical staff is to take the right attitude to tribal medicine and the tribal priest. "The most successful doctors have been those who have interested themselves in what we may call medical sociology, in such things as the tribal pharmacopoeia, the tribal theory of the influence of dreams on health, tribal methods of diagnosis" (Report of the Scheduled Areas and Scheduled Tribes Commission).

Another problem in public health among the Indian tribes concerns the shortage of medical personnel and qualified nurses in the face of continued belief in the old system and a steadily rising faith in the new. A majority of men and women of the medical profession are very reluctant to offer their services in the rural and tribal areas. This is due to a number of problems. There are difficulties of housing, education for their children and contact with the glamorous world outside. According to Dhebar Commission, the solution lies in having a special cadre for a period of twenty years to secure the medical personnel required for the tribal areas. Simultaneously, efforts must be made to train the local people, so that after twenty years or so, they will be able to staff their own hospitals. Besides, the use of Ayurvedic and herbal medicine should be encouraged because of the fact that the tribal people are already used to herbal remedies and hence there will be little problem of acceptability.

Due to local geographical and ecological condition and relatively not easily accessible areas of tribal habitations, the mobile dispensaries and health centres shall be more purposeful than the static one. However, it is also not realistic to provide these mobile centres with ambulance or large vans which often cannot get along the rough roads or tracks even in fine weather. An ordinary jeep is quite sufficient to take a doctor with his staff and medicines to a number of outlying villages. It might even be considered that an improved type of bullock cart could be sometimes used for the mobile units. In the north-eastern region these units have to move about in the most difficult countryside on foot, and doctors there perform successful operations under the most adverse circumstances in the village camps. It requires sincerity and dedication to work under such conditions.

The rules and procedures of indenting for medical supplies in the remote areas is very frustrating. The scrutiny of stock is made on the basis of the normal requirements of the plains areas. It is forgotten that the medical personnel in tribal areas have not only to treat the patient but also brave the rigours of climate and on many occasions to meet the urgent requirements they require the maintenance of stocks of special remedies at hand.

Another very important problem concerning health in the tribal areas is the addiction of the tribals to spirituous and highly intoxicating liquors and drinks. The indigenous liquor is prepared by fermentation of the rice, millets and other grains. This is the traditional liquor of the tribals which is prepared within the four walls of the home and consumed by all the family members. The second variety is the distilled liquor which the licence holders from the government sell. It is really an intoxicant and carries little food value. The poor tribals, in most cases, are coerced to discontinue the preparation of homemade liquor and made to purchase the distilled liquor from the contractors. After making them addicts of this variety of liquor they are made to part with the property or enter into exploitative bargains. The only practical solution is the banishment of liquor contractors and the harmful liquor from the tribal areas so that they may be left free to brew their own liquor and fulfil one of their important nutritional and cultural needs by themselves.

Drug addiction is another serious health problem with several tribes. Singpho tribe of Arunachal Pradesh is a case in point. From 40,000 about 150 years ago, the Singphos have been reduced to around 1,000. Though recurring wars, disease and malnutrition have played a role but deadly addiction to opium is the chief culprit for their fast dwindling population. It is said that opium has diminished the tribe's fertility, increased the death rate and contributed to the vicious circle of poverty. Almost every house of the Singpho has a small hearth in one of the corners above which hang a blowpipe, a large spatule, a packet of raw tea leaves, opium and tobacco. At any time of the day haggard, skinny tribesmen can be seen making the tobacco-opium concoction that they smoke along with generous swigs of the bitter tea liquor. Opium has become an inseparable part of Singpho life. You can tell a Singpho by smell. They have become too indolent to look after their cattle and lands yet they must buy the opium, mostly by selling the elephants they trap. They have smoked it for decades and their forefathers were induced to it by the British. Official agencies and more importantly some devoted and sincere reformist Singphos and voluntary social organizations have begun a serious campaign to wean the addicts away from opium. Let us hope that they succeed in their efforts.

The speedy spread of health education among the tribals is very crucial. As most of the tribals are illiterate, various audio-visual methods may be adopted to put across to them the basic principles of health and sanitation. Needless to say that for raising the standard of health of the tribals, cooperative endeavour is necessary among the States, the Centre, the non-official organizations and the medical personnel.

Drinking

Drinking among the tribal communities has been widely prevalent. The sentimental attachment of the tribals with one kind of liquor or the other is evident from the fact that mahua tree is treated as sacred by many of the tribals and is worshipped. Drinking can be said to be a part of their social milieu from the times immemorial and has to be considered in that context. In an essentially subsistence non-monetized economy, a healthy drink is as much a produce of the land as any other article of food. It is also seen that most of the locally prepared beverages are not intoxicants. It is an invigorating effect and has some food value also and hence it can be said to have acclimatized to their social situation.

The indigenous beverage prepared by fermentation of rice and millets has been the favourite liquor of the tribals. It is called by different names in different regions. In Madhya Pradesh it is known as Handia, in Assam as Pong, as Zoo in north-eastern region, as Ludgi in Punjab and Himachal Pradesh, as Kalhi in Andhra Pradesh, Pachawe in Bihar and with a variety of names in other tribal areas of the country. The tribals have been preparing and consuming this type of liquor on festive occasions, marriages and funeral and other ceremonial occasions. Even during normal days when the urge for liquor becomes imperative, home brew may be prepared either at home or in jungle and is enjoyed in the company of a few friends.

THE description given above provides a fairly clear picture of the traditional situation. But with the advent of British administration in tribal areas the tribals lost this sort of independence and their mental peace too, in the process. The colonial administration introduced a system of liquor administration alien to the tribal people. Unfortunately, the government and the liquor lobby became interested parties in the drinking of the tribal. Despite their repeated denials that this policy was aimed at increasing the revenue, it was crystal clear that this policy virtually forced the tribal to drink. Tribal Development in the Fifth Plan : Some Basic Policy Papers (1975) quotes W.B. Grickson who stated that introduction of an alien system of outstill in Bastar, not suitable to the local condition, introduced the contractor who was interested in maximising his profit. The old system of a village folk preparing a drink when the village community so desired was discontinued. This resulted in a level of drinking unparalleled anywhere else and untold misery. It quotes another enquiry in Bombay Presidency in 1938 by D. Synington which reveals that "the excise policy of British administration, in making the sale of liquor a source of revenue in the State, had devastating effect on the tribal people."

Now, let us review the situation in the post-independent period. Article 46 of the Constitution enjoins upon the State to protect the members of Scheduled Tribes from social injustice and all forms of exploitation. Article 47 of the Constitution casts a duty upon the State by prescribing that "the State shall regard the raising of the level of nutrition and the standard of living of its people and improvement of public health as among its primary duties and, particular, the State shall endeavour to bring about prohibition of the consumption of liquor, except for medicinal purposes, of intoxicating drinks and of drugs which are injurious to health." Furthermore, removal of poverty has been the core of approach of various plans and the first pre-requisite for the removal of poverty is elimination of exploitation. Keeping this objective in mind, our planners have given highest priority to the elimination of exploitation in all the programmes of tribal development. Unfortunately, one of the worst forms of exploitation of the vulnerable tribals is the prevalent practice of liquor vending.

While studying and analysing the problem of drinking among the tribals and its consequent effects on the tribal economy, Dhebar Commission was surprised to find out that in some places distilled liquor has entered tribal areas after independence. They observed that "we do not understand the need for this type of an arrangement when the tribals have their own favourite beverage which, from social as well as ceremonial point of view, they regard as quite sufficient." Prof. N.K. Bose, the Commissioner for Scheduled Castes and Scheduled Tribes (1970-71) describes liquor vendors as "agents of exploitation" in the tribal areas and the Dhebar Commission recommended the discontinuation of the sale of distilled liquor at once.

The present system of liquor vending is proving to be disaster to the tribal economy. The introduction of distilled liquor sold under licence issued by the government has heaped untold miseries on the poor tribals. It has been observed that "the liquor shops have served as a funnel through which anti-social elements from the advanced areas of the country find easy way into these backward communities. They indulge in all sorts of undesirable activities. The owners of these shops are reported to engage lathaits (muscle men) and create a state of terror in the region. It is alleged that they forcibly enter Adivasi huts without any fear of authority, to check and detect illicit distillation. The licenced shops are also alleged to engage in a large number of Pherrywallas (vendors) who go from village to village and establish informal sub-shops in almost all villages. The tribal community has no relief against these illegal activities. These illegal shops in almost every village become a great temptation to the Adivasi youth. A tribal gets into debt, sometimes imaginary : Land alienation begins notwithstanding the law against it. There are allegations of informal official pressure on the contractor to raise their auction bid. Once the contractor obliges the administration, he takes the administration for granted and does anything he likes in these areas. It is reported that in certain areas there are almost compulsory levies per family or per plough or per marriage in the form of minimum consumption of liquor on the point of threat that if he failed to pay he will be hauled before law for real or imaginary cases of illicit distillation. The strongmen of the liquor trade are able to keep on the right side of lower bureaucracy belonging to various departments, including excise, police, revenue, forest. The tribal considers himself to be alone against this alien groups. Some recent studies tend to show that higher State revenues of excise are positively correlated to high incidence of indebtedness and land alienation (Tribal Development in the Fifth Plan: Some Basic Policy Papers)."

The preceding description clearly shows that the tribal addiction to the distilled liquor is a source of many of his miseries and if the tribal is to come out of his age-old slavery to moneylenders he would have to be weaned away from liquor. But the evils of sale and consumption of distilled liquor are nothing to do with indigenous liquor, because this brand of liquor has been their part of life from times immemorial without causing any disruption in the fabric of their social and economic life.

The pro-distilled liquor lobby in the administration has been raising the bogey of increased consumption of liquor in case the contract system is abolished. On the other hand, genuine protagonists of tribal welfare strongly maintain that since a social norm tends to be within limits, in the present situation the local community will decide when to prepare the beverage. It is likely to be limited to special occasions only. No individual will have the freedom of going and getting the liquor as and when he wishes. Besides, physical limitation of availability of mahua and millet will impose an upper limitation on its consumption.

The picture shall remain incomplete without a brief review of another school of thought. On the other extreme stand protagonists of total prohibition even in tribal areas. Such elements are free to propagate their philosophy but they display their complete ignorance of the ways, values and life of the tribals. They fail to understand that home brew liquor has been a way of life with the tribals and the indigenous beverage, apart from fulfilling some their religious and ritualistic needs, also supplements some of their nutritional deficiency and adds a little cheer to their hard life. Anyway, if they have to give up their own traditional liquor, the initiative has to come from their side. Many of the tribal communities are aware of the evil effects of liquor addiction and consequently in a number of tribal areas strong movements have arisen from time to time which have dissuaded the tribals from consuming distilled liquor. The Bhagat movement in Bihar may be cited in support of the social forces opposing consumption of liquor. Until such a movement spearheaded by the tribals themselves gains ground, nobody should interfere with the normal home brew liquor that the tribals are accustomed to take. Let them attain the consciousness that rice and other cereals can be more suitably utilised and they will give up this habit. But as a first step to prove their concern for the plight of the tribals, the administration will have to banish the liquor magnates from tribal areas and hit their lobbyists harder than ever.

Housing

The problem of housing for the tribal has to be viewed from the aspects of (a) shelter, (b) sanitation, (c) aesthetic tastes, and (d) comparative cost.

Environment occupies an important place in the above mentioned scheme of things. Variations in climate coupled with difference in economic conditions of tribes and types of architecture pose a number of problems. A large number of tribal people are fortunate that they have been endowed with natural bounty. They are living in ideal climatic conditions. To the Chota Nagapur plateau, classic home of a dozen tribes, come many visitors anxious to escape the heat of the plains. The lovely Khasi Hills around Shillong and the Lushi or Naga Hills are cool, bracing and healthy. The Maikal Hills of Madhya Pradesh, though less elevated, are cool and invigorating for most of the year. The Nilgiri Hills, home of the Toda and Kota tribes, are famous as tourist resort (Dhebar Commission). But the Brahmaputra Valley of Assam inhabited by many of the plains tribals is oppressively hot in summer. Some of the dense forest districts are dry, airless and dusty and many areas like the plains of Banda and Mirzapur districts U.P., the abode of Kols, are dry, rocky, hot and always prone to water scarcity. At the opposite extreme, in the high mountain areas of sub-Himalayan ranges, the climate is extremely severe and the tribal people there have to face the rigours of snow and wind, rain and storm, glacier and avalanche. A number of tribes lives in the seismic belt, as in some areas of Assam, where they are exposed to the vagaries of earth movements. However, man knows how to adapt himself, even in extreme climates. His housing, like his clothing, is designed to keep out heat or resist cold. In hot areas of north-eastern regions, houses are built with bamboo framework which lets in plenty of air. Where the soil is consistently damp and the rainfall heavy, houses are generally arranged on piles well above the ground to keep them dry. In the cold areas, many of the houses are of stone or in the nature of log cabins.

House sense coupled with utility and artistic value is another aspect of housing among the tribal people. Many of the tribes have developed a real pride in having good houses. On the other hand, there are a number of small tribes who completely lack any houses sense. They are content to live in miserable hovels surrounded by insanitary conditions, while some other like the Birhors live in houses of leaves. They have perfected this art to such an extent that a Birhors tribal whose hut leaks is fined by the community. The Garo, Mishmi, Naga and Reang tribes of north-eastern region are famous for building beautiful houses combining utility and artistic value. They are raised well off the ground and are suitably ventilated. The people make good floors, weave bamboo expertly and keep their houses spotlessly clean. Same is the case with Gond houses in Madhya Pradesh, Bagata and Koya houses in Andhra Pradesh, Gadaba and Saora houses in Orissa and Oraon and Santhal houses in Bihar, which are usually well constructed with thick mud walls on which the people model or paint designs and pictures. Sometimes the floors and walls are washed with red or white clay or cow-dung.

Housing is one sector of tribal life which is not very gloomy but not all tribals are so fortunate. Particularly in the plains, some are landless and homeless and their plight is really miserable. A notable example of this situation is Yenadi tribe of Andhra Pradesh who live on the sufferance of climate, police and local landlords. It is tribes like the Yenadi who need special attention in any scheme of housing because they and their like make use of the vacant land on both sides of the P.W.D. roads and canals for housing purposes until they are driven away again.

The study Team of Planning Commission on Tribal Development (1969) is of the view that in the formulation of housing schemes for tribals a distinction should be made between plains tribals and tribals living in hilly areas, and that the housing should fully conform to the local needs, tastes and traditions. As a matter of example, it says that tiled houses are good but suitable thatched houses may be better in terms of comfort and cost. Further, a tribal knows to plug a leak in a thatched house but is helpless when a tile gives way.

Most of the houses provided by the government for needy tribals suffer from unimaginative and misfit designs. What generally happens is that some architect in the State capital who has never seen a good tribal house or visited a tribe, draws up a type plan which is followed automatically throughout the State. Any scheme of housing on stereotyped lines without taking into consideration tribal customs, practices and superstitions is bound to meet disapproval by the prospective inhabitants of the houses. Consultation with the tribals to ascertain their wishes regarding the designs of house should be made a condition precedent to the approval of any tribal housing scheme. This is not to suggest that houses built for tribals should not be improvements should be in accordance with their ideas and superstitions regarding layout and design. It may also be necessary that the selection of sites and construction of houses are preceded by the due observance of tribal rites and rituals.

The forest department is another great hindrance in solving the housing problem of the tribals. The unimaginative and reckless bureaucracy has posed such restrictions on the use of forest wealth by the tribals that the entire forest policy has become counter productive as far as the tribal welfare is concerned. It is very difficult for a tribal to obtain a permit from a forest official to collect the necessary material. In the absence of liberalised rules, the tribals have to faced a number of odds in obtaining their requirement of timber for house building or repairing purposes. This not only adds misery to their already hard life but also gives rise to sense of alienation and discontent often leading to separatist and secessionist movements.

Housing schemes for such small and impoverished groups as the Yendadis, Yerkulas, and Sugalis of Andhra Pradesh, Katkaris of Maharashtra, Dublas and Naiks of Gujarat, Gujjars of Himachal Pradesh, Paniyans of Kerala and Kurubas of Karnataka, etc., deserve top priority. But it should be kept in mind that even an extensive house is useless for a tribal if he feels uncomfortable in unfamiliar surroundings.

Education

Like all other sectors of socio-economic life, educationally the tribal people at different levels of development but, on the whole, formal education has made very little impact on tribal groups. In the light of the past efforts it is not shocking because prior to 1950, the Government of India had no direct programme for the eduction of the tribals. With the adoption of the constitution, the promotion of education of Scheduled Tribes has become a special responsibility of the Central as well as of the State Government.

The growth of formal education among the tribal populations of the country may be gauged from the facts yielded by the census data. The census figures of 1931 disclosed that only 0.7 percent of the tribal people were literate. This percentage rose to 32.60 percent in 1991 against 52.2 per cent for the entire country. The literacy rate among the tribal women is obviously much lower. So, the total picture of spread of education among the tribals is not very encouraging, barring a few tribes of north-eastern region like Khasi, the Garo, etc., who tremendously benefited from the vast network of Christian missionary institutions.

Since education is probably the most effective instrument for ensuring equality of opportunity, the tribal people are lagging far behind their more fortunate fellow countrymen due to lack of education. Let us analyse the reasons for this state of affairs.

Social Factors

More allocation of funds and opening of schools do not go far in providing education to the tribal people. Social factors play very important role in this respect. Formal education has not been necessary for the members of tribal societies to discharge their social obligations. Hence they should be prepared to accept education and it should be presented to them in such a way as to cut the barriers of superstition and prejudice.

Barring the tribal communities of north-eastern region, it is still a widespread feeling among the tribal that education makes their boys defiant and insolent and alienates them from the rest of their society, while the girls turn modern or go astray. Since some of their educated boys felt alienated and cut off their links with their families and villages after getting education and good employment, some of the tribal groups vehemently oppose the spread of education in their midst. Besides, some of their superstitions and myths also play their part. Some tribal groups believe that their gods shall be angry if they send their children to schools run by 'outsiders'.

Economic Factors

Some economic factors, too, are responsible for lack of interest shown by the tribal people in getting education. Since most of the tribal people are living in a abject poverty under subsistence economy, it is not easy for most of them to send their children to schools thus losing two healthy hands in their struggle for survival. Verrier Elwin (1963) very appropriately sums up the situation in the following way:

> "For a tribal family, to send its grown up girl or boy to school, is essentially a matter of economics; and entails dislocation in the traditional pattern of division of labour... many parents cannot just afford to send their children to school".

L.R.N. Srivastava (1968), on the basis of his survey of educational situation among the tribals, also supports this view by saying that poor economic condition of the tribal societies is a great hinderance to successful education. Almost all the tribes-whether food gatherers, hunters, fishermen, shifting cultivators, or settled agriculturists lack enough food to maintain the family for the whole year. Education, therefore, is a luxury to them which they can hardly afford. Each school going child in a tribal family is an economic unit and contributes to the family income. If the child is taken away from his normal economic work to attend school, the family is deprived of the little income which he brings. Instead, the parents have to feed the child out of their earnings which further reduces the economic stability of the family. According to the present system of education any economic benefit a tribal child can bring to his family will be only after ten or fifteen years of schooling. The parents have neither the patience nor the foresight to wait for such a long period. They can, however, be convinced easily if the education for them can be made productive right from the very beginning.

Lack of Interest in Formal Education

Sharma (1976) has rightly pointed out that the "urban middle class oriented educational system has got superimposed on the entire nation both in terms of its structure and content". In many states tribal children are taught through the same books which form the curriculum of non-tribal children of the urban and rural areas of the rest of the State. Obviously, the content of such books rarely appeals the tribal children who come from different cultural backgrounds. Stories of scientific and technological progress, founders of modern India, history and geography of the country, etc., of course, form necessary part of any curriculum but the situation demands that their education should start with the teaching of demography, history and ecology of their own region, their neighbourhood and the State. National consciousness should not be imposed from above or outside, but they should be made aware of it in a systematic manner. L.R.N. Srivastava (1968) puts the problem in a more lucid way by saying that "the tribal child who lives in an isolated and far off place untouched by the currents of modern civilization can hardly assimilate any information about history and geography of the country, about the industrial and technical development, uninteresting and out dated stores and about the important personalities unknown and unheard of in tribal areas. He has to be given a complete information about his neighbouring communities, his village life, social organization, belief and practices, and then pass on to the national scene where we can introduce him to India which is his country. Then only he can be able to grasp what is happening in his village, in his state, in his country, and if possible, in other countries of the world".

This is a well known fact that education in India has spread in a hapazard way without taking care of future needs. Tribal education also could not escape this anomaly and became instant failure due to apathy, indifference and lack of interest of the tribal people in formal education. S.N. Rath (1981) has put forward the following scheme which is not only recommendatory in nature but also analyses the malady with clarity.

1. Under the traditional tribal set-up a child enters adulthood with confidence. He knows his environment thoroughly, knows how to construct his own house, cultivate his field, weave his cloth; in short he acquired all the skills to lead a reasonably comfortable life within the limitations of his culture. The simple skill of reading and writing acquired in an overformal school is no match for this. We cannot afford to push him back to his environment naked. Therefore, a balance should be struck somewhere to evolve a system of curricula where the tribal school, in addition being a part of the national scheme, should have a supplementary curriculum adopted to the specific local conditions.
2. The supplementary curriculum should be biased towards crafts and should inculcate a sense of dignity of labour, qualities of cooperation and social discipline. Certain tribal activities like agriculture, dancing, hunting, tribal games and archery must be allowed to find fullest expression in the extra-curricular activities of the school, thus providing some continuity of the traditional values and forms of organization.
3. A scheme is to be worked out through which the school children shall be able to link up the school and the teacher with their parents and the tribal activities. The school has to act as a centre of dispersal of simple technical know how beyond the skills of reading and writing and become an effective agent of social change. This student-teacher-parent continuum should be able to generate a congenial atmosphere, so that the broad purpose of education, which is to enable an average citizen to comprehend the social, political, economic and other processes and forces around him, is fully served.
4. Needless to say this utopian scheme largely depends upon suitably trained and dedicated teachers.

Suitable Teachers

Lack of suitable teachers is one of the major reasons for the slow growth of education in tribal areas. Most of the teachers employed for imparting education to the tribal children show little appreciation of the tribal way of life and value system. They approach the tribal people with a sense of superiority and treat them as 'savage' and 'uncivilized' and hence fail to establish proper rapport with their students. The Scheduled Areas and Scheduled Tribes Commission's Report has analysed this situation in the proper perspective. It says that a teacher in the tribal areas must have a thorough knowledge of tribal life and culture. He must speak the tribal language. Only so can he be in a position to act as a friend, philosopher and guide to the tribal people. Actually the gulf between teacher and taught can be best reduced by appointing teachers from the tribal community itself or a separate cadre of teachers for tribal areas, with some inducements, should be created to serve the educational needs of the tribal society.

Lack of Facilities

One of the major problem in tribal education is that of language. Most of the tribal languages and dialects are in the most rudimentary stage and there is hardly any written literature. Hence, the problem of medium of instruction has been a great irritant. Most of the states impart education to tribal and non-tribal children alike through the medium of the regional language, thus making education uninteresting to many of the tribal people. It also hurts tribal sentiments for his own language. Hence, some way out has to be found to make education meaningful and productive for the tribal people.

Nature of habitat of the tribals is also responsible for slow growth of education. Most of the tribal villages are scattered. This entails long travels to attend schools. Unless the school is situated very close to their villages and its site approved by the local people the result shall not be encouraging.

School building, in some cases, also plays an important role in the growth of education among the tribal fold. Due to mis-management, bungling and sometimes financial constraints, the building is seldom suitable to run an educational institution. S.N. Rath (1981) has given a very graphic description of the situation by saying that dilapidated, often roofless structures standing as lone sentinels in the midst of a featureless sport away from the village are often pointed out as schools.

Another factor related with the problem is the number of teachers. Most primary schools in tribal areas are "single teacher-managed whose presence in the school is more an exception than a rule".

Overburdening may be one of the possible factors for this state of affairs. It will be unjust to expect a teacher to follow a non-stop six hourly schedule of teaching as a matter of daily routine.

The enthusiasm of tribal people in the education of their children also depends considerably on the timing of school hours in different seasons. The school timings should not clash with their important socio-economic activities and events. People running schools for the tribals have often killed their interest in education by their unimaginative planning. Local conditions and requirements of the people should get top priority in any scheme for running these schools and a balance has to be maintained between the needs of the family and the needs of education.

Stagnation and Wastage

To many observers of the situation, the problem of education in tribal areas is the problem of wastage. It is not that wastage and stagnation are peculiar to the tribal communities alone but the extent of wastage is much larger in their case. The problem of absenteeism is a serious one in tribal areas. One sees a large number of students on rolls but the actual attendance is really low, and the number of students passing out at the final examinations is even lower. The real problem is to create such economic conditions as could be conducive to the students developing sufficient interest in their studies.

Communication

Tribals have been living in isolation for centuries past. The main reason for this isolation is lack of communication. To develop the tribal areas and to improve their economic condition, communication is a sine qua non and its importance in the tribal economy hardly needs any reiteration and emphasis.

The problem of communication in tribal areas may be examined from two angles: (i) needs of the tribals; and (ii) development of the tribal areas as a whole.

It is seen that communication may not always prove to be a blessing. It also facilitates the entry of prospective exploiters and other anti-social elements from non-tribal areas, who, taking advantage of the innocence of the tribals, exploit them in a variety of ways. But at the same time, the march of events cannot be halted and the needs of defence, industrialization, mining and development can also not be ignored. However, one must keep the needs of the tribals in mind before throwing open any area.

No matter what the protagonists of the tribals' cause think, the communication has been spreading in tribal areas "muchmore speedily than we imagine. It may be that in a majority of cases the development of the tribal consciousness may not keep pace with the development of communications. Realistically speaking, therefore, balance will have to be struck so that this unprecedented expansion does not place an inordinate strain on the tribals and wherever the new roads go, the State will have to protect them against exploitation" (S.N. Rath).

According to the Scheduled Areas and Scheduled Tribes Commission, the problem of communications in that tribal areas may be considered from five aspects:

(i) roads and other communication indispensable for the national needs and defence;

(ii) roads and other communication indispensable for the industrial development

(iii) roads and other communication necessary for administration;

(iv) roads and other communication needed from the points of view of trade and commercial interests; and

(v) roads and other communication needed in the interests of the tribals.

According to the Commission, a correct approach will be to give the highest priority to (i) and (v); second priority to (ii) and (iii) and in relation to (iv) decide only after a close study on the basis of the trade and commercial data available and of the relative advantage to the tribal population.

Roads are the most important means of communication as far as the tribal population is concerned. If we view the situation from the aspect of comparative development, we see that there is a long leeway to be made up. The present all India average length of roads per hundred square kilometers in tribal areas is very poor in comparison with other rural and urban areas. Many of the rivers in scheduled areas are still unbridged and condititons are such that for several months in a year these areas are cut of from the rest of the world.

As far as the planning is concerned, a tribal will be more interested in connecting his village with the forest or the weekly market, hospital or the school for his children. If these roads can be used all the year round and can be widened to take carts and jeeps, it will be an added advantage. In fixing the relative priorities in this regard, consultation with the local people will go a long way in fulfilling the genuine needs of the tribals. Proper use of locally available materials, like lime and stone, may considerably lessen the cost and consequently open more avenues for fast expansion. If the road construction work is taken up in the off season when the tribals have practically nothing to do, they can earn some money to fulfil their needs for cash.

Many of the tribes are very good cultivators of some good varieties of rice, foodgrains and fruits. With a good network of roads, their production will be able to reach far off markets and they will be fetching handsome returns. In the absence of adequate means of communications they have to sell their produce at comparatively low prices and are easily browbeaten by the local non-tribal trader to sell their produce at throw away prices. Top priority should be given to the construction of village roads, bridle paths and motorable roads.

Post and Telegraph services are slowly percolating into the remotest parts of tribal areas but unfortunately the mail carrier (runner) and other staff are not regular employees of the Post and Telegraph department. The runners are usually engaged only for the period that the post can be carried, after which they are left to fend for themselves.

Post offices in these distant places are manned usually by teachers and no regular staff is appointed. Under such conditions the general public are the sufferers because those manning these services do not work with a sense of obligations. But if the tribal people are involved in the management of postal services in a meaningful way, it will go a long way in not only providing gainful employment to the tribal people but also in expanding and improving postal facilities in the hitherto neglected areas.

Telephones and air communication are the other sectors where much is left to be done. There are a lot of places that are neither connected with telephones nor by air communication. These facilities would be boon to the tribal village in distress. Although, many tribal areas are fortunate in having these services run by defence and police forces, they should be thrown open to the tribals free of cost in the absence of regular services.

Development of communications no doubt will provide greater opportunities for the tribal folk to develop national consciousness and a healthier intellectual horizon. Also, the importance of communication in the realm of tribal economy hardly needs any emphasis but what ought to be guarded against is the danger of greedy and cunning elements from the plains invading tribal areas to exploit the poor tribals. The history of expanding communications throughout the globe bears testimony to the fact that tribals everywhere have been thrown open. The best solution in such a situation seems to be taking all sorts of precautions and safeguards to protect interests before throwing any of their areas open.

Industrialization & Urbanization

Abject poverty and ruthless exploitation have been the plight of tribals everywhere and the Indian tribals are no exception. Ironically, the regions where our tribals people live are some of the richest in terms of natural bounties. They not only hold vast forest wealth but also contain endless deposits of minerals. With the advent of independence, numerous measures were taken to exploit them for raw materials and large power and irrigation projects. Rourkela, Bhilai, Ranchi, Bailadella, Hirakud, etc., are some of the milestone on the economic and industrial map of modern India.

The natural corollary of this development should have been tne economic upliftment of the concerned tribal population. But this did not happen. They were deprived of their lands under statutory conditions and were paid meagre amount in cash as compensation which they frittered away in drinking and celebrating tribal rituals. Most of them became landless and moneyless in the process. Since no steps were taken before hand to train tribal youths in the craft which was required in these industrial projects, they became losers from all angles. No doubt, these programmes are a boon to the nation, yet tribal interests cannot be sacrificed. In the initial stages a good number of tribals no doubt got employment in unskilled jobs but once the construction work came to an end they found themselves for skilled and semi-skilled jobs. Now, hordes of outsiders invaded these areas and settled there after getting employment. The bewildered tribals were left in the lurch to fend for themselves. Being unskilled, and untrained for any technical job and having no place to back to, they settled on the fringes and peripheries of these vast industrial empires as 'rejects'.

Marx, while writing on Indian tribals, has very sharply and rightly commented that in the process of industrialization he loses his original world but cannot derive any benefit from the 'new world' which only adds an element of agony and melancholy to the whole episode.

THE problems confronting the tribal people as a result of industialization in their areas may be discussed and summarized in the following way:

Displacement and Rehabilitation

The expectation that the industrialization of tribal areas would help in improving the economic condition of the tribal communities has proved to be largely illusory. Major industrial projects like the mammoth steel plants located in tribal territory far from providing employment opportunities to the tribals, have operated to their detriment by uprooting them from their hearths and homes and offering them no satisfactory alternative to the traditional methods by which they eked out a living in their old geographical and technological environment. The attitude of the projects, even in the public sector, has been that their responsibility to the tribals ended with the payment of compensation for the land acquired from them. A meagre cash compensation is on frittered away on drink and useless rituals and destitution is the price the poor tribal has had to pay for the establishment of industries in the areas inhabited by them.

The major power and irrigation projects, such as Maithon, Konar and Panchet in Bihar, Mandira, Machkund and Hirakud in Orissa, the steel projects of Rourkela, Durgapur, Bhilai, Ranch and Jamshedpur in Orissa, West Bengal, Madhya Pradesh and Bihar respectively are among the many undertakings that have resulted in a substantial displacement of the tribal problem of deep moral significance. The situation is far from happy for the following reasons:

(a) Very few of them have taken advantage of the agricultural facilities offered in the reclamation camp. The attraction of easy money and industrial employment has been too strong, especially for the younger generation.

(b) The alternative land offered by the authorities for cultivation is not irrigable and cannot offer adequate return to maintain the families on it.

(c) The cash compensation that is given is seldom utilized for productive purposes. It is almost invariably used up on daily living expenses until alternative employment is found.

Further, no space is provided to the tribals in the newly constructed township on the site of the project. They are left to construct and inhabit dirty slums on the outskirts or on the vacant lands in the township itself. Needless to say, these slums are without any civic amenities like tap water, garbage disposal, drainage etc.

Psychological and Social-Cultural Adjustment

Industrialization throws open the entire area for all sorts of people and the iron curtain of isolation and secrecy is shattered to pieces. Das and Banerji (1964) have enumerated the following changes coming up under the impact of industrialization with which the tribals have to adjust themselves:

(1) Being agriculture-minded for generations, the tribal factory worker has not yet been fully reconciled to factory life where he works for economic gain only.

(2) Being accustomed to lighter and seasonal work as farmer for generation, a tribal factory worker at heart does not like the hard labour or routine factory work, and this affects his productivity.

(3) Industrialization has tended to produce mostly nuclear type of families among the tribals living in an industrial area leading of inter-personal of individualistic attitude and consequent lessening of inter-personal attachment in the family. This is mostly due to economic pressure and lesser faciiities not pcrmitting maintenance of large family in an industrial area.

(4) Traditional authority of the elders in the family has been considerably weakened.

(5) Traditional restrictions about marriage are often being flouted by the younger generation, sometimes even to the extent of marrying outside the tribe. Divorces have become more frequent.

(6) Traditional pattern of ritualistic observances in marrying has been much simplified or shortened on financial grounds and from lack of sufficient leisure.

(7) Contact with people of different communities and different regions has broadened the view of the tribals and helped them get rid of superstitious beliefs and customs to a great extent. This has further accelerated the understanding of other peoples and their cultures which has been imperceptibly imbibed by them to an appreciable extent.

(8) Tribals are generally advancing towards integration with the general mass of people, but at the same time they are rapidly losing their traditional social-cultural characteristics.

Another point with which the tribals are trying to adjust is the change of unit of labour. In their traditional agrarian economy, the family was functioning more or less as a unit of labour. In the factories, however, it is the individual who is wanted. Since not much data are available about the problems of psychological and social-cultural adjustment it is difficult to gauge the impact of industrialization from this particular angle. But one thing is fairly clear. From the membership of a closed society he is being induced to accommodate himself in a universal pattern of cosmopolitan society without education, equipment and resources. There is a crisis of identity.

Migration

Deep emotional attachment with one's native place or traditional habitat has been a universal phenomenon. Simple societies or primitive groups are more attached with their land because of their traditional relative isolation. Thus, one may safely conclude that migration does not, usually, take place under normal circumstances.

Migration is not an old practice among the tribal communities. The possibilities and avenues of migration have increased only with advent of fast and easy means of transport and communication. The tribal migration may be understood from two angles. The first is through Pushed Out Factors and the second is Pulled Into Factors that force the tribals to leave their lands. In the first category come such factors as socio-economic exploitation, starvation, diseases and natural calamities like drought, food, epidemics etc. In the second category come attractions of employment, better income and better living conditions. Sometimes, the migration is the result of both these types of factors and a number of tribes have migrated to cities, townships and other far off places.

Tribal migration is not a very recent phenomenon and the examples of the tribes of Bihar and Bengal like the Oraon, Santhal, Ho, Munda etc. going over to the tea plantations of north Bengal and Assam bear testimony to this fact. But an organised type of migration through the middlemen and the contractors is definitely a new phenomenon not going back beyond 20-25 years. The enclaves of prosperity and 'green revolution' have been attracting the poor and exploited tribals. There has been large scale migration to Punjab, Haryana and Delhi from the tribes of Bihar, Orissa,

Madhya Pradesh and West Bengal; because of disturbed conditions in Punjab, migration to its big farms alongwith the Haryana's has virtually come to an end but migration to other regions continues. Previously, it was largely 'seasonal migration' but of late the tendency of 'Permanent migration' is more visible. According to the surveys undertaken by the concerned agencies and the newspaper reports the plight of many tribal migrants is not good. They have fallen victims to all sorts of exploitation including sexual abuse. Many of them are made addict of opium or other narcotics by the landlords or brick kiln owners and are forced to work for prolonged hours against meargre wages.

A number of social scientists are of the view that migration is a natural and rational phenomenon in which migration taken place from the labour surplus areas to the labour deficient areas. Whatever may be the interpretations the fact remains that the tribal people are much more vulnerable to exploitation than the other segments of the society. One of the reasons of it is that they are not organized but wherever they become united and get radical left leadership they are able to fight exploitation.

Depopulation

Depopulation presents a tragic aspect of tribal India. It can be understood through two angles the social-cultural aspect, and the biological aspect. If a human group leaves its traditional habitat and migrates to an unknown place in such a way as not to leave any clue to their whereabouts, they become a case of total depopulation for their erstwhile neighbours, administrators and social scientists. Many a tribal groups have 'vanished' in this way because of exploitation, deprivation, negligence or natural calamities. In the district and region wise compilation of tribes, castes and communities done by such British administrators as Thurston, Crooks, etc. we come across the descriptions of many tribal communities we do not come across these days. But here, we shall be focussing our attention on the biological aspect of depopulation which is universally accepted.

It is a paradox that on the one hand the population of large tribes viz. Bhil, Gond, Santhal etc. has been increasing on the average national rate, a number of other tribes are moving towards total extinction. The majority of such depopulating tribes inhabit different regions of south India. Most of these tribes are primitive food gatherers - hunters and they have been recognised by the administration as primitive tribal communities. Special projects have been launched for their socio-economic development so that they are able to survive. This special category consists of about 80 tribes. Some of the most glaring examples of depopulation are the Chero, Mal Pahariya, Birhor etc. from Bihar, Chenchu from Andhra Pradesh, Kadar from Kerala, the primitive tribes of the Andaman and Nicobar islands especially Onge. Jarwa and Great Andamanese and the Raji of Uttar Pradesh. In this category the tribes like the Toda of Tamil Nadu and the Jounsari (Khasha) of Uttar Pradesh may also be included whose populations have been either stagnating or showing only marginal increase.

The main factors responsible for the depopulating trend of such tribes are radical changes in ecological conditions, abrupt disturbance in man-nature equilibrium (mainly because of rapid deforestation) and the dehumanization of the forest policy and its cruel and faulty implementation. Paucity of safe drinking water, malnutrition and undernutrition and a number of diseases as epidemics have virtually become the fate of these tribes.

In the welfare administration is really serious in doing something for the tribal populations they should not allow or introduce abrupt and sudden changes in their socio-economic life. The forest policy should be rationalised and humanised, health care schemes should be launched on war footing, ruthless exploitation should be checked and education should be taken on top priority to break the barriers of fatalism and superstitions.

FOREST RELATED PROBLEMS, LAWS, POLICIES AND RELATED ISSUES

Chapter 14

The Tribal people everywhere have lived in intimate relationship with forests and their entire existence has been linked with forests due to historical factors. Forests have been sustaining their inhabitants. In fact there existed a 'symbiotic relationship' between the tribals and the forests. Forests have been their abode and source of livelihood. Thus, it has been a unanimously held view that forest economy is tribal economy and vice versa.

Not only their economic life but the religious and religio-magical beliefs of the tribal people have been rotating round the forests. Many a flora and fauna have been their objects of worship (Totems). Thus, the tribal people were able to achieve such a harmony that has always been a matter of envy for the non-tribals.

In the mid 19th century the importance of relationship between wildlife and botanical wealth and soil, moisture, rainfall and general environment was realised and it was decided to extend the authority of the state to the hitherto neglected parts of the territory. Following gradual extension of states' authority the 'lords' and 'masters' of forests were continually put under lot of pressures and inconveniences. Following is the chronicled narration of evolution of forest policy alongwith various measures taken by the state to manage the forests.

The First Forest Act of 1865:

This Act was the first attempts in the direction of regulation of collection of forest produce by the forest dwellers. In the process, the socially regulated practices of the local people were restrained by law.

The Forest Act of 1878:

This was the second step in the direction of further extension of states' authority over forests. The control over forests was further tightened by prohibiting certain acts such as trespass or pasturing of cattle and declaring certain activities as forest offences. Imprisonment and fines were also prescribed for these offences.

The First Forest Policy 1894:

The First Forest Policy envisaged, for the first time, the regulation of rights and restriction of privileges of the users in the forests. These regulations and restrictions were justified only when the advantages to be gained by the general public were great and the cardinal principles observed i.e., the rights and the privileges of individuals must be limited in the larger public interests. It is to be noted here that it was only in 1894 that the forest officials seriously appeared on the scene and claimed the authority to limit and regulate the traditional tribal rights over forests.

The Indian Forest Act 1927:

In continuation of the measures already taken, this act was an attempt to regulate further people's rights over forest land and forest produce. Through this act, elaborate provisions were made in the direction of further extension of states' authority and control over the forests. Forest offences were defined as offences punishable under the act. This Act created an extremely powerful and adequately protected executive consisting of Forest Officers of Indian Forest Service, State Forest Service, Rangers, Foresters, and Forest Guards. This Act gave the powers to the executive to make rules which were not necessarily permanent in nature. These officers enjoyed legal powers. For example Section 64 of Indian Forest Act states that any Forest Officer without a warrant could arrest any person against whom a 'reasonable' suspicion exists of his motive to pilferage forest or forest wealth and his act was punishable with imprisonment for one month or upwards. Section 68 deals with power to compound the offences while Section 70 deals with the power to seize and impound the cattle of the offender under Cattle Trespass Act 1871.

Scuh provisions, as stated above, made even some of the lower level officials of forest department like Rangers and Forest Guards very strong. Since it is these officials who regularly come in contact with the forest dwellers, they used their power arbitrarily and played havoc with the lives of the tribal people. The story of their interaction with the tribals is replete with the instances in which these officials claimed indemnity for acts done in good faith according to Section 74 and got away. It further states that no suit shall be against a public servant for acts done in good faith and that all forest officials are deemed public servants. In 1935 Forest was transferred to the state list according to the Government of India Act 1935.

The National Forest Policy 1952:

When the post independence India formulated its first National Forest Policy in 1952, it belied all hopes of a just and generous treatment of the tribal people. It followed, by and large, the limes of the British administration where the tribals had virtually no statutory right but enjoyed only certain concessions/privileges such as right to take water for agricultural purposes, digging of wells and canals for agricultural purposes, free grazing in open forests, removal of timber, bamboos, reeds, canes, etc. for construction and repair of houses and for agricultural implements, collection of dead word for domestic use as fuel, collection of grass for cattle and for thatching their huts, fishing and hunting ***excluding*** the protected fauna and cultivation of forest land.

The President of India under the Article 339 of the Constitution of India appointed a commission in 1960 under the chairmanship of late UN Dheber, popularly known as Dhebar Commission. In its comprehensive analysis it also studied the forest policy vis-a-vis tribals. The Commission noted that the tribals who had hitherto treated himself as the lord of the forest was made subservient to the forest department. The traditional rights of the tribals were no longer recognised as rights. "In 1894 they became rights and privileges and in 1952 they became rights and concessions. Now they are being considered as concessions only."

The Recommendations of N.C.A. -1976 and Tribal Rights

The Commission recommended a drastic reduction in the people's rights over forests and forest produce. It was stated that the free supply of the forest produce to the local people and their rights and privileges have brought destruction to the forests so it is necessary to reverse the process. The local people have not contributed much towards the maintenance or regulation of the forests. The Commission recommended strengthening of the forest legislation by the enactment of a revised All India Forest Act. The recommendations of the Commission were rejected by the Forest Ministers Conference in 1982. In 1976, the Forests subject was brought in to the concurrent list through the Constitution 42nd amendment empowering the Centre to make laws. Consequently, the Forest Conservation ordinance was promulgated in October 1980. Later, it was passed by the Parliament and became an act.

B.K. Roy Burman Committee on Forests and Tribals

The Ministry of Home Affairs under the Chairmanship of Prof. B.K. Roy Burman, an eminent anthropologist appointed a committee in 1980 to re-orient the forest policy to serve the tribal economy. The Committee submitted its report in 1982. It emphasised the importance of forests in tribal life. Besides getting free fuel, fodder and wood for house construction the tribals also earn one third of their income from the sale of the Minor Forest Produce.

The Committee noted that the forest operations, by and large, are the revenue earners for the Government. The tribal economy has figured little among the parameters of the forest policy and, at best, the tribals continue to be the wage earners. The Committed pointed out that the benefits should flow to the tribal people through the imaginative forestry programmes and conservation and recognition of their traditional skills. In other words, the individual tribal, the local tribal community and national interest should be regarded as the three corners of a triangular forest policy. Forest policy must fulfill three sets of needs. These are a) ecological security, b) food, fruit, c) fuel, fodder and other domestic needs of particularly the rural and tribal population.

The Committee also recommended that wherever the community rights exist on the forest land they should be recognised and adapted to serve the urgent needs of the soil and water management and reafforestation of tracts by suitable species.

National Committee on Development of Backward Areas (1980)

The Planning Commission appointed a committee on development of backward areas in 1980. The Committee followed the view expressed by the National Commission on Agriculture and recommended for the curtailment of the rights of the tribal communities over the forest land and forest produce.

The Committee was of the view that the rights in the forest could be sustained only if there was a comprehensive frame for the protection, use and development of forests in which the community and the individual must assume the responsibility for creation of the new forestry wealth and its protection.

The Committee further pointed out that the Minor Forest Produce should not be treated as source of revenue for the state but it should provide maximum return to the tribal so that the economic interests created in the maintenance of forests with the possibility of sustained income accruing to the individual regularly from its collection. All leases for collection and marketing of Minor Forest Produce should go to the cooperatives of tribals.

The Committee For Review of Rights and Concessions - 1980

The Ministry of Agriculture constituted a Committee to review the rights and concessions of tribal under the chairmanship of Shri M.S. Chaudhary, the former Chief Secretary of Madhya Pradesh in 1961. All other members of the Committee were the former forest officials.

The Committee observed that the concessions and privileges granted to the tribals in respect of fuelwood, timber, grazing, etc. were confined only to the villages in and around the periphery of the forest areas and generally only in respect of non-reserved forests. The rights, privileges and concessions in areas not under the British rule were mostly undefined. The Commission recommended that the exercise of rights and concessions should be restricted only to those tribals and other rural people residing within the distance of 8 K.M. from the existing forests.

The Committee also recommended that the beneficiaries should not enter the forest to remove the forest produce and that the supplies should be made available through the departmental depots opened outside the forest for this purpose. It also recommended that the barter or the sale of the produce obtained through such concessions should be stopped. The Committee further stated that the total quantum of rights and concessions be restricted to what the forests can bear. The Committee also recommended that the grazing of cattle in the forests should be severely restricted to the carrying capacity of the forest.

New National Forest Policy -1980 and The Tribal Rights

It states that the principal aim of the forest policy must be to ensure environmental stability and the maintenance of ecological balance including atmospheric equilibrium, which are vital to the sustenance of all life forms - human, animal and plant. The derivation of the economic benefit must be subordinated to the principal aim.

One of the striking features of the new forest policy is its reference to the relationship of the tribal communities with the forests. It states that having regard to the symbiotic relationship between the tribal people and the forests, a primary task of all the agencies responsible for the forest management including the forest corporations should be to associate the tribal closely in the protection, regeneration, and development of forests as well as to provide gainful employment to the people living in and around the forest While safeguarding the customary rights and interests of such people the forestry programmes should pay special attention to the following :

1. To reduce the illegal cutting and for the exploitation of the forest the contractors should be replaced by the forest corporations, labour cooperatives and the tribal cooperatives.
2. Special attention should be paid to the protection, regeneration and optimum collection of the minor forest produce along with institutional arrangements for its marketing.
3. Family oriented schemes for improving the status of the tribal beneficiaries.
4. Integrated area development programmes to meet the needs of the tribal economy in and around the forest areas.

The above mentioned provisions are some of the important provisions of the new forest policy with regards to the tribals.

As far as the rights and concessions enjoyed by the tribals the new forest policy categorically stated that the rights and concessions enjoyed by them should be fully protected. Their domestic requirements of fuelwood, fodder, minor forest produce and construction of timber should be allowed to be fulfilled through forest produce. This is the most welcome feature since it emphasises the needs of the forest dwellers for the first time since the forest administration began in India (the draft of this policy is enclosed in the annexure (XIII) part of this book).

Forest Conservation Act - 1980 Vs. Forest Policy 1988

Recently, the Central Government has brought some amendments in the Forest Conservation Act 1980 which are almost in contravention with the National Forest Policy 1988.

Under these amendments the state governments cannot, without previous sanction of the centre, assign by way of lease or otherwise any forest land or any portion thereof to any person or to any authority, corporation, agency or any other organization not owned, controlled or managed by the Government (Sec.2a). This goes against the provisions of the forest policy resolution that wherever possible, degraded lands should be made available for tree farming on either lease or on the basis of a "tree patta scheme". The provision in the amendment specifically dis-allows the lease to any non-government agency except with the prior approval of the Central Government. This restricts the giving of degraded land to the tribal cooperatives and organisations for the purpose of afforestation.

Another amendment in the forest conservation act is the offering of the explanation regarding the non-forest purpose. This explanation is very restrictive. The forest department cannot allow the use of forest land by the individuals or organisations even for horticultural crops or medicinal plants. The provisions cover all forest lands including degraded lands. These provisions are bound to raise hostilities amongst the tribals and the Government. The recently appointed committee by the Prime Minister and the Parliament should pass the revised comprehensive forest act in tune with the National Forest Policy resolution.

Destruction of the Forest Environment and The Tribal

Prior to the advent of the British rule, the forests remained communal property with no individual staking any claim to them. Individuals had resource to the forest for their needs and protected them as their natural heritage.

For the forest dweller-the tribal-the forests remained his life blood, the symbiotic relationship of the forest and the tribal constituted the foundation of his independence. The mutual interdependence as the basis of his relative seclusion was an expression of his independence from the outside world for his survival.

For the British, the forests were the treasure groves and with one stroke of the executive pen, the colonial administration took over the vast forests in the name of the people. The guardians of the forest then set-out to exploit its natural wealth. The people of the forests were now aliens or intruders on the state property. But they were undisturbed from their habitat since they provided cheap labour by which the forests could be cut, the timber, thus, removed could serve the colonial interests. The forests began to be felled and the timber hauled to the distant markets.

The Forest Policy of 1952 with minor changes continued in essence as laid down by the colonial rulers. The revenue from the forest exploitation was increasing year after year. The profit of the state turned out to be the doom for the tribal. For him the relationship with the forests meant more than food, fuel, fibre and fodder and was closely related to their survival. The satisfaction of their basic needs was considered as illegal and attracted penalty. Their symbiotic relationship was never understood properly. Their proximity to the forests encouraged their use as forest labour. This helped their rapid alienation from the forest. Their survival was increasingly put in jeopardy by the contractor, moneylender combine; they provide cheap labour and a safe cover for illegal felling.

Unwillingly, due to his innocence, the tribal became a tool for his own destruction. His hunger for land pushed him into cleaning fresh areas for encroachments. His encroachments resulted in the low productivity due to the impoverishment of soil nutrients since the soils were exposed and got eroded.

The importance of forests for mining and carrying construction of multipurpose projects, thermal projects, and industries depending on the ore's availability in forest areas and the preservation of wildlife made the government to dispossess the tribals land. This resulted in the dislocation of the traditional habitats of the tribals ruining their traditional economy and driving them to the fringes of the urban or industrial areas ultimately living as paupers at the mercy of the anti-social elements. Often the compensation was meagre. The tribals who were affected were illiterate. They did not know the laws. Since their land was held under the traditional rights and in the interior of the forests, they did not have legal documents to prove their titles, their lands were never surveyed. Their titles were never registered. The customary rights of the tribals over their land is in the form of community ownership. They have no record of rights. Even while recording their rights they get dispossessed. Wrongly recording the chief as the owner and not as the manager of their common property was another reason. The government while recording the rights looks for the records and no general rights on a community basis are recognised.

Due to the continued land alienation from whatever ancestral lands the tribal cultivated, he slowly lost the consciousness of the fact that the jungle was his security. Therefore, he had little stakes for the protection and preservation of the forest. Neither he resisted the destruction nor he visualised the preservation. In the name of the scientific forest management the fruit trees, the medicine trees were fit for fuelwood only, and hence were replaced by monoculture such as teak and eucalyptus plantations which are almost of no use to the tribals or support any wildlife.

The Government of India report on the Himalayas in 1959 said, "The Himalayan forests, for instance, are the greatest national asset and to them we owe the richness of the country. The denudation of the Himalayan slopes leads to a greater intensity and frequency of floods, cause recurrent erosion, and to cause detritus being deposited in the fertile sub-mountain tracts. The process inflicts immeasurable loss and misery on the unsuspecting millions in the Indo-Gangetic plain, and brings about the progressive and permanent impairment of soil fertility and the cumulative reduction in the agricultural potential of the whole land."

This is a self professing doom. But with the deforestation which has reduced the tree cover by over 60% we have,

1. **Floods :** The flooding area has doubled from 1971 to 1981 and an annual loss of over Rs. 2000 crore due to floods.
2. **Erosion :** Around 175 million hectares are erosion prone. Pastures turned out to be the wastelands. Every year the loss through top soil and soil nutrients is more than a 1000 crore rupees.
3. **Siltation of Irrigation Projects :** Soil erosion in the hills leads to siltation of the reservoirs, in which we have invested more than 10000 crore rupees. The life of these reservoirs has been reduced to almost half due to siltation.

The effects on the tribal life have been tragic. Drastic reduction of humus has reduced the productivity of their land and forced them to migrate in search of seasonal employment or fall in the trap of illegal timber merchants. The women take recourse to carrying firewood to nearby towns for sale. Monoculture has driven away the wildlife, his only source of animal protein. Forests, the life line of tribal, with their destruction has ruined his life. According to a report of the Planning Commission, India may soon face the Ethiopian type of crisis for water.

The ecosystem is self-regulating and interdependent. The destruction of one part such as forests affects all the other parts. The key to the protection of the ecosystem, here , is the saving of the natural forests as well as afforestation on a massive scale.

Need For Reforms in The Forest Act to Save The Tribals

It is necessary to outline the issues that are actually at stake in the forests. These are mainly three,

1. Justice to the people, both the tribals and the non-tribals.
2. Justice to the nature, (vegetation and wildlife).
3. Justice to the coming generations, so that natural resources are available in the long run.

The forest act is, however, not aimed at protecting the forest dwellers as amongst the other living things and their products. Any future legal reforms in "the forest act must first aim at doing justice to the people and only subsequently at doing justice to the nature and the future generations. It does not mean that doing justice to the nature is the second priority. The law is inter-related as the parts of the ecosystem. The only way by which the flora and the fauna can be protected is by protecting the people, the tribals. If they are protected and made saviours of the forest, natural forests will be saved and justice to the nature would be done, the obligation to the future generations follows from this because we would have not destroyed what is meant for all. Thus, by setting our priorities right, all the three aspects of the justice would be simultaneously accomplished.

Now the question arises as to from whom the people are to be protected. They have to be saved from the contractors, industrialists, money-lenders and the wrong policies of the government and the administration.

Having settled the priorities the immediate issues are :

1. What is the exact nature and extent of the rights that the tribals have over the forests, their resources and the-benefits arising from them?
2. What rights they should have?
3. The criterion of justice to determine the rights.
4. Who will provide the people with such rights? What is the position in the present act?
5. The remedies available to the people when their rights are not met.

The above issues call for reforms in the present forest act. According to the Indian Forest Act 1927, no person can claim a right to private property in the forest land merely because he has domiciled there, or even if his forefathers have lived there for centuries. Nor do such people have any rights over the forest produce, vide Sec.3 of the act. The government may constitute any forest or waste land which is the property of the government or over which the government is entitled, as a reserved forest. Tins section presupposes that forest land is the state property though the tribals co-habit the forest. Section 4 of the forest act provides for elaborate provisions for obtaining the common land as the forest land. It directs the Forest Settlement Officer to issue notice in the official gazette about the government's intention to declare the forest land as the reserved forest so that any person who has any right over any part of that land may claim it as his private property. Section 5 puts a bar on all rights if they are not claimed within three months of the issue of the notification in the official gazette. Where private property rights are claimed, the government can further invoke the land acquisition act 1894 for the public purpose. Asking the people to claim rights in private property when they are unaware of such a concept amounts to playing with people's ignorance. The section 5 of the forest act further directs for the notification of the rights to the individual private property alone, not to rights in common or the communal rights of the tribes. The forest dwellers have been continually using the forest and the forest produce. Hence, despite the fact that they did not claim rights to land and resources section 6 to 16 of the Forest Act deals with the claims to partial rights such as grazing, water resources, shifting cultivation and the use of the forest produce, etc. Such rights depend entirely on the discretion of the Forest Settlement Officer. Hence, they become only privileges granted to particular persons or groups.

CONCLUSION

After a just and rational analysis presented above Subhash C. Babu, IFS (1994) raises some important issues.

How to save the tribals and the forest is a big question. Till today, they have no stakes in the preservation of the forest. Their own poverty has made them an easy prey to the vested interests and, thus, degraded the forest environment. A local vested interest in protecting the forest should counteract the powerful timber lobby. The Chipko Andolan is a clear manifestation of this. It is futile hope to expect regulation and penalty to deter the, illegal timber trade, especially when the stakes are high and risks are low, the forests cannot be policed, they can only he protected and that too by the local people only.

The new forest policy rightly points out at the involvement of the tribals in the preservation, protection and re-generation of the forests and that the first charge on the forest produce should be the needs and aspirations of the tribals and the local people. Unless they are taken into confidence and made the partners in the development of the forest no massive afforestation will re-cloth our denuded forests and hill slopes. Hence, it is essential to meet the priorities and requirements of the tribals. The tribal does not or would not like to consider himself an object of compassion and charity. He feels, on the other hand, that he has been the victim of the extraneous forces, which have taken advantage of his relative innocence in worldly matters and duped him of his birth right.

As far as the foresters and the forest department are concerned the change of attitude is a must. The present concept of ownership and monopoly of the forester and their produce will have to relent to create a feeling of co-ownership or partnership between him and the tribals. The change of foresters' present attitude may not be very simple as it may involve legal and administrative complexities. Nevertheless, the forester's cooperative spirit towards the tribals, in view of the peculiar circumstances, must assume some concrete shape to inculcate mutual trust, confidence and goodwill among the tribals towards the forest administration.

The provisions in the National Forest Policy 1988 with regards to the tribals are alone insufficient. Hence, a revised All India Forest Act is the need of the hour. Under persistent pressure and advocacy of tribal rights the government of India passed a landmark Act in 2006. Now the pressure should be for its sincere implimentation (see Act in annexure).

The Scheduled Tribes and other Traditional Forest Dwellers (Recognition of Forest Rights) Act, 2006

Millions of people live in and near India's forest lands, but have no legal right to their homes, lands or livelihoods. A few government officials have all power over forests and forest dwellers. the result? Both forests and people die. This Act recognises forest dwellers' rights and makes conservation more accountable.

Why is this law necessary?

What are called "forests" in Indian law often have nothing to do with actual forests. Under the Indian Forest Act, areas were often declared to be "government forests" without recording who lived in these areas, what land they were using, what uses they made of the forest and so on. 82% of Madhya Pradesh forest blocks and 40% of Orissa's reserved forests were never surveyed; similarly 60% of India's national parks have till today (sometimes after 25 years, as in Sariska) not completed their process of enquiry and settlement of rights. As the Tiger Task Force of the Government of India put it, "in the name of conservation, what has been carried out is a completely illegal and unconstitutional land acquisition programme."

What are Conditions like in the forest areas?

Because of this situation, millions of people are subject to harassment, evictions, etc. on the pretext of being encroachers in their own homes. Torture, bonded labour, extortion of money and sexual assault are all extremely common. In the latest national eviction drive from 2002 onwards, more than 3,00,000 families were driven into destitution and starvation. In Madhya Pradesh alone, more than 125 villages have been burned to the ground.

The situation is so bad that the then Commissioner for Scheduled Castes and Scheduled Tribes, in his 29th Report, said that "The criminalisation of the entire communities in the tribal areas is the darkest blot on the liberal tradition of our country."

Why were people's rights not respected when these forests were declared?

The Indian Forest Act, 1927, India's main forest law, had nothing to do with conservation. It was created to serve the British need for timber. It sought to override customary rights and forest management systems by declaring forests state property and exploiting their timber. The law says that, at the time a "forest" is declared, a single official (the Forest Settlement Officer) is to enquire into and "settle" the land and forest rights people had in that area. These all powerful officials unsurprisingly either did nothing or recorded only the rights of powerful communities.

The same model was subsequently built into the Wild Life Protection Act, passed in 1972, with similar consequences.

Mistakes may have been made, but surely these laws are the best way to protect our forests?

It is not just people who have lost. The very purpose of the Forest Acts was to convert forests into the property of a colonial department; and when you convert an ecosystem into someone's property, there will always be stronger claims to that property than conservation. To destroy a forest today requires nothing more than either a bribe to the local forest officer or an application to a committee in Delhi. The results include:

The loss of more than 90% of India's grasslands to commercial Forest Department plantations.

The destruction of five lakh hectares of forest in the past five years alone for mines, dams and industrial projects;

The clearing of millions of hectares of forest for monoculture plantations by the Forest Department;

Recent proposals to privatise "degraded" forest lands for private companies' timber plantations.

Moreover, the forest laws destroyed all the community management and regulation systems that had existed before, forcing people to choose between either abandoning the forest entirely or living as 'criminals' within or near it, this day it is a criminal offence for you or I to plant a tree in a reserved forest; but it is legal for the Department to fell the entire forest so long as it has Central government permission.

What does the Forest Rights Act do?'

The Act basically does two things:

– Grants legal recognition to the rights of traditional forest dwelling communities, partially correcting the injustice caused by the forest laws.

– Makes a beginning towards giving communities and the public a voice in forest and wildlife conservation.

Who is a forest dweller under this law, and who gets rights?

There are two stages to be eligible under this Act. First, everyone has to satisfy two conditions:

1. Primarily residing in forests or forest lands;
2. Depends on forests and forest land for a livelihood (namely "bona fide livelihood needs")

Second, you have to prove:

— That the above conditions have been true for 75 years, in which case you are an Other Traditional Forest Dweller [s.2(o)];

OR

— That you are a member of a Scheduled Tribe [s. 2(c)]; and

— That you are residing in the area where they are Scheduled [s. 4(1)].

In the latter case you are a Forest Dwelling Scheduled Tribe.

What kind of rights do forest dwellers get under this Act?

The law recognises three types of rights:

Land Rights

No one gets rights to any land that they have not been cultivating prior to December 13, 2005 (see section 4(3)) and that they are not cultivating right now. Those who are cultivating land but don't have document can claim up to 4 hectares, as long as they are cultivating the land themselves for a livelihood (section 3(1) (a) and 4(6)). Those who have a patta or a government lease, but whose land has been illegally taken by the Forest Department or whose land is the subject of a dispute between Forest and Revenue Departments, can claim those lands (see section 3(1)(f) and (g)).

There is no question of granting 4 hectares of land to every family. If I am cultivating half a hectare on December 13, 2005, I receive title to that half a hectare alone; and if I am cultivating nothing, I receive nothing. If I am cultivating more than 4 hectares without documents or a dispute, I receive title to only 4 hectares.

The land cannot be sold or transferred to anyone except by inheritance (see section 4(4)).

Use Rights — The law secondly provides for rights to use and/or collect the following:

a. Minor forest produce things like tendu patta, herbs, medicinal plants etc "that has been traditionally collected (see section 3(1) (c)). This does not include timber.

b. Grazing grounds and water bodies (sections 3)

c. Traditional areas of use by nomadic or pastoralist communities i.e. communities that move with their herds, as opposed to practicing settled agriculture.

Right to Protect and Conserve

Though the forest is supposed to belong to all of us, till date no one except the Forest Department had a right to protect it. If the Forest

Department should decide to destroy it, or to hand it over to someone who would, stopping them was a criminal offence.

For the first time, this law also gives the community the right to protect and manage the forest. Section 3(1) (i) provide a right and a power to conserve community forest resources, while section 5 gives the community a general power to protect wildlife, forests, etc. This is vital for the thousands of village communities who are protecting their forests and wildlife against threats from forest mafias, industries and land grabbers, most of whom operate in connivance with the Forest Department.

How are rights recognised?

Section 6 of the Act provides a transparent three step procedure for deciding on who gets rights. First, the gram sabha (full village assembly. NOT the gram panchayat) makes a recommendation - i.e. who has been cultivating land for how long, which minor forest produce is collected, etc. The gram sabha plays this role because it is a public body where all people participate, and hence is fully democratic and transparent. The gram sabha's recommendation goes through two stages of screening committees at the taluka and district levels. The district level committee makes the final decision (see section 6(6)). The Committees have six members - three government officers and three elected persons. At both the taluka and the district levels, any person who believes a claim is false can appeal to the Committees, and if they prove their case the right is denied (sections 6(2) and 6(4)). Finally, land recognised under this Act cannot be sold or transferred.

— (Courtesy: forestrightsact.com)

DEVELOPMENT, DISPLACEMENT & REHABILITATION

Chapter 15

Development has become a nightmare for many in the Third World Countries because it continues in such a way that the so called 'target group' or beneficiary becomes 'victims' of progress and development. Though it is an established fact that throughout history, rearrangement in human settlement patterns have been "a companion of development" but the process should be just, humane and as voluntary as possible.

Development involves changes in land and water use patterns, and in some instances, these changes require that people be displaced. But, as Michel Cernea puts it, involuntary displacement must be avoided or minimised as much as possible. If involuntary displacements are, to a certain extent, inevitable they must be carried out in a way that will protect the livelihoods of the displaced people. If this is not done, then some people will share the gains, while others only in the pains, of development. We have to adopt a 'people centered' resettlement approach in dealing with the displaced. "Anthropologists were the first to document the disruptive social impact of forcible displacement. As a research theme with practical significance involuntary resettlement has long enjoyed great popularity among other social scientists as well. Many studies have lately been sponsored by planning agencies. Non-governmental organizations (NGOs) and even social activists have carried out their own studies of the displaced, enriching the existing knowledge on the subject" (H.N. Mathur, 1995).

Since independence, development projects of the five year plans have displaced lakhs of persons each year primarily as a direct consequence of administrative land acquisition. This does not include displacement by non-plan projects, changes in land use pattern, acquisition for urban growth, and loss of livelihood caused by environmental degradation and pollution. Hydro-electric and irrigation projects are the largest source of displacement and destruction of habitat. Other major sources are mines, super thermal and nuclear power plants, industrial complexes as well as military installations, weapons testing grounds, railways and roads, expansion of reserved forest areas, sanctuaries and parks and technological interventions which cause the large scale displacement of traditional fisherfolk and handloom weavers. Thus, artisan communities are also badly hit.

In the scenario of development and displacement the majority of the affected are obviously tribals and other economically morginal rural populations who have historically been dependent on the natural resource base for their subsistence. A significant point to be noted here is that the tribal communities are roughly 8% of the total population of the country, yet over 50% of those displaced belong to this section of our population. The implication is obvious - the tribal people are disproportionately affected by our 'developmental' policies and the resultant displacement. The 29th Report of the Commissioner of Scheduled Castes and Scheduled Tribes and the Report of the Working Group on Development and Welfare of Scheduled Tribes During the Eighth Five Year Plan (1990-95) testify to this fact.

In most of the cases people's consciousness and awareness of tribal displacement and impoverishment awakes largely when they come across news about the struggles and movements of the affected people. Among the major struggles at present in the Chotanagpur tribal belt are those against the Netarhat Pilot Project Test Firing Range (the case now suspended because of the fierce opposition from the affected people) in Gumla and Palamau districts which threatens to displace about three lakh people, the Koel Karo dams in Ranchi and Gumla districts threatening to displace about one lac people, coal mines in the North Karanpura Valley of Palamau district that may cause displacement of about a lakh of people, and the Subarnrekha dams in Singbhum district threatening to displace another one lakh tribals. Prevailing conditions in other states point towards the similar trend. Agitation against the Narmada Dam is now known internationally. The Palavaram dam in Andhra Pradesh shall be displacing an estimated three lacs people majority of them being tribals. In Karnataka, resistance is building up against the Nagarahole wildlife sanctuary. Agitations have been there in Orissa against the Gandhmardhan bauxite mines and the Chilika project.

Impact of Displacement and Rehabilitation:

When we look into various aspects of displacement, the displaced persons or the 'oustees' may be categorised on the basis of the degree of impact of displacement. L.K. Mahapatra (1994) divides them into the following categories:

(a) people who lose their house, homestead land, and their farming land or other productive assets in full.

(b) people who lose their house and homestead and their farm land or other productive assets in part.

(c) people who lose their house and homestead only.

(d) people who lose farm land only in full or in significant part.

(e) people who lose their base for plying their arts and crafts or selling/bartering their specialised services or skills.

(f) people who lose their base for earning their livelihood front the local forest or other eco-system including fishing in the river.

(g) people who lose their base for earning their livelihood through wage labour.

(h) people who lose their house or land or both for making room for constructing the township to house the project employees or for construction of the canals or ancillary structures for completion or maintenance of the project.

"But, unfortunately, in India as also in many developing countries, the 'oustees' are normally considered to properly cover a few categories - (a), (b) and (c) - but all the other categories - (d) to (h) - are not included under 'oustees' legally in order to stake their claims for compensation or rehabilitation".

In most cases, the only legislation that is applied is the Land Acquisition Act, 1894 (amended in 1984) which only makes the state liable for cash compensation, in the process legitimising the gross injustice and social violence in reducing rights and interests into claims and complex systems into monetary compensation. Significantly the Act only recognises individual and not collective or community rights. Much of the land attempted to be taken away from the tribals is Common Property Resources (CPRs). If it is a forest land, the law gives no rights whatsoever to the people even though they might have used it as their livelihood for several generations. Traditionally no compensation has been paid for it. "Besides, most tribals live in regions that have been administratively neglected and are considered backward. They cannot, therefore, hope to get a remunerative price for it and the compensation offered to them for the little individual land they own is very low. Besides, the tribals have traditionally lived within a self sufficient, subsistence economy that depended on the natural resources. They had relatively little exposure to the economy outside their region. Except in the

North-East arid parts of Chota Nagpur, literacy among them is extremely low. As a result they cannot hope to get many jobs in the new project" (Walter Fernandes, 1995).

Studies by several anthropologists have shown multiple effects of displacement. Involuntary resettlement leads to increased stress, both psychological and socio-cultural and also heightens morbidity and mortality. Another unfortunate outcome is a feeling of alienation, helplessness and powerlessness. "Moving away to new places is just unthinkable to the tribal people as they are deeply attached to their ancestral lands. The word 'resettlement' does not exist in many tribal languages". (H.M. Mathur, ibid). The widespread consequences of displacement include "dismantling of production systems, desecration of ancestral sacred zones or graves and temples, scattering of kinship groups and family systems, disorganization of informal social network that provide mutual support, weakening of self management and social control, disruption of trade and market links, etc. "(Lokayan Bulletin, 1995). Further, these patterns have been equated with national progress where public purpose and national interest have been used interchangeably. It is this mindset that justifies the labelling of those who criticise these projects as not only anti-project or anti-development but also anti-national.

The more unfortunate part of the story is the case of multiple displacements. It has also happened that several tribal groups after having made the painful transition and settling into a new life style were again uprooted and displaced. The case of Singrauli in Uttar Pradesh and New Mangalore Port are the examples. If displacement is inevitable, resettlement must include reconstruction of production systems, raising standards of living and minimising the conflict with host community. "The commitment therefore has to be not just for resettlement but for rehabilitation which should be an entitlement and not an act of reluctant generosity" (Smitu Kothari, 1995). Moreover, the cost of project should always include the cost to be incurred on resettlement and rehabilitation. All these projects should be open for public debate. Implementation of any project which does not include satisfactory arrangement for resettlement and rehabilitation.

LETTER OF Dr. B.D. SHARMA

(Commissioner
Scheduled Castes & Scheduled Tribes)

to

THE PRESIDENT OF INDIA

(Through the Union Minister of State for Welfare)

Chapter 16

This is an extract from the letter written by Dr. B.D. Sharma, IAS, to the President of India as part of the 29th report (1987-89) submitted by him as The Commissioner for Scheduled Castes and Scheduled Tribes. This is a historical document and has been made part of the text of this book so that every reader reads it. Popularly known as 'IAS Gandhi', B.D. Sharma has given voice to the voiceless and helpless tribals. Currently, after his retirement, he is working through his organization *Bharat Jan Andolan*. ***Author***

I am presenting herewith the Twenty-ninth Report on the condition of the Scheduled Castes and Scheduled Tribes under Article 338 of the Constitution for the year 1987-89, In the last report, which was my first report, I had reviewed the situation of the Scheduled Castes and Scheduled Tribes in broad terms. In that report one major aspect which came to the fore was that a dualistic system is getting established in our country. The modern organised sector comprises the upper segment. Consequently, even amongst the Scheduled Castes and Scheduled Tribes, two different segments are getting established exactly in the same fashion. The modern organised sector is the leading sector of our developing economy. Therefore, all eyes are set on it and everyone is looking at it with fond hope. It was in this context that I had made extensive recommendations in the earlier report so to ensure that the members of the Scheduled Castes and Scheduled Tribes get an equal opportunity and honourable position in both the segments, particularly in the organised modern sector. The real partnership in the grand procession of development cannot remain confined only to reservations in services but must extend to all segments of national life. Only then the system can truly be considered to imbibe the spirit of the Constitution implicit in the protective provisions and the right to equality.

1. The irony, however, is that such a dualistic system is by its very nature inequitous. Therefore, if we see the above plea for equity and justice in the broader context of national economy it will mean a plea merely for sharing of non-justified benefits of an inequitous system. Secondly, even after the policy of equitable sharing is implemented with full responsibility and honesty it will

benefit only a small segment amongst the weaker sections of our society. And here is an extremely regrettable aspect of this scheme. If the system continues as it is, the burden of deprivation and exploitation will continue to increase and will, to a large extent, fall on the members of the same community, bulk of whom happen to be located in the lowest stratum of our system. In this Way, a highly anomalous situation is being created. This partnership in injustice in the name of justice acquires appearance of justice. But by the same token in such a milieu, not only ignoring broader issues of justice and equity but even opposing the same also tend to be justified. Therefore, unless the question of equity and justice is considered from the perception of the people located at the lowest rung of our society, which accounts for bulk of the members of the Scheduled Castes and Scheduled Tribes excepting a small section who have joined the organised sector, the safeguards in the Constitution for these communities will remain, more or less, meaningless.

2. The life of the vast majority of our people is linked with three elements, viz., the right over resources, the right over means of production and the entitlement for labour. These aspects unfortunately have either not been properly discussed or in case there is some discussion it is mostly superficial. The reason is that the moment such issues are seriously considered, the very foundation of the vested interests, which are flourishing in the name of modernity, progress and development, gets shaken. But these are the questions which are crucial for the welfare of the members of the Scheduled Castes and Scheduled Tribes. And what is more, they are also crucial for the quality of national life, basic principles and human values. It is in this context that I had decided to undertake a special review of the national scene with regard to these three elements. The present report and the previous one taken together in a way make for a comprehensive frame. This frame can provide the basis for a life of honour and dignity for all members of the Scheduled Castes and Scheduled Tribes. Moreover, the frame can also become the frame for establishment of a social order imbued truly with the ideals of equity and justice.

The Three-tiers in National Life

3. The situation in our country with regard to the establishment of an appropriate system and suitable manner for enabling the common man to lead his life with honour and dignity is rather

unhappy. The polarisation in our national economy is becoming increasingly sharper. On the one end we have the carefree setting of the modern organised sector. The moment a person steps in this sector, he is free from all worries about his ordinary living for all times. In that worryless life, the only worries are how to retain one's position, how to get as large a share in the comforts and luxury-goods characteristic of that sector and how to somehow move along the high tide of so-called development. On the other extreme is located the unorganised traditional sector. The question before the ordinary people here is that of just two square meals. The only wish of those people, however, in this sector who command the resources and also those who understand the new world, is somehow to join the modern sector, or else to amass similar artifacts of comforts and luxury there itself. Therefore, the general scenario in this sector is that of strife, loot and raw struggle for existence.

4. In this milieu the growing centralisation in our economy is adding fuel to fire. Whatever is left with the ordinary people is being snatched away on the strength of law or sheer use of force and money power. Whatever is being snatched away from this side is getting accumulated at the other end. Is this way not only a dualist but a three-tier structure is getting consolidated comprising *India, Bharat and Hindustanva"*. The bulk of the members of the Scheduled Castes and Scheduled Tribes are included in this lowest tier of *Hindustanva*.

5. It is clear that this process in our national life is not in keeping with the intention of our Constitution. It is also against the declared principles. But then how is it happening? I have tried to look into this question in some details with a view to find a possible solution. There are two basic aspects. One concerns the texture of our legal structure and the other related to the paradigm of development. So far as the paradigm of development is concerned, we have accepted the path adopted by the western countries as the ideal. Moreover, in a hurry for development we have accepted the questionable premise of "development first" and given social equity a secondary position. In this approach an important fact of the global system was overlooked that the "dustbin" of the third world was a necessary concomitant of the process of development in the first and the second worlds. In the same continuation, the third world now requires a "dustbin' of "fourth world". Today in our country *Hindustanva* has become that very dustbin of development.

Dissonance between Law and Constitution

6. The present system is patently inequitous. But unfortunately our legal structure has also proved to be its compeer. The wasp and weft of our legal system was broadly set during the British period. The basic premises of the system established by the British were those of their own society and its objective was to strengthen the foundations of their empire. The people were subject and the system was symbol of the Raj. After in dependence we prepared and adopted a Constitution dedicated to the establishments a socialistic society based on our own traditions and basic human values. But the structure of the system, over which this crown of Constitution was placed, was totally dissonant with its basic spirit. This dissonance not only continued in the coming years but the situation became still worse. Firstly, the nascent ruling elite came to relish the old system. Secondly, in the hurry for development the incongruities were first ignored and later on they were accepted even as necessary for the maintenance and advancement of the new system. There was yet another important reason for the continuance of the **inconfruous** situation. The law and the rules are concrete and functional while values are abstract. The latter are generally a good subject of thought and discussion which by itself can be a matter of satisfaction. Consequently big mountains of violation of Constitution and human rights could remain hidden behind the small straws of the legal frame.

Right to Life

7. The most sacred and primary amongst all human rights is the right to life. The right to life does not only mean the right to bare animal level subsistence; it really means right to live with human dignity. And two crucial elements for a life with dignity are personal liberty and adequate means of livelihood. The form of these elements in real situations can be quite different depending on the specific economic and social situation. For example, in the modern sector they comprise what are known as the fundamental rights. But when it comes to the tribal people, who are located on the other end of the spectrum in the traditional sector, these formal principles in the present context have no meaning. In their situation a self-governing system based on their own tradition and within the understanding of the ordinary people is essential for enjoyment of these rights in the real sense.

8. The situation in relation to appropriate means of livelihood is very complex. Moreover numerous anomalies have plagued the system. So far as the adequate means of livelihood in the organised sector is concerned the formal form is dominant. Every member of this sector has a specified position and whatever the role of that person, irrespective of its utility or non-utility for life be not only can claim due entitlement just by virtue of the membership of the organised sector but can also openly claim entitlements which are not really justified. But in the case of unorganised sector no body is sure about what a member of that sector will finally set. And the situation of each member in the sector may be quite different. Nevertheless, it can be said that broadly command over resources, ownership of means of product and due entitlement for labour are three such elements which together determine the situation of an individual and also the community with regard to the appropriate means of livelihood.

9. Thus, there are five elements which are necessary for life with dignity, self-management at the community level, command over resources by the community, ownership of means of production by the worker, equitable entitlement of labour and personal liberty. These are the basic rights for the human society. These are also the soul of a democratic system. These values have been enshrined in our Constitution in unequivocal terms.

..... And Its Denial

10. Even though the position about the right to life in the Constitution is crystal clear, yet so far as the right to life of the common man is concerned, it is not only being ignored in practice but is being blatently violated. The main reason for this situation is that during the British period the natural resources were accorded the status of property under the law rather then being recognised as the basis of life of the people. The irony is that even after the right of property was removed from the list of fundamental rights and in the face of clear enunciation by the Courts about the real intent of the right to life enshrined in the Constitution, the legal frame in that regard in practice remained unchanged in its original colonial form. That is why there is a direct clash at almost every step in the national life between the Constitutional and human right of right to life of the common people and the legal right of property of the more powerful groups. It can be said that in the inequitous distribution of resources during the British period the state and a groups of selected people along with the state become

the owners of all natural resources including land. But by the same token the common man, who was using those resources for making a living through the ages was deprived of his natural right to make a living from them. This process unfortunately has become still more stronger after independence.

11. In view of this denial of the basic right to life, a big question arises about the nature of responsibility of the state itself. After all in our Constitution the State has been given a special responsibility in relation to social justice. Then how is this all happening ? To answer this question we will have to review the different roles of the State in the complex modern situation and the priorities adopted by the State in that regard. The State can broadly be said to have three primary responsibilities, viz., law and order, protection and development. In the anxiety to maintain order and in the hurry for development as also in the dazzle of its glitter, the dark lanes of the State's responsibility for protection of the poor, particularly the Scheduled Castes and Scheduled Tribes, have been often forgotten. Moreover there is no hesitation in supporting the vested interests entrenched in the old as well as the new structures under the cover of policies, principles and laws and even in striking against those whom the State is expected to protect. In some areas, it appears as if law, Constitution, human rights and state's responsibility are all non-existent. This is the biggest irony of our national life which I have tried to present in this report.

12. This phenomenon is an integral part of the inhuman processes of deprivation and destitution which has been continuing for ages. But its scope became much wider and its intensity much higher during the British period. A careful review of the present situation clearly brings out five levels of deprivation, viz., —(i) non-recognition of rights over resources and restrictions on their use, (ii) Alienation of worker from the means of production, (iii) denial of due entitlement of labour, (iv) bartering of personal liberty and finally (v) the psychological state of accepting deprivation and destitution as justified and proper and demise of self-respect and dignity. It is unfortunate that the processes of deprivation have not only continued at all these five levels throughout our national life, with the bare exception of the organised sector, but at many places it has become much more intense. It will be necessary to start our review with the last level.

Social Prestige and Dignity

13. The honour and dignity of a person is dependent on his work, his right over means of production and his right to manage the system. The condition of the members of the Scheduled Castes and Scheduled Tribes on all these counts was deplorable from the very beginning. Hard work fell in their share while command over resources was enjoyed by others. But after independence these people were rendered still more helpless and vulnerable in the face of unholy collusion between the system and the more powerful groups. Firstly, whatever means of production had remained in their hands are also gradually slipping through their fingers. Secondly, there is also a state of near lawlessness in the villages. In this milieu, the remaining resources of the village community are being commandeered in some cases by the stronger people of the village in some other cases by small and big companies and finally in some cases by the State itself ignoring the fact of dependence of the people on those resources for their living and their traditional rights. Who cares and who knows where these people should go? In this raw struggle for existence prestige and dignity for the ordinary people are at best images of a dream world.

14. The biggest irony with regard to dignity and prestige of a people in our country is that the condition of the tribal communities, who are most conscious about self-respect and honour, is the worst. These communities have become completely helpless in the face of the omnipotent system on account of the 'criminalisation' of their social and economic system itself, denial of their rights over resources and non-recognition of their traditional self-governing systems. The forests are the property of the State; therefore it is an offence for the tribal, who has been living in those very forests for the ages, to make a living from these forests. His very presence in the forest is against the law. If a tribal enters the forests with his bow and arrows, it is an offence. If his cattle as usual graze in the forest, they are taken to a kine house. If he takes his traditional brew after worshiping his Gods or in social functions according to his tradition he still becomes a law breaker. He is branded as an offender in all matters concerning his social and economic life only because the law is against him. The criminalisation of the entire communities in the tribal areas is the darkest blot on the liberal tradition of our country.

15. And the saddest thing is that all this has happened and is happening in the name of principles, claiming authority from the Constitution and the law. That is not all. This is being done by a system, which considers itself to be a symbol of justice, rationality and modernity. Those who have been given the responsibility under the Constitution for correcting this anomalous situation have almost no realisation about that responsibility. The first attempt of the system ordinarly is to assert its own position as right and to prove that the others are on the wrong. It is expected that the tribal society should change and adapt itself in accordance with the frame of the modern system. And finally, an attempt is made to convince the people that this what development really is!

16. Thus, firstly no action has been taken to correct this basic anomaly and even if some action is initiated, one can never be sure as to where it might get stuck. The result is that today there is a state of confrontation in almost all the tribal areas. In this connection I have reviewed in some detail the Excise Policy in the tribal areas. There are clear policy guidelines of the Central Government in this matter. But even after 16 years of their issue they have not been adopted in full by any State so far. Even where they have been adopted, something or the other gets incorporated at some stage of implementation or the other such that the basic spirit of those guidelines cannot be realised. Moreover when people demand implementation of the policy guidelines, they have to face the wrath of the system.

17. I have discussed the issue of Excise Policy in some detail because this issue touches the personal and social life of every tribal. In this case even when a tribal strictly follows the social norms of his community he breaks the law, he is an offender before the law and legal action can be taken against him. Can there be a more regrettable situation than this? Any law in the tribal areas, which makes the social tradition of the tribal people a criminal act, is against the spirit of the Constitution. If social prestige and personal dignity in the tribal areas are to be upheld all these legal anomalies must be done away with immediately.

Entitlement of the Common Man

18. The biggest question in relation to the right to life is the entitlement of the common man for his labour input. What can be the meaning of honour and what can dignity signify to a

hungry person? The present situation in this regard is unjust. The members of the organised sector first take away from the gross national product what they consider is due to them on the basis of highly inflated and arbitrary entitlements. The members of the unorganised sector have to be content with whatever is left thereafter. The fact is that not even proper valuation has been made of the work of ordinary labourers outside the organised sector including the framer. It is an irony that the agricultural labourer in our agricultural country whose work is the most skilled, the most arduous, and whose working conditions are the most difficult has been graded as an unskilled worker. This is also the case with other workers in the unorganised sector. Their skills are deemed to be 'non-skilled' and their knowledge as 'ignorance'. And all the skilled workers in the traditional sector are gradually becoming a motley crowd of unskilled people, a process which was set in motion as a part of imperial design during the British period. In the case of most of these workers, deprivation has reached the ignominious level of 'biological exploitation', which is not even alluded to.

19. I have referred to in my last report the unconstitutionality of the dualistic system in the determination of wages and salaries for the organised and unorganised sectors. But this serious constitutional issue has not been even discussed so far in any forum. This duality is at the root of inequity in our country. If the question of justice for the common man is considered in the real sense, then the first step will inevitably have to be equitable determination of wages of the agricultural labourer. It will directly lead to a substantial rise in the price of agricultural commodities. In the end, it will boost the entitlements of all workers in the unorganised sector. Thus a new relationship will be established between the organised and the unorganised. The natural outcome of this process will be that the entitlements of people belonging to the organised sector at the other end will be significantly reduced compared to what they are enjoying today. The members of the organised sector will not easily accept this new deal. But this simple logic and this stark reality about injustice in our national life have to be got accepted by them whether they like it or not. Or else, how can the common man expect to get justice without changing such glaring unjust relationships in our national economy?

20. This is the plain reality about our economic structure. If this reality is ignored it will not possible even to present the correct

analysis of our national problems. And if the disease itself is not correctly diagnosed how can we expect a real cure? For example, from analysis presented in the report it is clear that there is no unemployment in our country. The reality is the so-called unemployment is a part of a big conspiracy by the vested interests which has only one objective, that is, to extract maximum work from the ordinary man with a minimal wage which may be just sufficient for his bare physical survival so that he can contribute his bit until his limbs can move and in the end he is obliged to withdraw from the stage after providing a "substitute". It is here that deprivation in our country descends to the abysmal level of biological exploitation.

21. The members of the Scheduled Castes comprise a substantial segment amongst the workers in the unorganised sector. In the present situation when the members of the Scheduled Castes do not have anything which they can call their own except their labour and their skills, their struggle for entitlement for their labour is the real struggle for justice; it is also a struggle for the right to life. The first step for social justice in this context has to be due recognition of the skills of the agricultural labourers and conferral on him the status of skilled workers. Moreover, his wages should be fixed in accordance with the principles accepted for organised sector such that his wife and children are not forced to go out of their homes in search of work and as a respectable citizen he can also maintain his family with his own earnings.

Rights over Means of Production

22. Most of the members of the Scheduled Castes and Scheduled Tribes are dependent, in some way or the other, on agriculture. But their muddle in this regard has been in the tribal areas, which is continuing even now. Firstly, in many areas there are no authentic papers. Therefore, the position about land such as the size of holding, its precise location, is not properly recorded. Secondly, the laws are much too intricate which are beyond the understanding of the people. According to the present law, any land which is not recorded in the name of an individual is deemed to belong to the state. Therefore the government can do whatever it likes with regard to such lands. On the other hand the ownership, in a way, is bestowed automatically in favour of a person the moment his name is entered in the records in an appropriate column. The outsiders have taken full advantage of these legal stipulations. Today not only the record

is against the people, the entire system is against them. The correct information about cultivation, ownership, etc, concerning land is available only in the village, yet all disputes about land are decided in courts outside. It is well-known that a simple person has no hope of getting justice there. But he cannot do anything, he is utterly helpless.

23. In many areas, particularly where industrial complexes are being established, there is a state of near lawlessness. The case of Sonbhadra in U.P. is extremely regrettable; the area is witnessing open loot in the name of settlement. The instructions of government and even decisions of Courts are unable to protect the tribal lands. Unless, there is a basic change in the present system such that all matters concerning land are decided in the open, in the presence of village people, the tribal people cannot get justice. To leave the entire tribal community at the mercy of an outside formal system in matters concerning land, which is the only basis of their life, is patently unjust and in violation of Constitutional safeguards. A people's movement has been launched on this issue in Sonbhadra. The demands of the people in this vital matter must be conceded. In fact, that proposition should be accepted as the norm for preparation and maintenance of land records for all tribal areas in the country.

24. The most basic question about land concerns entitlement of the tiller of land. Even though the right of the tiller on the land he tills has been accepted in principle in our country. Yet in reality his position is the weakest. In my previous report, I had made extensive recommendations with a view to give the principle of 'land to the tiller' a real form. In this context, unfortunately the position at the moment is that it is not even certain that the tiller of the land can continue to till the land, the question of bestowal of ownership rights remains a far cry. In some states, it is almost impossible even to get the fact of cultivation by a tenant entered in government records. I have given two examples in this regard-one from Bihar (Sole Daltanganj) and another from Andhra Pradesh (Pulimamidi). In both these cases the people, most of whom belong to Scheduled Castes, are cultivating the land but their names do not find a place in the record. They have asked the government to provide protection for their cultivation about which the concerned governments have not taken a clear stand. Therefore, they have resolved to protect for themselves their basic right to till the land.

25. In these cases the issues concerning land record and cultivation appear to be very simple. But some of them involve basic question's. If a person is cultivating a place of land, then should this fact be not recorded in government papers? Whatever is on the ground must get reflected in the record in someway or the other. If even this simple thing is not being done as a conscious policy in our system it has only one implication. An easy way has been found to ignore the due entitlement on land of the poor people. This position may be legal, but it cannot be said to be just and cannot be accepted as being in accordance with the spirit of our Constitution. Here lack of consonance between the law, justice and constitution become glaring. And this is not the clutches of zamindars-absentee or otherwise. The person who tills that land and subsists on it has no relationship with it under the law.

26. All struggle concerning cultivation of land are basically a conflict between two rights. On the one side is the right to life and on the other the right to property. The right to life is basic and much higher than the right to property. Where a person is earning a living by cultivating the land, its ownership cannot be bestowed on him straight away for some reasons, the minimum which can be expected from the government is to ensure that he continues to remain in possession of that land his right to make a living from it is effectively protected.

27. The first step for protecting the right to life related to land will have to be to ensure that, whatever may be the law, or even if the law is silent on this issue, the person who is cultivating a piece of land continues to be in possession of that land. This principle should be openly promulgated and the fact of possession through cultivation should be entered in government records. Moreover, if a zamindar tries to evict a person ignoring this right, the government has the responsibility to provide full protection to the victim. And if a government cannot protect this basic right, no one can take away the right of an individual for self-defence. This is the message of our Constitution.

Bonded Labour

28. The worst disregard of the right to life is being perpetrated in the case of bonded labourers. Their condition is extremely pitiable notwithstanding governmental statistics and comprehensive plans for their liberation and relief. The coffee plantations of Tamil Nadu are gold mines for their owners but

the tribal, who nurtures them through his sweat and blood, is a 'prisoner' there. The limbs of labourers working for big landlords in Daltanganj and Champaran are chained in lieu of five *kathas* (measures) of agricultural land. In many areas on the border of U.P. & M.P., working in the stone quarries is the destiny of the people; they can lose their life should they dare to refuse to go to work; their limbs can be crushed; beating is an ordinary thing. Such oppression and such exploitation even after 14 years of enactment of the law for liberation of bonded labourers, which is in the knowledge of administration, about which even sensitive social workers out of sheer helplessness cannot but turn their face saying 'what to do?' is abominable. It is an open disregard of human rights, which is not merely a matter of regret, but is a matter of national shame for all of us.

29. It is clear that there is one basic defect in the policy about liberation of bonded labourers. The plan of liberation of the bonded labourer, instead of cutting the fetters of his slavery, cuts him away from the support of his life. What is necessary is to cut the shackles of slavery of the bonded labourer besides ensuring that in doing so he is not alienated from his life' support. He has a right on the life support system or the enterprise in which he may be engaged. This fundamental right of his must be protected at any cost, yet the inhuman bondage must also be snapped forthwith. But even this will not be enough. The owners, who are responsible for this crime against humanity, should be externed from those establishments and the labourers must be given the ownership right on the same. This will be the real liberation of bonded labourers.

Right over Resources

30. The primary resources other than agriculture in the traditional economy are forests, pastures (waste land and water) on which the ordinary people depend for their living. The wrong entitlements over resources of all descriptions started getting established during the British period. It was in that period that the intimate relationship between the resources and the local community which was like that between the mother and the child, was ended and the State acquired monopoly rights thereon. This Colonial process of centralisation has unfortunately got further reinforced under the tutelage of the new paradigm of development which has been adopted in our country after independence. The full implications of this colonial-

developmental process are becoming clearer only now. Everywhere the life support system of the local community and the common man at the moment is being snatched away by the abstruse state institutions and big people without any qualms of conscience. In this situation, the people are engaged in a fierce struggle of their right to life. But the system is branding their current use of these resources as illegal and is driving them away taking undue advantage of its authority.

31. The first fundamental change which was effected in this process related to forests. In the new frame, the symbiotic relationship between the forests and the forest dwellers was not recognised and the forests became property of the State. After the state acquired monopoly rights over the forests, a normal system was established for their management which gradually became increasingly comprehensive and also strong. The biggest irony of this change was that the forest-dwellers who has a life-long relationship with forest — which are their very homes, their religion, their culture and their everything — was conspicious by its absence in that frame. In this formal structure, which recognises only administrative and market relations, an all-out effort has been made to see that these life-long mother-child relationships are transformed into market relationships. How can this be possible? It is on account of this basic lack of understanding, that there is state of confrontation and regime of destruction in almost all the tribal areas which in final analysis means great injustice to the tribal people.

32. The British enacted the Indian Forest Act with a view to acquire formal control over the forests. At the time of reservation of forests, legal formalities were no doubt complied with, but there was no question of people getting justice. Most of the tribal people were forcibly evicted from their homes. The memory of that forcible eviction now remains only in their folk tales. Whosoever could do, prepared agricultural land outside the forests. Even then their living relationship with the forests still continued. Those communities, which are totally dependent on forests have not been able to come over this great tragedy even now. The primitive tribal communities and the shifting cultivators in many areas are still engaged in a struggle of life and death. Similarly, the right to life of the nomadic communities has also been disregarded. Their problems have so far remained altogether unnoticed.

33. It is clear that the right to life at the individual level and the human right of maintaining the identity at the community level in the case of the tribal people have been ignored in the Indian Forest Act. Therefore, this law is not in consonance with the spirit of our Constitution. But since the state itself was one party in this deal, there was no change in it even after the Constitution was adopted and the situation remains as it was before it. In this way, the Constitutional provisions for protection of tribal people as also the human rights have been ignored in the system of management of forests adopted in our country. This is also the most sore spot for the tribal people; this is also the most pathetic tale about the condition of these communities.

34. All the tribal areas were incorporated after independence in larger state units. In this process, no special attention was paid to the existing administrative arrangements and everywhere the system of the largest unit as it is was gradually extended to the tribal areas. Wherever forests were not reserved, the process of reservation was started. The private forests were taken over by the State. In this way, all special features of the earlier management systems that evolved in keeping with the local traditions stood derecognised in the new system. But people's life does not automatically change simply because a new system may have been adopted. Therefore, numerous anomalies arose in the field and people really could not accept the new system from the core of their hearts. Consequently there is confrontation in many areas on this count.

35. The process of reservation of forests after independence was largely pursued in a routine fashion. In some cases, mere formality was observed just for the sake of it and even the fact that some people were living in the forests was not taken note of. In this way, the spirit of the law itself was violated. For example, in some cases of Jagirdari forests the original inhabitants were deemed to be encroachers without any enquiry as soon as these forests were taken over by the state. In some cases, the officer did not visit the spot yet recommended reservation of the area. Similarly, there were a variety of local practices in each area, like warkas in Thane, dali in Raigarh and green manure leases in Karnataka, etc., which were not even looked at. Therefore, the old legal arrangements became illegal in many areas just with the passage of new law without any consideration and without any thought. And the tribal became a law breaker.

36. This reservation of forests predictably failed to protect the forests. Firstly, the internal pressure on forests has been rising incessantly on account of growing population and increasing needs of the people. But the biggest devastation was caused by external pressures. Extensive plantations of mono-culture species after clearing the natural forests in the name of scientific management, establishment of tea, coffee and cardamom plantations, leases of forests produce at throw away prices in the name of promoting industries and establishment of industrial and mining complexes in the name of development, construction of highways, heavy influx of outsiders, eviction of tribals, supply of forest produce for meeting new demands, everything in the end proved to be a big burden on the forests. Consequently, there was ruthless destruction of the forests. The worst effect of this mindless destruction has been on the life of the tribal people. The very basis of their life is getting destroyed. But unfortunately no attention has been paid to this aspect of denudation of forests. For example, food production in our country has increased manifold, but how much loss have the tribal communities sustained in terms of non-availability of food articles from the forests due to their destruction does not find a place in national accounting. In all campaigns for the protection of forests the real culprit, who has destroyed them for quick gains and who continues to destroy them even now, is left out and the full wrath of the system falls on the tribal, who is already under tremendous pressure.

37. While discussing management of forests, besides the issues concerning the life of the people, those relating to environment and national development cannot be forgotten. But a direct consequence of non-recognition of even the existence of the community and not associating it in the management of forests, the position of forests has become very vulnerable. They are like that public property which has no one to look after and, if at all there is one, he too is far away from the scene and has no significant role to play in its protection. It is true that the internal pressure on forests has increased. But the tribal after all brings only a pole or two for constructing his hut, a small branch for making his plough and dead wood for lighting the fire to protect him from worms and insects, wild animals as also from cold during the winter. Nowhere he has built grand mansions. When the tribal clears the forest and cultivates forest land it is under compulsion of his circumstances. If he can be provided an alternative, he will happily accept the same.

38. The main reason for the depletion of our resources is the growing inequality and the rising tide of consumerism. But unfortunately these facets are not even alluded to anywhere. Therefore, the greatest need today is to put stringent check on the consumerist life-style and ensure equitous entitlement in the use of natural resources. For achieving this, it will be necessary that all those vested interests, who have entered into forests for quick gains and establishing big jagirs, are ruthlessly suppressed. All plantations, small and big, legal and illegal for example those which have mushroomed in Karnataka, should be taken over by the government and handed over to the labourers. If a poor person gets due entitlement over the natural resources, he will be relieved of the problems of the day; only then he will be in a position to think for tomorrow; in that frame he will become the greatest friend of environment. There are some good experiments of partnership of the people in protection and development of forests from West Bengal which are worth emulation. In many areas, people are taking initiative on their own, which deserves to be strongly supported.

Minor Forest Produce

39. The minor forest produce has an important place with regard to people's partnership in forestry. I had recommended in my previous report that the people should atleast be given full rights over the minor forest produce. The rights presently claimed by the government on minor forest produce even with reference to the provisions of the Indian Forest Act, are not legal and royalty levied thereon is unethical. The declarations of the Government of Madhya Pradcsh and Bihar last year recognising the tribal people as owners of minor forest produce instead of mere labourers engaged in collecting the same, was the first major step towards ending the historical injustice with regard to forest against the tribal people. It is, However, a matter of deep regret that regressive forces got active immediately after this declaration in Madhya Pradesh. And today the situation is that even this great decision is being dented. This regressive step is a mockery of the entire Constitutional ground plan in which the State has been given with great confidence the responsibility of protection of the interests of the tribal people. Will the Governor and the President keeping aside all sorts of formalities in this regard, ensure that this just decision is not negated and that the subsequent regressive decision does not became a blot in the history of our social justice.

Wild Life

40. A highly anomalous situation has also arisen in the management of wild life on account of ignoring certain basic facts about the tribal scene as the tribal people and the wild animals have co-existed reasonably well from times immemorial, that wild life has not been destroyed by bows and arrows and that the real culprit responsible for their destruction is the outsider. Consequently, unnecessary restrictions are being placed on the activities of the tribal people and in many cases they are being forced to move out of their homes. Their plea is that they have been living with the tigers through the ages and they can still live with them quite well. But nobody is prepared to listen to them. In many areas their economy has been greatly damaged through measures which are not legal. There is open violation of their right to life, which is not in keeping with the spirit of our Constitution. There is an urgent need for serious review in all these cases both at the level of law and also in terms of actual practice.

Displacement

41. The other side of the issue of the rights over resources, in the context of their alternative use for development, is displacement. A comprehensive review of the situation about displacement clearly brings out that we have reached a critical stage in the journey of development, particularly in the tribal areas, which can no longer be ignored. The greatest loss in the wake of development has been caused to the tribals and the resourceless people, bulk of whom belong to the Scheduled Castes. Their rights over resources either have remained completely unnoticed or have been only partially recognised because all resources have been treated merely as property. The biggest irony is that a 19th century colonial law like the Land Acquisition Act is being used indiscriminately in the great voyage of development. This law does not admit the concept of the right of life and the will of the Raj has been accorded the hoary status of 'public purpose.'

42. The Land Acquisition Act, in a way, is functioning like an indomitable, inanimate instrument for the transformation of the agriculture based traditional system into a modern system. This instrument, in that process, is snatching away from the poor all those natural resources which have formed the basis of their life so far, with the characterstic unconcern and mechanicality of an

instrument, for presenting the same to be used as raw material by the new system. The sharecropper, agricultural labourer, shephered, hunter, *kevat* and such like do not even exist in the eyes of this law which is concerned only with the so called owners of those resources. Moreover, the owner of land himself gets compensation only for his ownership right, following the principle of market price or capitalisation of net income. It is not even realised that land to a farmer is the source of making a living with skillful use of his personal labour. The stark reality about the wanderings of a proud farmer, whose honour is inexorably linked with his land, for vending his labour and his deep agony are not even alluded to. Meaningless are to the new world the questions of his honour, his sentiments and even his future!

43. Whatever may be the law on this point but, in my view, the means of livelihood of a citizen and his right to life cannot be taken away. Mere exchange of property is the concern of Land Acquisition Act, the concept of right to life simply does not exist so far as this Law goes. The law governing the acquisition of land, therefore, is not in accordance with the spirit of our Constitution, this law is unconstitutional. That is not all. The process, which is being adopted for the acquisition of land in the field, is unethical and anti-people. Acquisition of land becomes a certainty, once a decision is taken about establishment of a project. Invitation of objections in accordance with the law thereafter, is a mockery of the whole system. Thus, even though the letter of law may be followed but its intention is not being honoured. Therefore, the entire process is illegal.

44. The situation in the tribal areas in relation to the displacement is especially a matter of grave concern. The rich natural resources located in these areas are today required for development. But the traditional rights of the people who are fully dependent on those resources for their living, are not recognised simply because they are not formally recorded. The biggest irony is that the existence of the community and its relationship with the habitat are not even alluded to in any law whatsoever. Moreover all those aspects of life, which cannot be captured within the frame comprising formal rights concerning property and market relations, are conspicuous by their absence. The emotional world of the tribal people is as real as the modern world of concrete jungle, it is much more sublime. Therefore, the protection of this sublime 'world' has also been recognised in the global context as a human right. The present process of land acquisition is not

only violative of the Constitutional rights but even that basic human right. The biggest irony is that the state does not hesitate in disowning even the Constitutional responsibility of providing protection to the simple tribal communities, simply because it has taken on its shoulders another grave responsibility of the so called development.

45. An important question, which arises at this stage, is whether the tribal people should have an opportunity of participation in the fruits of development. It would have been a matter of great happiness for me if effective measures had been taken for this purpose. Today even rehabilitation depends on the mercy of the state. The entitlement of a displaced person is limited only to compensation and that too in respect of that property alone which may be in his name. But even so, what will he do with that money? Some islands of affluence do appear in the tribal areas with development, but they are surrounded by an ocean of misery, social disorganisation and personal destitution. When the tribal, after the loot of his resource base runs towards the forests for refuge, he is not allowed to set his feet there; they are out of bounds for him. He is obliged to join in the end the army of landless labourer in the countryside elsewhere or to seek the 'security' of city slums and their sidewalks. This is the plain reality of the so called development in the tribal areas nothing short of a great human tragedy!

46. The fact is that the paradigm of development adopted in our country and its compeer life style are themselves incogruous with our socio-economic situation. So long as they are accepted as ideals, establishment of a 'Fourth World' and biological exploitation of the people comprising 'Hindustanva' are inevitable. Therefore, the very foundation of the new structure is wrong. The minaret of development, which is being raised on the ruins of the economy of the ordinary people with utter disregard of their fundamental rights, cannot be a lasting structure. The people, who are victims of injustice, are now rejecting this paradigm. Whatever may be the formal position about land acquisition, to the ordinary tribal it is nothing but forcible occupation of his land. There is nothing new in this. This has been his experience through the ages, it is his experience even now. There is, however, a difference. Earlier other people were aggressors, today the assault is by government itself. Then where is he to go ? And it is here that he revolts - from the core of his heart — against the entire system.

47. A precondition for any new use of natural resources should be that the concerned institution or the government should not only provide an alternative economic base for the people, who may have been depending on them for their living, but should ensure that the new life is better than the earlier. Moreover, the government must proceed with honesty, it must be fully convinced that whatever is being promised is real and-feasible. What is still more important is that the affected people should themselves be able to realise that the alternative will be better for them and they are prepared for it of their free will. If these principles are ignored, any action in that situation which may cause displacement will be against the democratic values and also against the spirit of our Constitution. And any use of force in the name of law and order against the people, who are fighting for establishing their right to life, who are struggling against the paradigm of development which is not only inequitous, but is violative of the law of the land, is against the spirit of our Constitution and against human rights. In fact, it is a mortal affront to the cultural sensitivity of our country. And bulk of the affected people comprise the simple tribal people, members of the Scheduled Castes and other resourceless people, who have been suffering for ages and whose protection has been entrusted to the State by our constitution!

48. Here we face a rather confusing and complex situation. All actions by the people described above are deemed to be violations of law and are being dealt with as such by the state authorities. If this approach continues, the solemn resolutions by the people will continue to be perceived as a form of revolt against its authority by the state. In that process the people will become still more disoriented and confrontation will get further accentuated. There is no doubt that in the end the system will have to bow before the people's will, but only after a great human tragedy. Can there be a more ridiculous situation than the one when a tribal is asked about the extremist activity in his area, his natural response with a sense of gratitude towards the extremists is that "if nothing else, at least atrocities of the administration have ended after the coming of the 'dadas'? What should one say about a system in which the Constitution itself has bestowed on the President and the Governors unlimited powers for protection and welfare of the tribal people, yet they have not been able to save the people from exploitation and oppression of their own servants, and this historic task has been accomplished only by the Naxalites in some areas? What is the

instrinsic nature of that system in which the law itself has become the biggest terror for the common man? Under the cover of that law, he is being deprived of everything - right to life, his honour and even his freedom And the law is being used for exploitation, oppression and finally even to wipe out their social identity itself. Exploitation, terror and tyranny are experienced reality of the common man, particularly the members of the Scheduled Castes and Scheduled Tribes.

49. This is the tragedy of our national life. Those who *ate* operating the system are helpless before that system, they are prisoners of its logic. They are also perhaps to some extent assured about its premises to the poor. But the common man now has no faith, whatever faith is lingering is also disappearing. There is only one way to come out of this tragic situation, that is, to acknowledge, as the first step, the basic anomaly of our national life viz., the ritual of a legal process can strangulate justice—and give high regard to the wisdom of the people and follow them. The resolutions of the people referred to in this report, should not be seen in the narrow legal frame but must be viewed in the broader perspective of human rights and democratic values. Moreover it was Tilak and Gandhi who pronounced that "Swaraj is my birth right" and 'Toleration of injustice is a sin'. If the Government is helpless in removing the basic anomalies and ending the unjust situation, it can atleast do one thing, that is, not to brand those, who are struggling for justice as offenders. Self-governance is the soul of democracy. Supporting those, who are struggling for that principle, is the duty of all citizens. I hope that the Government will support the people's resolution for protecting their right to life in general and for establishing self-governing system in keeping with their tradition in the tribal areas. I further hope that the government will also adapt the formal system in accordance with the wishes of the people, even though with so much of delay, which alone will make the Constitutional scheme a living reality.

Five Tasks......

50. An important objective of this Report is to establish, through you, a dialogue with the common man who, in the ultimate analysis, is the source of all reasons, all processes and finally all objectives. I have not made any formal recommendations. What recommendations can be made when the foundation of the system itself is faulty? The law and the system itself are against the spirit of the Constitution and basic tenets of natural

justice; moreover the right to life of ordinary people is being violated at every step. The whole report itself is one substantial recommendation.

51. So long as a process of basic change in accordance with the spirit of the Constitution does not begin, isolated measures will serve merely as patch work. It will be like dressing a wound while the root cause of the disease remains as it is. Nevertheless, some elements are vital. If consensus can be engendered about them, if every person located at different levels in the national life can contribute according to his situation, it will be possible to fulfill, even though partially, the national goal and social obligation concerning equity and justice.

Firstly, our legal frame should be restructured with the right to life of the common man as the central point so that the gross dissonance between the law and the Constitution can end. As a first step, all unconstitutional elements should be identified and removed from all the laws particularly those concerning the command over resources, ownership of means of production and entitlement for labour. A new legal frame should be evolved which is truely equitous.

Secondly, in whatever way the common man may be making his living, that should be recognised as a right and the state should provide protection to his right to life in that form removing all discordant elements. This should in particular cover bonded labourers working in different establishments, share croppers and agricultural labourers, forests dwellers and people depending on the marginal resources of village.

Thirdly, a system of self-governance should be established at least in the tribal area in which the local community should have the full responsibility for managing their day-to-day life including the maintenance and use of all the resources.

Fourthly, so long as the State is unable to discharge the Constitutional obligations, the people's resolve for recreation of their system based on those basic values should be honoured and their peaceful struggles should be supported. Any use of force, direct or indirect, against the people's struggles for establishing their right to life should be prohibited.

Fifthly, certain basic questions have arisen concerning the right to life, paradigm of development and the style of life within the broads frame of the existing law, Constitution, human rights and the responsibility of the State particularly in the tribal areas. The movement in Narmada Valley has become a symbol covering all these questions. It will be necessary to find a satisfactory solution to these problems rising above the clamour amongst different interest groups in the immediate context to a higher level and broader frame of our civilisational obligation and human values. The paradigm of development and style of life must be redefined so that they are in harmony with the condition of our country and our national objective.

......And also a Resolution

52. And there is a need for national resolution as well for creating a climate of goodwill, particularly in the tribal areas. A unilateral process of development should not be imposed on the voiceless people. Their life should not be put to stake in the name of national development and high ideals. Today, the tribal people have nothing but the backlash of development in the name of development which has lead to disorganisation as a community and destitution as individuals. Everywhere the tribal is pleading with folded hands — 'do not burn my hut'... 'save me, where I will go ? ... 'Our *maiya* (Mother) will be left behind' 'or else bomb and finish us ?'.. But there is no one to listen to him. The moving words of his pathetic pleas will keep wandering filling those hills and forests; they will continue to reverberate perhaps eternally laden with the chilling message of the helplessness of man in the face of an inhuman system ....

53. If a climate of goodwill is to be created, the war waged against the tribal people in the name of development must be stopped forthwith. Instead he should be extended an invitation for participation in the great voyage for achieving real development. This is a difficult task. This will be possible only when we decide that a 'Fourth World' shall not be allowed to come into being as a concomitant of development in our country. It will be necessary to give a fresh look to the paradigm of development and the style of life. A climate of confidence and goodwill can be created in the tribal area only if attention is paid immediately to those people who have already become victims of development and the new system, who are in great agony. Instead of being concerned about moving ahead in a great hurry, the tribal people should be given, as the first step, the responsibility of managing their own socio-economic life on the one hand and should be made partners in the larger national development on the other. It is possible that the pace of change and development may have

to be slowed down to some extent. It is also possible that we may have to stop for a while in some places. But this is necessary and also desirable. If this caution is not exercised, the wheel of development itself may crumble in the face of bubbling discontent and erupting revolts in the tribal areas.

Rights and Responsibilities

54. I cannot say what will be reaction of the system to this Report of mine. But when the question is of the very identity of one-fourth of the people in the country, when the issue is about their basic right to life, when the people themselves are struggling for the establishment of that right, not to present a clear picture about the situation would have been the biggest crime. It would have been dereliction of my duty. I had suggested in my earlier Report that the National Development Council should especially consider this whole situation about the Scheduled Castes and the Scheduled tribes separately. I had also requested the judiciary that they may review the situation in the context of the way the system has been functioning that whether the denigration of the rights of the people can be justified simply because the State did not discharge its responsibility entrusted to it by the Constitution and the tribal is facing its consequences. I will like to renew this request of mine once more.

55. But I will also like to urge on all those people, who are a part of the modern system, that after all they also have a duty in their individual capacities. They may do whatever may be possible for fulfilling that obligation in relation to the people's struggles for fundamental rights and basic principles. If they cannot participate directly in their struggles for the right to life, the minimum which they can do is not to oppose them. Similarly, I will again urge on the political parties that the issues concerning basic principles should be kept separate from the politics of vote. The members of the organised sector and those having command over resources comprising the so-called 'Bharat', may also look at the logic of the present system from the perspective of the bulk of the people who are resourceless comprising 'Hindustanva'. I hope that the man of learning will ponder over the simple analysis which has been presented here and guide the people to cut through the illusive obsession of development and inspire them to search for a new path so that we can establish a socialist society in its true sense. And there

is only one power — the youth power - which can bring about the vital qualitative change in the entire system. It is not merely a wish, but I am fully confident that our young people, implied by the spirit of dedication, sacrifice and driven by the dream of creating a new society will come forward to accept this great challenge in this unique phase not only in the history of our nation but in the history of the human civilization itself.

56. Finally I, as the Commissioner for Scheduled Castes and Scheduled Tribes, myself have a responsibility that the people, for whom the Constitutional safeguards have been provided and the review of whose functioning has been entrusted to me, are made aware about the exact position in this regard. But the common man does not understand the abstract language of principles and policies. He is fully engrossed in the problems of the day. Unless the substance of all principles and policies is presented to him in the context of his day-to-day problems, they will have no meaning, they are of no significance. What I have said in this report will perhaps echo for a while in some assembly halls and then disappear in the void around. Only a dialogue concerning the struggle for life of the people themselves can be its real and lasting expression.

57. Today, when the ploughman who makes a living by tilling the land has no right over it, when the tribal is a stranger in his own home, when the workers and the tribals in many areas are fighting their battles all alone, when the state has no hesitation in using force against people struggling for establishing their right to life oblivious of the fact that it has not only been entrusted the full responsibility of their protection but whose very existence as a people depends on its good will, a highly anomalous situation has been created. Today, these people may get some real relief, even though quite meagre, only from the extremists and thereafter they are unwillingly caught in the holocast of a crossfire. In this situation, if a dialogue has to be established with them for discharging, even though symbolic, the obligation as a part of the system and also in relation to the constitutional responsibility there is no other alternative but to get directly linked with their life struggle. It is within this frame of affection and obligation that it is now obligatory for me to get associated with the struggles of the common man, particularly the members of the Scheduled Castes and Scheduled Tribes, for the establishment of their right to life. I am presenting this report to you with this solemn resolve. It is

also with a fond hope that there will be a serious discussion at the national level on the fundamental questions concerning human rights, democratic values and constitutional scheme raised in this report which may contribute in making a decisive turn in the national life and building up of our nation in the image of the dreams of the founding fathers of our Constitution.

SOME OTHER FACETS

They made us many promises, more than I can remember, but they never kept but one - they promised to take our land, and they took it.

— Dee Brown

From Bury My Heart At Wounded Kee

I have my bow and arrow and they, their guns; let's see who wins.

(From Santhal Rebellion)

— Verrien Elwin

TRIBAL WOMEN:
'Liberated' with Restrictions

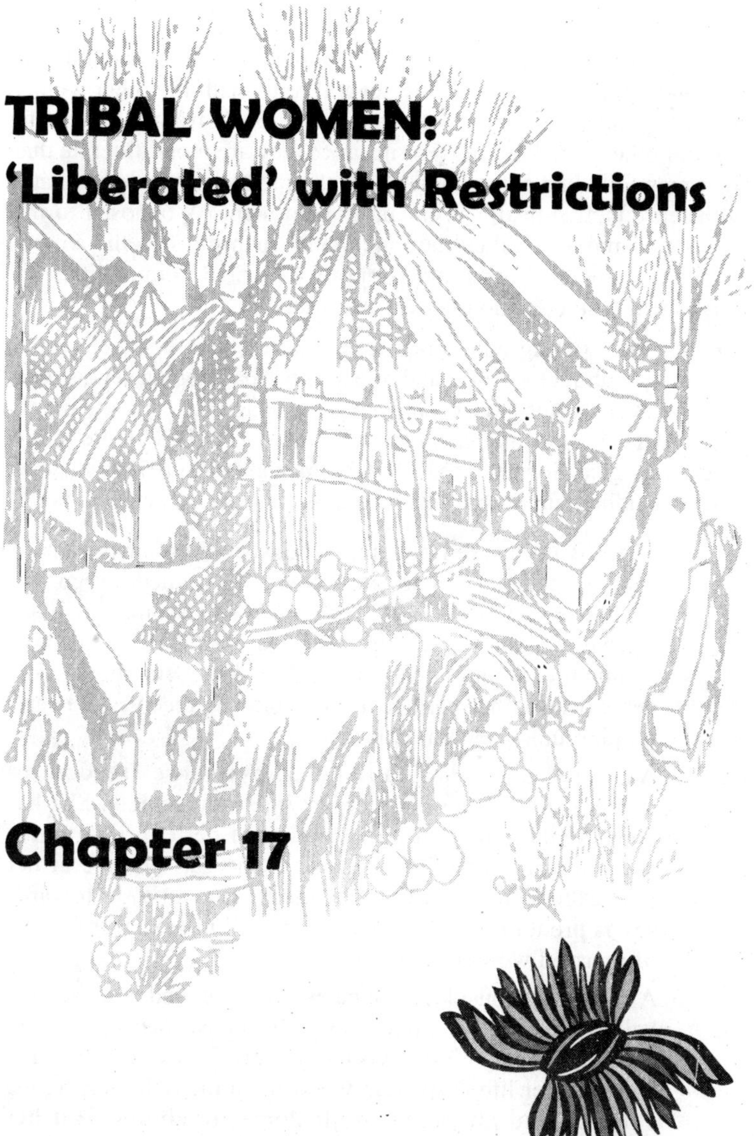

Chapter 17

Like any other social group the tribal women constitute about half of the total population. They share several traits with the other women but at the same time different in several respects from their counter parts of other social groups. For instance they are more illiterate than their men folk, like other women have their share of problems related with reproductive health, work more than men. As opposed to this they enjoy more social/cultural autonomy than most of the women from other social groups and some of the tribal communities are matrilineal unlike the non-tribal communities.

Though the existing ethnographic literature does not yield much information about the status and role of the tribal women across India yet whatever studies have been done provide a fairly clear picture. In one of the earliest volumes on tribal women published by the Indian Anthropological Society titled Tribal Women in India (1978), whatever N.C. Choudhry summarised is, broadly speaking, true even today:

1. There is no marked preference between a boy and a girl in tribal societies. Both are almost equally wanted, exceptions are in few societies (Gaddi, Toda) but then, in some situations, a girl is more preferred than a boy (Garo, Khasi). She receives as much care and attention as a boy gets. But she is more dependent on her mother from whom she receives the early training in household duties.
2. As a girl and a woman she enjoys more freedom of movement than her counterpart in Hindu society. She has considerable voice in the selection of her (life) partner if she does not actually select him. She can divorce at her will except in very few instances. Her attitude towards sex is predominantly free and natural but sexual infidelity of married women is frowned upon .
3. A woman is considered an economic asset and considerable value is placed on a hard working, industrious and dutiful wife. There is a clear division of work between a man and woman. Her life is spent in working on the field, raising the children and attending to all domestic chores. But her important economic role does not give her a very high position

in the society at par with man. She cannot fully inherit property except in matrilineal societies, she has little religious duties and she cannot hold any public office. Her loss in position is compensated by granting her sufficient freedom in her movement and action.

One of the best indicators of social status of women in a society is the sex ratio. As per 2011 Census, sex ratio among the scheduled tribes is 991, ranging between 981 to 1020 which is much better than the rest of the population. Hardly any cases of female foeticide or infanticide are reported from among the STs. J.J. Roy Burman (2012) writes that "Occupational differentiation and emphasis on status and hierarchical social ordering that characterise the predominant Hindu culture are generally absent among the tribal groups." Though most of the tribal communities are patriarchal and patrilineal there are tribal groupe like Khasi, Garo, Jaintia, and Lalung of Maghalya who still follow matrilineal system and where property is passed on from the mother to the daughter and traditionally, the husband comes to reside in the household of the wife. That does not mean that men are subordinated to women and as per the customary law she may not be owning the land. Yet, they are running small business like running shops in the markets. In Mizoram they may be seen managing even big stores and larger business.

In a very judicious and incisive analysis of the matrilineal tribes of north-east Tilput Nongbri(2016) tells us though, "factually,even in these tribal societies unequal relationship between men and women prevails.Matriliny gave them(tribal women) comparative autonomy and influence and provided them with institutional support and security not available to their counterparts in patrilineal societies.However, matriliny,far from being a liberating force,in fact, adds to women's vulnerability." He further tells us that by vesting descent rights on the mother, women are not only objectified as symbols of the culture and tradition, they also become subjected to a strict social and moral code to uphold the honour of the family. He writes:

"As children are recruited into the descent group through the mother, a woman's sexuality becomes the concern not only of the family but also of the community.......Perceived that women are the entry point through whom outsiders could gain access to their social and material resources, men have come up with strict normative codes to regulate their conduct"

Women in most of the tribal societies contribute significantly to the family economy by performing agricultural chores, fetching water, collecting minor forest produce, looking after cattle etc. Hence they are considered as economic asset. Because of this reason among most of the tribal communities the practice of 'bride wealth'/bride price has been prevalent in which the bridegroom gives to the bride's parent money, cash or kind like cattle. In recent times the practice of dowry has also entered into some tribal communities especially wherever economy has undergone changes and the role of women decreased and also the impact of neighboring Hindu communities as well as entry of migrant male labour. Roy Burman (ibid) highlighting the role of Christianity in north eastern region tell us that "Christianity has brought about a significant emancipation of the tribal women. While earlier the women were restricted from attending schools, it is the missionaries who opened schools and encouraged the girls to attend them. They also opened up Church forums where women could participate and also take the lead. The Protestant Church took lead over the Catholic Church in these matters."

Generally speaking we observe contradictions and contrasts with reference to the status and role of tribal women. On the one hand the women enjoy a greater cultural autonomy- right to visibility, right to mobility, right to choose spouse as well as to divorce him, mixing freely and among some of them greater freedom to have premarital sex relations and in the others restrictions also exist. In most of the tribal communities women have hardly any role to play in the social and political spheres – no place in village councils or traditional panchayats. After the promulgation of PESA ,Panchayat (Extension to Scheduled Areas) Act, 1996, women were conferred this right but like the case of the rest of the country, in many cases, the husbands or male relatives of the 'elected' representative wielded power. There are very few tribal women MLAs or MPs in the country.

The issue of lack of political representation of tribal women attracted national attention when in 2018 a controversy erupted over the reservation for women in Nagaland's urban governance bodies. The Naga tribal organisations vehemently opposed the reservation on the basis of their customary laws while the critics of this opposition termed those opposing this move as regressive and too traditional to allow any relaxation in the traditional power structure. Sooner or later the tribal communities living with modern democratic institutions will have to reconcile to these changes.

Women constitute a larger share in the work force in most of the tribal societies and hence they also migrate along with their men to different regions in search of livelihood. Though it is true that tribal labour migration is poorly recorded by the scholars, whatever scant information we have reveal that the women tribal migrants are concentrated mainly in three sectors- agriculture, brick kilns and construction. Many of those who migrate to the cities, especially big cities, work as domestic help. Usually they get this employment through contractors or placement agencies. They live between two cultures-their own as well as the culture of the urban centre. Several of them are vulnerable to all sorts of exploitation including sexual exploitation while a small and more fortunate minority of them are able to achieve upward mobility through education. They are the women who settle down in these cities and may or may not maintain any contact with their native places and prefer to get assimilated in the new socio-economic environment.

INDIGENOUS KNOWLEDGE SYSTEM AND TRIBAL INDIA

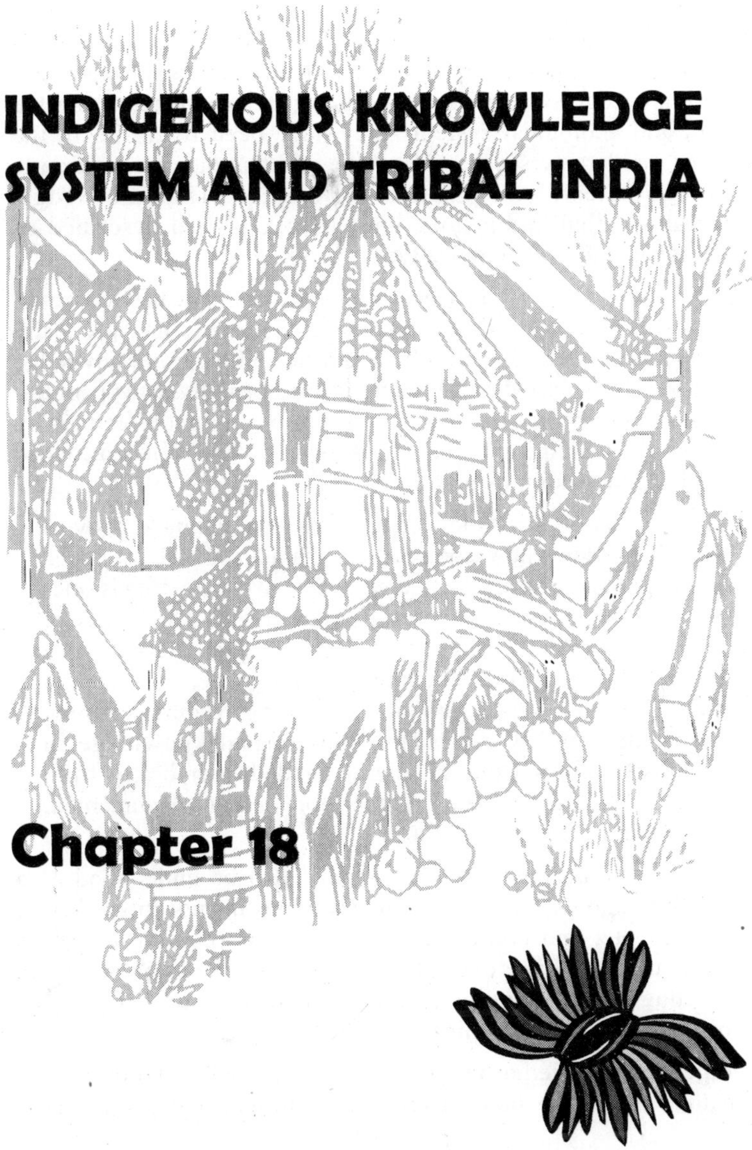

Chapter 18

Even before the advent of modern civilization, based on modern science and technology, people from all over the world had their own knowledge systems derived from their experiences from the world and ecological systems they have been living in. In the present, modern perspective it may be said that they are the people who know, learn and practice 'differently'. This knowledge, generally called 'indigenous knowledge', is also described as 'traditional' and 'folk' knowledge.

As Devy (2014) says, "their perspective reveals how they construct the world through their understanding of space, time, joy, pain, life and death." It is difficult to define indigenous knowledge because it is as varied as the many groups of indigenous peoples/ tribes around the world. Yet, there are some common features on the basis of which it may be understood. UNESCO has provided a working definition as under:

> "Indigenous or local knowledge refers to a complete body of knowledge, knowhow, and practices maintained and developed by peoples, generally in rural areas, who have extended histories of interaction with the natural environment. These sets of understandings, interpretations and meanings are part of a cultural complex that encompasses language, naming and classification systems, practices for using resources, ritual, spirituality and world view. Non- formal knowledge in contrast to formal knowledge is handed over orally from generation to generation, and therefore seldom documented. (Boven and Morohashi, 2002)

Indigenous/traditional knowledge may also be understood as a network of knowledge, beliefs, and traditions intended to preserve, communicate, and contextualize indigenous relationships with culture and landscape overtime. This knowledge is often passed on through regular indigenous performances – oral traditions, song, dance and ceremonies.

Indigenous knowledge should be looked as traditional or 'native' wisdom. Since the indigenous communities/tribal people have been inhabiting all types of eco-zones- hills, forests, coastal areas, arid and semi-arid desert zones, they accumulated vast experience in coping with environmental hardships and developing sustainable livelihoods.

Ethno-botanists tell us that India has more than forty five thousands species of wild plants that may be divided into plants of medicinal properties being used for indigenous health practices, thousands of plant species are used by tribal communities as food of high nutritional value, roots, tubers, fruits, flowers, etc. The tribal communities have intelligently attached religious/ spiritual value to a number of flora and fauna. For instance among several central Indian tribes it is believed that god Vidyadhar resides in mango trees, Brahma in Arjun tree, Lakshmi in Basil or Tulsi etc. The totem of several tribes also presents an important aspect of conservation. Several tribes in almost all the geographical zones declare the endangered species of flora and fauna as their totem. This is the tribal way of conservation and maintaining ecological balance. Because of their rich knowledge of medicinal value of a number of plants they use them with great effect. They have antidote of snake and scorpion bite using the parte of leaves of drum stick tree or silk cotton tree. The tribal communities of north- eastern region such as Khasi, Garo, Jaintia etc. know how to conserve highly nourishing varieties of food grains. Wherever vanda plants grow the local tribal communities use the root, stem and leaves of this plant and some others for setting bone fracture.

The tribal communities know the importance of conserving biodiversity. In the central as well as north -eastern regions the tribes maintain 'sacred groves' from which not even a twig of grass can be removed as per their religious beliefs. Their knowledge of environment and marine life is amazing. When Tsunami hit large parts of the world including India in 2004, everybody was sure that the depopulating primitive tribes of Andaman & Nicobar Islands would be wiped out. To the amazement of all, except a minor loss of life, all of them survived. Observing the restlessness of marine animals, birds, and air, they knew that something serious was going to happen and they protected themselves in safe hideouts carrying food and water of several days. The scientifically advanced countries could not apprehend the coming disaster and paid a heavy price of life and property but most of the tribes living in islands and coastal areas survived with minimal losses.

The vast treasure of knowledge related with ethno-medicine finally attracted the attention of our scientists and Indian Council of Medical Research have taken up a big project of documenting the indigenous medical system of the tribal communities before it is lost or get patented by the outside agencies. Moreover, the indigenous knowledge is also to be protected under intellectual property laws.

Intellectual Property Rights of the tribal people are not being respected, much less guaranteed anywhere in the world today. Apart from plants tribal people have drawn attention to new varieties of crops, organic pesticides, sweeteners, new fruits, perfumes, etc. Multinational companies have infiltrated deep into the tribal areas and they are 'gene hunters' and 'gene grabbers'.

PROTECTION of indigenous/tribal languages is also crucial in conserving indigenous knowledge as most of it is contained in these languages and transmitted orally from generation to generation.

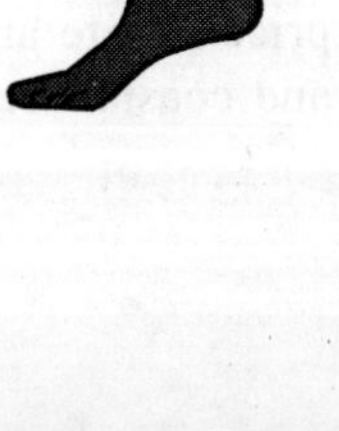

DEBT BONDAGE AND BONDED TRIBES

Chapter 19

Chronic indebtedness among tribals is a universal phenomenon. Indian tribals too seems to accept indebtedness as an inevitable and inescapable aspect of their existence but debt bondage as an economic arrangement is found only in some of the tribes. "Debt bondage is a system whereby a debtor pledges his labour or the labour of somebody else close to him in lieu of the interest to be paid on the loan advanced to him by the creditor. Usually the pledgee or his nominee is released only on the discharge of the debt. Since the man gets only food and very little or no money, he has to depend upon someone else in the family to procure the sum required for his release and this, of course, is rarely available. The relationship may therefore last for months and even generations, frequently involving the male heir." (Saxena, 1978)

Debt bondage is an outcome of the situation in which the tribals are becoming or have become part of peasantry. The reasons of this state of affairs may be enumerated as follows:

(i) uneconomic holdings;
(ii) poor soil;
(iii) primitive techniques of cultivation;
(iv) lack of irrigation facilities;
(v) lack of credit facilities for so called 'unproductive, purposes'
(vi) lack of alternative economic avenues in their immediate vicinity;
(vii) presence of strong cultural values of 'honesty and truthfulness which do not allow them to disown any debts howsoever old.

The roots of all these reasons may be found in the transformation of economy to wholly or partially a cash economy. Saxena further states that certain social institutions of tribal society also contribute towards pushing the tribals into debt bondage. The ceremonies connected with the tribals' life cycle involve sacrifices, feasts, and gifts. When tribal economy was barter based and slightly more prosperous, these ceremonies did not attain much financial strain. With increasing contacts with other cultures, and change over to money-based economy, the expenditure on such ceremonies has been fast increasing. This situation provides an unlimited scope to the exploitative operations of money-lenders and traders. Their dealings with ignorant and simple tribals are such that the debt once incurred becomes very difficult to be cleared and telescope infinitely into the future. The tribal people do not know any other agency which can help them so readily and even at off hours. Being illiterates, they can never scrutinise the accounts.

The annual report of the Commissioner for Scheduled Caste and Scheduled Tribes indicates that the areas where the debt bondage is prevalent are scattered almost throughout the country.

This type of debt bondage is known by different names in different areas.

The Kolta: Bonded for ever

The Kolta are one of the worst examples of bonded labour among the Indian tribes: They inhabit Jounsar bawar, Rawain and Jounpur area of districts of Dehradun, Uttar Kashi, and Tehri Garhwal respectively—a more or less compact region of now Uttarakhand. The economic system of this region is technologically primitive and cultivation of land is a tradition and a way of life for the people of this region. In the local caste hierarchy, the Kolta occupies the lowest place, being untouchable with artisan groups occupying the middle rung and brahmins and rajputs standing at the apex by virtue of their being higher caste landlords. The traditional local code, i.e Dastur-ul amal prohibits the Kolta from owning land but its abolition by the state government has helped the Kolta to a considerable extent in acquiring the cultivating land as owner-cultivator.

State	Local name of the system/practice	Tribes affected
Andhra pradesh	Gothi, Vetti	Koya Dora, Konda Redde, Konda Kumare
Bihar	Kamia	Korwa Bhuyia
Gujarat	Hali	Dubla-Halpati
Kerala	Vasloorkava Panam, Nilpu Pannam	Paniyan, Adiyan
Karnataka	Jeetha	Adi-Karnataka
Madhya Pradesh	Hervahi, Mohidari Hali,	Adi-Dravida
	Kamia	Sehria, Gond, kol

Maharashtra	Vet, Begar	Dhor Koli, Katkari Vorli, Bhil
Orissa	Gothi	Kondh Paroja
Rajasthan	Sagri	Bhil, Bhil-Mine
Tamil Nadu	- -	Paniyan Kuttunakany Sholaga, Arin
	Thatiyar,	Pulayar
Uttar Pradesh	Mat Harvahi	Kolta, Kol

Of all the handicaps the Kolta suffer from, the institutions related to land ownership and tenure provide the foundation for their "institutionalised" exploitations. Though as a result of governmental efforts a large number of Kolta have got some land but these holdings are so small, so meagre and usually of such low quality that they are uneconomic and insufficient to provide their owners with two square meals a day throughout the year.

For the Kolta the implication of having little or no land is that almost all households remain impoverished. They are unable to generate any surplus from their agricultural activity. Their bare minimum consumption expenditure exceeds their income. They have to depend on others to sustain themselves and have to borrow money from Brahmins-Rajput landlords at usurious rates of interest varying from 25-60% per annum with another 6¼% deducted from the loan as initial commission for "Ganth khulai", literally meaning opening the not of cloth in which the moneylender traditionally keeps his money. Even those who succeed in obtaining loans from co-operative societies for agricultural purposes usually do not spend the entire money for the specific purpose and a large part of it is consumed for 'unproductive' purposes, like marriage, treatment of sickness, consumption expenditure at festivals, etc.

Always ready to exploit and keen to engage the labour of his debtor, the landlord moneylender agrees to advance the loan on the well known conditions. Since most of the Kolta are illiterate, they have no idea of what is being entered in the account books of the moneylender. They put their thumb impression very submissively and that seals their fate. In many cases these transactions are oral, and they cannot afford to approach a court of law for seeking redress.

But even those transactions which are recorded in the account books are nothing but legal fiction. Wrong entries and inflated amount are quite common and the most a Kolta can do is to call the village panchayat (which is dominated by the Rajputs). The panchayat instead of helping him usually finds some pretext to fine him for trying to "backout' of the loan maligning his 'savior' landlord moneylender. The debtor the poor Kolta in these circumstances, has no choice but to pledge his services as bonded labour. He is not even in a position to pay the interest not to speak of the principal amount. And therefore, his bondedness may, as it often does, continue for generations. He has to suffer great privations and work for his master from dawn to dusk under conditions of semi-starvation.

The first and only comprehensive study of the bondage of Kolta carried out by present author, (Hasnain, 1982) shows that their chronic indebtedness and the resultant bondedness lead to the following consequences:

(i) loss of personal freedom and utilization of their labour almost free of cost;
(ii) change in occupation and loss of money;
(iii) land alienation and its acquisition by the creditor
(iv) conversion of their wives, sisters, and daughters into posititutes sold and resold in near and distant cities for ending the debt bondage; and
(v) chronic veneral diseases. Proprietor

Thus, we see that the process of bondedness which begins as an economic transaction under the cultural and the ecological conditions, results in servitude for not only the borrower but his generations to come.

Re-visit after 25 Years

The fieldwork for this study was done between 1973 to early 1976. By that time the Bonded Labour System (Abolition) Act 1976 was not promulgated. This piece of legislation did make some difference in the lives of bonded labour in different parts of the country in various ways and degrees.

Let us first take a look at this Act before making commenst on the changes coming into the lives of the Kolta bonded labour - the population under study representing one of the worst cases of bonded labour in the country.

India ratified ILO convention No.29 (forced Labour Convention 1930) on 30.11.1954. Tragically, it took almost 22 years for the Government of India to pass a legislation called Bonded Labour (Abolition) Act 1976. Yet, India is the first country in South Asia to enact such a legislation. In pursuance of this, some institutional mechanisms were developed in the form of vigilance committees at the district and sub-divisional levels under the chairmanship of District and Sub-Divisional Magistrates. Executive Magistrates were empowered under the Act to conduct summary trial of offences, to release the bonded labourers and to issue release certificates. The Act also lays down stringent penal provisions against the offending employers. The penalties include imprisonment for a term which may extend upto three years and also with fine which may extend upto Rs. 2,000/-. In order to assist the State Governments in their task of rehabilitation of released bonded labour, the Ministry of Labour has launched a centrally sponsored scheme since May 1978 for rehabilitation of freed bonded labour, under the scheme, the Government of India extends rehabilitation assistance at the rate of Rs. 10,000/- per freed bonded labour. The Supreme Court in its order, dated 11.11.1997 requested the National Human Rights Commissions to be involved in dealing with the issues of bonded labour. In pursuance of this order of the Supreme Court, a Central Action Group was constituted in the National Human Rights Commissions. The CAG held regular meetings/sensitization workshops at various places in collaboration with the Ministry of Labour and Employment and the matter is being pursued with the State Governments.

The Bonded labour System (Abolition) Act defines bonded labour as 'the system of forced, or partly forced labour under which a debtor enters, or has, or is presumed to have, entered, into an agreement with the creditor to the effect that:

(i) in consideration of an advancer obtained by him or by any of his lineal ascendants or descendants (whether or not such advance is evidenced by am documents) and in consideration of the interest, if any, due on such advance, or

(ii) in pursuance of any customary or social obligation, or

(iii) in pursuance of an obligation devolving on him by succession, or

(iv) for any economic consideration received by him or any of his lineal ascendants or descendants, or

(v) by reason of his birth in any particular caste or community, he would-

1. render by himself or through any member of his family, or any person dependent on him, labour or service, to the creditor, or for the benefit of the creditor, for a specified period or for an unspecified period, either without wages or for nominal wages, or
2. forfeit the freedom of employment or other means of livelihood force specified period or for an unspecified period, or
3. forfeit the right to move freely, throughout the territory of India, or
4. forfeit the right to appropriate or sell at market value any of his property or product of his labour or the labour of a member of his family or a person dependent on him, and includes the system of forced, or partly forced labour under which a surety for a debtor has, or is presumed to have, entered, into an agreement with the creditor lo the effect that in the event of the failure of the debtor to repay the debt, he would render the bonded labour on behalf of the debtor.

This Act locales Indian slaver as forced labour in adverse debtor-creditor relationships in employment, but primarily in inter-generational customary bondage in agriculture and its effect, in terms of the forfeiture of constitutional and legal rights of the person

Centre for Education and Communication in its report. "Labour Vulnerabilities and Debt. Bondage in Contemporary India (2005) has demystified bonded labour as identified in Bonded labour System (Abolition) Act. 1976 as:

* Bonded labour as agrestic and inter-generational customary bondage with emphasis on semi-feudal characters of social and economic relationships no longer adequate to comprehend and address contemporary phenomenon.
* Bonded labour is flexible and adaptive.

Bonded labour is ingrained in employer-employee relationship. It institutionalises and operationalises labour vulnerability which is done through the medium of debt. Bonded labourers invariable enter into a contract-forced or of own will. Contracts are one sided, opaque to the workers, to be observed in contravention of law and always as an instrument of control and exploitation of workers.

Bonded labour in India is rooted in history- customary forced labour extracted from the members of the marginalized and socially discriminated groups such as Dalits and Adivasis exploited by the caste landlords in the feudal society. The practice not only continued after independence but multiplied as a result of increased poverty, reinforcement of social/caste discrimination and displacement of the poor, mainly tribal communities, from the laud and forest based livelihood by the very process of 'development'.

The passing of the 1976 legislation straight away meant that those bound by an outstanding debt no longer needed to keep working with the creditor. It made the binding of labour against a debt a legal offence. It also made it legally binding on the Stale

Governments to identify all the bonded labourers in their suites, organise release from the wily employers and provide them with a viable rehabilitation package. To accomplish this, the State governments intiated several measures and instituted new administrative setups. Official surveys enumerated the incidents of bonded labour and special commissions were set up to formulate strategies for the eradication of the system. "The opening up of labour markets, the increasing linkages with towns and the growing political conciousness have made it difficult for employers to bind labour for generations. In some instances, employers, in order to circumvent the law have found other ways of subjugating labour" (S.S. Jodhka. ibid). The decline of the old system, however, did not translate into an) kind of substantive empowerment of the labour class. In some cases, it just meant a greater degree of eausalisatioin, or simply, unemployment. Freedom without economic security means little and brings other forms of vulnerabilities. We need to make a concerted effort to understand and conceptualise the newer, and increasingly elusive forms of bondage relations.

The debt bondage may also be seen as a legacy of colonial of British and Capitalist legal concepts. "Such bondage", far from being a relic of pre-modern times, was constructed by the colonial discourse of freedom, namely a past enlightenment emphasis upon equality in nature, and the extension of money as a basis of social relations" (Peter Robb. 1994).

II

The situation of Kolta of Jounsar bawar (Dehradun). Jounpur (Tehri Garhwal) and Rawain (Uttar Kashi), if analysed with reference to the "dominant caste" theory if M N Srinivas (1955), provides us a new insight different from the situations in other parts of rural India. In Jounsar bawar, the Kolta are a part of Jounsari tribe (a scheduled tribe) while in the remaining two geographically contagious regions they are scheduled caste. The common cultural indicators are their untouchable status and polyandry- the entire region being a traditionally polyandrous tract. Jounsar bawar presents, a complex situation where people live along a caste hierarchy- Brahmins and Rajputs (popularly known as Khasa) occupying the highest rung in the caste hierarchy while Bajgi, Lohar and other occupational groups are placed at the middle rung while the Kolta, etc. being untouchables have been placed at the lowest rung- yet declared as a scheduled tribe. In the other two regions they are simply a caste group- an untouchable caste. Though, it is true that even in Jounsar bawar they are simply a caste group in the local caste hierarchy, they have been declared a scheduled tribe under Article 342 of the Constitution- a sociological reality super imposed by an administrative-constitutional arrangement. Thus, it would be theoretically pragmatic if we analyse the situation of domination of Rajputs even in Jaunsar Bawar under the conceptual umbrella of dominant caste. The social situation under study may be analysed, for example, within the framework of social, economic and political connections between Jats and scheduled castes in Haryana. Rajasthan and Western Uttar Pradesh or Thakurs and Scheduled Castes in Eastern Uttar Pradesh. In this way an analysis of domination and resistance may also be done.

Rajputs in this region possess over 90% of the agricultural land and here comes the requirement of the use of agrestic serfdom. Here, the dominance of the Rajputs/Brahmins is perpetuated and legitimized through religion. As principal landowners, the dominant Rajputs achieved a privileged position within the local system of exchange of goods and services between castes on the lines of loosely traditional Hindu Jajmani System.

III

The last thirty years witnessed some changes in the life of Koltas especially since 1980s - after the promulgation of the abolition Act. These changes are more visible in the villages located on the periphery of the roads. With the construction of more roads and pathways new markets have emerged increasing employment avenues and new avenues of livelihood. Wages have also increased. There is now increased movement and migration towards Himachal Pradesh in several villages in Jaunsar area. Not only new schools have been opened hut the rate of enrollment in schools has increased appreciably. Yet, the rate of dropouts among the Kolta children has not dropped appreciably. This is largely due to economic vulnerability of the Kolta. It is a universal phenomenon that wherever children contribute to family economy, they are not sent to schools. Why would the poor people deprive themselves from the earning or contribution of their children? No matter free education has been enforced yet the incentive to send the children to school is still very weak. True, the aspirational level of the Kolta has moved a little upward yet the means to achieve the goals have not increased proportionately. Thirty years ago the author hardly found a Kolta aspiring beyond a bus conductor or office peon or lowest level revenue official. Nor you come across dozens who want to become a government officer. This is definitely a good omen.

Participation of the Kolta in the political process also shows substantial increase. In atleast five villages the author visited after 30 years the Kolta are no more deaf and dumb driven cattle. They demonstrate an increased will to participate and assert themselves not only in village or Khat panchayats but also in elections to the Slate Assembly. During my last visit a Kolta from village Navy dared to contest election in panchayat in the face of stiff opposition, ridicule and threat. Though he lost but blazed a trail for others to follow. This trend is more visible especially in Tehri Garhwal where the local Communist Party worked among them, mobilized and galvanised them to resist all such pressures from the Rajput land lords. I still vividly remember the days dining 1973-76 when during my Ph.D. fieldwork it was almost impossible to talk freely with the Koltas. Hence, most of my interviews had to be conducted during nights. In some of these villages the Rajputs were so aggressively hostile to any 'outsider' talking and mixing with bonded Kolta that it was almost impossible to conduct fieldwork. There were all sorts of harassment and intimidation to demoralize any outsider. This situation does not prevail in most of the villages anymore, though the landlords are still apprehensive and curious to know about any such interactions, the increasing self confidence and assertiveness of the Koltas prove to be a deterrent for them.

One aspect of life that has not changed much is the continuing prostitution and trafficking of women among the Kolta and Bajgi. Because of economic vulnerability it continues unabated. The pimps and brothel keepers of Delhi. Meerut and other cities are still active and taking advantage of their poverty they continue to tempt them to send their women folk to the brothels for earning some money. Such women stay at the brothels for periods ranging between 3-10 years and bring back with them sexually transmitted diseases and at the same time serving as catalytic agents for other vulnerable women from their group. Thus, both types of factors- "pushed out" factor as well as "pulled into" factor may be seen working to the detrement of the Koltas and Bajgis. One is really lucky if one is not a Kolta/ Bajgi woman of Jounsar bawar and Garhwal.

Because of a flurry of interventions by the civil society organizations supported by judicial activism the stranglehold of drudgery and helplessness has loosened a lot yet the lack of political will on the pan of the government is not able to galvanise the administrative set up to effective action. The initial euphoria and enthusiasm of the NGOs has also abated in the lace of the sluggish and halfhearted efforts of the bureaucracy. Landlessness of the Koltas is still rampant while land based livelihood as long term rehabilitation measure is crucial for effective rehabilitation of the freed bonded Koltas. Moreover, creation of a strong alternative credit agency and innovative measure's such as 'self help groups' is imperative for the over all empowerment of the Koltas. It is also necessary to make release and rehabilitation sustainable. This is crucial in the face of 'freed' bonded Kolta going back to bondage and agrestic serfdom in a different form.

Inter-generational bondage is no longer a typical characteristic of bonded labour. In the lace of globalization, bonded labour may exist as pan of community production for the Indian or global markets, whether the product is brick and stone, garments of embroidered cloth such as zardozi. Same is the case with Kolta. Wages for them are not sufficient to satisfy their needs, or be sufficient to repay the amount that they owe the employers. Thus, their economic vulnerabilities and the desired empowerment remain the most crucial factors reshaping their lives.

Remedial Measures

Some of the states have recently enacted laws providing severe punishment against such anti-social and inhuman practices and also including long-range preventive measures to stop accumulation of old debts. A central law with the following important provisions was also promulgated:

(i) bonded labour system has been abolished and such labourers stand heed;

(ii) punishments provided for its contravention are substantial;

(iii) civil courts have no jurisdiction to pronounce upon or issue injunction in any matter connected with this law;

(iv) vigilance committees at district and sub-divisional levels are to be set up to advise the implementing authority.

But inactment of laws is no solution. The bureaucratic apathy and lack of political will on the part of the government can never translate decisions and laws into action. Absence of vigorous and meaningful schemes of rehabilitation and their honest implementation, has converted these laws into damp squibs. Many of those who were bonded are still bonded and probably they will remain so until some radical steps are taken to their betterment.

TRIBAL MOVEMENTS

Chapter 20

A number of tribal movements have been studied and documented in around five decades but there was a point of debate whether these should be described as tribal or peasant movements.An important point to be noted is that the tribal movements were a mix of political, economic and cultural issues as against economically motivated peasant struggles. Nandini Sundar (2016) while tracing the study of tribal movements says that "one major influence on the study of Adivasi movements was the publication of the subaltern studiesvolumes(Ranjit Guha edited1982-7) as well as the individual monographs by the subaltern historians such as Ranjit Guha's Elementary Aspects of Peasant Insurgency in Colonial India(1983) and David Hardiman's Coming of the Devi(1987) which explored many of the cultural, religious and economic dimensions"

There are various interpretations with regard to movements broadly described as pertaining to the cultural domain.Virginous Xaxa(2008) referring to the multiple interpretations says that KS Singh(1983,1993) uses the term 'Sanskritisation' and 'Cultural' to describe such movements depending on the overall thrust while Surajit Sinha(1972) employs the term 'Reform' in place of Sanskritisation and 'Ethnicity' in place of cultural to refer to such movements.Xaxa(ibid) proposes his own classification as:

1. Sanskritisation movement
2. Cultural and Identity Movement
3. Land and Forest based Movement ; and
4. Autonomy Movement.

BK Roy Burman in MSA Rao edited Social Movements in India(1984) envisages several parameters turning to the specific manifestation of restlessness among the tribes which are as follows:

1. Response to threats to the privacy of habitat
2. Response to threats to access to and control of resources

3. Response to disruption of traditional roles in the total interaction setup.
4. Search for new meanings of the relationship between man and nature
5. Search for new meanings of the relationship between individual and society.
6. Search for new frontiers of identity
7. Search for a more satisfactory system of control over resources
8. Search for a more satisfactory system of organization of community power at all levels.

Following are a brief narration of some of the past tribal movements that could be understood in the light of various classifications given above.

Reform and Revitalization Movements

When we talk of tribal movements, sometimes it becomes imperative to distinguish between a tribal movement and a non-tribal peasant movement. This becomes necessary because despite the fact that though the bulk of tribal population has transformed itself into peasantry as a result of the 'peasantization process', it still retains some of its charac-teristic features. Because of their concentration in certain regions and a strong element of ethnicity involved, the core issues, leadership pattern and nature of political mobilisation differ from those of non-tribal peasant groups. Further, while the peasant movements tend to remain purely agrarian as peasants lived off land, the tribal movements have been both agrarian and forest-based, because traditionally, the tribal's dependence on forests has been as crucial as their dependence on land. Another important point is that the tribal revolts were directed against feudal lords, money lenders and petty government officials not because they exploited them but also because they were aliens. K S. Singh's (ed.) Tribal Movements in India (1982-83, 2 Volumes) is a very important work in this field. He has divided this work into two parts dealing with the North-Eastern tribes and Central and South Indian tribes. While the North-Eastern region and the central Indian tribal belt have been rich in tribal movements, the tribes down south are too small in numbers, and too isolated in their habitats to organise movements in spite of their exploitation and the resultant discontent. L.K. Mahapatra (1968) also agrees with this assertion and shares the view that we do not find any significant social movement—religious, status mobility or political among the numerically small, migratory tribes, like Birhors, Korwa, the Hill Kharia or the shifting cultivators like the Hill Maria, Saora or the more primitive Kond.

Ghanshyam Shah (1990) has published a very important and well documented review of literature on social movements of India in which, beside other dimensions, different typologies of tribal move-ments have also been described. LK. Mahapatra (1972) applies the typologies widely used for social movements to tribal movements. He describes these as (1) reactionary (2) conservative, and (3) revisionary or revolutionary. The reactionary movement tries to launch a movement to bring back 'the good old days'; whereas the conservative movement tries to maintain the status quo. The revisionary or revolutionary movements are those which are organised for 'improvement' or 'purification' of the cultural or social order by eliminating 'evil' or 'low' customs, beliefs or institutions. Surajit Sinha (1968) classifies the movements into (1) ethnic rebellion (2) reform movements (3) political autonomy move-ments within the Indian Union (4) secessionist movements, and (5) agrarian unrest.For brevity Ghanshyam Shah (ibid) has reformulated the typologies as follows: (1) ethnic movements (2) agrarian movements and (3) political movements. Not only is there a great deal of overlapping among all three types, but they are also interconnected and one leads to the other. As for as the issues are concerned the tribal movements may again be viewed from several angles. K.S. Singh (1985) divided the tribal move-ments into three phases viz. (i) between 1795 and 1860 which coincides with the rise, expansion and establishment of the British Empire (ii) between 1860 and 1920 which coincides with the intensive phase of co-lonialism during which merchant capital penetrated into tribal economy affecting their relationship with the land and forest, and (iii) the third phase between 1920 and 1947 i.e. till the achievement of independence. During this phase the tribals not only began to launch the so called 'separatist' movements but at the same time participated in nationalist and agrarian movements. In some areas like Jharkhand,Gujarat and Maharashtra, social reform movements led tribals to participate in the nationalist movements against British rule.

Exploitation of all sorts—land alienation, usury, forced labour, har-assment in forests-continued to be the main issues of tribal movements on the eve of independence and thereafter. The tribals of Andhra Pradesh actively participated in the Telengana movement and fought against the landlords. In the late sixties the main constituents of the Naxalbari movement were the tribals who fought against exploitation. Demand for a separate political entity as a state or a district, within or outside Indian Union has been made by various tribes of eastern and north-east frontier tribes. The movement of Naga, Mizo, Boro-Kachari, etc. may be included in this category. Sometimes the seemingly political demands camouflage the demands of ethnic and economic nature. N.K. Bose (1967) characterises these movements as the growth of 'sub-nationalism'. As Shah (ibid) rightly points out the nature of tribal movements in terms of their solidarity and the issues that they raise depends upon a variety of factors. The tribals of eastern and central India have close interaction with the Hindu peasantry and most of them do not occupy peripheral international borders. Therefore they do not demand political status outside the Indian Union despite extreme forms of persistent exploitation. The tribals of north-eastern region have been isolated from the 'mainstream' society and moreover they are located on the international border. They are more prone to secessionism. Thus, was see that the nature and the degree of involvement of tribal groups in solidarity movements depends upon a number of factors, such as the locale of the tribal groups vis-a-vis the core peasant matrix, the numeri-cal strength of tribals, the degree of their exposure to and inter-relations with the non-tribals.

Although a number of tribal groups have been airing their griev-ances through uprisings and revolts, only a few of them could organise movements and sustain them over a substantial period of time. The Santhals, Munda, Ho and Bhumij of the Chhotanagpur-Santhal Par- gana region, the Kondh, Koya and Savara of Orissa-Andhra, the Bhat- tra, Parja and Muria of Bastar, the Bhil, Koli, Juang, Bhuiya, Konda Dora etc. of the adjoining regions are the glaring examples. Among the north-eastern tribals the Mizo-Naga and Bodo are the main tribal groups. Among a multiplicity of movements, only a few of them cut across local and community barriers and developed into regional and nation-wide movements.

Tribal Movements in Central Indian Tribal belt:

In terms of their concentration central Indian tribal belt occupies the most important place in tribal India and in this belt Madhya Pradesh-Chattisgarh and Bihar-Jharkhand occupy a place of crucial importance.

Madhya Pradesh - Chhattisgarh

Though Madhya Pradesh-Chattisgarh may not boast of the top position in terms of tribal movements (the so called Maoist Movement is a recent phenomenon described in chapter Two) ,Bihar-Jharkhand is more pronounced but the issues involved have been the same. Interference and exploitation by the outsiders have their bearings on tribal movements in Madhya Pradesh-Chattisgarh too.

The Bastar Movement is the most talked about one in this category. The Gonds are the main tribal community in the erstwhile Madhya Pradesh. The areas they occupy have popularly been known as gondwana pradesh whose nerve centre has always been Bastar. Outright economic exploitation by the non-tribal landlords, sahukars, moneylenders has been their main problem; yet like the tribal groups of Bihar-Jharkhand their discontent and frustra-tion could never take the form of rebellious movements. Perhaps their deeply rooted belief in a messiah or prophet always curbed them to take any radical measures. Several sub-groups of the Gonds still believe that such a prophet shall appear one day, rid them of their miseries and revive their traditional culture. Interestingly the tribal groups of Madhya Pradesh have always been less hostile to the outsiders mainly Hindu peasantry.

The substantially 'Hinduised' Raj Gonds have been the chief propo-nents of several reformatory and other movements which largely began around 1920. Verrier Elwin pinpoints a regional organisation called Suryavanshi MahaSabha as the chief reformatory body. This body maintained a critical attitude towards the ancient and traditional Gond values and customs. It further propagated Shiva worship and donning of sacred thread. Mandla became the focal point of this movement But after some time many Gonds realised that this new life style and philosophy of life was not in consonance with the ground realities confronting them. For example, because of the imposed curbs on the mobility and rights of their women folk, their participation in the economic realm decreased substantially putting lot of strain on their socio-economic life. Change in the food habits also did not suit their traditional life style. The new 'morality' became a joke for them. More-over, they realised that it contributed minimally towards their efforts of status elevation. With many of the so called 'reformatory' steps proving counter productive a new movement surfaced led by an uneducated Gond woman Rajmohini Devi in Sarguja, north Gondwana. It called for the giving up of curbs against women and adoption of alien practices. But this movement too was of local nature and hence could generate only short lived influence. A significant point to be noted here is that all these movements, directly and indirectly, also resulted in the adoption of many Hindu cultural elements by the tribals.

The Raja of Bastar always maintained lot of influence on the Gonds. These Rajas were regarded as the Rajas of the Gonds too. But there were always disputes regarding dynastic successions and palace intrigues were the order of the day. The tribals had to endure lot of hardships. The last Raja of Bastar Praveen Chand Bhujangdeo took the reigns in 1947 but had to merge his 'Kingdom' with the Indian Union. He indulged in all sorts of propaganda about his super human status. His supporters spread the myth that he was an apostle of Rama and Krishna. The curtailment of his rights and privileges angered him and his staunch supporters. Because of corruption and misutilization of public exchequer his estate and property were confiscated by 'court of wards'. This was the breaking point as for as the 'Maharaja' was concerned. He started organising a tribal movement against the government and tried to make a common cause with the other erstwhile princes; Abhujmarh was decided as the headquarter of this 'princely' struggle. The Gond tribals were exploited to the hilt to promote his whims. This movement culmi-nated in the firing on a mob of around ten thousand tribals gathered in Lohariguda. More than a dozen tribals were killed and hundreds injured. In order to keep his support base intact he further propagated the myth that the tribals not owing allegiance to him would invite the wrath of Danteshwari Devi, a local deity. The headquarter at Jagdalpur became a scene of dharna by thousands of tribals. On March 10,1966 a bloody clash followed between police and Maharaja Praveen Chand and his supporters in which some tribals and the Maharaja himself were killed. By and large this movement revolved round the personality and personal interests of the Maharaja; hence this should not be equated with the movement of Bihar-Jharkhand and West Bengal led by Birsa or Siddhu Santhal.

Bihar-Jharkhand

Among the tribal movements organised in Bihar-Jharkhand and the adjoining areas Birsa Movement is the most widespread and best known. After Birsa movements, Tana Bhagat Movement occupies the most important place because of its multidimensional significance of far reaching socio--political implications.

The neighbouring tribe of Oraon was the focal point of Tana Bhagat Movement. This carried social implications of far reaching importance. The Oraon have a distinctive religion, complete with their own pan-theon, priesthood, festivals, elaborate rituals etc. Dharmesh is their presiding deity. Interestingly, in parts of Bihar-Jharkhand the term Bhagats is often employed for sorcerers and magicians but among the Oraon the name is applied to those who subscribe to the cult of bhakti and observe certain rules of ceremonial purity.

A number of anthropologists are of the view that the entire Bhagat movement may be conceived as an attempt to raise the status of its members in the eyes of Hindu neighbours by Sanskritization which also included the inculcation of Hindu beliefs and practices. As the story goes, it was started in April 1914 by a youngman of twenty five named Jatra Bhagat. It is also believed that one Hanuman Oraon too was the co-founder of this movement. Jatra Bhagat was undergoing training to become a mati (witch doctor) when he started the movement. Like Birsa, he also had the vision of a luminous figure from whom he had a revelation. This vision of Dharmesh, the supreme god of the Oraon, occurred at night while he was returning home after his lessons. It asked him to give up his training in ghost finding and exorcism, to echew his faith in such deities and spirits that called for animal sacrifices, and to give up meat eating and liquor. His attack on the belief in spirits, insistence on 'ritual purity' in food and drink, the agrarian and anti-government stance reminds one of Birsa Movement. The first manifestation of defiance began when he exhorted his follow-ers not to work as coolies in the local construction activities. This followed his arrest and imprisonment and the message of the new faith spread like wild fire. Among the Tanabhagats (that included non-Oraon tribals too) the belief in the coming of the Messiah had been quite strong. The Tana Bhagat Movement may be said to have developed in two phases. The first phase was that of the eradication of existing beliefs and practices in ghosts and spirits. The second phase had a constructive programme, because it consisted of the promulgation, formulation and codification of its doctrines, beliefs and rules and regulations for the conduct of followers of the new religion.

Initially the followers of the new faith were neither anti-government nor anti-outsiders/non-tribals and they were merely trying to reform their society but they had to retaliate in the face of anticipatory hostility on the part of petty government officials and outsiders. Then came 1921- 22 and Mahatma Gandhi's non-cooperation movement and the whole Bhagat movement was transformed. Mahatma Gandhi and his teach-ings had a profound impact on the followers of the Tana Bhagat Movement .They participated in it in great numbers. Jatra Oraon was jailed in 1921 and the discontent exploded in violence. The uprisings had to be crushed through military power but it again surfaced in full fury during the Second World War. The Bhagats cooperated with the nation-alists and revolutionaries.

Presently there are Bhagats of various shades. The Bacchidan Bhagat largely come from the well to do Oraons who are relatively more Hinduised. They employ Gosain or low grade Brahmins as their guru. They are known as Bacchidan Bhagat because they gift a calf to their guru for cleansing them of their sins and ritual impurities. The Bacchi-dan Bhagats who take Vaishnava as their guru are called as Vishnu Bhagats. The Nemha Bhagats exhibited a fusion of tribal and Hindu beliefs and practises and they observe all the rules very strictly. Then there are Kabir panthi Bhagats with a system of having spiritual preceptors who may or may not be Oraon. They neither worship idols nor use any visible symbol of divinity. Analysing the nature of the Tana Bhagat move-ment in the perspective of dissent, protest and reform, it is apparent that the movement was a spirited protest against the prevailing social order. It had borrowed heavily from the Hindu and Christian ideas of simplicity and piety. This simplicity became a value all the more because of the impact of the social movement under the leadership of Mahatma Gandhi. Conceptually the movement may be viewed within the framework of nativistic or revitalization movements taking place in tribal India. The Tana Bhagat movement may be viewed as a resistance, and also as an emulative movement. Conditions for resistance already existed in the excessive exploitation and social degradation of the Oraon.

Movements in North-East Region

Ethnicity has been the most important issue in the north-eastern region of India and this region continues to exhibit violent ethnic conflict.Several rounds of division and reorganization of Assam and the emergence of seven states could not totally solve the problem. Ethno-political movements have been most pronounced in this part of India. Even today Kuki-Naga conflict in Manipur,Khasi-Garo rivalry and frictions in Meghalya and violence in Bodoland in Assam sometime make the north-east as an 'ethnic cauldron.'

Naga Movement

The Naga and Mizo rebellions are two of the important examples of a long series of armed rebellions on the north-eastern fringe of India. The present Nagaland lies on the extreme north-eastern fringe of India, adjacent to Burma. Designated as Naga Hills during the British administration, it was for long one of the least accessible regions of India.

The State of Nagaland is inhabited by numerous Naga tribes such as Angami Naga, Ao Naga, Sengma Naga, Konyak Naga etc. Despite their poverty and economic backwardness, they are proud of their cultural heritage. Shifting cultivation, locally known as jhum, is their main source of livelihood. Traditionally, the Naga tribes do not bow before anybody's authority, in some cases not even their chieftain's. The Nagas resisted the British onslaughts for a long time and after a century of repression and bloody struggle the British empire could establish any semblance of authority in Naga Hills only in year 1885, As usual the area was thrown open to different shades of missionaries who did pioneering work in spreading literacy and providing them basic medical amenities. The practice of head hunting, a symbol of social prestige, was discontinued but the bloody warfare and vendetta which had taken deep roots among them could not be subdued. To acknowledge defeat, even against much stronger opponent, without offering stiff and bloody resistance, is against the very nature of brave Naga. They had also fought, before British rulers, Mughal and Ahom empires for interfering with their freedom. Till the initial decades of 20th century, they had been fighting with their traditional weapons-spears, swords, bows and arrows but they entered the era of firearms much earlier compared to the other tribal groups.

This happened during the Second World War when the Japanese army had surrounded Kohima and Japanese soldiers had infiltrated deep into Naga territory. While retreating, the Japanese soldiers left vast quantities of arms and ammunition behind. It is largely believed that the familiarity of present Naga rebels with the firearms and modern techniques of guerilla warfare is the direct result of this experience.

After India attained independence and Nagaland along with other tracts of north eastern hill area became a part of Indian Union, a concerted move was undertaken by the overambitious and the politicised section of the Nagas to secede from India and form an Independent country. The seeds of this separatism were probably laid when Charles Pawsey, Deputy Commissioner of Kohima in 1945, established the Naga Hills District Tribal Council to unite the Nagas in the task of reconstruction after the war. "A small newspaper called, significantly, The Naga Nation was published and later The Naga Herald, subsequently banned in 1953. Dr.Zapu Phizo himself and most of the Phizo's top lieutenants seem originally to have been initiated into politics by Pawsey. The mentorship of Pawsey was so effective apparently, that in June, 1947 Phizo was able to declare boldly that the Naga Hills would cease to be a part of India after India's independence. "Before he made his declaration behind the scene parleys between the British authorities in India and their principals in London are said to have favoured a future for the Nagas separate from the rest of India" (RakshatPuri, 1972). Briefly, in months that followed, an agreement was arrived at between Sir Akbar Hyadari- the governor, and Assam's Chief Minister Gopinath Bardoloi, on the one hand, and the Naga National Council led by Phizo on the other, the last clause of which was interpreted by the Nagas to mean that they would have the choice of separation after ten years. Official statements made it clear that this was not so. Pandit Nehru, described the Naga demand as "unwise, impracticable and unacceptable"

Phizo and his followers, well versed in guerilla warfare, took to the jungle and the rebellion for secession from India started in a systematic way. It continued unabated for a decade or so with full support of Naga masses who were providing all sorts of assistance and shelters to the insurgents against the security forces of India. Meanwhile the state of Nagaland came into being in 1962 and this satisfied a considerable section of politically conscious Naga people. Commenting on the deterioration of relations between the Nagas and the Government of India after 1952 onwards,M.Alemchiba Ao, himself a Naga, says that the main cause that led to unfortunate conflict was Government's lack of knowledge of the tribes and their failure to appreciate the basic requirements of the hill men (1972).

Dr. Phizo, apprehending arrest, took to exile and settled in London and his followers back home formed a government in exile in the difficult terrains and jungles of Nagaland and adjoining Burma and the erstwhile East-Pakistan. They formed their own army, parliament, cabinet, courts, etc. The Naga rebels also got training arms, money and political support from the countries unfriendly to India, especially China and Pakistan.

Disillusioned with the secessionist movement, increasing number of Nagas started turning to the constitutionally elected State Government and its democratic institutions. Seeing their movements petering, out the rebel Nagas struck again with full ferocity in 1972, just after the elections through which a new government had come into being. The security forces of India also retaliated with full force. Many underground insurgents were flushed out, a vast area was intensively combed, organizations sympathetic to rebels were banned and many persons suspected to be harbouring the rebels were arrested and tortured. Gradually the new wave of insurgency subsided but did not end.

The Government of India has no doubt shown utmost restraint in dealing with the insurgency in Nagaland. On the administrative front, massive amounts of money have been invested on a variety of developmental activities and for providing them gainful employment. All such schemes are being implemented through Naga people themselves. They form their own government on the basis of adult franchise. The result of this attitude has started bearing fruits. The rebels have almost been isolated and they are able to show their presence and defiance only through sporadic cases of ambush on government officials and convoys of security forces. The indigent Christian missionaries have undertaken the mission of reclaiming their tribal flock to the Indian nation unlike the foreign missionaries who were either indifferent or instigating the Christian Nagas to secede from India. It is a great tribute to the dedication and zeal of the Christian missionaries that the literacy among many of these tribes is much higher than the average in the rest of the country.

The so-called "separatist" tendencies among the Nagas and other north-eastern tribes were initially only natural attempts on their part to define their socio-cultural identity vis-a-vis others in new circumstances of independence. "For most tribes in north-eastern hill areas the experience of being integral part of nation is relatively recent and their difficulty in quickly and unqualifyingly accepting this fact needs to be sympathetically reviewed."(Srinivas and Sanwal, 1972). To some other anthropologists a great deal of what is happening in north-eastern hill areas today, can be related to the tribal elite's fear of losing their cultural identities in the ocean of Hindu nationalism. Thus, attempts to produce cultural uniformity and integration through induced assimilation can be dangerous. India has always being heterogeneous in terms of race, language, religion and culture. The essence of Indian unity lies in diversity, and any attempt towards unity to succeed must be in the framework of this cultural, religious and ethnic pluralism.

In order to achieve peace the Government of India has been negotiating with the most powerful and popular Naga faction National Socialist Council of Nagaland(I-M).It seems most of the issues have been resolved but a final peace accord has not been achieved so far.

Concluding one may say that the present problem with the Naga is not merely economic though economic steps for their betterment have certainly diffused the situation to a great extent. It is political problem and needs a political solution.

Mizo Movement

The unrest and uprising among the Mizos is another example of simmering tribal unrest and discontent on the far north-eastern fringe of India. There is hardly any need to dilate on the nature of the threat that a weak, strife-torn and isolated northeast spells for India.

The Lushais constitute an important tribe inhabiting the Lushai hills adjacent to Bangla Desh and Burma. Traditionally, the Lushai people call their place of habitation as Mizoram and hence the inhabitants of Mizoram are called Mizos. They have been as much alienated from the rest of India as those of Naga Hills, thanks largely to inaccessibility and lack of communication in an area many points of which are linked only by helicopter. Backed and protected by British administration, the western missionaries converted the Mizos to Christianity in large numbers and 'reclaimed' them to 'civilization', but in the process raised yet another wall, cultural and religious. Educational and medical facilities were extended to far flung areas for the first time and many of the missionaries served them with dedication and compassion. They were assured a better future if they embraced Christian religion. Being satisfied with such assurance, they cooperated with British authorities. It is on record that about three hundred Mizo headmen extended all sorts of help to the British rulers when the Japanese army attacked Assam during the Second World War.

Like the Naga rebellion the nature of Mizo uprising, too is highly political. Unlike the Santhals and Munda rebellions, it was not the result of exploitation by the outside elements backed by British authorities. Accustomed to free life Mizos did not like any political interference from any side. They resorted to guerilla warfare whenever an attempt was made to put them under any political authority except their own. The geographical and ecological conditions like deep forests and difficult mountainous terrain further encouraged their defiant temperament. They live under geographical conditions ideal for guerilla resistance. Burning with political ambitions and instigated by the unfriendly China and Pakistan, the Mizo leadership raised the banner of revolt just after India attained independence and they were put under the political authority of Indian Union.

The demand for "Mizoland" and for single entity comprising the hill districts of Assam around Shillong, were originally one movement, and the movement was for a separate state, not for separation from the country. It took shape in 1954, with the formation of Eastern India, Tribal Union subsequently giving shape to the All Party Hill Leaders' Conference. "There followed the usual cycle of verbal assurance from New Delhi, unexplained delays, and obstruction by interests-usually Assamese-opposed to the aspirations of the hill leaders and their followers "(RakshatPuri, ibid). In the process, elements in the Assam Congress Party are said to have attempted to divide the hill leaders by supporting the dissident Mizos, who were apparently encouraged to form a Mizo National Front, under the leadership of Laldenga. This move spiralled into secessionist movement and the Mizo National Front began to demand complete separation from India and mounted a guerilla terrorist campaign to make the demand effective.

In April, 1970 was created a new state of Meghalaya out of Assam. The hill leaders were satisfied so is the case with their followers the Khasi, Garo and Jaintia peoples. To fulfill the political aspiration of the Mizo, Mizoram was declared a Union Territory—independent of Assam— along with Arunachal Pradesh reorganising the state of Assam in 1971 under the North-Eastern Areas (Reorganisation) Act, 1971. However the guerilla warfare continued though officials sources claimed success in a programme of resettlement of Mizo villagers. "The Mizos were regarded as good soldiers when the British were in India. Many of hard-core guerillas are said to be demobilized soldiers who fought in Burma campaign during the Second World

War, and who have not been able to find gainful employments in the hills and have no access to the opportunities elsewhere in the country.

For some time Laldenga remained underground in the hill with his government in exile and led the movement from hidings. But later opted to go to West Germany and London to mobilize support for his demands. In the absence of Laldenga from the scene disillusionment grew among the large sections of his followers-guerillas and non-guerilla Mizos— and they started cooperating with the constitutionally elected government of Mizoram and various institutions of the democratic government. The Indian security forces too made the lives of secessionists miserable and demoralization started settling in. Meanwhile the Government of India pumped massive doses of developments grants to this tiny Union Territory. The seventies witnessed fast pace of spread of education, medical facilities and employment opportunities. The popularity of Laldenga and the secessionist movement led by him declined appreciably but the hard-core and the dedicated section of the Mizos remained sympathetic to their leader and the movement. Acknowledging the potentiality of such a situation, the Government of India once more opened the door of peaceful settlement and invited Laldenga from West Germany with the guarantee that he will be provided free and safe passage out of India in case the talks failed. The delicate parleys continued for more than a year in New Delhi in 1981 and the first half of 1982. Finding itself helpless before the rigid attitude of Laldenga, the government terminated the talks, and allowed Laldenga to go wherever he liked: In this way the Government of India honoured its promise.

Although, the extremist section of Mizo National Front continued the guerilla war but its intensity declined to a great extant. Declining support of the Mizo masses, the emergence of Bangla Desh in place the erstwhile East Pakistan dealt a serious blow to the whole movement. While the growing disillusionment of the people deprived the guerillas of their mass base, the dismemberment of Pakistan also deprived them of the strategic support. Later an accord was reached with the Mizo National Front, Laldenga became chief minister of Mizoram, elections were held, he ruled for a while and died of Cancer. Rest is History.

Present Situation

The very nature of mobilization, movements and objectives have undergone changes. The secessionistic movements in the north-east are now part of history and whatever remains is confined to the demands for more political autonomy within the framework of Indian Constitution. However,in the central Indian region and the adjoining states the so called Maoist Movement is different for its objectives. The ongoing Pathalgadi Movement insists on the honest implementation of the constitutional provisions for the scheduled tribes and Sarna Movement is directed towards the restoration of tribal identity.

Pathalgadi Movement

This is a unique tribal movement different from the previous ones as it is based on the awareness of constitutional rights of the tribal people. Pathalgadi literally means 'carving a stone'. Carving stone plaques is an ancient tradition among the tribal people of Jharkhand region. They usually erected engraved stones to mark the birth or death of a member of the community. This practice took a new meaning after some tribal activists led by Late BD Sharma, a former IAS officer and one of the greatest advocates of tribal rights and an IPS officer Bandi Oraon initiated the practice of erecting stone slabs on the entry of villages after the promulgation of the Panchayat (Extension to Scheduled Areas) Act in 1996. This act passed after great struggle empowers the tribal people in gram sabha panchayats to preserve and safeguard their traditions, public spaces and cultures. Significantly, it gave them the mandatory right to consultation and approval in land acquisition. Green painted stone slabs were engraved with the excerpts from the PESA Act and the Fifth Schedule of the constitution dealing with the administration of Scheduled Areas.

The Pathalgadi Movement caught the imagination of the scheduled tribes of not only Jharkhand and even beyond. In order to counter the assertion of the constitutional rights of the tribal community, the central government in 2016 issued two ordinances to amend the Chotanagpur Tenancy Act, 1908 and Santhal Pargana Act, 1949. These amendments enabled commercial use of tribal land and made it easily transferable. It empowered the government to procure agricultural land from the tribals for non-agricultural purposes. The movement became stronger and more local after these ordinances and tribal people, in increasing number, erected new stone slabs as mark of protest now warning the outsiders not to enter these areas without any justifiable reason. It led to violent clashes between the local tribal communities and government authorities. Individuals and NGOs in the forefront of the movement were arrested and penalized. As per reports the BJP led state government booked thousands of tribal citizens on charges of sedition between 2017 and 2018 when the movement was its peak.

After the Jharkhand Mukti Morcha (JMM) led government came to power and Hemant Soren, a Santhal, became chief minister, order was issued to release the activists of Pathalgadi Movement arrested under sedition Act. This movement may be taken as the beginning of similar movements in the Fifth Scheduled Areas for demanding their rights enshrined in the Indian constitution.

Sarna Movement

This is another movement on the part of the tribal communities to assert their identity separate from the 'imposed' Hindu identity. Since long, a number of tribal communities have been trying to assert their tribal/adivasi identity. On Noveember 11,2020, during a one day special session convened by the state assembly, a resolution was passed for the provision of a separate 'Sarna Code' for members of the the tribal communities. If approved by Central government, the coming census of 2021 may have a separate column allowing members of these communities to identify themselves as belonging to a distinct religious community. The word Sarna in the local tribal language refers to the place of worship and a white red flag flutters over these platforms or places of worship. Moreover, in a number of villages and towns of Jharkhand, one may see a number of these flags fluttering on cross roads and public places. In the Sarna Code there is no idol worship and instead Nature is worshipped through natural objects. Though there was no separate column for Sarna religion, more than forty lakh tribal people of Jharkhand, West Bengal, Orissa and Bihar (majority of them from Jharkhand) had recorded their religion as Sarna in 'other religion' category.

Another point related with the tribal identity and consciousness is related with Paingudi known as abode of tribal gods. Thus Paingudi is the natural abode of tribal gods popular in tribal areas of Chattisgarh and adjoining areas. In 2020 the Chattisgarh government initiated a programme of 'recovering/ rediscovering' Ram's forest movement (Ram van gaman path) in his journey during his exile. In this project hundreds of huts having natural objects symbolising Nature/

god are being renamed as Ram's forest abodes after altering the very nature of these abodes. The adivasis of this region look at it as the attempt to 'Hinduise' them by force. This is yet another attempt by the adivasis to counter the attempts to transform their identity.

TRIBAL RESISTANCE, VIOLENCE, LEFT WING EXTREMISM and STATE'S RESPONSE

Chapter 21

The so called Maoist/Naxalite movement going on from Srikakulum in Andhra Pradesh upto Sonbhadra district in Uttar Pradesh, especially in the Central Indian Tribal belt, is being seen as one of the most serious problems being faced by Indian nation since independence. On the basis of its coverage in media, discussions, and debates by the State and non-state agencies, two perceptions prevail:

1. It is posing threat to internal security with national security implications. For those who view it like this, a security-centric and law and order approach would lead to a 'solution'.
2. Others view it as a genuine socio-economic problem compounded by exclusion, discrimination, and marginalization. For them it is a social movement for social justice. Moreover, it is not a problem but consequence of several problems. It is not a sudden eruption and its' origin and roots may be traced to colonial times that witnessed a number of tribal revolts in response to the oppression and exploitation of the Adivasi population.

The gravity of the situation may be gauged from the fact that it has taken under it's shadow around 200 districts in 15 states. It has spread over 35-40% of the geographical area of the country. The most affected regions are Southern Orissa, South and Central Chhattisgarh, South Bihar, Eastern Andhra Pradesh. Eastern Maharashtra and upto Southern Uttar Pradesh. The tribal population of the country is around 8% of the total population and almost 50% of the total tribal population lives in Bihar and Jharkhand, Madhya Pradesh and Chhattisgarh and Andhra Pradesh. This means that Central India is the largest tribal belt of the country. Significantly, the areas inhabited by the tribal people are the poorest, most underdeveloped, and most economically backward where they are living under severely oppressive conditions. The problem not to be missed is that the ultra-left extremism and violence is most visible in these areas.

Though, tribal problems vary from state to state but mostly, the common problem are land alienation, chronic indebtedness, food security, health, education and displacement. Nobody can deny it that in areas like Bastar, people even today have no access to potable and safe water fit for human consumption. There are no schools and if schools are there, there are no teachers. Either hospitals are not there and if these are there, there are no doctors or medicines and people's representatives are hardly concerned about the state of affairs. Lakhs of tribal boys and girls are unemployed despite many of them being educated. They go to the nearby cities but return frustrated. Agrarian situation is so bad that agriculture is hardly productive and employment oriented. Their livelihood is severely jeopardized. Under these circumstances when they come across the gun totting Maoists showing sympathy towards their problems the tribal youths are naturally attracted towards them. When the Maoists loot food grains from government agencies and distribute it to the starving tribals, they become heroes. When they redistribute land to the landless, they become gods.

Of all the problems enumerated above displacement has emerged as the single most serious problem, ironically, most of the tribal areas are very rich in forest, water, and mineral resources. In the post-independence period a number of developmental projects have come up resulting in large scale displacement. Hydroelectric and irrigation projects are the largest source of displacement. Other major sources of displacement are mining, super thermal and nuclear power plants, industrial and military installations, weapons testing grounds, railways and roads, expansion of reserved forest areas, sanctuaries and parks and technological interventions which cause the large scale displacement of traditional fisher folk and hand loom weavers. In the scenario of development and displacement the majority of the affected are obviously tribal communities who have been historically dependent on the natural resources for their subsistence. A significant point to be noted here is that the tribal communities are roughly 8% of the total population of the country, yet over 50% of those displaced and ousted belong to the tribal communities. The implication is obvious the tribal people are disproportionately affected by our developmental policies and the resultant displacement. What about rehabilitation? Documents of the Planning Commission admit that not even 20% of the displaced have been properly rehabilitated. Who will protect the livelihoods of the displaced people?

Will it not be right to conclude that the tribal people have been made 'victims of progress'? Moreover, among the non-economic consequences of displacement, dismantling of kinship network, mutual support system and desecration of sacred groves are the important ones. Unfortunately, these tribal communities were hardly made partners in progress. Previously, as a result of colonial exploitation they suffered for more than two hundred years at the hands of land grabbers, money lenders, forest and liquor contractors flourishing under the patronage of governmental agencies and in the post-independence period they were made to suffer as the sacrificial goat' at the alter of 'development'. That is why a number of tribal leaders have been asking an inconvenient question: "Are we an internal colony of India?"

The founding fathers of the constitution formulated a number of provisions for safeguarding their interest. Almost all the state governments, in pursuance of the constitutional provisions, have come out with a number of legislative measures such as Prevention of Land Alienation Act, Regulation of Money lending Act etc. Moreover, the Fifth and Sixth Schedule of the Constitution have laid down a number of provisions for the administration of the tribal areas and protection of their language and culture but they continue to be oppressed and exploited and their interests unprotected largely because of lack of political will on the part of the State to eliminate all forms of exploitation and social injustice.

It is said that folk songs never lie because these are the spontaneous overflow of powerful feelings. It will not be out of place to mention two of the popular folk songs from the Jharkhand region:

> "They made us many promises, more than I can remember but they fulfilled just one-they promised to take over land and they took it."
>
> "When they (diku/outsiders) came to our land they were as thin as the eye of a needle. Sucking our blood, they have become as fat as the ploughshare."

Such folk songs speak volumes of injustice and exploitation, it's a classic case of a whole population being made 'legally dispossessed.'

II

The Expert Group of Planning Commission in 2006 came out with a report titled "Challenges of Development in Maoist Affected Tribal Areas." This report is a first of its kind in the last twenty two years by the centre. It has tried an open approach rather than a security-centric one. This report also argues that land related factors play an important role in the growth of Maoism. Pointing out that thousands of acres of land remain fallow, the expert group has asked the government to devise legal means to ensure that the landless get land. It recommends that The Scheduled Tribes and other Traditional

Forest Dwellers (Recognition of forest rights) Act, 2006 be implemented in full earnest: in order to ensure people their land rights. It acknowledged that left radicalism has emerged as a result of deficit planning. "Constant alienation has made people take up arms and it is time one understands the problem as not just a law and order problem but one whose foundations are socio-economic." The report relates extremism to deeper faults in governance, land alienation, unemployment and inequalities in society.

This is an undeniable fact that the tribal economy has been forest economy and vice-versa. The situation has been further compounded by a heavy use of the coercive apparatus of the state in the forests negating all democratic principles. The forest department, armed with the powers of the police, and the police itself rules the forests much like an occupation army. Arbitrary imprisonment, unpaid extraction of food etc. (eggs, chickens, goats, milk, forest produce etc), unpaid labour, forced extraction of money, down right looting of houses and settlements, rape and arson are regularly used to keep the tribes in subjugation. It is worth noting that normal laws do not operate in the forest areas.

Cross misuse of Land Acquisition Act is one of the sorest points in this tragic situation. This situation reminds one of colonial India where the imperialist power laid claim on the property of the common people in the name of service and public purposes. But the fact of the matter is that they indirectly served their colonial interests only. The same policies still persist in independent India where the government has the power to acquire any property in the name of 'national interest'. In this so called 'public interest' and 'national interest' where does the tribal people figure? Are they not part of- the 'public' and 'nation'? Who would protect their interests? Are we dealing with alien/enemy people from another land?

Multinational Corporations have been given access to the natural resources in tribal areas in a big way especially in the mining sector. As Gautam Navlakha [2006] points out when the Central government speak of Maoists obstructing development in tribal areas it means the Maoist presence is obstructing corporate exploitation of minerals, forests, water and land resources of the adivasis. Corporations come with capital intensive, low job creating investment which necessitates import of skilled labour from outside and token employment for locals as members of an unskilled low wage labour force. The National Mineral Development Corporation's Kirandul and Bacheli mines in Dantewade district of Madhya Pradesh do not employ local people.

The entire iron ore mined here is exported through a dedicated railway line to Visakhapatam and then exported to Japan at low cost. The so called 'Red Corridor', (areas under the influence of ultra-left forces) is full of minerals where the adivasis have been residing for centuries. The Multi-national companies are eyeing the minerals of these regions and the government is all set to sell it on the market rate and therefore it has signed hundreds of Memorandums of Understanding (MOUs) with these multi-national companies. Since the tribal populations in these areas strongly feel that they have been betrayed, neglected and dispossessed in the name of development, industrialization and 'national interest' they are resisting against unjust displacement. They also believe that in the name of fighting insurgency the government wants to capture the land and hand it over to the multi-national companies, justice demands that the Land Acquisition Act should be limited to national security and public welfare and should not be stretched to acquisition for companies, cooperatives and registered societies. The Act need to be further revised to minimize displacement and secure the rights of the affected displaced persons.

III

On March 13,2006, the Union home minister tabled in parliament a status paper on the problems of left wing extremism. The policy, as laid down in the paper, to deal with 'Naxalite Menace' contains the following points:

(i) The Government will deal sternly with the naxalites indulging in violence,

(ii) Naxalism being an inter-state problem, the states will adopt a collective approach and pursue a coordinated response to counter it.

(iii) The states will need to further improve police response and pursue effective and sustained police action against the naxalites and their infrastructure individually and jointly.

(iv) There will be no peace dialogue by the affected states with the naxal groups unless the latter agree to give up violence and arms,

(v) Efforts will continue to be made lo promote local resistance groups against the naxalites but in a manner that the villagers are provided adequate security cover and the area is effectively dominated by the security forces.

(vi) Keeping in view that naxalism is not merely a law and order problem, the policy of the government is to address the menace simultaneously on political, security, development, and public perception management front in a holistic manner.

(vii) Political parties must strengthen their cadre base in naxal affected areas so that the potential youth there can be weaned away from the path of naxal ideology.

(viii) The slate governments will need to accord a higher priority in their annual plans to ensure development in these areas. The focus areas should be to distribute land to the landless poor as part of the speedy implementation of the land reforms, ensure development of physical infrastructure like roads, communication, power, etc. and provide employment opportunities to the youth in these areas.

Of this agenda of action the government has taken up on top priority the modernization of state police, supply of mine protected vehicles, long tern deployment of central para-military forces and recruitment in central para-military forces. The tribal and forest related issues, effective implementation of land reforms and creation of employment opportunities are the issues always talked about but never taken up seriously Should we hope this will be taken up in urgency now?

The idea of promoting local resistance groups against the left militancy took the form of Salva Judum in which some local people were trained in warfare and given arms.

This is like creating a situation of civil war. This policy has been condemned by all peace and justice loving people. They demanded that this should be scrapped as it delegitimises politics, dehumanizes people and degenerates those engaged in their security. Above all, it means abdication of the state's responsibility itself. A better alternative will be to encourage civil society groups, having knowledge of and sympathy with the local tribal population in assisting this task force for wider participation of people in the implementation of various laws.

As a response of the civil society the points raised by B. D. Sharma in his letter to the President of India dated May 17, 2010 also deserve serious consideration. Among other points, he quotes the former president or India, late K R Narayanan: "Let it not be said by the future generations that the Indian Republic has been built on the destruction of green earth and the innocent tribals who have been living there for centuries". B D Sharma further says that:

(i) The tribal people are the most democratic people on earth. The found Jug fathers, therefore, especially bestowed them with a protection shield, the Fifth Schedule, described as 'constitution within constitution' Yet these communities were virtually criminalized on the dot with the adoption of our constitution. They have no place for the community and its customs and traditions. The Governors endowed with limitless powers for removing such dissonance, have remained unaware till date about the catastrophic impact of this lapse on their part on the life of the tribal people.

(ii) The Union should be persuaded to publicly state its special responsibility towards the tribal people.

(iii) Proposal for 'Peace Now' should be initiated immediately.

(iv) Honour, within one year, honestly all the promise that have been made to the tribal people and broken by the state.

(v) Work out a comprehensive solution to confront the existing violence and chaos.

In order to ensure peace and justice, the following measures should be taken up urgently :

(i) Land records in the tribal areas must be maintained properly so that the affected tribal don't have to suffer in case of any litigation,

(ii) Eliminate Benami land holdings

(iii) Surplus and reclaimed land be distributed among the tribals along with financial assistance to rejuvinate productive agriculture. In this task proper utilization of Waste land Reclamation Board will go a long way to mitigate the sufferings of the tribals.

(iv) Draconian and colonial Land Acquisition Act should be reviewed and amended.

(v) Ensure the payment or minimum wages.

(vi) Scheduled Tribes & other Traditional Forest Dwellers (Recognition of Forest Rights) Act, 2006, should be implemented in letter and spirit.

(vii) Abolition of Bonded Labour Act 1976, should be implemented strictly.

(viii) Ensure easy and favorable credit facilities so that the moneylenders may not exploit the tribal people.

(ix) Implementation of forest laws should have a human face, putty cases of violation of forest laws withdrawn, and proper implementation of the scheme of joint Forest Management (J. F. M.) should be ensured.

(x) Customary laws of the tribals should be codified and respected.

(xi) Protect and promote tribal languages.

Indigenous knowledge System of the tribal people, especially related to environment, medicine, and water management, should be documented and protected under Intellectual Property Rights.

(xii) State to shun the obsession that whosoever supports the tribal cause is a Maoist or waging war against the State.

(xiii) Restoration of peoples' right to live in dignity and freedom.

Today tribal cultures all over the world including India are 'wounded cultures'. Given the number, the tribal voice will remain marginalized in national politics. The local tribal communities arc trapped in unending cycles of brutal violence unleashed by Maoists, the State (security forces) and vigilante armed civilian groups such as Salva Judum and its incarnations by other names. Each group claims that their attacks are retributive and defensive, and that they have not initiated violence but none- of the groups can defend such a claim Further even armed struggle does not mean a license to loot and kill.

Rightly or wrongly the left extremists have emerged as the voice of the oppressed tribal population. The Adivasis are not necessarily being inspired by Marxism/Maoism. They are with them because these ultra-left forces have mobilized the oppressed tribals and provided political leadership, fighting for the tribal rights. By all means, fault the left extremists for their shortcomings and crimes but they have to be respected for fighting against exploitation and oppression which should have been done by the State. Why should the exploited tribals wait patiently for a change in their lives while the prosperity of the already privileged rise astronomically and exponentially?

(a) ... management of forest laws should have a human face ... [illegible] ... Forest Management ... should be ensured.

(b) ... [illegible] ... should be modified and respected.

(c) ... against outside ... interference.

... [illegible] ... protected ... [illegible]

(d) ... [illegible] ... wherever suggested ... [illegible] ... the State.

(e) ... of practical path of ... [illegible] ... and economy.

Today if all authorities ... [illegible] ... would ... [illegible] ... national politics. The local tribal communities are ... [illegible] ... the State ... [illegible] ... by other ... claims that ... [illegible] ... armed ... [illegible]

... because the ... have ... as the ... [illegible] ... are not necessarily ... [illegible] ... their ... [illegible] ... exploitation and oppression which should have ... by the State. What ... [illegible] ... tribals ... [illegible] ... economically and ... [illegible]

DENOTIFIED TRIBES

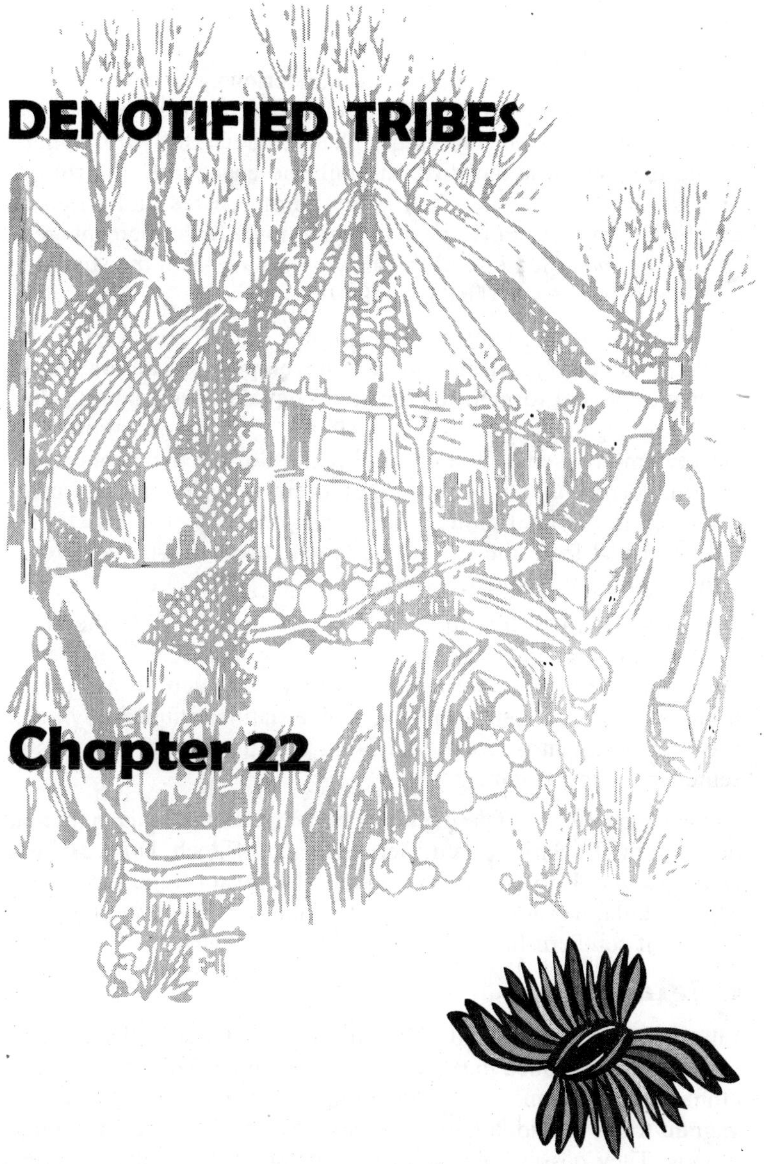

Chapter 22

That crime is hereditary no one would seriously believe, but that men are born to crime is at least an Indian reality. Criminality cannot go by groups. It is an individual phenomenon. But with a single stroke the British authorities, through the enactment of Criminal Tribes Act in 1871, branded some whole castes and tribes as criminals. "In fact, it may be said that a much larger percentage of these tribes were led into criminality by giving them the stigma of criminal tribes" (A.V. Thakkar, 1949).

The tribes in India, known as "Criminal Tribes", regarded crime as their hereditary calling and had developed an elaborate code of discipline and formalities for this. They adopted crime as their trade and engaged in anti-social activities. "Criminal activities are largely emphasised by the cultural pattern of the tribe concerned. Certain criminal tribes have got their sanction for criminal activities in their religious beliefs and practices. The sanction is often derived from their tribal gods who are believed to revel in crime" (D.N. Majumdar, 1949).

During the British rule, these tribes were made to bear the brand of criminality by the accident of their birth and were subjected to restraints on their movements so harsh that even an accidental failure to report to their respective police stations at unearthly hours was treated as an offence, justifying the imposition of a savage sentence of imprisonment.

Among such tribes wandering in northern and central India, important ones are the Bawaria, Bhatu, Beria, Bhedkut Biloch, Dom, Habura, Harni, Kanjar, Karwal, Mina, Mahtam, Pakhiwara, Tagu and Sansia. The Yerkula, Yenadi and Sugali are some of the important tribal groups of southern India falling under this category.

Origin

Like many other castes and tribes, the origin of the so-called criminal tribes is also shrouded in mystery and very little is known about their ethnic composition. Majumdar opines that these wandering and vagrant tribes are not a homogeneous lot; ethnically they are mixed groups. They possess physical traits characteristic of the important racial stocks in varied proportions. B. S. Bhargava (1949) is of the view that the criminal tribes have never cared to preserve their separate identity or purity like other more zealous castes and tribes of India. Their numbers have been swelled by recruits from all classes, consisting generally of adventurets, refugees, and outcastes, who are always welcome into their fold.

According to one view they have descended from the Gypsies. Gypsy tribes are found all over the world and are believed to have emanated from a common origin. But there is little evidence to show that the criminal tribes of India belong to the same stock as the Gypsies found in the present day Europe or other parts of the world. Again, it is held by some that the criminal tribes owe their origin to the aborigines of the old, who had been displaced from time to time by the incursions of the inhabitants of Central Asia. According to this view, those aborigines who could not find suitable habitations had to roam from place to place. In due course of time wandering became a way of life with them and they began to feel quite at home in the nomadic mode of life. Some of them found it convenient to supplement their honest earnings by petty thefts and pilferings. As Bhargava (ibid) tell us, most of the Hindu criminal tribes of upper India trace their origin from Rana Pratap of Chittorgarh in Rajputana. By a legend they generally date their social degradation from the time of the siege of Chittorgarh by Allauddin Khilji in 1308 AD. They ascribe their nomadism chiefly to their efforts to save themselves and their religion from the inroad of Islam.

The existing evidence before us goes to prove that the nomadic tribes have always been recruiting their members from practically all sections of society, and naturally, therefore, the social origin of different criminal tribes differ in various particulars. Definite historical information about their past are meagre or unobtainable. However, Bhargava has collected some legends which throw some light on their origin and antecedents.

Some scholars have derived the word Bawaria from the Hindi word Baola or Baora meaning crazy. It is said that after the capture of Chittorgarh a number of Rajputs ran away into the jungle and began to live a nomadic life. One of them fell in love with a Rajput maid and married her. But he could not give up his nomadic mode of life although the parents of his wife strongly disapproved of it. They began to call him Baola meaning mad or crazy and later on his descendents came to be known as Bawaria. In the time of the

Marathas, they took to dacoity on a large scale. A note on the 'Bhavri tribe published by the Madras police, derives the word Bhavri from Bavdi or Baoli meaning a pond. It is said that these people originally used to settle on the banks of a large Baoli meaning a pond and hence the name Bawaria.

A good number of Bhatus have recently come under the influence of Christianity and Islam. Some authorities are of the opinion that the name of the tribe has been derived from the Sanskrit word Bhanti, meaning varieties. Nesfield is of the view that the word Bhatu is derived from the Hindi word Bahutor, meaning arm-breakers, referring to their favourite device used against their opponents. The Muslim Bhatu differ in their social life from other Bhatus only in this respect that they bury their dead instead of cremating them, and contrary to the Islamic faith they do not hesitate to eat pork.

Kanjar is a name usually applied to a number of nomadic tribes of Gypsy origin. Crooke derives it from the Sanskrit word Kannanchara-a wanderer in the woods. The Kanjar residing in the Punjab and Rajputana profess that they originally served the Jats and the Rajputs as bards. By and by their profession became less remunerative and perforce they had to supplement their income from other sources.

Similarly other criminal tribes also carry some legends about their origin but it is very difficult to verify them due to paucity of historical material and conflicting and some time contradictory claims and counter claim.

Habitat and Population

Criminal tribes were concentrated in the present Uttar Pradesh, Madhya Pradesh, Maharashtra, Tamil Nadu, Andhra Pradesh and Karnataka. They were not present in appreciable number in the States of Assam and Jammu and Kashmir in the North and Kerala in the South.

Population statistics for denotified tribes are not available since they are not separately counted during the Census. The Criminal Tribes Act Enquiry Committee estimated their population at about 35 lakhs. The Special Working group on Cooperation for Backward Classes estimated their number and distribution in different States to be 35.13 lakhs as below—

States	Population of Denotified Tribes (In Lakh)
Uttar Pradesh	16.70
Bombay (including Maharashtra and Gujarat)	6.30
Madras (including Tamil Nadu and Andhra Pradesh)	5.90
Mysore (Karnataka)	2.10
Punjab (including Haryana)	0.80
Madhya Pradesh	0.80
Orissa	0.70
Areas of former Hyderabad State	0.70
Rajasthan	0.70
West Bengal	0.26
Bihar	0.13
Delhi	0.04
TOTAL	**35.13**

At Present, according to one estimate, they number about 560 lakhs. STATES are empowered to notify communities considered as 'Denotified Tribes' in their respective State. The list of communities varies from State to State. Some of the communities listed as 'Denotified Communities' are also included in the list of Scheduled Castes/Scheduled Tribes in the respective States based on criteria followed for the purpose. The number of Denotified Communities in different States is given below—

States	No. of Communities
Andhra Pradesh	65
Bihar	10
Gujarat	34
Haryana	6
Himachal Pradesh	1
Madhya Pradesh	41
Orissa	8
Karnataka	106
West Bengal	6

Maharashtra	35
Rajasthan	26
Uttar Pradesh	36
Tamil Nadu	66

Legislative Measures

The Encyclopaedia of Social Work in India (Vol. III) giving a detailed chronological description tells us that the early years of the nineteenth century witnessed unprecedented insecurity in northern India owing to the criminal activities of **thugs** and dacoits. It led the then Government of India to undertake special measures to suppress such organised criminal acts. Consequently, in 1839, a Thagi and Dacoity Department was created to handle this task. The special operations of the Department, conducted through specially appointed Superintendents for the purpose, brought to fore that certain tribes in Northern India, like the Meenas, were primarily responsible for organised crimes and offences against property. To keep a check over the activities of these tribes, the first Criminal Tribes Act was passed in 1871.

Earlier, under Regulation XXII of 1793, Magistrates were empowered with summary powers to punish specified tribes which were committing systematic crimes, vagrants and suspected persons. With the adoption of the Indian Penal Code in 1860 and the Criminal Procedure Code in 1861, however, the above summary powers were withdrawn.

The Criminal Tribes Act, 1871

It was mandatory, according to this Act, before declaring a gang, a tribe or a class of persons as criminal, to report to the Governor General in Council giving adequate reasons for declaring it as such. It was also stipulated that satisfactory arrangements be made for settling those criminals who did not lead a settled life. The report was also to state the arrangements made for enabling the tribe to earn its living when it was settled in any fixed place of residence. There was, however, no provision in the Act to separate the children of criminal tribes from their parents, although its necessity was emphasised during the debate on the Bill in the Council. Although the provisions of this Act were helpful in controlling the criminal tribes who were settled, other predatory tribes could not be tackled in view of the stipulation that necessary arrangements should be made to the satisfaction of the government for settling them in some specified place.

The Government of the North-Western Provinces appointed a Police Committee consequent on the serious crimes committed by the Sansi tribe coming to light while implementing the Act. On the basis of the recommendations of this Committee, the Government of India decided to amend the Criminal Tribes Act, 1871.

The Criminal Tribes (Amendment) Act, 1897

Inter-alia, the amending Act provided for minimum penalty on second and third convictions of members of criminal tribes for specified officer. The local governments were also empowered to separate children between the ages 4 and 18 from the criminal tribes and place them in specially established reformatory '.settlements'.

The Criminal Tribes Act, 1911

The Indian Police Commission appointed by the Government of India in 1902-03 brought to the notice of the Government some of the defects in the 1871 Act which stood in the way of its wider application. It recommended that a special clause be inserted in the Criminal Tribes Act to authorise simple registration of notified criminal gangs and the taking of the finger impressions of the adult male members. In view of the recommendations of the Indian Police Commission, a Bill, to replace the Act of 1871, was introduced in the Council. It was felt that the criminal tribes could not be clubbed together for the purposes of containing their criminal activities as they fell into three main categories, viz. those who were originally criminals but had settled down to honest occupations with the exception of a few members; those who had settled abodes but continued to do crimes; and those wandering tribes who committed crimes when opportunities arose.

Under the new Criminal Tribes Act, 1911, local governments were given wide powers to declare a tribe to be a criminal tribe without requiring its settlement or provision for means of living. The members of the tribe could be registered and their finger impressions taken for observation and supervision, after due notification. Even the more criminally minded members could be restricted to any specified area or interned in special settlements made for them. Under this act, the minimum age of children to be separated from their parents was raised to 6 years.

The Criminal Tribes (Amendment) Act, 1923

The Criminal Tribes Act was a Central Act but could be adopted by-local governments by framing suitable rules to suit local conditions. In its operation, however, local governments encountered number of problems. This led to the convening of a conference in 1919 to evaluate the experience gained by the operation of the Act. The Indian Jails Committee of 1919 was also asked, inter alia, to examine the functioning of the Criminal tribes Act, 1911. Based on the recommendations of the Indian Jails Committee and the said conference, the Criminal Tribes (Amendment) Act, 1923 was passed. The amended Act empowered local governments to settle tribes either in its own territory or in another province with its consent, prescribing an enquiry before any criminal tribe was interned in a settlement or transferred from the British Indian provinces to the Indian States. As regards the policy to be followed in the operation of the Act, the Government of India made it clear that the Provinces would not be interfered with but the administration of the Act should be carried out in such a way as to ensure effective prevention of crime, proper treatment of the tribes in the matter of wages, housing etc., and their reclamation.

The Criminal Tribes Act, 1924

By 1924, a number of Indian States had also enacted legislation to deal with the criminal tribes in accordance with the provisions of the legislation in the Provinces. Important amendments were also effected in the Criminal Tribes Act, particularly the Amendment Act, 1923. These developments prompted the consolidation of the entire legislation relating to criminal tribes and, accordingly the Criminal Tribes Act, 1924 was passed.

The Criminal Tribes (Amendment) Act, 1947

As a result of the implementation of various legal measure and the greater awareness among the members of the criminal tribes, they gradually got themselves educated and started settling down in lawful occupations. This attitudinal change among the criminal tribes received considerable sympathy from the government and the people at large, particularly social workers and an atmosphere of goodwill was generated in respect of the need to dispense with some provisions of the Act. Accordingly, a private members' Bill was admitted in 1946 which sought to amend section 23 of the Act providing for minimum enhanced punishments for those convicted for a second or third offence. It was also felt that a whole tribe should not be dubbed as criminal. The Criminal Tribes (Amendment) Act 1947 was thus passed which abolished the minimum punishment prescribed for the second and third convictions.

Criminal Tribes and Notified Tribes

The Central Act of 1924 was also applicable to the Provinces with suitable modifications. Accordingly, the Governments of Madras and Bombay made certain amendments' to the application of the Act at different periods. The Criminal Tribes (Amendment) Act, 1943, of Madras was the first amending Act to liberalise the provisions of the Act, including naming the 'Criminal Tribes' as 'notified tribes'. Provisions were also made for relaxation of punishment, placing the accused in settlements and removal of children from parents to certified schools, etc. Some States opted to use the then Habitual Offenders Act in place of the Criminal Tribes Act.

Repeal of Criminal Tribes Act

Attainment of independence brought in a favourable change in the outlook of governments vis-a-vis the deplorable conditions of the so-called criminal tribes and it was felt that the provisions of the Criminal Tribes Act were inconsistent with the dignity of free India, As a first step, the Government of India, therefore, appointed in September 1949 a Criminal Tribes Act Enquiry Committee, under the chairmanship of Mr. Ananthasayanam Ayyangar to enquire into the working of the Act and to offer recommendations for its modification or repeat.

On the basis of the recommendations of the Ayyangar Committee, which were of socio-legal in nature, the Criminal Tribes Act 1924 was abrogated in 1952 and replaced by the Habitual Offenders' Act, which took cognizance of only those individuals who habitually indulged in crime. This brought about a fundamental change in the basic approach in as much as responsibility for crime was transferred from a whole community to the individual offenders.

with the abrogation of the Criminal Tribes Act, the groups which were previously notified under the Act came to be termed as Vimukta Jatis or ex-criminal tribes. The Backward Classes Commission appointed by the Government in 1953 also considered the question of the status of the ex-criminal tribes and their welfare needs. It recommended that such communities should neither be called 'criminal' nor 'ex-criminal' tribes thereby attaching any stigma to their name. It also suggested that they should simply be termed as 'denotified communities'. Similar suggestions were also received from some social workers. As a result of these suggestions and with a view to removing the stigma of criminality attached to these tribes, they are now officially referred to as 'Denotified Tribes'.

Cultural Environment and Initiation into Crime

Poverty, of course, is the chief reason with all such resultant evils as low standard of living, absence of anything approaching moral or civic consciousness and sense of deprivation and marginality. Their mode of life which releases them from all such obligations as binding on the members of a settled human group is also a crucial reason for their criminality. These circumstances are enough to turn even ordinary people with normal instincts into criminals. The perverted notion of crime that develops under these circumstances completes the vicious circle. Here crime is idealized and glorified. They are actuated not only by the blind adherence to the traditional profession but also by the natural desire to supplement their meagre income by crime as a sort of subsidiary occupation. To these, we should add the joy of the wandering life, the call of the adventure, the dread of a humdrum and settled life which is so strong with all nomadic people. Standing beyond the pale of society, they rejoice in waging a remorseless war on it.

They do not rest content by leading the life of crime for themselves. They consciously and deliberately subject their children to a strict and systematic course of education and training in crime. So long as a child is not sufficiently grown up to accompany them on 'active duty', the best possible theoretical training is imparted to him by the womenfolk and the menfolk alike. The moral background for the commission of crime is strengthened by the conviction instilled in them from their childhood that it is their birthright and sacred duty to earn their livelihood by committing anti-social acts even though by so doing they put society to great inconvenience and hardship. They take pride in committing crimes and in their society honour and respect for a person varies according to his success in his criminal career. A person having no taste for crime is looked down as a coward and he commands no respect.

The Bawarias justify their crime by saying that they do not commit the so-called anti-social acts of their own accord. When they receive inspiration from the gods or the ancestral spirits, they have to comply.

Bhargava (ibid) narrates that nearly every child is taught the art of hiding small things such as a gold rings or a few coins in his throat. The female children are taught to hide articles in certain pockets of their underwears, so that it is not easy to detect them: Some women are able to hide article even in their vaginal cavity.

It is evident from the narration given above that the initiation into crime commences at an early age and abetted by the cultural environment, expertise is obtained within a short time. Just to have a 'feel' of their lives, description of the criminal life as lived by two of the important tribes viz., the Kanjar and the Bawaria, is given here in some detail.

Crime Among The KANJAR

Among the so-called ex-criminal tribes, the Kanjars occupy an important place in view of their numerical strength and vastness of their area of movement. Mostly they live in Madhya Pradesh, Rajasthan, U.P. and parts of Maharashtra. They also visit places in Punjab and Andhra. Those in the south are known as Dakshmi Kanjars. They are also known by different names as Bijoria Nat, Kabutari Nut, Bhanmat and Banchchade in different parts of the country. The females among them used to go about begging and showing physical feats accompanied by their males who played on drum.

Basing their mode of life on thieving and pilfering, the Kanjars became hard and bold, sure of eye and swift in striking and getting away. J.C. Dikshit (1964) has provided a graphic and detailed account of the nature of crimes and modus operandi of the Kanjars wandering in Madhya Pradesh.

The main types of offences committed by the Kanjars are: (i) dacoity, (ii) highway robbery, (iii) house-breaking, and (iv) thefts, including cattle thefts. In dacoities, the modus operandi is mostly uniform. Before starting for a raid they usually get complete information in about the topography of the village they propose to raid. Then they visit their priest and consult him regarding the most auspicious time for the commission of the crime. After offering the sacrifice of a fowl to the deity, they get heavily drunk and start for the excursion, armed with lathi, pharsa and firearms. Their women do not accompany the raiding party. The selection of the day is also important. It is usually two-three days after the full moon. They usually reach the village at dusk time, catch hold of an innocent villager and compel him to show the house they have to raid. On reaching the place they fire a few shots in the air and throw stones along the street by means of slings.

Thus, after scaring away the villagers they start looting. After committing the dacoity they soil the ground at the spot. They believe that by doing so, they will not be caught. After the mission has been completed, they leave for their abode. On the way they commit as many dacoities and robberies as they can. The time is so adjusted that they get the advantage of moonlight during their escape. On reaching their abodes they hand over the property to their womenfolk. After successful campaigns, there are usually big feasts and heavy drinking.

The road dacoities and robberies are usually committed on market days at dusk time when persons returning from market are deprived of their cash and belongings. They usually start 'their campaigns after Dashehra festival when crops are standing in the fields providing them good hiding places.

Dikshit (ibid) tells us that they commit house-breaking by means of nakab, meaning making a whole in the wall. Some of them have also taken to gimlet, window bar wrenching and roof cutting. They slip their hands through the small opening left between door, windows, etc., and are also skilful in sliding of the locks and chains. They are also experts in removing ornaments from the persons of sleeping women and children.

They are very swift in their moments. After committing a series of offences in quick succession, they immediately move on. They are rapid travellers and when pressed cover as much as forty miles in one night. Their women play very important role in the disposal of stolen property. The property is usually buried in the jungles, away from their camp and only the women know the spot. According to their requirements the property is dug out and passed on to receivers in whom they have implicit faith. In case of arrest of male members the women engage lawyers and fight the cases. Each camp is headed by a women known as Patelan who directs their activities and looks after their interests when they are in jail or absconding.

The Kanjars are so much hardened that even third degree methods have little effect on them. They do not easily break down after arrest. For this they are trained from early boyhood. The father would often beat a son mercilessly and keep him tied and without food for days, just to toughen and harden him.

Crime Among The BAWARIA

In the past the Bawarias were notorious for committing daylight dacoities. They have now adopted less violent forms of crime and, more shrewd methods which render their detection difficult. Though, they are mostly illiterate and are scattered all over India, they have kept intact distinctive language, customs and code words. And thus they are able to be in close communication with the entire tribe throughout the country.

B.S. Bhargava (1949) tells us that the Bawarias of northern India have been notorious for committing thefts from camps, specially of Government officials and are probably the most clever of camp robbers and tent cutters to be found in India. They are equally adept in nakabzani—removing goods from a building by gaining entrance through a hole made in the wall. He narrates that they have an interesting custom connected with this. On reaching the house they plan to burgle, they throw three small stones one after the other to ascertain whether the inmates are fast asleep. While this is probably no more than a measure of precaution or safety, they say that in this way they decide their course of action. According to them, if a man gets up on this warning, it shows that he has earned money by hard and honest labour; if he continues to sleep, they conclude that he has acquired money by dishonest means. Hence, if one does not wake up, they consider themselves justified in robbing him and distributing his wealth among those who have a better claim to it. Sometimes they enter the camps of pilgrims in the guise of ascetics and steal ornaments and other valuables when the inmates are asleep.

Burglary is their speciality and they commit it only when they are sure of a large haul. Before preparing for an expedition omens are sought by counting grains of boiled wheat. If the omens are favourable they set out on the expedition in guises best suited to their requirements. At the time of committing the offences they usually put on a mask to avoid chances of recognition.

For breaking into the houses they make use of the two devices known as Bagli Naqab and Naqab. In the first device, a hole into which a hand can be inserted is made in the wall at the side of the door frame and at the level of the latch. The arm is entered through this hole and the door is unfastened from the inner side. The second device is resorted to when they are aware of the exact place at which a certain property is placed in a room and are sure that the property can be removed from outside without personal entrance. They simply make a hole at the place in question and secure their booty through it. During a single night a gang of Bawarias can successfully commit a number of offences. Usually they do not indulge in criminal activities in partnership with anyone who does not belong to their tribe.

When Bawaria camps are searched one invariably hears a peculiar sound produced from the throat which is considered as a warning to others to escape if possible. While going to a place one of them so drags his stick on the way that it leaves a track behind. Their accomplices easily follow the track so left and reach the rendezvous at the appointed time. This is especially helpful to the absconders. Where the road is metalled or the ground is such which cannot conveniently be marked, they make small piles of stones and leaves alternately every few furlongs to guide other accomplices.

According to Bhargava (ibid), they use a regular and widespread system of signs when they are engaged in their criminal activities. Some of the signs used by them are :

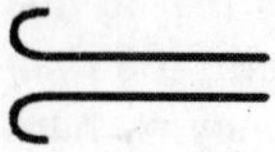
– The curved arc points out the direction the gang has chosen

– Three persons are hiding in the vicinity

– Four persons have gone in the direction of the arrow

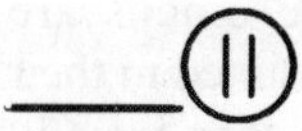
– Two persons are hiding in the well

– There are four persons in the temple

– Property has been secured and the gang has escaped in the direction of the line

– The gang is encamping in the village

– The gang encamped in the vicinity for three days and has now left for the new destination.

– The gang has in its possession property worth Rs. 400 and has gone towards the direction denoted by the arrow.

Reform and Rehabilitation

The permanent solution of the problem of the so-called criminal tribes will depend upon continued improvement of their economic and social conditions, the education of their younger generation and also an effective supervision and check on their criminal activities. Due to some anomalies and overlapping, the task of reform and rehabilitation has not been moving ahead smoothly. Now designated "Denotified Communities", these criminal tribes appear to possess all the characteristics of tribals but not all have been included in the list of Scheduled Tribes. The Backward Classes Commission, set up under Article 340 of the Constitution had, in their report submitted in 1955, rightly recommended that these communities should be divided into Scheduled Castes, Scheduled Tribes and other Backward Classes as the case may be. Nothing significant, however, appears to have been done to give effect to that recommendation. This has resulted in the anomaly on the same community being treated as a Scheduled Tribe in one region and as a "Denotified Community" in another in the same State.

The Shilu Ao Committee Report (1969) regards the denial to such of the members of "Denotified Communities" as are in every way tribal benefits admissible to their Scheduled brethern, as invidious and contrary to the spirit of the Constitution.

The absence of public sympathy is the greatest drawback in implementing any scheme of reform and rehabilitation of these tribes. Unfortunately, the abolition of the Criminal Tribes Act, instead of improving their status, gave them a free licence to commit more crimes. 'The repeal of the Act followed by abolition of all criminal settlements without any serious effort on the part of the Government to rehabilitate them, only vivified the old instinct of crime which they committed with redoubled vigour. It has been observed that during the last few years they systematically started their depredation with such vehemence that all the labour put in by the criminal tribes settlements appeared to have been a waste" (Dikshit, 1964). It was, therefore, decided to make a new approach to this problem. It was decided to pursuade them to settle down to peaceful ways of life, to make them realize the futility of the kind of life they were leading and to reform them economically, socially and culturally, so that they could live as good and responsible citizens.

Welfare Measures for the Denotified Communities

Early Measures—Besides welfare measures introduced in accordance with the provisions of the Criminal Tribes Act, welfare and reformative activities were also implemented, although to a limited extent, by various states. The 'settlement treatment' given to the criminal tribes made them amendable to discipline, and welfare activities carried out in the settlement and even outside the settlements improved their social and economic status to some extent.

Under the provisions of the Criminal Tribes Act, various State Governments/Provinces established colonies meant for members of criminal tribes. Punjab had 9 such colonies, Rajasthan 17 and Bhopal 5, while Uttar Pradesh, Bihar, Hyderabad and Delhi had one each. Besides, Uttar Pradesh had 4 settlements and Punjab, Bihar and Madhya Pradesh had one settlement each set up under Section 16 of the Act.

In these colonies and settlements certain facilities for agriculture, cottage industries and other avocations were made available. In most of them, facilities for education were also made available both for children and adults. In some colonies there were facilities for vocational education, recreation and games. Some of the children were enrolled in Reformatory Schools in some States. While the colonies were under the surveillance of the police department, the settlements were managed directly by the government, but welfare measures were operated either by the government or through voluntary organisations.

In some states like Bengal, Punjab, Uttar Pradesh, Madras, Bombay, Delhi, Bihar and Orissa, reformative work was well organised and, therefore, there was perceptible change in the conditions of the settlers. In Bengal, for example, they were placed in industrial settlements. Punjab provided lands for cultivation, made available agricultural inputs and organised cooperative credit societies, besides provision for education of children and adult literacy classes. In Uttar Pradesh, there was provision for free education, facilities for higher education, organisation of 'reform panchayats' for eradication of evil habits, employment facilities in small scale industries, irrigated agriculture and tailoring, and facilities for recreation and games in settlements. Special officers were also appointed to look after the welfare measures for the settlers and for reclamation colonies.

Welfare schemes in Delhi included compulsory education for children, establishment of an adult education centre, cleanliness drive in the colony, establishment of a cooperative thrift and credit society and a cooperative store. Attempts were also made to find suitable occupations for the inmates. In Bihar too, lands were allotted for cultivation, besides organising a cooperative credit society.

In Madras, higher elementary schools (separate for boys and girls in some settlements) were established with provision for free education, mid-day meals, books and clothing. In Bombay, attendance in day school was compulsory for all children, while night school attendance was compulsory for males in the settlements. The school children were provided with all facilities free of cost. More vulnerable children (orphans, children of irreclaimable parents, etc.) were separated and placed in children's home. Punjab too had facilities for reformatory schools where children of criminal tribes were sent. Besides the British Indian Provinces, some of the princely States also had provision in their Criminal Tribes Acts for welfare measure like colonisation, education, etc.

Later Measures

The problem of rehabilitating the 'denotified tribes' and weaning them away from criminal associations is a complex one. In addition to the criminal tendencies, they were educationally and economically back-ward, especially as they were communities with nomadic habits. After the abrogation of the Criminal Tribes Act, 1924, in 1952 the government was keen to undertake such schemes as would accelerate the process of integration of the denotified tribes into the mainstream of society. However, for want of preparation, only a small beginning could be made in the First Five Year Plan. An expenditure of Rs. 102 lakh was incurred on training towards a settled way of life for nomadic and semi-nomadic communities. One of the schemes implemented during the First Plan was opening of Ashram type schools to provide, besides free education, boarding and lodging arrangements for the children so as to keep them away from the bad influence of the older generations. Members of the denotified tribes were also entitled to get post-matric scholarship.

During the Second Five Year Plan period, welfare schemes for denotified tribes were undertaken partly under the Centrally sponsored programmes and partly under the state sector. A provision of Rs. 202 lakhs was made under the State sector and of Rs. 110 lakhs under Centrally sponsored programmes. During the Third Plan period, in view of the urgency of early rehabilitation of these tribes, all the schemes were implemented under the Centrally sponsored programmes. Economic development and social progress of these communities were, therefore, given emphasis, for which Rs. 419 lakhs was made available. In the Fourth Plan period all these schemes were continued with an allocation of Rs. 439 lakhs.

The pattern of implementation of schemes was again changed in the Fifth Plan period when all the welfare schemes for the denotified tribes were transferred to the State Plans Sector. Accordingly, the States were also advised to include the developmental programmes for these communities in the general sectors of their plans. Gujarat, Himachal Pradesh, Karnataka, Maharashtra, Punjab, Rajasthan, Tamil Nadu, Uttar Pradesh and West Bengal included programmes for these communities under the backward classes sector of the State plans with an outlay of about Rs. 600 lakhs.

In the Sixth Five Year Plan onwards these schemes continued. The programmes undertaken for the welfare of the denotified tribes can be grouped into three broad heads: educational, economic development and other schemes.

From the expenditure incurred on the welfare of denotified, nomadic and semi-nomadic communities during the Fifth Five Year Plan, it would appear that educational programmes got paramount importance, having utilised three-fourths of the total budgets. They included granting of scholarships and stipends to eligible students, grant of tuition and examination fees, provision of mid-day meals and establishment of Asharm schools, residential schools and hostels. For the economic development of these communities schemes like rehabilitation/colonisation , assistance for agriculture development, animal husbandry, poultry farming, cottage industries and organisation of cooperative societies were undertaken. Other miscellaneous schemes included setting up of community welfare centres, Balwadis, Sanskar Kendras, digging of drinking water wells etc.

The schemes implemented by different States have varied. The Government of Andhra Pradesh, for example, has provided housing facilities, scholarships and open schools and hostels, for which non-Plan provisions have been utilised. Very few educational and economic schemes have been taken up for these communities in Bihar outside old Champaran and Darbhanga districts where non-Plan provisions have been drawn upon. Schemes like financial assistance for small traders and cottage industries, assistance for development of agriculture, imparting of training to artisans, assistance for purchase of milch cattle, and educational programmes are among the welfare schemes undertaken by the State of Gujarat. The denotified tribes of Haryana are being helped both in the field of education and economic development. They are being given land for agriculture and also for housing. Subsidies are also provided for the purchase of pigs, buffaloes, goats, etc. Recently the State Government has set up a committee to make an indepth study of the problems of the denotified communities and to suggest measures for their socio-economic development. No specific scheme has been drawn up by the Himachal Pradesh Government. The state Government, however, proposes to start a few schemes for the educational and economic development. For education, Ashram Schools and ordinary schools have been established by the Maharashtra Government. Development of agriculture, colonisation and digging of irrigation wells are some of the economic activities undertaken for them. To ensure employment, training facilities are provided, and subsidy for procuring milch cattle is granted by the State Government. Among the economic activities undertaken by the Government of Orissa are establishment of rehabilitation colonies, allotment of agricultural land, assistance for agriculture, irrigation facilities, assistance for goat rearing, piggery and setting up of small scale industries. The State Government of Rajasthan undertakes both education and economic programmes for the denotified tribes. Important among the educational programmes are award of scholarship to pre-matric students, and incentives to students at the elementary stage. Economic schemes include housing grants and training in crafts. In the field of education, Uttar Pradesh provides pre-matric and post-matric scholarships and assistance for technical education. Agricultural development and encouragement of cottage industries are also undertaking for the economic upliftment of these communities. Rehabilitation programmes are implemented by providing houses and agricultural land.

As already stated the absence of public sympathy is the greatest hindrance in their rehabilitation. It is seen that the villagers, in the vicinity of their settlements, are still suspicious of them and do not take to them kindly. They still refuse to give them employment. Confidence in them has to be established. It is possible that tendencies to relapse into occasional criminal activities may still persist even among the reformed and settled groups, and there may be occasional lapses on their part. But they will have to be dealt with patience, sympathy and compassion and efforts to reform them shall have to be continued with missionary zeal.

Furthermore, these unfortunate people, as a result of their past experiences, also view with suspicion efforts on the part of any outsider to approach them and help them in settling in gainful occupations. According to M. K. Venkatesan (1964), a study of Denotified Tribes in various centres has shown that they are not interested in settling on occupations which will yield some return over a period of years and require steady application or efforts. They are more interested in trades or occupations which all give them a quick return and that too of comparatively higher amounts than that received by ordinary unskilled labourers. A study of the Denotified Communities in Baroda revealed that they are quite adept in various trades, such as diamond cutting, selling of brass and stainless steel utensils in exchange of old clothes, carpentry, blacksmity, retail selling of vegetables, pulling rickshaws or carrying head-loads for hire. They are interested only in having some sizable earning every day.

They are very chary of taking new ideas, as their experience so far has only been of maltreatment at the hands of the police. They have reached the stage when they cannot believe that government or any other agency is interested in their well-being. In overcoming this psychological resistance, the planners and administrators dealing with their rehabilitation should constantly keep in mind that they are dealing with an intelligent and enterprising set of people who could be provided with such schemes as interest them.

ART in TRIBAL India

Chapter 23

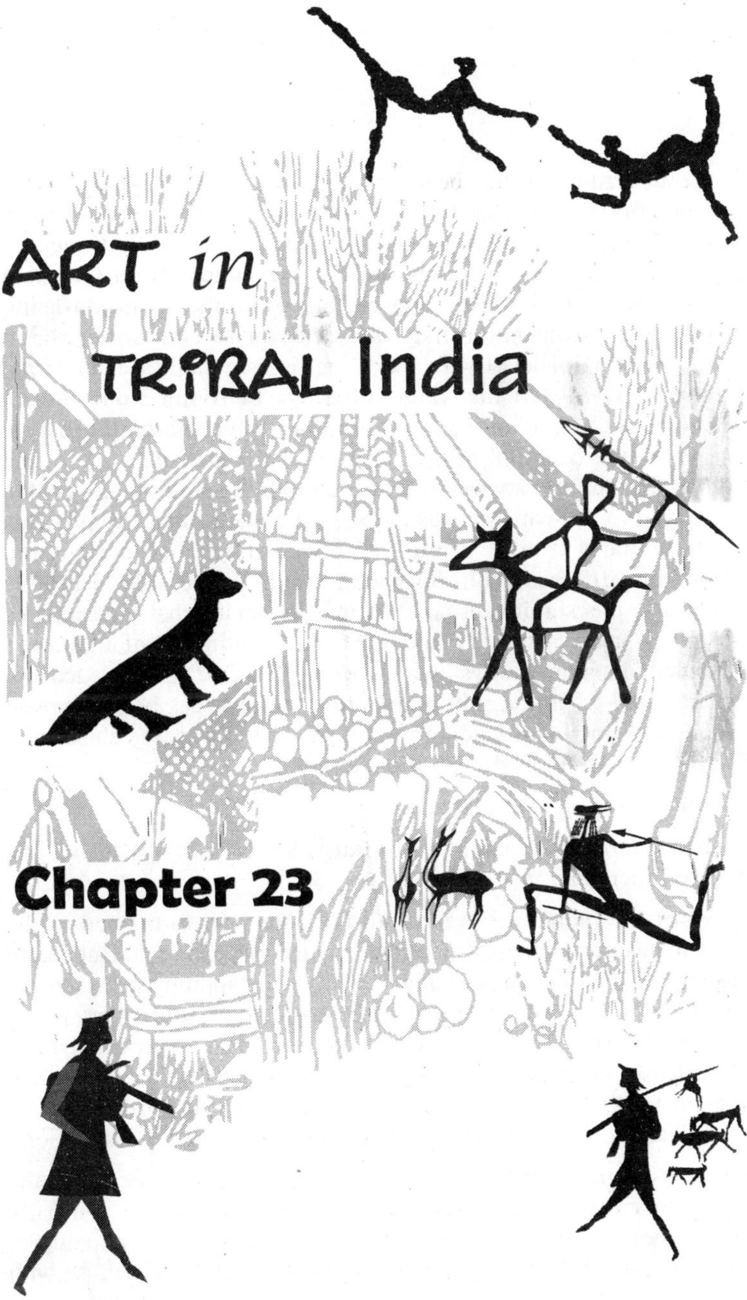

Not much attention has been devoted to a scientific study of the artistic efforts of the Indian tribes. However, whatever data we have reveal that in these tribes various types of art are present. Generally the "art of primitive peoples runs a wide gamut from technical clumsiness to high skill, from childlike simplicity to confusing complexity, from naturalism and realism to conventionalized abstraction" (Hoebel, 1949). The tribal is essentially a man of the nature, deriving all his traits and ways of living from natural phenomena. To a non-tribal layman most of the objects of tribal art may not look beautiful or artistic. But as a matter of fact, "for the full appreciation of a work of art it should be seen as far as possible in the setting for which it was created" (Leonard Adam, 1949). This is particularly true of primitive art because of its strange and altogether different cultural background. Verrier Elwin (1973) elaborates this significant point further by saying that the statue of an ancestor or of a deity under African conditions of light, and intended to remain always in the gloom of a shrine or temple, cannot be expected to produce the same effect when it has been removed from its original surroundings and displaced in a glass cabinet in a European room or an Indian room either.

The art forms of the tribal art are :

(i) plastic art (ii) graphic art, (iii) music art, (iv) art of dancing and (v) oral literature.

Most of the Indian tribes have all the above art forms and in the present chapter, all these aspects will be discussed in brief. But before discussing the tribal art of India it seems quite appropriate to remark that the primitive art is the most pure, most sincere form of art, partly because it is deeply inspired by religious ideas and spiritual experience, and partly because it is entirely unselfconscious; there are no tricks " which can be acquired by the unworthy, and no technical exercises which can masquerade as works of inspiration.

The most significant aspect of the art of India's tribal folk is that the art is interwoven with religion and the distinction which is usually drawn between the sacred and the secular by more sophisticated people ceases to exist. Thus, both art and religion "tend to fuse with each other into a unified whole" (N. K. Bose, 1971). The tribal artist is not ashamed of what might be regarded by others as crude'. He remains true to the impression which an object has produced upon him, and tries to reproduce it faithfully. Interestingly, the tribal artist may be 'untutored' but he is not uninitiated.

Plastic and Graphic Art

Under the heading of graphic and plastic art among the Indian tribes, mention may be made of painting, wooden and stone sculpture and statuettes.

Significantly, as Elwin observed, the worship of idols and images, which has been so potent as source of inspiration in other parts of the world, is weak in tribal India. It is extremely rare to find any representation of the tribal gods. The great tribes the Gond, the Santhal, the Bhil, the so-called Naga groups-represent their deities, if they make them at all, by stones, lumps of earth, bits of unshaped wood. Indeed, their shrines are nearly always empty in view of the fact that tribal gods are imagined in essentially anthropomorphic terms. Images are in fact made not to represent the gods but as offerings to the gods. In Bastar for example, the Murias offer at their shrines attractive little brass images of horses, elephants and human figures. Other tribes make offerings of birds, horses and elephants of clay. Besides, the representatives of demons, dummies and other products of fantasy are also artistically produced.

Terracotta animals and the like are also popular with many of the Indian tribes and one can see heaps of terracotta figures in tribal villages under trees. Year after year, the figures go on piling. They may strike an outsider by the monotony of their form or by lack of any arrangement among the offerings. These are no more than tokens of memory, the symbol of an experience through which one has passed.

Some of the tribal artists are remarkable painters. They paint on walls. The Saoras of Ganjam are almost obsessed by gods, ghosts and ancestors. Since they believe that these unseen things may interfere with the course of their lives, they have developed and elaborate system of sacrifices and actions intended to flatter their vanity. Among such actions is the custom of making paintings on the walls of the houses. These are made in honour of the dead, to drive away disease, to promote the fertility of the crops and on the occasion of certain festivals. Most of the tribal painters acts under the inspiration of a dream. The paintings are of great variety and some of them are extremely striking,

Marriage is another event in their life that has inspired art. In order to avoid evil spirit, baffling patterns are drawn on ground using a variety of colours. Some Central Indian tribes display a riot of colours on earth on such occasions. Besides diagrammatical representation on the ground, beautiful crowns for the bride and groom and a variety of lampstands are also made to decorate the site of marriage in making beautiful heads of deer and other animals. Some other tribes make it on wood. Among the tribes interested in indulging in various artistic activities on the occasion of marriage, Santhals appear to be the most enthusiastic. They are famous for making beautifully decorated palanquins in which bride and groom are carried from house to house.

El win (ibid) while surveying the tribal art concerned with death has provided us very vivid narration. He saw the Marias of Bastar making splendid wooden pillars for the more important of their dead.

These are carved with the things that interested the deceased: we see dancers in their finery, women serving rice beer from pots, hunting scenes, shamans in the act of divination. But it is the Phoms and Konyaks of the north eastern region who excel in making grave effigies.

These are believed by some anthropologists to provide either temporary resting places for the soul of the dead or more permanent receptacles for their soul-essence. The figures are realistically carved with the usual tattoo marks and ornaments of the dead person, and are placed in little shrines which are decorated with spears and other weapons. But while on the one hand death encourages art, on the other it is its enemy not only because its relentless fingers stifle the creative purpose forever, but because some tribes believe that anything beautiful that a man has made must perish with his body. Thus, the Santhals bury or cremate any fine piece of carving, a favourite decorated flute or a splendidly ornamented fiddle with the dead. "Many of the tombs of the Chang, Phom and Konyak have the appearance of regular museums. On the bamboo platforms, upon which the corpse is exposed, are hung a great variety of ornaments, pieces of cloth, baskets, weapons, traps, etc. These are allowed to rot in wind and rain and I have often been tempted to remove them and so save them from oblivion. It is a real waste, tragic waste, but even to touch them would be a major breach of a strict taboo" (Elwin).

The artistic taste of the tribal folk also finds expression in the decoration of their houses, in the clothes they weave and wear, as well as in the simple ornaments with which they decorate their own bodies. Though the range of colours is limited and mostly they are yellow, red, blue, green and deep black but we see a riot of colours even within this limited range.

Most of the Indian tribes are very fond of tattooing. To the womenfolk of such tribes as Maria and Muria of Bastar, tattooing is like having gold and silver ornaments. They have a wide range of designs, figures, and pictures to select their favourite one and that will also fascinate her lover. Many of the Maria and Muria women have almost all of their body tattooed.

Ornaments present excellent opportunity to the Indian tribal folk to express their artistic creativity. A variety of hairpins and combs made of bamboo and wood are proudly exhibited on their head. Besides, the way they decorate their hair, waist, neck and forehead with flowers, beads and cowries is a feast to the eyes. The Bhils with huge bangles, bronze anklets, necklaces and other jewellery made of white copper, lead, bronze, beads, nuts, straw, grass and silver present a very colourful and attractive look. Ornaments made of wheat straw and grass provide a special type of spring decor of Bhil girls. Various types of head-gears also add charm to a tribal's personality. The tribals of the north eastern region are famous for their beautiful and tastefully decorated head-gears made of feather and fibre. The Oraons make artistic costumes and ornaments from peacock and bhangara feathers. The head-gear of the Bison-Horn Marias of Bastar is a rare artistic piece made of the horns of bison. The scarcity of bison horn has made it all the more valuable and important. 'The cowarie decorations, and peacock feathers artistically tied around it make it artistic and gorgeous. All these costumes, jewellery, head-gears, hair dressing styles etc., are manifest in almost all their functions, dances and festivals" (D.L. Samar, 1964). The bone decorations done by the Naga and other Manipur tribes, though look a little grotesque, are artistically designed. Since most of the north-eastern tribes live mostly on hunting, the hides and bones left as residue are made use of as decorative pieces for their homes and other places of collective activities. In Madhya Pradesh, Bihar and Orissa where flowers grow in abundance they from the principle medium of dress and hair decoration. The tribes of Rajasthan use metallic ornaments made of white copper, bronze and silver.

Even hunting implements and weapons of war could not escape the artistic urged of these people. The Naga tribes are very well-known for decorating their weapons of war and the human heads they keep as trophy (remnants of the head hunting days) in very artistic ways. The hunting implements like the arrow and the bow of the Bhils and other central Indian tribes and the spear of Manipur and other north eastern tribes are kept not as utility implements alone but also as decorative article of show value.

Apart from the above mentioned articles, some more items of daily use may also be cited as art pieces. Stools, chairs and cots (wherever they are in use) also come in for decoration through engravings. Basketry and pottery also come in for occasional ornamentation. Totemic flags and emblems too are always products of artistic effort. The Nagas make beautiful wooden drinking mugs and spoons.

Music, Dance and Oral Literature

Music and dance include types of instrumental and vocal music, and also various types of dances and dance dramas. Oral literature includes folktales, folksongs, riddles, proverbs, myths and common sayings.

Most of the Indian tribes have evolved one type of collective dance or the other accompanied by music. Karma dance of the Gonds arid the bihu of the north-eastern tribes are very famous. Bhils of Rajasthan are also justly famous for their gauri dance-drama.

Among the musical instruments used by Indian tribes mention may be made of drums of various types, pipes, flutes, horns, brass plates, Kartals, Jhahjh, etc. The Maria mradang, the Bhil modal, the Naga khol, the Bhilala dhol and nakkara used in their dances and other ceremonial occasions are also examples of excellent craftmanship. The decorations, paintings and designs done over them by tribals themselves are attractive and fascinating. Other musical instruments like the special type of drum and the pungi of the Maharashtra Bhils too are known for their musical and artistic value. The gourja of Garasiya tribe of Rajasthan is also worth mentioning. It is temporarily made with ordinary clay for use in their famous gangore festival. It is artistically decorated with conch shells and cowries and is taken in procession followed by dancing and singing.

D.N. Majumdar (1967) observes that in the myths and folktales heard in the tribal villages of the country is enshrined, in a poetic and imaginative garb, the philosophy of these simple folks. Every tribe has several myths, often mutually contradictory about its origin. In these myths gods and men live together in an amoral world. But there are other types of myths the sole function of which is to compel obedience to some customs by pointing out how so and so was punished by the super-natural powers for such and such offences. The world of vegetation, the animal kingdom and man's dependence on them supply the subject matter for many myths current among the Indian tribes. Folktales are frankly imaginative and more entertaining than awe inspiring. In fact, their main functions appear to be entertainment. They are short like our short stories and long like our novels. They deal with human situations in which suspense, ghosts, heroes and heroines have their due place.

Poetry, dramatic stories and music generally go together. All kinds of poetry have been found among the Indian tribes; they have lullabies, nonsense rhyms, devotional songs, love lyrics, satiric verses and epic ballads. They have seasonal songs, marriage songs, dance songs, hunting songs, incantations, and funeral chants. Songs are sung in solos, in duets and also in choruses. Riddles, proverbs and sayings also are common among all tribes.

Majumdar (ibid) rightly laments that there is so much in the everyday life of the Indian folk that requires to be changed; there is so much in it that has to be preserved and nourished for the good of the country as a whole, and that includes tribal art in all its forms. Verrier Elwin (1973), too, sadly comments that to study tribal art in modern India is a melanchol task. The march of civilization, for some reasons, has a paralysing effect on tribal people. The tribal people of India conquer the sorrows of daily life by discovering their own soul in the depth of religious and artistic experiences. As such, tribal art is everyone's art but this everyone's art has started fast losing its richness in the bewildering mosaic of the fast marching industrial civilization.

Young Boys and Girls from Munda Tribe of Jharkhand

Dhankul Tija Jagar — painting of the folk tale of Bastar

Goncha from Bastar - the local tribal version of lord Jagannath

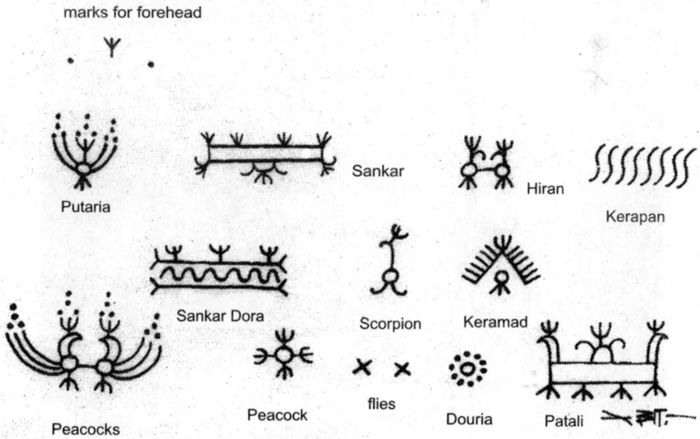

Tattoo marks for enhancing beauty (Bastar)

SOCIAL CHANGE AMONG THE TRIBES DURING COLONIAL PERIOD

Chapter 24

Tribal societies like other societies have also been undergoing change. However, the fact remains that powerful forces of change were released for the first time only during colonial period and that is why colonial transformation of the tribal society forms an important area of study and investigation in anthropological studies in the Indian sub-continent. The most apparent aspect in any such study is the fact that with the extension of authority of the state to the forest regions largely inhabited by the tribal populations, a number of minor and major tribal uprisings occurred.

Before taking up the emerging dimensions of tribal transformation that began more or less with the advent of colonial rule, it would not be out of place to take a brief look at some features of pre-colonial situation. In any such analysis we should, first of all, give up the popular notion that before the advent of the British Colonial rule the tribal communities have been leading the existence of total isolation-geographical and cultural-from the centers of Indian civilization. The presence of ant mahamatya during Mauryan period, whose reference is found on the rock edicts of Asoka, bears testimony to the fact that the polity of even such an ancient period had contacts with the communities living in hills and forests (Girijan. & Vanvasi). There was a definite orientation of the adivasis towards the larger Hindu population though the tribals were not "Hindus" following then-customs and traditions including their animistic beliefs. A number of anthropologists brought out classification of tribal communities focussing on cultural process. This exercise was largely in terms of the orientation of the tribal communities towards the Hindu Society. B.K.Roy Burman (1970) classified the tribes as follows:

(a) Tribes incorporated in the Hindu social order
(b) Tribes positively oriented towards the Hindu social order
(c) Tribes negatively oriented towards the Hindu social order
(d) Tribes indifferent towards the Hindu social order

Amplifying his position, Roy Burman observed that the tribes like the Bhil, Bhumij, etc. may be considered to be incorporated in the Hindu social order. They had accepted the ethos of the caste structure and now can hardly be differentiated from the neighbouring Hindu peasantry. The tribes like the Santhal, the Oraon, the Munda, the Gond etc. can be considered to be positively oriented towards the Hindu social order. Though, the bulk of their population were not in caste frame and they are still not, to a considerable extent they have adopted the symbols, ethos and the world view of their Hindu neighbours. Tribal communities like the Mizo and the Naga can be considered to be negatively oriented towards the Hindu social order. They definitely rejected caste as a frame for social organization. Most of the tribal communities in Arunachal can be considered to be indifferent to Hindu social order. They were and still are hardly aware of the tenets of Hinduism. Many of them traditionally eat beef and their moral constraints and systems of pollution and purity do not appear to bear any significant degree of resemblance to those of the Hindus. Yet, as Roy Burman (1994) himself acknowledges, positive and negative orientation towards dominant cultural influences is not a rigidly fixed pattern for all times to come. The situation has definitely changed in varying degrees. In later years, Roy Burman has disassociated himself with this approach but as a referrant to the precolonial or colonial set up this can still be used to understand the socio-cultural situation vis -a-vis tribal communities.

In order to understand the colonial and post-colonial situation vis-a-vis social-cultural change the classifications of L.P.Vidyarthi (1977) and S.C. Dube (1977) may also be referred to which talked about different levels and stages of acculturation vis-a-vis the larger Hindu society, more precisely Hindu peasantry in different regions of the country.

Commenting on the pre-colonial situation, K.S. Singh in his essay on **Colonial Transformation of the Tribal Society in Middle India**, agrees with the view that most of the ethnographers described the pre-colonial situation as static. Through his case study of the tribal communities of Middle India, K.S. Singh relies on historical evidence and says that three major trends were visible during pre-colonial period. His analysis is largely oriented towards politico-economic dimensions. Citing three major trends, he says that the first was colonization and establishment of settlements **(bhums)** by peasant castes, who were encouraged by the Mughal rulers and zamindars to reclaim lands and offered various incentives for this purpose, or by other categories of immigrants. Trade and strategic routes passing through the jungle regions acquired a new significance, The Jharkhand and Gondwana emerged as historical regions in the medieval period. Secondly, many tribes, such as Bhils, Mina, Kols and Gond were recognised as dominant communities by the Mughal empire. Thirdly, we witness the rise of state either out of the tribal matrix as in the case of the Gond and Chero or as a result of the imposition on the tribal system of the authority of the Rajputs and other castes which established their power in the highlands of Orissa, Central India, Gujarat and Rajasthan. A crucial precondition of the formation of state in middle India was the extension of cultivation through the reclamation of land and the introduction of a new agricultural technology by the peasantry from plains. The Gond, Nagabansi and Chero chiefs encouraged the settlement of non-tribal peasant communities such as Kurmi, Keori and Kunbi, who with their superior agricultural technology, alone could generate the agricultural surpluses that the new states required, A new mode of production thus emerged. A consequence of the imposition of the feudal super structure on the tribal society was its breakdown and fragmentation into distinct social strata, based on corresponding distribution of power and economic interests in land and defined in terms of ritual status. The new states acted as the agents of sanskritization but they also strengthened the sense of tribal identity. State formation stimulated commercial activities, developed trade routes and promoted small scale urbanism. A variety of castes ranging from the Brahmins, who were tempted by generous grants of land, to the artisan communities flocked to the new fort cities. All in all, a complex social-economic system had emerged in certain parts of tribal middle India even before the colonial System was established there."

Thus, with the establishment of the colonial rule the relative (geographical/cultural) isolation of most of the tribal societies in India came to an end. Radical changes in tribal situation occurred. The British Colonial rule created new problems by replacing the old social organization, agrarian system and socio-economic values with the new ones the tribals were not familiar with. Old forms of social controls and agencies of social change were revised. New forms of commercialization began. Not only land became property but significantly private property. A new rule of law was established. The colonial rule "initiated commercialization of production, consumerism and money/cash economy to precisely serve their exploitative interest. The State power played a decisive role in determining the future of the people and during the British period It experienced a basic transformation. As a result, the self contained subsistence economy based on agriculture and forest produce was weakened and destroyed" (S.R. Sharma, 1999). The customary law of tribal communities was replaced by the new law of the centralised state power during the British rule and this continued even after that. The new law operated through it's administrative and judicial organs and helped the process of Hinduisation to some extent. This process progressed in proportion to the urbanization and transformation into capitalist economic development.

The most striking feature of this period was the breakdown of the communal mode of production and the emergence of private right in land. A further stage In the development of the peasant system was the penetration of tribal economy by market. The colonial system created a demand for money in largely non-money economies to pay land revenue and other levies, to defray expenditure of various kinds, and to buy necessities, "The traditional form of barter exchange died away. There was some evidence that sections of the tribes took to commodity production on at a limited scale." (K.S. Singh, ibid). Even the most primitive economies came gradually within the operation of the market system. With the market came the middle man, merchants and moneylenders. Here the concept of **diku** (the aliens, outsiders) becomes crucial to the understanding of agrarian relations. A diku was the creature of the colonial system who performed a variety of functions as a middle man in administrative matters, as a moneylender, as a trader who controlled production of foodgrain through the system of advance credit, and as a land grabber.

During this period the process of peasantization and depeasantization operated at the same time. Several tribal communities who were not peasants were coming into the fold of peasantry while a number of tribal people after losing their land were entering into a different economic system. Substantial sections of tribes from middle India such as Santhals, Oraon and Munda had to migrate to the tea plantations of Assam and the adjoining areas while others became industrial labour, share-croppers etc.

Inter-tribal markets had been traditionally an institution of socio-cultural importance. These were not the places only for economic transactions. It also served as agency of Culture Change. With the entry of new market forces and creation of demand for new commodities triggered by the outsiders the traditional tribal markets either declined or were transformed into places of formal economic exchanges and activities. Profit making had never been the dominant value in tribal economy. Rather, reciprocity, redistribution and cooperation were the bases of the traditional tribal economy. All these values were eroded. Now the tribal society was moving closer and closer to the peasant/ caste stratified system. This strengthened the role of sanskritization. Several tribes of middle India unitedly moved towards the Varna system and laid their claim over Kshatriya status mainly because the Kshatriya model of Sanskritization or Kshatriazation was the easiest and most popular process. The Santhals and the Gonds are the most obvious examples of this process.

The role of Christianity as an agent of change also deserves some discussion mainly in the north-east regions as well as astray pockets of Madhya Pradesh, Bihar and Bengal. Since Christianity was perhaps the earliest agency of welfare in a number of tribal areas, it took a back seat as an ideology. The modernizing role of Christian missions is also an important feature of social change in those tribal areas where it had a deep impact. But unfortunately there always existed a close link between Christianity and Colonialism. "At the political level, the missionaries, in close collaboration with the colonial administrators, rationalised the raj (British rule) and sought to create a new bastion of support for it among the backward communities of India. In the initial phases, the missionary activities were disruptive of the tribal system. Evangelisation was inherently ethnocentric. The missionary imposed a puritanical ethic on the permissive tribal society, though the approaches of various denominations (of missionaries) to social questions markedly varied depending on the exigencies of the situation." (K.S. Singh, Ibid). In the north-eastern region and middle India they mainly worked on the tribes and elsewhere on non-tribal communities mainly the lower social strata of Hindus and Muslims. Under the impact of Christianity, a number of values and institutions of the affected tribal communities wilted. The fate of 'Youth Dormitories', a very popular institution of tribes declined. Obviously, the missionaries wanted the churches only to be the places of congregation. At the same time it is also true to an extent that the Christianity gave a new sense of self-respect to the tribal peasants and sought to create a separate identity for them.

In any analysis of social change among the tribal communities during the colonial period the role of tribal movements cannot be ignored. Many tribes reacted to the changes brought about by the colonial administration in a variety of ways. Because of their prolonged relative isolation the tribal communities had developed their own social structure and mechanism of social control and they were quite sensitive to them. Perhaps that is why they reacted to these changes more strongly and often violently than other populations. We have got a chronicled description of tribal movements and revolts-minor and major, and studies of unrest and disturbances. Most of the tribal movements could be covered under the headings of 'Anti-Colonial', Anti-Diku' and 'Pro-Ethnic'. Analysing the nature and consequences of these tribal movements in Middle India K.S. Singh (ibid) write that 'the first phase (1795-1860) coincided with the rise, expansion and establishment of the British empire. It saw the rise of what we may call the 'primary resistance movements'. It was led by the traditional chiefs and their subordinates who had been dispossessed of their property and thrown out of their occupations by the new system. The Chuar rebellion (1795-1800), the uprisings of Chero and disturbances in Chotanagpur in 1820, the Kol and Bhumij insurrections, the resistance offered by Gond zamindars in 1819 and 1842 and the Khond resistance of mid 1830s are some of the examples of this phase. The Santhal insurrection (1855-59) was both a resistance and agrarian-cum-revivalistic movement. All these movements sharpened the tribal ethnicity and gave them a new identity. The second phase (1860-1920) coincided with the intensive phase or colonialism, which saw a much deeper penetration of tribal and peasant economies by merchant capital, higher incidence of rent etc. All gains registered during the first phase of the movements were washed away. Not only those who were expelled came back but many more also came, intensifying the exploitation of tribes. Unlike the peasants, the tribal movements developed a religious and political overtone. The failure of the first phase of movements had made the tribals look inward. They sought to restructure the entire social system. This was the beginning of revitalization movements. The Munda-Oraon Sardar Movement (1869-1895) led by Birsa Munda, the Tana Bhagat I Movement (1895-1901) and the Bhil's movement led by Govind Giri may be the examples of this phase which were largely socio-cultural in nature. It involved participation of the tribes in the national and 1 agrarian movements and emergence of a seperatist movement in Chotanagpur. It also reflected a deep yearning end craving for the roots and a sense of pride in tribal cultures. The followers of Mahatma Gandhi sprung up among the Bhils, Gonds, Hos, Oraon, Mundas and Santhals. It also coincided with the politicisation of the tribes bringing them into the mainstream of national Politics and Political process (for details see the chapter on Tribal Movements). The tribal movements of the colonial period had a deep imprint on the struggle of the tribal people in the post-independence period.

Peter Gardner (1978) in his review of social-cultural change among the tribal peoples of India has selected five tribes namely the Garos of Assam now of Meghalya (studied by Burlington, 1963), Bhumij of Bengal (Sinha, 1957, 59, 62, 65), Konds of Orissa (Bailey, 1960) Kotas from the Nilgiri Hills (Mandelbaum., 1954,55,60) and Paliyans from the southern extremity of Tamil Nadu (Gardner, 1966, 699 72). Talking about the Garos, he says that " basically there are two broad phases to the recent history of the Garos as Burlington recreates it. First, there was a protracted period during which endemic head hunting in the hills and other war like behaviour kept outsiders at arm's length. It did not prevent active market links between the Garos and plainsmen in market towns at the foot of the hills but it did prevent even the most concerted efforts of zamindars from bringing any but the edge of the plateau under their authority. Burlington describes the border as being in constant turmoil. Phase two began abruptly. In 1867, the British moved troops onto the plateau, nine years later, by a symbolic gesture in which they destroyed two hundred skulls. It brought headhunting to a sudden end. As for as the other areas of society and culture they adopted change on their own terms. Except some changes in the life of the converted Christian Garos they remained largely unaffected. Moreover, one way or the other, Garos did not comply with whatever pressure there might have been from their Hindu neighbours to give up widow remarriage, slaughtering and eating of beef, or casual handling of cooked food. They chose to judge behavioural propriety in their own terms.

In many superficial ways the Konds of Kondmals, in northern Orissa, live in circumstances startlingly like those of the Garos. The East India Company, repelled morally by the practice of Kond human sacrifice, waged a twenty year war in the mid-nineteenth century to bring the whole Kond area under it's jurisdiction. Protective policies enunciated in 1855 amounted to little at first. Between 1875 and 1924, a great deal was done by way of road building and vocational education. And in 1897 Konds were offered special compensatory rights and privileges under laws to ensure them justice in the face of Oriya exploitation. They were protected, for example, from loss of their land (Bailey, 1960). Bailey sums the situation up in terms of two trends, the results of different administrative policies: (a) assimilation through opening up of the area and (b) protection from exploitation through education, laws, reserved jobs, and general "uplift". The area did open up, exploitation was not severe, but educational advances in retrospect have to be viewed as modest. Other outcomes of change during the period include improvement of the medical situation, articulation with the world of caste, establishment of regular dominance-submission relationships with other peoples, and retention with changed functions of territorial clans and lineages.

The Bhumij of Barabhum, in the Eastern foothills of the Chotanagpur Plateau, have been associated with the Barabhum kingdom since the thirteenth to sixteenth century (Surajit Sinha, 1962), A century ago there were fewer non-Bhumij in the area and the land was more forested. While they are known to have been speakers of a Munda language in the past, by the early nineteenth century the Bhumij were reported to be speaking Bengali, the language of the great agricultural plain around them and by the 1880s they were said to speak only Bengali. A century ago, there were no weekly markets in the area, only itinerant traders. With the general opening up of the area to Hindu immigrants gradual Hinduization of the Bhumij began from the apex of their society downward. They claimed a true Rajput-Kshatriya ancestry. New festivals to major Hindu deities, and the much admired behavioural model of the Rajput-Kshatriya were the obvious features of this transformation. The link with an interfering external British administration was to stay and Hinduization was to continue.

The Kota have been studied several times by David Mandelbaum who has published a steady stream of articles on their changing relationship with the outside world. As he reconstructs the past, Mandelbaum gives some credence to a folk-historical idea that, once, the Kotas who are artisans, the Todas who herd buffaloes, and the Kurumbas who are food collectors were the sole occupants of the Nilgiri plateau. Then, centuries ago Badaga cultivators arrived from Mysore as refugees of War. The four people worked out a small social system of their own with caste like economic and ritual interdependence and with a distinct hierarchy in terms of both power and considerations of purity. The new era began with a peaceful influx of Britishers and plainsmen having special interests in the plateau. When the British arrived to establish hill stations in the early nineteenth century, traders were already visiting the area and labourers were infiltrating from the plains. There was some missionary and government education of Kotas. The Kotas gradually became sophisticated. A reformist faction of the Kotas undertook to sanskritize their behaviour, especially that which other Nilgiri tribes took to be demeaning. Mandelbaum contends that these changes have been slow and self determined.

The Paliyans are, largely, a food collecting people of southernmost India who have been known for centuries as shy honey-collectors. They live in bands scattered along the east slope of the ranges dividing southern Tamil Nadu from Kerala. For many centuries, Paliyans have maintained sporadic, tangential contact with the Tamil plainsmen around them. In it's most circumspect form this contact has been silent barter of forest produce for commodities such as metal implements, cloth, and condiments. Forest contractors, however, pursued Paliyans into their inhospitable dry thorny forest to arrange for special kinds of labour such as the extraction of soap, nuts, hemp, and elkhorn. Paliyans had to enter into contract labour under threats, even at gun point, and some bands, after experiencing episodes of such bullying retreated into an almost fully nomadic existence. Thus, the variation between contact and isolation is best seen as cyclical. The second phase of Paliyan contact with outsiders could be thought of in quantitative terms rather than qualitative. Mandelbaum attributed this to (a) increased exploitation of forest produce, (b) development of plantations in the lower valleys which Paliyans have long Inhabited, (c) entry of benevolent development officers, malaria eradication crew, etc., and (d) the lure of material advantages (Peter Gardner, 1972). But a qualitative change does take place when Paliyans settle down.

The colonial administration was, by and large, law and order oriented administration. It certainly acted as a catalytic agent but the pace of social change increased manifold in the post-independence period. Some aspects of change under the impact of welfare and developmental measures could be seen in a separate chapter in this book captioned as 'Social Change and the Contemporary Tribal Societies'.

IMPACT OF HINDUISM, BUDDHISM, CHRISTIANITY AND ISLAM ON TRIBAL SOCIETIES

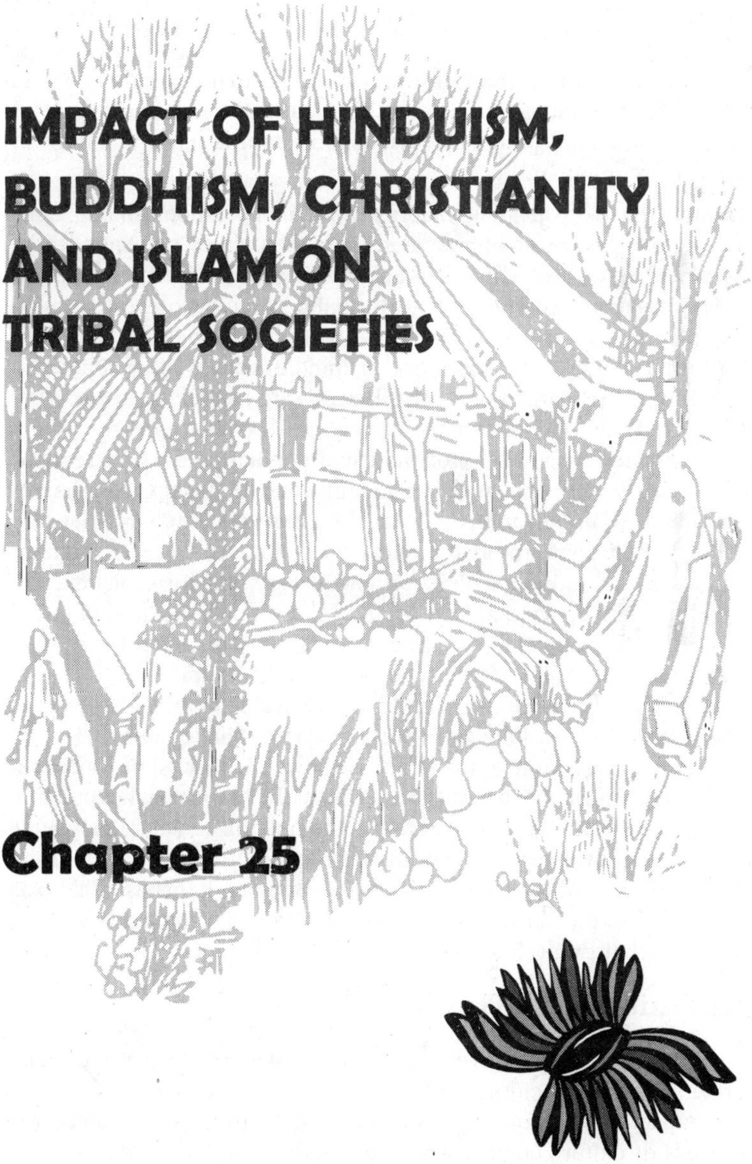

Chapter 25

India is the home of the followers of all the major religions of the world. This religious pluralism has added to the rich and colourful mosaic of cultural pluralism. Tribal India too, is not a monolith in terms of religious following.

Though, the overwhelming majority of tribal population still maintains it's exclusive beliefs and practices, more than ninety percent of them are oriented towards Hinduism and passing through different stages of Hinduisation. More than 95% of tribal populations of western India (Rajasthan, Gujarat and Maharashtra), southern India (Andhra Pradesh, Karnataka and Tamil Nadu), middle India (Madhya Pradesh), eastern India (Bihar,, Orissa, West Bengal) are Hinduized, while other Hinduized tribal populations are scattered all over the country. On a rough estimate around 5% of the tribal population are adherents of Christianity and are largely concentrated in Assam, Meghalya, Nagaland, Manipur and Mizoram. In astray pockets Christianized tribal populations are also found in Kerala, Andamn & Nicobar Islands, Bihar, Madhya Pradesh and Orissa. As for as Islam and Buddhism are concerned, followers of these faiths are around half a per cent (0.21% to 0.89%) each of total tribal population of India. Other religious faiths hardly figure in tribal India and their followers may be there in insignificant and inconsiderable numbers. The Siddi of Gujarat, Gujjars of the north-western Himalayan regions, Bakrewal of Jammu & Kashmir, some Bhils, Kotis and Dhankasi of Rajasthan are the examples of Muslim tribes. Almost the entire tribal population of Lakshdweep is Muslim and this is the only place where they have any significant presence. The impact of Buddhism may be seen on the Bhots of north-west Himalaya, the Bhutias, Lepchas, Chakmas and Nagas of the north-east Himalayan region and some of the tribes of Arunachal Pradesh and Ladakh.

Hinduism and Tribes

Except some of the relatively geographically isolated tribes the social organizations and cultures of almost all the tribes of India exhibit the impact of Hinduism. Establishment of British rule hastened the process of culture contact with the outside world as a consequence of increased communication. Many of the tribal areas hitherto closed were thrown open. The so called iron curtain over the tribal areas was removed. But this is also significant that despite the adoption of many values of Hinduism, Buddhism, Islam and Christianity the distinctive features of tribalism and tribal ethos remained.

The increased culture contact between the tribal societies and the outside world has been largely in the form of peasantization. When any tribal society comes into contact with the neighbouring Hindu peasantry (as has been the case with most of the tribes) it not only learns the art of cultivation but also adopts popular and local Hindu beliefs and practices in this process of peasantization. Even otherwise except the tribes of north-eastern region, Bay of Bengal and some other isolated areas the tribes though mariginally have been a part of the culture process of Indian civilization. Their references in the great epics of Ramayana and Mahabharat and the presence of the local versions of Hindu pantheon and mythology in many tribal societies bear testimony to this fact. More than two dozen versions of *Rama Katha* among many tribes has been indicative of the forces of Hinduization influencing the tribal societies in a variety of ways.

Even otherwise in most of the cases the adoption of Hindu beliefs and values has been quite a smooth process without any element of planned missionary activity. Major religions such as Christianity and Islam have fixed dogmas and their adoption simply means that a tribe has to give up it's tribal values, rituals and total cultural ethos. It is like giving up one's past and enter into a hew world. In contrast Hinduisation seems quite smooth and compatible to the local tribal cultures. A tribe can continue with many of its values and beliefs and at the same time adopt some new ones such as a new god or deity. This has been the core of tribe-caste continuum in Indian society. A number of tribal communities have been transforming themselves into caste and become sufficiently Hinduized to be described as Hindus but they still do not maintain social contact with the higher castes. Tribes of central India such as Gonds, Bhils, Bhumij etc. may be fitted into this category.

But there may be yet another category of tribes who has been totally assimilated with the Hindu society. " This is the level where a tribe has taken the form of caste (specially of scheduled castes), have adopted the elements of Hinduism but have retained several elements of tribal values and ethos. Here Religion and magic have assimilated into each other and the forms *of gotra* is more totemistic than vedic" (GS Bhatt, 1963). Here we come across not castes but 'tribe castes'.

This is the stage where the tribe is gradually transformed into castes. This is the meeting point of Hinduism and tribalism.

Surajit Sinha (1962) on the basis of historical and ethnographic studies of the Bhumij puts forward the concept of "tribal-Rajput continuum", He speaks of the diffusion of the Rajput model among the tribals of central India like the Bhumij, the Munda, and the Gond and their changing self-image and identity accordingly. Way back Griffiths (1946), while speaking about the process of Hinduization of Kol Tribes (of U.P. & M.P.) expresses the view that they are apparently forming miniature caste system within the tribe, modelled some where after the Hindu caste system.

Recent ethnographic studies of tribes of northern, western and middle India have left little doubt that many of them have become Hinduized to the extent that they have been assimilated with different castes at different levels in the caste system. The Tharu (S.K.Srivastava, 1958) and the Khasa (D.N.Majumdar, 1962) have largely succeeded in getting themselves accepted as Kshatriya. Moreover, the process of Kshatriyization has been the most popular form of Sanskritization in the Indian society. Sachchidanand (1964) gives an elaborate account of Hinduization among the Oraon and the role of Tana Bhagat Movement in the transformation of the Oraon society.

As a result of the impact of Hinduism and culture contact with the Hindus the tribes adopted Hindu customs, traditions, beliefs gods and goddesses, festivals and rituals and new taboos. In several cases they had to undergo some social disabilities, had to give up beef eating and drinking. G.S. Bhatt (ibid) describing the contribution of the Brahmins in this transformation tells us that the Brahmins have diffused and propagated Hinduism through two ways. On the one hand they offered their services to the tribals, introduced Hindu beliefs and practices to them and on the basis of mythological evidences justified and legitimized their claim to a caste. The Brahmins propagated the view that the genesis of every tribe is caste and they supported their assertion through evidences from the *Purana* and *Mahabharat.* If any tribe or caste had a low social status, they expressed the view that they are of Kshatriya lineage and their present plight was the result of their ignoring vedic rituals and taboos. Thus, they rekindled the hope among the tribal communities that they could still regain their past glory and retrieve the lost ground in terms of social status by 'readopting' and reviving the lost cultural elements. One of the popular mythological stories among several sub-tribes of the Bhils is a case in point. The genera! condition of Bhils has been and still very bad. Steeped in poverty and exploitation many of them have taken to crimes and criminal activities like theft, gambling, dacoity etc. as a way of life. They believe that Parvati was a Bhil and when they demanded bride price from Shiva for their marriage Shiva refused on the ground that he was a pauper and unconcerned with accumulation of wealth. In order to get the money, they killed Nandi, Shiva's bullock because the had heard that Nandi's shoulders contained lot of precious pearls Consequently, they were cursed to lead a life of poverty and hardship but at the same time Mahadev gave them a *Vardaan* that if they resorted to theft to earn their livelihood, it would invite no sin or curse That is why some sub-tribes of Bhils consider them as thieves of Mahadev.

One of the 'negative' features of the impact of Hinduism on tribes is the replacement of simple tribal rituals by highly complicated and cumbersome Hindu rituals requiring money and the services of a priest Child marriage has never been a feature of tribes. The youth dormitories have declined and it has given rise to tensions. The tribal are losing faith in their religio-magical beliefs and practices but it has not been replaced by any new basis of faith. Wherever pre-martial and extra-marital sex-relations were socially sanctioned the outsiders have taken advantage of this permissiveness and it has resulted in the ruthless exploitation of the tribals. As long as these relations were confined within the domain of the respective tribal communities these were not social problems. Today, it has become responsible for their moral degeneration leading to prostitution. The practice of bride wealth has been replaced among many tribes by the dowry system and even if it remains it is being demanded in cash with inflated amount leading to their indebtedness. Among several tribes the bride wealth has assumed the dangerous proportions of dowry with the result that a number of eligible girls from Chotanagpur region are forged to remain spinsters if no prospective bridegroom could manage high amounts of bride-price.

Wherever the tribes have adopted Hinduism freely, unhindered and according to their own genius it has given rise to a new sociocultural system based on the amalgamation of Hinduism and tribalism, which is Hindu, as well as tribal. The Rajvanshi of Bengal, on the one hand, have reached the level of a caste society by adopting Hinduism, on the other hand they have retained their traditional social organization. All the Rajvanshi claim to belong to the same *gotra (Kashyap)* but practice *gotra* endogamy which is not sanctioned in Hinduism. The

Lambadi of south India take the services of a Brahmin priest in marriage rituals. Earlier they did not marry with mother's brother's daughter or father's sister's daughter but now they have taken to this practice because several Hindu castes follow this practice. The Gonds, Bhils and several tribes around Chotanagpur region have also adopted some other practices prevalent among the local Hindus.

Another fact that deserves mention seems to be quite significant, Unfortunately the first representatives of Hinduism and the Hindu in the tribal areas were the exploiters-money lenders, traders, contractors and officials. The tribals hate them but not the Hindus or Hinduism. Perhaps the sages *sadhus, Mahatma, Sanyasis* were too benign and helpful whose roles convinced the tribals that the Hinduism had nothing to do with their exploitation.

Buddhism, Islam & Christianity

The impact of popular Hinduism and the process of Hinduization have been so pervading over tribal India that the role of other religious ideologies and religious systems seems to be marginal. However, as the impact of Buddhism, Islam and Christianity is concerned the roles of Buddhism and Islam is seen as marginal and not very significant as compared to Christianity. Even otherwise Islam and Christianity may never be very popular among the tribes because adopting either of these means severing one's ties from the past. Being based on certain fixed dogmas they demand total rejection of many of the tribal beliefs and practices so dear to the tribal people whereas adopting Hinduism does not pose any such dilemma. Being highly flexible and free from fixed dogmas the tribal could always adopt Hindu beliefs and practices even partially as per their preferences and compatibility.

As for as Buddhism is concerned only some tribals came under it's impact. These are mainly Bhots of north-west Himalaya and the Bhutias, Lepchas, Chakmas and Nagas of the north-east Himalyan region. Some tribal communities of Arunachal Pradesh have also come under the impact of Buddhism and the tribal population of Ladakh (Jammu & Kashmir) have also been adherents of Buddhism for quite some time.

An important fact to be noted here is that perhaps no tribal community has adopted a new faith in toto. In every such tribe the converted and the non-converted members live together. If we take up the case of Arunachal Pradesh we find that the tribal population can be divided into Budhists and those who continue to abide by their beliefs in spirits. The tribes of Western Arunachal Pradesh inhabiting the high hills of Kamang and Subansiri and Siang districts are the followers of *Mahayana* or Tibetan Buddhism. The Khamti inhabiting the foothills of Lohit district follow *Hinayana* version of Buddhism. Those who have taken to Buddhism maintain a *gompa* - a very sacred place where the images of Budha are installed and the holy books are kept. One or more sacred specialists known as *Lama* are attached to a *gompa.* Almost every Khampti and Singpho village has a monastry locally known as Bapuchang. The Singophos living as neighbours of the Khamtis have followed them and the majority of them have accepted *Hinayana* Buddhism. Commenting on the general tribal situation in Arunachal Pradesh, Haimendorf (1983) says that "Unlike the Christian converts among the Nishis those Khovas who are attracted by Buddhism do not opt out of the social life of their community and continue to participate in the traditional tribal rituals. In the some way the Sherdukpens combine their adherence to Mahayana Buddhism with the communal worship of tribal deities whose cult lies in the hands of priests entirely distinct from the lamas incharge of the larges *gompa* furnished and decorated in the style of Tibetan *gompa.* Among the Monpas too elements of the ancient Bon religion coexist with the dominant Budhist faith and the parallel practice of both religions within conflicts comparable to those which threaten to destroy the social fabric of Nishis affected by religious siralries. This shows that even the adoption of Buddhism could not cut through the traditional beliefs and practices. Though, Buddhism is gradually penetrating their society in the realm of ethics and social organization but the local little traditions are too deeply embedded to be given up easily.

As for as Islam is concerned it could never penetrate into the tribal regions mainly because of it's highly dogmatic nature and lack of patronage from the Muslim rulers. It hardly ever enjoyed the official or imperial patronage because the Muslim rulers were not missionaries but largely pursued their imperial and political objectives. Hence, it was left to *sufi* saints and preachers to spread it. That is why we find that it has had marginal impact on tribal regions. The Siddis of Gujarat, a section of Gujjars of the north-western Himalayan region, and sections of the Bhils, Dhankasi and the Kotis of Rajasthan have embraced Islam. Some small pastoral communities such as Gaddi and Bakriwal of Jammu and Kashmir have also adopted Islam largely because of the highly benign role of the *sufi* saints. Lakshdweep is the only example where wholesale conversion to Islam has taken place but even then the tribal population of India which has adopted Islam still remains less than one percent.

The tribal population of Lakshdweep consists of seven Muslim tribal communities namely, Koya, Malmi, Melacheri, Manikfan, Thakrufan, Thakru and Reveri. Recently as part of *People of India Project* Lakshdweep society has been studied thoroughly and we have latest ethnographic data about them. K.S. Singh (PIP, 1993) tells us that it is by now well established that Islam came to the Arabian Sea Islands from Southern Arabia and carried it's own idioms and structures. The Islamic structure of the Lakshdweep Islands was also part of the South Indian Muslim society. However, it seems that Islam came to the Islands from the Malabar coast. The location of the mausoleum of the venerable saint Ubaidullah at Androth is significant because this Island is closest to the coast. Not only the Arabic words assimilated into Malayalam but the Arabic script was also used for the Malayalam language." The matrilineal descent household unit is known as *tarawad.* The institution of matriliny that exists in Lakshdweep has been well investigated, particularly in the context of Islam (Leela Dube & Kutty : Matriliny in Islam) and other studies. The scholars have reported the decline of the matrilineal groups and matrilineal ideology as a result of the ideology and practice of Islam which, as a religion born in Semitic ambience, upheld patrilineal norms and paternal authority.

There has been a progressive Islamization of the life cycle rituals. For example, puberty rites for the girls similar to those of the Nair have been given up because they were considered repugnant to Islam. The father has come to assume a new responsibility. Kinship terminology also indicates the influence of Islam. One aspect of Islamization is the rise of new religious fervour seen in the observance of festivals such as Prophet Mohammad's birthday. Practices in conformity with the *Shariat* are insisted upon. Old rituals are disappearing. Folk dances are on the decline though the Mopilla folk song cassettes are very popular. Islamic Personal Laws prevail. Cross-cousin marriages are now preferential marriage type among all the seven groups. Women enjoy high status and have powerful say in the decision making process.

Among the entire population Islamic Great Traditions are paramount but the local little Traditions of pre-conversion times are still popular. This is not the case only with the people of Lakshdweep, rather this is a universal phenomenon. Yogendra Singh (1996) is largely right when he says that Islamization cannotes increased tendency among the converts towards new identity formation based on an increase in orthodox Islamic principles in cultural life. It also results In the conscious rejection of many syncretic elements which had thus far persisted in their culture as remnant of their Hindu (or tribal) past. Such orthodox organizations as the *Tableeghi-Jamaat* (preaching fraternity) have been in the forefront in their endeavour to 'weed out' the Pre-muslim/islamic cultural elements in the name of Islamic purity. However, the opposite trend is also visible among not only Muslim tribes but among the general Muslim population too. This is to achieve a symbiosis or integration of fusion of Islamic Great Traditions with the largely local Hindu Little Traditions.

Despite it's highly dogmatic nature Islam was able to find some adherants in tribal societies. It was largely because of the reason that Islam developed in a nomadic socio-cultural milieu and it's social structure had tribal egalitarian character. However, Muslim tribal societies themselves may well show marked internal differentiation in structure and organization.

The impact of Christianity, after Hinduism and the process of Hinduization, has been the most important area of acculturation studies among the tribes of India. The spread and impact of Christianity may be traced back to the establishment of the British colonial rule which led to the establishment of mission organisation and Churches in tribal areas especially in the north-eastern part and parts of Bihar, Orissa and Bengal. The missions on the one hand took to propagation of Christianity and on the other laid down an extensive network of social services such as education and healthcare. Thus, Christianity is the earliest agency of welfare in the tribal areas.

Introduction of Christianity, no doubt, gave the tribal people a sense of confidence to tackle the new world and a sense of self-respect but at the same time it added to the complexities of their social-cultural life. It divided the tribal societies, wherever it succeeded, into vertical divisions. For example the Khasi of Meghalya were divided into Christian Khasis and non-Christian Khasis. The non-converted Khasis often looked at the converted Khasis contemptously. Wherever the Christian Khasis dominated in population they became a dominant community but wherever they were in small numbers they could not cope up with the pressure of the non-converted majority and had to migrate to the urban centres or got themselves absorbed in the employment of missions.

THE spread of Christianity led to a number of problems in the process of acculturation. When any tribal community takes to the process of Hinduization, they find it a gradual process the changes are not sudden. Alongwith Hinduization the tribal beliefs and practices continue but adoption of Christianity leads to a sudden and radical departure from the past. Many of the traditional tribal beliefs and practices are denigrated and discarded. When we look at various aspects of culture change among the tribes as a result of adoption of Christianity, we find that the spread of Christianity encouraged right in personal or private property, patriarchal family system and doing away with such of their traditional institutions as 'youth dormitories'.

In certain situations Christianity was adopted by the tribal people as a sign of revolt or as a reaction to their ruthless exploitation by landlords, moneylenders, and traders who happened to be Hindus. The Kol rebellion (1932) and spread of Christianity in and around Chotanagpur region may be a case in point. Christianity has also been the earliest channel of westernization in a number of tribal communities and regions. A new and western life style involving the western style dress, taking food on chair-table and going to Churches on Sundays attired in western dress are a common feature in a number of Christian tribal communities. Use of Cosmetics, perfumes, soap and shampoos, western music etc. may also be seen in a number of areas among the Christian tribals.

In the north-east region the spread of Christianity has brought about most radical transformation. The advent of Christianity in Mizoram may be traced back to the first quarter of twentieth century. The spread of Christianity and spread of formal and modern education in Mizoram were complimentary to each other. The missionaries started formal education in the Lushai Hills. They wrote books both for general education and Christian religion. Tribal languages were also promoted and developed along with spread of English language. With the spread of Christianity, belief in spirits and their appeasement through sacrifices and rituals were replaced by the new faith. "Under the old Mizo Customs marriages and divorces were easily gone through. With Christianity marriage has attained a religious overtone. Monogamy has been accepted totally. Before the advent of Christianity, if a mother died at child birth, the child would also be buried with the mother. The missionaries started homes for motherless babies which would take care of such infants. With better medical cover such deaths of mothers at child birth have been eliminated" (Animesh Ray, 1993). It is regarded as fashionable to become a Christian and get educated and westernized among several Naga tribes such as Konyak Nagas and the Ao Nagas. The Church associations advocate abstinence from drinking country rice beer *(Zu)* or any other alcoholic drink. They also advocate monogamy and discourage divorce.

K.N. Sahay (1963) made a detailed study of the tribal Christian converts of Chotanagpur. This study helps us to understand as to how Christianity has brought about a change of self image and identity among the tribal converts. He tells us that the immediate result is that the tribal converts begin to consider themselves different from the non-Christian and acquire a "sense of superiority" over the latter and think that they practice the "best religion of the world". The catholic converts consider themselves to be the true adherents of Christianity. It is significant that the oraon society which was culturally homogenous has come to be divided now because of the working of various denominations of Christianity. With conversion their self image and identity have also undergone tremendous transformation.

When we look at the role of Hinduism or Hinduisation, Christianity and Islam and their protagonists in a holistic way we find that by and large these were detrimental to the cultural autonomy and socio-economic interests of the tribal people. The British colonial role followed the policy of isolation of the tribal people, the missionaries were interested in their conversions to Christianity, the Hindus demanded their total assimilation into the, larger Hindu society, the social workers's endeavour has been to 'civilize', them and make them their carbon copies, the freedom movement and its leaders wanted to bring them into the stream of national movement by creating a political consciousness among them. Every school of thought tried to understand the tribal people and their problems in their own ways and through their respective angles, The anthropologists had a clear vision of the tribal ethos and they wanted to understand the tribal people at the ideological level in consonance of their discipline "The British anthropologists on the governmental pay roll advocated isolationism, missionary-anthropologists like Stephen Fuchs saw tribal's larger interest and welfare outside the domain of Hinduism, while anthropologists like Verrier Elwin were the advocates of tribalism and tribal revivalism. Anthropologists like D.N. Mazumdar emphasised upon the protection of tribal cultures so that they become a part of the larger Indian "federation of cultures (G.S. Bhatt, ibid)."

The tribal cultures in India can be protected, preserved and find a special and unique place in the vast sea of Indian culture only when acculturation is not imposed over them. When foreign missionaries convert them into Christians they rob them of their cultural autonomy. When Hindu organisations make them Hindus, they too, are guilty of attacking their cultural autonomy. Under these circumstances the assimilation of the tribal people take a political shape. In the interest of national unity the tribal people should be left alone to decide their fate and future so that they can achieve, if they like a cultural milieu in consonance of their requirements by way of mingling of Hinduism, Christianity, Islam and tribalism. As long as the foreign missionaries remain among the tribal populations the Hindu 'missionaries' and the dogmatic social workers too cannot be prevented from disturbing the harmony of tribal life. The tribal cultures need to be protected from all sorts of missionaries, Christian, Hindu or Muslim. G.S. Bhatt (ibid) rightly calls for the indianization of Church in tribal areas to avoid several complications discussed in this chapter. When a prominent sociologist like G.S. Ghurye took the stand that the tribals were 'Backward Hindus' and needed to be brought into the Hindu fold through mass-scale and total assimilation, the activities of the foreign missionaries might also have played a part in his thinking. A popular opinion based on 'Hindu Nationalism' supported Ghurye's contention. Unfortunately the competition and rivalry in propagation of faith has resulted in clash between minority and majority.

Competition in the propagation of religious faiths in secular India has dangerous potentiality of promoting the worst type of communalism. Let the tribal people enjoy their cultural autonomy, make their own decisions and participate in the nation-building process as equal partners in progress retaining their self-respect and keeping their heads high.

CONSTITUTION, ADMINISTRATION AND TRIBAL DEVELOPMENT

It is no easy task for an outsider to get people to change their pattern of doing things.

— Arensberg and Niehoff (1964)

Perhaps it would be useful for public health specialist to start talking about a new category of diseases.... Such diseases could be called the "diseases of development" and would consist of those pathological conditions which are based on the usually unanticipated consequences of the implementation of developmental schemes.

— Hughes and Hunter (1972)

A BRIEF HISTORY OF TRIBAL ADMINISTRATION

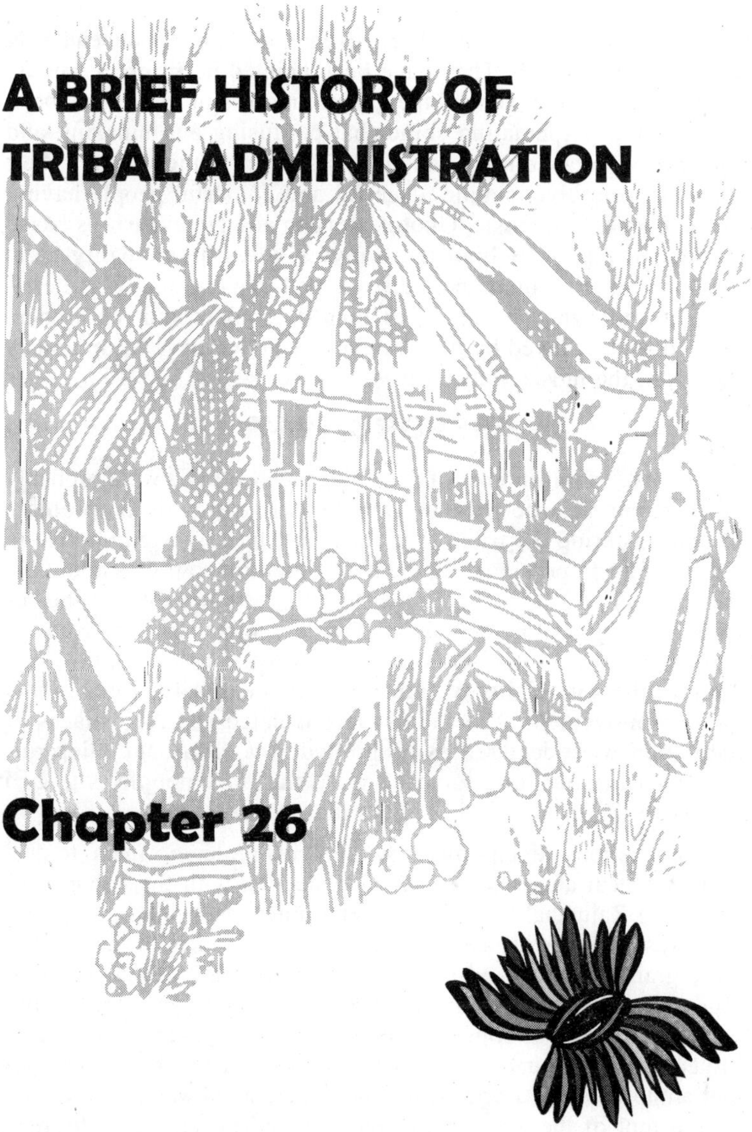

Chapter 26

The so-called aborigines had been, even much before independence, a subject of research. They have been painted in different colours by different people. Hence, the general masses in India have been holding and perpetuating somewhat confusing and amazing and sometimes fantastic myths about this section of the society. Their image of primitive, simple, cheerful and colourful people having exotic dances and music, Ghotul, Rorung and Dhumkuria is based on several myths. Behind these myths lies a bitter reality-heart breaking poverty, ignorance, disease and exploitation. It is heartening to note that a number of honest scholars and researchers refused to be swayed by mere romanticism and have scrupulously portrayed the ugly reality as it is.

BEFORE 1947

The British administrators of pre-independence India were probably the first people who tried to grapple seriously with the problem of administering the tribal areas and they had a vested interest in cultivating and perpetuating the above mentioned myths about the tribal people of India. They did everything to ensure that the so-called aborigines, the Scheduled Tribes, remain isolated from the rest of the Indian masses, because, the British imperialists had realised the potentiality of Indian tribes as explosive force in any national movement. The tribals were isolated and their places of habitation were declared as prohibited area. Thus, the alien rulers and Christian missionaries were the only people who had access to the tribal areas in the initial stages.

The first serious attempt made by the British rulers in India, to deal with the local aborigines, was in connection with the Paharias or Malers of Rajmahal Hills. The implicit intention behind this beginning was to deal with 'tribulent' tribes only. Leaders of these tribes were granted Sanad and they were assigned the responsibility of reporting all outbreaks. Ghurye (1963) writes that those leaders living near the lines of communication were to be paid a fixed sum to protect the mail runners. The payment is described by the competent authorities as "a bribe pure and simple as in Musalman days". At the foot of the hills, lands were granted to retired or disabled soldiers, and thus a ringfence of military minded people was created round the marauding Paharias. Slowly working through the corps that were raised, a court was appointed from among the officers of the corps for purpose of justice. Encouraged by its utility, the government was approached to withdraw the Rajmahal Hill tract from the jurisdiction of the ordinary courts. Thus in 1782, this tribal tract was withdrawn from the jurisdiction of the ordinary courts and the heriditary leaders of the tribe were called into a sessions courts which was to meet twice a year and try all offences. The council came to be known as' Hill Assembly and it had the power to inflict or rescind even capital punishment.

Having achieved the objective of internal justice and peace through the creation of the Hill Assembly; Cleveland, the clever administrator tried to solve another important problem, the problem of encroachments by the hated "foreigners". The lands held by the Paharias were "formed into government estate, held by them direct from Government and free from rent. These measures induced those Pahariya Chiefs, who had still held out, to join in and accept the rule of the British, which for all practical purposes was their own rule. The whole tract, thus unified and specially treated, came to be known as Daman-e-koh" (Ghurye, 1963). In this way the turbulent and problematic Paharias or Malers were pacified and the rules were made Law as Regulation I of 1796. With the passage of time, the prestige of Hill Assembly dwindled and the Regulation I of 1796 was repealed by Regulation I of 1827.

At this stage some other tribal groups, graoning under the yoke of exploitation, rebelled. In this context such uprisings as Ho mutiny of Singbhum in 1831, Khond uprising of 1846 and famous Santhal rebellion of 1855 are worth mentioning. The British Indian Government was also forced to send punitive expeditions to Assam, Nagaland and Jaintia Hills between 1850 and 1890 and repeatedly to the Lushai Hills, Naga Hills and to the Abor during the last decade of the 19th century and the first decade of 20th century.

The underlying causes of these uprisings and disturbances were almost always the same: the deep resentment and dissatisfaction created as a result of exploitation by their technologically and culturally more advanced neighbours.

At this stage the idea that "distinct and special arrangements were necessary for isolated tribal regions gained acceptance. The findings of anthropological researches seemed to support it" (Report of the Scheduled Areas and Scheduled Tribes Commission, Vol. I., 1960-

61). The British Government finally decided on a policy of segregating the tribes into special areas where their lives and interests could, supposedly, be adequately protected. Keeping this purpose in mind, an Act was passed in 1874 to specify tribal areas into, Scheduled Districts'. These areas were reconstituted under Section 52A of the Government of India Act of 1919. This Act provided for the appointment of officers to administer civil and criminal justice, to superintend the settlement and collection of public revenues and all matters relating to rent, and otherwise to conduct the administration within the Scheduled Districts. It also provided for the extension, by notification to the Scheduled Districts, laws in force in any part of British India, with such special restrictions and modifications as were deemed fit. Thus, wide powers of legislation by simple executive order were vested in the Executive. With the freedom movement gaining momentum, there was increasing anxiety on the part of the British administration to isolate the tribes from the national mainstream. The Indian Statutory Commission (Simon Commission) suggested that on financial and constitutional grounds the responsibility for the tribal tracts should be entrusted to the centre. In the subsequent years and upto 1947 numerous Acts and Regulations were promulgated and various reforms introduced. Thus in 1935, more stringent provisions for a special treatment of the tribal areas were in-corporated by converting them into "Totally and Partially Excluded Areas".

AFTER 1947

With the dawn of independence, the nation witnessed a considerable awakening about the welfare of the tribal people, This was reflected in various provisions of the Constitution independent India adopted by the Constituent Assembly on January 26, 1950. It visualised a policy of progressive assimilation of the tribal people in the national mainstream. In order to promote the integration of the tribal people with the rest of their Indian brethren, the Constitution provided special safeguards for the tribal communities for a period of ten years. This period continues to be extended till now.

A tribal welfare department was instituted in 1951 for the protection and advancement of the Scheduled Tribes and with the help of various provisions of the Constitution, a new line of administration was chalked out. Article 244 of the Constitution provides for the administration of "Scheduled Areas" in accordance with the Fifth Schedule and (in Assam) "Tribal Areas" under Sixth Schedule.

The Schedule Areas, thus defined, are administered as part of the stated in which they are situated but the Governor is given powers: (a) to modify Central and State laws in their application to them; (b) to frame regulations for their peace and good government and in particular for the protection of rights of tribals in land, the allotment of waste land and their protection from moneylenders. In the framing of the regulations the Governor is required to consult the Tribes Advisory Council in the state. The governor is further required to submit to the President of India an annual report or a report at such intervals as may be required by the Union Government. Thus in the Constitution ample provisions exist to protect the rights of the tribals in land, to protect them against exploitation by moneylenders and to preserve their social and cultural life.

The Scheduled Areas have been constituted with two ???? objectives. One is to assist the tribals in enjoying their existing rights and the second is to develop the Scheduled Areas and promote the economic, educational and social progress of Scheduled Tribes.

The Fifth Schedule visualises a division of responsibility between the state governments and the Union Government in the matter of administration of the Scheduled Areas. The State Government is directed to screen legislation unsuitable for extension to the tribal areas and to frame regulations for peace and good government. It is also the responsibility of the state government to implement special schemes of tribal welfare and general development of the Scheduled Tribes inhabiting within its boundaries. The Union Government takes the responsibility of providing guidance to the state government regarding administration of the Scheduled Areas and also to make available additional funds required to raise the administrative capability and standard of living of the tribal people. The Union Government also enjoys power to give directions to the state governments regarding the implementation of any particular scheme, laying down priorities in their implementation and in regard to the general administration of the tribal areas.

The Union Government's responsibility for the administration of the Scheduled Areas is not limited only to the provisions of funds for their development but extends to guiding the state governments and giving directions to them. This crucial role is provided for in Article 339(2) and Para 3 of the Fifth Schedule of the Constitution. It augers well for the tribal communities that The Union Government have relied upon persuasion and the good sense of the state government to adopt a uniform policy for the development of Scheduled Areas and rarely the situation demands a directive to the state governments. It is better if the unfortunate tribals are not dragged in unnecessary bickering and tug of war between crucial administrative agencies. Further, periodical conferences are held with the Planning Commission and the Ministry of Home Affairs to review the progress in regard to the programmes and to consider difficulties in their implementation.

Laws in the Scheduled Areas

In the matter of laws applicable to the Scheduled Areas the Governor has been given powers to make regulations for their peace and good government. He has also the powers to direct that State and Central laws shall not apply to the Scheduled Areas or shall only apply with modifications.

Role of the Traditional Tribal Council and the Advent of *Panchayati Raj*

The institution of traditional tribal council is as old as the tribal society. Their functions have been primarily to decide social and religious matters in the light of their customary laws and, in some areas, to determine judicial matters also on the basis of the consent of the people as a whole. This does not mean that the tribal councils did not decide economic questions. This has been a part of their social irresponsibility. These tribal councils were not elected bodies. Heredity was often the basis, but many times character and the personal life of an individual elevated him to his coveted position. Despite such constraints, every adult had an equal right to argue and put forth any question and thus issues used to be settled through consensus. The decision of the councils are law to the tribals because they are based on their social customs and religious rites.

Introduction of statutory panchyati system throughout India has weakened the traditional tribal councils at some places, but generally speaking, these statutory panchayats have adopted almost all the functions of the traditional tribal council with the added responsibility of implementing developmental work too. The functions of the statutory panchayats are, broadly speaking, administrative, economic and social. Amongst the administrative functions are included watch and ward, control and regulations fairs, market, grazing grounds and village farm lands and functions pertaining to sanitation and health. Amongst the economic functions are included functions relating to development of agriculture, irrigation, conservation, promotion of cottage industries and development of animal husbandry. Amongst social functions are included education and recreation, maternity and child welfare, etc. Commenting on the expansion of panchayati raj, the Report of the Scheduled Areas and Scheduled Tribes Commission, 1961, rightly remarks that the foundations of tribal life should not be destroyed. The "traditional tribal councils should not disappear. They should be revived where they are weak and encouraged where they are strong. They have evolved naturally out of the conditions of life in the tribal areas and they command a ready allegiance from the people who are naturally more willing to co-operate with institutions which have an established position among them through long usage and convention.

CONSTITUTION AND SCHEDULED TRIBES

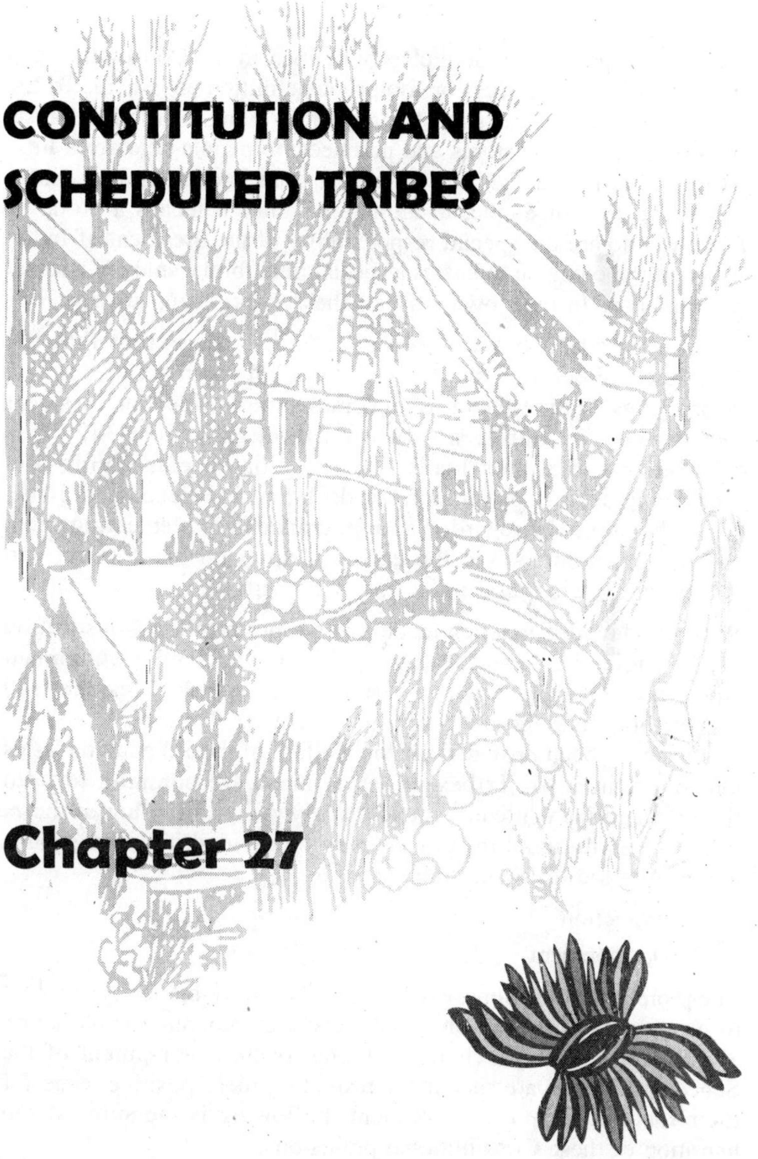

Chapter 27

The term 'tribe' is nowhere clearly defined in the Constitution and in fact there is no perfect or foolproof definition anywhere. To the ordinary man the word suggests simple folk living in hills and forests with their 'exotic' customs and practices; to people who are a little 'better' informed, it signifies 'colourful' folks known for their dance, songs and folk medicine; to an administrator it means a group of citizens who are the special responsibility of the President of India; to an anthropologist it indicates a special field for the study of a social phenomenon. In their own way all these impressions are correct.

The Constitution has defined a 'tribe' to the extent that the Scheduled Tribes are "the tribes or the tribal communities or parts of or groups within tribe or tribal communities" which the President may specify by public notification through Article 342. This ambiguity sometimes leads to confusion in classifying and identifying a tribal population for declaring it a Scheduled Tribe, but it should not be regarded as a hindrance in implementing tribal welfare programme (see the earlier chapter on the concept and definition of 'tribe' and issues involved with it).

With the dawn of independence and adoption of the Constitution of free India, the responsibility for their welfare and development was placed on the popular government through the President and Governors. In pursuance of the Directive Principles, special articles have been provided for the welfare of the Scheduled Castes and the Scheduled Tribes. Most of these are common to both these categories while a few exclusively meant for either of these. These Constitutional provisions may be divided into two groups underlying the following themes:

1. Protection
2. Development

The protective provisions, essential for their development, are meant to provide them protection from social and economic exploitation and injustice. The provisions relating to the development of the Scheduled Tribes are meant for providing them positive steps for their socio-economic development. Following is the summarised narration of these Constitutional provisions.

Protective Provisions

Article 15(4) -Promotion of Social, Economic and Educational Interests :

Though Article 15 prohibits any discrimination on grounds of religion, race, caste, sex or place of birth but the clause (4) of this Article provides an exception to this. It empowers the state to make any special provision for the advancement of socially and educationally backward classes of the citizens or for the Scheduled Castes and Scheduled Tribes. This provision is in accordance with the policy envisaged in Article 46 that the state should promote with special care educational and economic interests of the weaker sections of the people and protect them from social injustice. This clause has been especially incorporated to prevent any special provision made by a state for the advancement of socially or educationally backward classes of citizens from being challenged in the law courts on the ground of its being discriminatory.

Article 16(4) - Reservation in Posts and Services and Article 19(5) : Safeguard of Tribal Interest in Property :

While the right of free movement and residence throughout the territory of India and of acquisition and disposition of property are guaranteed to every citizen, special restrictions may be imposed by the state for the protection of the interests of the members of the Scheduled Tribes under Article 19(5). Since they are vulnerable to all sorts of deceivement and exploitation, hence there are various provisions disabling them from alienating even their own property except under special conditions. In their own interest, laws maybe made restricting the right of the ordinary citizen to move freely or settle in particular areas or acquire property in them.

Article 23 : Prohibition of Traffic in Human Beings, Forced Labour, etc.

It prohibits traffic in human being, begar or forced labour and other similar forms of forced labour. This is a very important provision because the Scheduled Tribes being much vulnerable to economic exploitation may be made bonded. In fact a substantial number of tribal population in the country has been leading a miserable life in bondage (for details see the chapter on debt bondage and bonded tribes).

Article 29 : Cultural and Educational Rights :

Article 29 (2) is controlled by the clause 4 of Article 15,

Incorporated in the Constitution by the First Amendment Act, 1951. This has brought Article 15 and 29 in line with Articles 16 (4), 46 and 340 and made it constitutional for the State to reserve seats for the backward classes of citizens, in public educational institutions. According to Article 29 a cultural or linguistic minority has a right to conserve its language or culture. This article provides protection to Scheduled Tribe communities to preserve their languages, dialects and cultures. The State would not by law enforce upon it any other culture or language.

Article 46 : Promotion of Educational and Economic Interests of Scheduled Castes, Scheduled Tribes and other Weaker Sections :

Article 164 : Minister Incharge of Tribal Welfare in the states of Bihar, Orissa and Madhya Pradesh :

This Article provides for a Minister incharge of tribal welfare in the states of Bihar, Orissa and Madhya Pradesh. These states have substantial tribal populations and special provision of a Minister looking after tribal welfare is an evidence of the concern of the framers of the Constitution for safeguarding the interests of Scheduled Tribes.

Article 330,332 and 334: Reservation in the Lok Sahba and the Vidhana Sabhas,

Article 335 : Limits of Reservation,

Article 338 : Special Officer:

There shall be a special officer for the Scheduled Castes and Scheduled Tribes to be appointed by the President. It shall be the duty of the Special Officer to investigate all matters relating to the safeguards provided for the Scheduled Castes and Scheduled Tribes under the Constitution. He shall report to the President upon the working of these safeguards at such intervals as the President may direct. The President shall call all such reports to be laid before each house of Parliament. Such an officer has been designated as Commissioner for Scheduled Castes and Scheduled Tribes.

By virtue of the Constitution (Sixty-Fifth Amendment) Act, 1990, the post of 'Special Officer' has been substituted by the National Commission for Scheduled Castes and Scheduled Tribes. The

Commission shall consist of a chairperson, vice-chairperson and five other members to be appointed by the President. The Commission shall have the power to regulate it's own procedure. (The duty of the Commission and other matters have been dealt with in detail in the chapter on Administration and Institutional Setup alongwith the details regarding the former 'Special Officer' i.e., 'Commissioner for Scheduled Castes and Scheduled Tribes' for the readers to compare these and understand some shifts and departures from the past).

Through, another amendment to the Constitution (89th amendment in 2003), National Commission for Scheduled Castes and Scheduled Tribes was bifurcated into two Commissions and the National Commission for Scheduled Tribes (NCST) was established.

Article 339(1) :

Appointment of a Commission :

The President may, at any time and shall, at the expiration of 10 years from the commencement of the Constitution, by order appoint a commission to report on the administration of Scheduled Areas and the welfare of the Scheduled Tribes in the States. Such commission, namely Scheduled Areas and Scheduled Tribes Commission, was appointed on 28th April, 1960 and it submitted its report in October 1961. It was headed by late Shri U.N. Dheber and it is popularly known as Dheber Commission.

The second such Commission was appointed by the President on 18th July, 2002 under the chairmanship of Sri Dilip Singh Bhuria (now Known as Bhuria Commission) which submitted its report in 3 volumes on 16 July, 2004.

Provision Meant For The Economic Development

Article 275 and 339 :

Provisions relating to economic development of Scheduled Tribes are mainly contained in Articles 275 and 339. Article 275 of the Constitution provides for assistance of the States for the implementation of the provisions of the Constitution. Article 339 lays down that the 'executive power of the Union government extends to the giving of directions to a state as to the drawing up and execution of schemes specified in the direction to be essential for the welfare of the Scheduled Tribes in the state."

Fifth And Sixth Schedule :

Articles 244 and 244(A) under Part-X of the Constitution provide for administration of Scheduled Areas and Tribal Areas. Under the Constitution the terms Scheduled Areas and Tribal Areas have definite connotations. The Scheduled Areas are governed by the provisions contained in the Fifth Schedule and the areas thus covered may also be called the Fifth Scheduled Areas. The Tribal Areas are governed by the provisions of the Sixth Schedule.

Fifth Schedule:

The Scheduled Areas and their administration fall under the Fifth Schedule. Here, it means such areas as the President may, by order, declare to be Scheduled Areas. The Parliament is empowered to make any amendment in the Schedule and it shall not be deemed to be an amendment of the Constitution for the purpose of Article 368.

The history of the Scheduled Areas may be traced back to 'The Scheduled District Act, 1874" which provided for the appointment of special officers to administer civil and criminal justice, to superintend the settlement and collection of public revenue and matters relating to rent and otherwise, to conduct the administration within the Scheduled Districts. Passing through "Government of India Act, 1910", Government of India Act, 1935" (Excluded and Partially Excluded Areas Act) it is under the present Constitution known as Fifth Schedule.

The Scheduled Areas have been constituted with the clear objectives to (a) assist the tribals in enjoying their existing rights without any hindrance by others and (b) to develop the Scheduled Areas and protect and promote the interest of the Scheduled Tribes.

Under the Presidential order certain tribal areas have been declared as Scheduled Areas in the state of Andhra Pradesh, Bihar, Gujarat, Madhya Pradesh, Maharashtra, Orissa, Rajasthan and Himachal Pradesh. The main features of the Fifth Schedule are the (1) special legislative powers of the Governor (b) Governor's Report to the President and (c) Constitution of a Tribes Advisory Council.

Sixth Schedule:

The Sixth Schedule applies to Tribal Areas within the States of Assam, Meghalaya, Mizoram and Tripura. Among the main features of the Tribal Areas are (a) their full autonomy in respect of matters falling within their jurisdiction. In other words these areas may be described as 'states within a state', (b) power of self management to the tribals through autonomous district and autonomous regions and (c) autonomy of these areas to such an extent that the writ of the Parliament or the state legislature does not run automatically unless the Acts in whole or part are specifically extended to the Tribal Areas by notification of the Governor.

There are nine autonomous districts in Tribal Areas of the four states mentioned above. The Governor enjoys unique position vis-a-vis autonomous districts. In several respects his position may be equated to that of the President's in relation to states.

Special Provisions with Respect to Tribal Areas and Hill Areas of Nagaland, Assam and Manipur:

Article 371 - A (Nagaland):

As per provisions of this article, no act of Parliament in respect of the (a) religious or social practices of Nagas (b) Naga customary laws and procedures (c) administration of civil and criminal justice involving decisions according to Naga customary law and (d) ownership and transfer of land and its resources, shall not apply to the state of Nagaland unless allowed by a special resolution of the Nagaland Assembly.

Article 371-B (Assam):

The President may provide for the Constitution and functions of a committee of the legislature assembly of the state consisting of members of that Assembly elected from the tribal areas as specified in the Sixth Schedule and such other members of that assembly as may be specified in the order. This committee has been provided to look after the interests of Tribal Areas at the state level.

Article 371 - C (Manipur):

This article provides for the constitution and functions of a committee through a Presidential Order. The committee shall consist of members of the legislative assembly elected from hill areas of the state. The Governor has been required to submit an annual report to the President regarding the administration of the Hill Areas in the state of Manipur. The Union Executive has been empowered to issue directions to the state as to the administration of the said areas.

After going through this summarised narration of the Constitutional provisions for the Scheduled Tribes one may visualise a very rosy picture of the state of affairs. Sadly the lofty ideas of the framers of the Constitution could never be translated into reality. The plight of the tribal people during the last four decades after independence as portrayed honestly in the pages of this book bear testimony to this bitter reality.

TRIBAL DEVELOPMENT

Chapter 28

The Indian Constitution enjoins on the State the responsibility to promote, with special care, the educational and economic interests of the scheduled tribes, and to protect them from social injustice and from all forms of exploitation. Their development is a special responsibility of the President; the Governors are responsible for reviewing the administration and development of tribal areas and for reporting to the President.

The problems of development of tribal areas is primarily linked with the backwardness of these areas, poverty of the people and the concept of integration of tribals with the rest of the population. For promoting the welfare of scheduled tribes and for raising the level of administration of scheduled and tribal areas to the State level, Article 275 of the Constitution provides for grants-in-aid from Consolidated Fund of India to states for implementation of developmental programmes. Also, special funds have been provided in each plan for welfare of scheduled tribes in the sector of welfare of backward classes. The assumption behind such an arrangement is that these funds will be additive to general developmental outlays which will accrue to the tribal people and areas.

Apart from concentration of population of tribes in different states, individual tribes and sub-tribes vary from bare handful to several lakhs. They subsist on a variety of economic activities, belong to several ethnic stocks and speak a large number of languages and dialects. They are also at different levels of political, economic and educational development. According to the Report of the Task Force on Development of Tribal Areas (1975), an important document, handicaps of tribal people in different zones in the country may be summed up as follows:

(i) Northern zone stretching from. Ladakh in north-east to Tarai region of Uttar Pradesh has tribes who have been neglected by the authorities since British days, mostly due to remoteness of their habitat and difficult climatic conditions. It is only since the Chinese invasion in 1962 that along the Himalayan mountains, attention has been drawn to their plight.

(ii) In the eastern, central and western zones, comprising of States of West Bengal, Bihar, Orissa, Madhya Pradesh, Uttar Pradesh, Gujarat, Maharashtra, Rajasthan, problems of tribal development are related to pressure of population on land, problem of land tenure, indebtedness and rights of tribals in forests and practice of shifting cultivation coupled with lower production level. Tribals of this area suffer from chronic scarcity of food, water and employment. Added to these, is the problem of Modernization due to growth of industrial complexes in the heart of tribal areas which has disrupted the traditional style of life. This has also led to group tensions due to large scale population movement which industrialisation entails compounded by resettlement of refugees from erstwhile East Pakistan among the tribal people especially in Dandakaranya.

(iv) Problems of southern zone tribes are mostly based on their primitive economy of Podu culture (shifting cultivation), or food gathering habits and prevalence of Muttadari system of land tenure.

(v) Tribals living in the Islands of Andaman and Nicobar, Lakshwa-deep and Minicoy have their problems arising out of their subsistence economy based on fishing and cultivation of coconut.

In spite of differences in problems between different zones are a few common features of tribal economic and social life which merit consideration in formulating development programmes in tribal areas. Some of these common features may be listed as given below:

(i) their habitats have been in isolated and difficult terrains with primitive transport system and roads, bridges, culverts, etc., are still scarce and do not link the tribal villages even to the nearest market available or the ' block headquarters;

(ii) Agriculture and collection of forest produce together contribute major portion of the income of tribals;

(iii) barter system of services and commodities still exists in several tribal areas, the market remains unorganized and commodities loans predominate, making it easier for moneylenders to operate;

(iv) tribals spend large amounts of their income on social and religious ceremonies, as a result of which they are perpetually indebted to the moneylenders;

(v) tribals still depend on natural growth of crops with a view to achieve self-sufficiency and lack motivation for making profits;

(vi) their low rate of literacy makes them vulnerable to the unscrupulous personnel in the bureaucracy or forest contractors.

Planned and Systematic Development

The advent of independence saw a plethora of governmental programmes launched by various official and non-official agencies for the welfare and development of the tribal people. But the first systematic effort for the development of tribal areas was initiated in 1955 in the form of Special Multipurpose Tribal Development Blocks. A modified version of this programme was taken up on a larger scale during the Second Five Year Plan when the tribal development blocks were started. This programme was further expanded during the Third Five Year Plan and all areas with more than two-third tribal concentration were covered by the end of this period. About 38 per cent of the total tribal population of the country spread over 504 tribal development blocks was covered. Although, it was agreed in principle to extent the programme to all those areas which had more than 50 percent tribal population, it is not possible to do so during the Fourth Plan. The developmental effort in then existing tribal development blocks was consolidated by extending the period of their operation. The area coverage, therefore, remained practically unchanged upon the end of the Fourth Plan. In the meantime, this programme was reviewed on a number of occasions, notably by a study team appointed by the Planning Commission under the Chairmanship of Shilu Ao. It was felt that the tribal development block was too small a unit for planning and execution of long-term developmental programmes. It was also found that the developmental effort from the general sector programmes was not adequate in those areas, particularly in the context of their comparatively lower economic base. It was, therefore, decided to evolve a new strategy for the development of tribal areas.

As a follow-up action, the Planning Commission appointed a Task Force on Development of Backward Classes which considered the problem in its numerous facets. The Task Force appointed a number of working groups, notably the one on personnel policies. The Task Force suggested a three-tier developmental structure at micro, meso and macro levels. The meso unit was suggested to be the main building block of this strategy. Area development and tribal development were to be suitably intermeshed in an integrated developmental programme. The strategy becomes clearer in the report of the Task Force and the various aspects needing special attention came into greater focus. [The strategy clearly spells out the problem of tribal development into two parts: (a) that of areas having more then 50% tribal concentration and the scheduled areas; and (b) that of areas with dispersed tribal population. Besides these two broad categories, primitive tribal communities at pre-agricultural level of technology were identified as a special group.]

The strategy for areas of tribal concentration culminated in the concept of a Sub-Plan for these areas. For this purpose the State and Union Territories have been grouped into three categories viz.:

(i) States and Union Territories having more than 50% tribal population: Meghalaya, Nagaland, Arunachal Pradesh, Dadra and Nagar Heveli and Lakshdeep, Minicoy and Amindivi Islands fall under this category,

(ii) States and Union Territories having large tribal population: Andhra Pradesh, Assam, Bihar, Gujarat, Himachal Pradesh, Madhya Pradesh, Maharashtra, Manipur, Orissa, Rajasthan and Tripura come under this category.

(iii) States and Union Territories having scattered tribal population: Kerala, Karnataka, Tamil Nadu, Uttar Pradesh, West Bengal, Andaman & Nicobar Islands, Goa, Daman and Dieu.

The state plans of States/Union Territories in category (i) are really tribal development plans and, therefore, no Sub-Plan has been considered necessary in their case. The Planning Commission requested other states, with some exceptions, to prepare Sub-Plans. A very broad frame of reference has been provided for the Sub-Plan in the note of the Planning Commission. The Sub-Plans are expected to: (i) identify the resources, for the sub-plan areas; (ii) prepare a broad policy frame for the development of tribal areas; and (iii) define a suitable administrative strategy for its implementation, [The Sub-Plan area in each State is to be divided into viable project areas, taking into consideration administrative boundaries, topography, level of economic development, ethnic composition, natural resources and potentials for development.] For each of the units so defined, an 'integrated tribal development project' with reference to the problems of that area is to be formulated within the policy frame provided by the Sub-Plan. The most important feature in the new strategy is that it recognises that there is no uniform solution to the variety of problems facing the tribal areas and communities which are at different levels of socio-economic development. However, certain common features also cannot be missed which will need immediate attention, though solutions will depend on the local situation. Elimination of exploitation is highest on the agenda. The integrated tribal development project will be a continuous effort for understanding the local situation, evolving suitable programmes, their effective implementation and a constant appraisal of the results on the "— touch-stone of their impact on the well-being of the most deprived sections of the community.

Development Programmes in the Plan

The pattern of central assistance for plan programmes depends on whether these are centrally-sponsored or state plan schemes. In case of centrally-sponsored schemes, states get 100% central assistance and for those in the state plan, central assistance is available as block grants and loans. Classification of centrally-sponsored and state plan schemes is as follows:

Centrally-Sponsored Schemes

1. Tribal development blocks;
2. Cooperation;
3. Girls' hostels;
4. Post-matric scholarship;
5. Coaching and pre-examination training schemes for competitive examinations;
6. Research, training and special projects;

State Plan Schemes

Education : Pre-matric scholarships, stipends, boarding grants, hostels, supply of free books, stationery, uniforms, mid-day meals, etc.

Economic Development : Subsidy for agricultural implements, seeds, fertilizers, etc., cottage industries, rehabilitation, communications, animal husbandry, horticulture, pisciculture, cooperation, minor irrigation, soil conservation.

Health, Housing and Others : Housing, drinking water supply, medical and public health, social and cultural activities, aid to voluntary agencies, and miscellaneous.

I. Special Multipurpose Tribal Blocks

As the first systematic effort for the development of tribal areas, Special Multipurpose Tribal Blocks were initiated in 1955. Forty-three such blocks were opened in different states for the first time in 1956 to speed up the process of development in the areas of the largest tribal concentrations. These blocks were jointly sponsored by the Ministries of Home Affairs and Community Development. The state governments were given charge of implementation of this programme. These blocks differed basically from the normal blocks on the following points:

(i) Developmental programmes to be implemented were more intensive in character;

(ii) The population and area coverage was to be much less than normal blocks;

(iii) Peoples' contribution had to be kept to the minimum and limited only to supply of the unskilled labour at a lower rate;

(iv) Loan funds were to be diverted as subsidies;

(v) Personnel appointed for these areas had to be suitably trained.

Various centrally-sponsored as well as state-sponsored schemes, as mentioned earlier, were taken up under these Special Multipurpose Tribal Blocks. However, after some time it, was realised that the programmes being undertaken under these blocks were not yielding desired results. In order to pinpoint the lacunae and suggest a better alternative, a committee was constituted under Verrier Elwin to go into various aspects of the programme. The main observations of the Elwin Committee were:

(a) Though, the programme suffered from the defects of all tension.

(b) In tribal areas; top priority should be given to agriculture and allied subjects, like irrigation, reclamation and soil conservation.

(c) There should be really serious attempt to relate the programme and the way of doing things to the tribal background, etc.

Now a modified version of this programme was taken up on a larger scale during the Second Five Year Plan when the Tribal Development Blocks were started.

II. Tribal Development Blocks

In the Third Five Year Plan period (1961-66), Tribal Development Blocks came into being, based on the general pattern of Community Development Blocks, but more intensive in character. The object was to bring about rapid improvement in socio-economic standard of the tribals.

These blocks were originally chosen with a population of one lakh (one hundred thousand) to become the units of formulation and execution of development programmes. Later on, this was lowered to twenty-five thousand and an area of 200 square miles. Popular representatives were associated with the block's governmental machinery, so that the programmes could be reflective of the needs and aspiration of the people. Till the end of 1966-67, 484 blocks had been set up in various states. Though, no rigid pattern was laid down, the guidance prescribed that 60% of funds should be earmarked for economic development programmes, 25% for communications and 15% for social services. High priority, assigned to communications programme, was in consideration of the difficult terrain and inaccessibility of tribal areas. An assessment of the programme made by the Vidyarthi Task Force indicated that it had fallen short of expectations, though it brought in a change in the outlook of tribals, particularly in the field of education and agriculture. The following programmes were planned and implemented according to the priorities prescribed:

Agriculture: Schemes for weaning away the tribals from shifting to settled cultivation; Establishment of grain goal for supplying fruit plants, grafts, vegetable seeds and seelings; Agricultural implements, loans and grants for soil conservation, minor irrigation, etc.; Demonstration farms to introduce improved agriculture practices.

Animal Husbandry: Piggery, poultry-keeping and sheep-breeding.

Cottage and Small Industries: Various types of cottage and small industries depending on local availability of raw materials.

Social Education: Promotion of existing village institutions into community centres.

Women and Children's Programme: Teaching of health and sanitation through recreational and cultural programmes.

III. Tribal Sub-Plan and Integrated Tribal Development Project

With some changes, the tribal development blocks continued into the Fourth Plan and beyond. These programmes, in practice, became too rigid, although varying conditions demanded different approaches to their problems. The tribal development block area proved to be too small a unit for large investments in infrastructures, economic development and social services. That these blocks could not accommodate schemes like soil conservation, major and medium irrigation, secondary and technical education, etc., is an instance in point.

In the Fifth Five Year Plan, attention had to be focused on the specific problems of each identifiable group and area, so that a definite perspective emerged for the course of their development. Broadly speaking, the situations in regions of tribal concentration and in areas of dispersed tribal population were quite distinct which required different approaches. In the regions of tribal concentration, area development approach had to be adopted, focussing on the problems of the tribal people. Keeping these factors into consideration, the concept of sub-plan was evolved. The sub-plan is not a scheme, it represents a new approach. [The strategy clearly spelt out the problem of tribal development into two parts- (i) that of areas of having more than 50 percent tribal concentration, and the scheduled areas, and (ii) that of areas with dispersed tribal population. Besides these two categories, primitive tribal communities at the pre-agriculture level of technology were identified as a special group.]

The region of tribal concentration, or the sub-plan in each state comprises a number of viable project areas, known as Integrated Tribal Development Projects. For each project an integrated area development programme, focussing attention on the specific problems of the area and people in that region, has to be formulated.

The long-term objectives of the sub-plan are : (i) to narrow the gap between the levels of development of tribal and other areas; (ii) to improve the quality of life of the tribal communities.

Among the immediate objectives are elimination of exploitation in all forms, speeding up the process for social and economic development, building up inner strength of the people and improving their organisational capabilities. In relation to the developmental programmes, the tribal sub-plans represent the totality of public sector effort in that area. The resources of the sub-plan are:

(i) State plan outlays;

(ii) Sectorial outlay in the central ministries;

(iii) Special central assistance;

(iv) Institutional finance.

According to the note on the preparation of sub-plan issued by the Planning Commission, a general strategy to achieve the objectives has to be evolved in the sub-plan keeping in view the special problems of the tribal region in each state. Some of the elements of this strategy are as follows:

Prevention of Exploitation

No developmental activity for benefiting the tribal population will succeed unless exploitation in various forms is prevented. Integrated credit-cum-marketing services, covering marketing of agricultural and minor forest produce, supply of inputs and essential consumer commodities, credit for production purposes as also for consumption and social needs etc., have to be set up. Redemption of past debts through legislative and executive measures will have to be taken up. Suitable measures may also be considered for dealing with the resultant liability. Programmes for the prevention of land alienation, restoration of lands already alienated, termination of practices, like bonded-labour, solution of the problems created in the zones of influence of modern industrial areas and review of excise and forest policies get special attention.

Development of Tribal Economy

Tribals, by and large, depend on agriculture and forests for their livelihood. Hence, development of agriculture is given the highest priority. The most, important components for the development of agriculture are held ownership and its development, provision of irrigation and improved, methods of cultivation. Completion of land records will have to be given a high priority. Shifting cultivators, forest villagers and forest labourers will be getting special attention.

Generation of Employment Opportunities

The level of economic activity in tribal areas is very low, yet the potential of their resource endowment is only partially utilised. Opportunities for better utilisation of available manpower have to be created through programmes of horticulture, animal husbandry, piggery and allied occupations. Cottage industries based on local raw materials have to be developed with a view to maximise the proportion of semi-processed and processed goods in the export-mix of the region.

Provision of Basic infrastructure

For speeding up the socio-economic development, basic infrastructure, legal, institutional and physical, are required to be developed on a priority basis. Growth centres, communication network, schools, rural health centres, marketing and credit organisations, rural electrification, manpower resources and training have to be planned in an integrated fashion, keeping in view the special conditions of the tribal areas.

Special groups and problems

As the sub-plan focuses its attention on the welfare and ; development of the people, special attention has to be given to areas and groups facing special problems. These include primitive tribal groups in extremely backward pockets, shifting cultivators and tribals affected by major projects. Those tribal groups, who have not received the benefits of development so far and are more backward amongst the tribal communities themselves, need to be identified. Special assistance is provided for such groups.

Preparation of the sub-plan involves - (i) identification and demarcation of areas of tribal concentration; (ii) Identification of socio-cultural barriers and promoters of change and development; (iii) Assessment of potentialities, special problems and felt needs of the tribal areas; (iv) Assessing the resource availability for the sub-plan; (v) Formation of sectorial programmes; and (vi) Devising a suitable administrative set up.

[The sub-plan area in each state is to be divided into various project areas, taking into consideration administrative boundaries, topography, level of economic development, ethnic composition, natural resources and potential for development.]

As the tribal development block was too small a unit for planning and coordination, it was decided to constitute a project area comprising a group of development blocks. Therefore, the entire tribal sub-plan area has been divided into a number of viable Integrated Tribal Development Projects (ITDP). As the situation varied from one state to another and from one area to another in the same state, the project size was decided, keeping in view the specific situation in a particular case. The project covers on an average, about three to four lakhs population and about six to seven blocks.

The project represents the total developmental effort in a particular area and has to accept the problem-solving approach, covering a large spectrum from protection to welfare. It has been conceived as comprising the totality of the existing administrative apparatus in the concerned area.

IV. Large Sized Multipurpose Societies

These cooperative societies have been set up since 1974 in tribal areas in the country with a view to supplying under one roof the various requirements of tribal people. Their credit-cum-marketing needs are particularly looked after by these societies. The policy of LAMPS is sought to be tribal-oriented by having tribals on the board of directors. Adequate share capital is being provided.

SCHEMES TAKEN UP DURING PLAN PERIODS

The following schemes have been taken up during different plan periods:

1. Protective Measures

(i) Legal Aid.
(ii) Marketing agricultural and minor forest produce.
(iii) Sale and supply of essential consumer commodities.
(iv) Bonded Labour.
(v) Non-productive credit,
(vi) Reorganisation of excise administration.
(vii) Strengthening of traditional panchayat.

2. Agriculture and Forests

(i) Survey and land records,
(ii) Agricultural research.
(iii) General agricultural development,
(iv) Credit for productive purposes,
(v) Landless labourers,
(vi) Training of young farmers,

(vii) Forest villages.

(viii) Development of forests and forest based economies etc.

(ix) Shifting cultivation.

3. Animal Husbandry

4. Irrigation

5. Communications

6. Electricity

7. Industry

(i) Small-scale industry

(ii) Medium industries and mining.

8. Special Programmes for Tribals affected by major projects.

9. Isolated small tribal communities.

10. Education.

(i) 100 percent coverage of children in age group 6-11 and 75 percent in age group 11-14.

(ii) Residential schools.

(iii) Provision of principal meals and uniforms.

(iv) Hostel accommodation.

(v) Pre-matric scholarships.

(vi) Post-matric scholarships.

(vii) Improvement of standards.

(viii) Teaching in mother tongue.

(ix) Extra-curricular activities.

(x) Physical education.

(xi) Construction of high school and middle school buildings.

(xii) Special programmes for youth in the age group of 15-25.

(xiii) Citizen education.

(xiv) Stipends to children of teachers.

(xv) Special pay to teachers working in extremely backward areas.

(xvi) Construction of residential facilities, specially for lady teachers.

(xvii) Recruitment programmes and refresher course for teachers.

(xviii) Development of tribal markets as centres for cultural activities.

11. Public Health.

(i) New Public health centres.

(ii) Free medicines.

(iii) Special clinics and mobile dispensaries.

(iv) Safe drinking water,

(v) Research on tribal housing.

(vi) Development of small model towns in tribal areas.

12. Administration and Voluntary Agencies.

(i) Strengthening administrative structure.

(ii) Housing for personnel in extremely backward areas.

(iii) Special pay for personnel belonging to development department working in extremely backward areas.

(iv) Aid to voluntary organisations.

The Shilu Ao Team on Tribal Development Programme had also expressed the view that the results achieved have not been commensurate with the expenditure incurred, and that much money has been wasted on schemes which have failed largely because of the failure of planners to take into account the stage of development of the tribals for whom they are intended and the conditions obtaining in the areas where they are to be implemented. The resources had been wasted on grandiose schemes of colonisation, housing, cooperation, etc. which had largely failed and had conferred no tangible benefits on the tribals. Failure of housing schemes is an instance in point. Tiled houses, involving considerable expenditure of public funds, constructed in the midst of forests on stereotyped lines have either remained untenanted or abandoned soon after construction because of the erroneous assumption of the planners that what is good for the people in the plains should be equally good and acceptable to the tribals. What is surprising is not the initial assumption which may have been due to ignorance but the persistence in the error in the face of accumulated experience which had demonstrated time and again that tribals will not 'stay put' in houses which do not conform to their ideas of layout and designs. If housing schemes have failed, colonisation schemes have fared no better. More money has been wasted on these schemes, with their ambitious housing adjuncts, than on any other single welfare activity undertaken for the benefit of the tribals. In one of the more important states which the Team visited, the failure was so complete that colonisation schemes were completely excluded from the Third Five Year Plan. The waste could have been avoided if planning had been preceded by a socio-economic survey to help the planners with the data concerning the felt needs of the tribals and the conditions obtaining in the regions which they inhabit. Among some other factors responsible for the unsatisfactory results of the tribal development programmes are:

(i) The delay in the implementation of considered recommendations made by the Scheduled Areas and Scheduled Tribes Commission and other high level bodies in the past to protect the rights of the tribals has worsened the position which these recommendations were intended to correct while the failure to pay attention to and profit by their advice on matters pertaining to the formulation and implementation of tribal development programmes had resulted in the failure of ambitious schemes and consequent waste of valuable resources,

(ii) No conscious attempt has been made by any of the state governments, with the solitary exception of Andhra Pradesh, to ensure that the tribals receive a reasonable share of the benefits from the general development programmes to which they, as citizens of the state, are legitimately entitled. Broadly speaking, the planners in the states have proceeded on the basis that the special provision is the only provision available to finance tribal development programmes.

(iii) Development effort instead of correcting the existing imbalance as between tribe and tribe has widened it as the benefits of the schemes undertaken have largely accrued to the more progressive sections amongst them.

(iv) The tribal development blocks failed to get any significant support from the general development programmes including community development programmes.

(v) The Schemes formulated for these blocks were not adopted to the felt needs of the specific areas.

The administrative set up is also, responsible for the unsatisfactory performance of tribal development programmes. When a number of departments, each providing its own particular input and each working more or less independently of the other, come into existence, the tribal people are forced to run from pillar to post to get what they need. The Planning Commission in this connection observed:

> Multiplicity of agencies has resulted in diffusion of responsibility, inadequate control, lack of coordination and from the people's angle, difficulty in identifying the officials concerned with specific programmes. The pattern of administrative organization will have to be worked out in detail for achieving functional coordination and efficiency. Delegation of authority, specificity of responsibility and adequate flexibility should be built into the system so as to enable the implementing authority to effect changes in the on-going programmes on the basis of concurrent evaluation. As a result of historical reasons, the administrative structure in tribal areas has continued to lack simplicity and thereby defying comprehension of the tribals and has failed to evoke substantial response from them. All that polemics, criticism and counter-criticism apart, there is a consensus that position of the tribals has improved, but in the absence of concrete data it is not possible to give a clear verdict on the extent of progress and say if it was appreciable or only marginal. In the light of our laudable objective but' not so good performance, it is evident that the entire question of tribal development needs afresh look.

Dr. Ram Dayal Munda, former Vice-Chancellor of Ranchi University and a tribal himself has the unkindest remarks for the government approach towards tribal development. In a frank interview (1988) he hits the nail straight on the head when he says that the "government is pumping money into a leaking system. What use is it anyway? There has been no significant result of these efforts. Land alienation continues unabated, outsiders continue to get preference in matters of training and employment, even loans. There is no evidence of decentralization. Corruption and favouritism continue to thrive under an alien political culture".

Procedure for Declaration as ST

The term Scheduled Tribes is defined in the Constitution of India under Article 366(25) as such tribes or tribal communities or parts of groups within such tribes or tribal communities as are deemed under Article 342 to be Scheduled Tribes for the purposes of this

Constitution. Article 342 prescribes the procedure to be followed in the matter of specification of Scheduled Tribes. In terms of Article 342(1), the President may, with respect to any State or Union Territory, and where it is a State, after consultation with the Governor thereof, notify tribes or tribal communities or parts thereof as Scheduled Tribes. This confers on the tribe or part of it a constitutional status invoking the safeguards provided for in the Constitution, to these communities, in their respective State/ UTs. Thus, in terms of Article 342(1), only those communities who have been declared as such by the President through an initial public notification will be considered as Scheduled Tribes. Any further amendment in the list is to be done through an Act of Parliament (Article 342(2)). Parliament may by law, include in or exclude from the list of Scheduled Tribes, any tribe or tribal community or parts thereof. The list of Scheduled Tribes is State-specific. In other words, a community declared as Scheduled Tribe in one State need not be so in another State.

Scheduling and De-Scheduling of Tribes

Thus, the first specification of Scheduled Tribes in relation to a particular State/ Union Territory is by a notified order of the President, after consultation with the State Governments concerned. The above Article also provides for listing of Scheduled Tribes State-wise/UT-wise and not on an all-India basis.

The criteria generally adopted for specification of a community as a Scheduled Tribes are:

(a) indications of primitive traits;

(b) distinctive culture;

(c) shyness of contact with the community at larger;

(d) geographical isolation i.e. backwardness.

These are not spelt out in the Constitution but have become well established. They take into account the definitions in the 1931 Census, the reports of the first Backward Classes Commission (Kalelkar Committee), 1955, the Advisory Committee on Revision of SC/ST lists (Lokur Committee), 1965 and the Joint Committee of Parliament on the Scheduled Castes and Scheduled Tribes Orders (Amendment) Bill, 1967 (Chanda Committee), 1969. There are over 700 tribes (with many of them overlapping in more than one State) as notified under Article 342 of the Constitution of India, spread over different States and Union

Territories of the country. It is worth nothing that no community has been specified as a Scheduled Tribe in relation to the States of Haryana and Punjab and the Union Territories of Chandigarh, Delhi and Puducherry.

Ascertaining ST Status of Individuals

Where a person claims to belong to a Scheduled Tribe by birth, it should be verified: (a) that the person and his parents actually belong to the community claimed; (b) that the community is included in the Presidential Order specifying the Scheduled Tribes in relation to the concerned State; (c) that the person belongs to that State and the area within that State in respect of which the community has been scheduled; (d) he may profess any religion; (e) that he or his parents/grandparents, etc., should be permanent resident of the State/UT on the date of notification of the Presidential Order applicable in his case; (f) a person who is temporarily away from permanent place of residence at the time of the notification of the Presidential Order—applicable in his case, say for example to earn a living or seek education, etc. can also be regarded as a Scheduled Tribe, if his tribe has been specified in that order in relation to his home State/Union Territory; (g) but he cannot be treated as such in relation to the place of his temporary residence notwithstanding the fact that the name of his tribe has been scheduled in respect of that State where he is temporarily settled, in any Presidential Order; (h) in the case of persons born after the date of notification of the relevant Presidential Order, the place of residence for the purpose of acquiring Scheduled Tribe status, is the place of permanent abode of their parents at the time of the notification of the Presidential Order under which they claim to belong to such a tribe. This does not apply to the STs of the Lakshadweep Islands for whom there is a requirement of being born in the UNION TERRITORIES in order to be eligible for ST status.

Scheduled Tribe claims on migration

a) Where a person migrates from the portion of the State in which his/her community is scheduled, to another part of the same State in respect of which his/her community is not scheduled, the person will continue to be deemed to be a member of the Scheduled Tribe, in relation to that State.

b) Where a person migrates from one State to another he can claim to belong to a Scheduled Tribe only in relation to the State to which he originally belonged and not in respect of the State to which he has migrated.

Scheduled Tribe claims through marriages

The guiding principle is that no person who is not a Scheduled Tribe by birth will be deemed to be a member of Scheduled Tribe merely because he or she has married a person belonging to a Scheduled Tribe. Similarly, a person who is a member of a Scheduled Tribe will continue to be a member of that Scheduled Tribe, even after his or her marriage with a person who does not belong to a Scheduled Tribe.

Issue of Scheduled Tribe certificates

The candidates belonging to Scheduled Tribes may get Scheduled Tribe certificates, in the prescribed form, from any one of the following authorities:

(i) District Magistrate / Additional District Magistrate / Collector / Deputy Commissioner / Additional Deputy Commissioner / Deputy Collector / 1st Class Stipendiary Magistrate / City Magistrate / Sub Divisional Magistrate / Taluka Magistrate / Executive Magistrate / Extra Assistant Commissioner [not below the rank of 1st Class Stipendiary Magistrate]; (ii) Chief Presidency Magistrate/Additional Chief Presidency Magistrate / Presidency Magistrate; (iii) Revenue Officers not below the rank of Tehsildar; (iv) Sub-Divisional Officer of the Area where the candidate and / or his family normally resides; (v) Administrator / Secretary to the Administrator / Development Officer (Lakshadweep Islands).

Punishments for officials issuing Scheduled Tribe Certificates without proper verification action is to be taken under the relevant provisions of the Indian Penal Code if any official is found to have issued a Scheduled Tribe certificate carelessly and without proper verification. This will be in addition to other action to which they are liable under the appropriate disciplinary rules applicable to them.

Migrants from other States / Union Territories Persons belonging to a Scheduled Tribe who have migrated from one State to another for the purpose of employment, education etc. experience great difficulty in obtaining ST certificates from the State from which they have migrated. In order to remove this difficulty, it has been decided that the prescribed authority of a State Government / Union Territory Administration may issue a Scheduled Tribe certificate to a person who migrated from another state, on the production of the genuine certificate issued to his father / mother by the prescribed authority of the State of the father / mother's origin except where the prescribed authority feels that a detailed enquiry is necessary through the state of origin before issue of the certificate. The certificate will be issued irrespective of whether the tribe in question is scheduled or not in relation to the State / Union Territory to which the person has migrated to Scheduled Tribe claims through marriages.

Ministry of Tribal Affairs

The Ministry was set up in 1999 after the bifurcation of Ministry of Social Justice and Empowerment with the objective of providing a more focused approach towards the integrated socio-economic development of the Scheduled Tribes (the most underprivileged section of the Indian Society) in a coordinated and planned manner. Before the formation of the Ministry, tribal affairs were handled by different Ministries at different points in time.

The Ministry of Tribal Affairs is the Nodal Ministry for overall policy planning and coordination of programmes for development of STs. To this end, the Ministry has undertaken activities that follow under the subjects allocated in the Government of India (Allocation of Business) Rules, 1961 and amendment(s) thereafter. The subjects allocated to the Ministry of Tribal Affairs are as follows:

It covers all tribal people and all areas with tribal population across the country.

- Social security and social insurance to the Scheduled Tribes
- Tribal Welfare: Planning, project formulation, research, evaluation, statistics and training
- Promotion and development of voluntary efforts on tribal welfare
- Development of Scheduled Tribes
- Scheduled Areas
- Monitoring of ST Welfare Grants, based on the framework and mechanism designed by NITI Ayog
- The National Commission for Scheduled Tribes
    a. Commission to report on the administration of Scheduled Areas and the welfare of the Scheduled Tribes; and
    b. Issue of directions regarding the drawing up and execution of schemes essential for the welfare of the Scheduled Tribes in any State.
- Implementation of the Protection of Civil Rights Act, 1955 and the Scheduled Castes and the Scheduled Tribes (Prevention of

Atrocities) Act, 1989, excluding administration of criminal justice in regard to offences in so far as they relate to Scheduled Tribes. Note: The Ministry of Tribal Affairs shall function as the umbrella unit for the overall development & well-being of the STs. However, the Sectoral programmes & Schemes for the development of these communities as well as their coordination will fall under the ambit of the concerned Central Ministries / Dept., State Govt. and/ or Union Territory Administration, where each Ministry/ Dept. is responsible for its concerned sector.

(Source: Website of Ministry of Tribal Affairs)

National Commission for Scheduled Tribes

The National Commission for Scheduled Tribes (NCST) was established by amending Article 338 and inserting a new Article 338A in the Constitution through the Constitution (89th Amendment) Act, 2003. By this amendment, the erstwhile National Commission for Scheduled Castes and Scheduled Tribes was replaced by two separate Commissions namely- (i) the National Commission for Scheduled Castes (NCSC), and (ii) the National Commission for Scheduled Tribes (NCST) w.e.f. 19 February, 2004.

The term of office of Chairperson, Vice-Chairperson and each member is three years from the date of assumption of charge. The Chairperson has been given the rank of Union Cabinet Minister, and the Vice-Chairperson that of a Minister of State

Functions and Duties of the Commission

The functions and duties of the National Commission for Scheduled Tribes have been laid down in Clause (5) of the Article 338A of the Constitution. Clause (5) states that it shall be the duty of the Commission:

(a) to investigate and monitor all matters relating to the safeguards provided for the Scheduled Tribes under this Constitution or under any other law for the time being in force or under any order of the Government and to evaluate the working of such safeguards;

(b) to inquire into specific complaints with respect to the deprivation of rights and safeguards of the Scheduled Tribes;

(c) to participate and advise on the planning process of socio-economic development of the Scheduled Tribes and to evaluate the progress of their development under the Union and any State;

(d) to present to the President, annually and at such other times as the Commission may deem fit, reports upon the working of those safeguards;

(e) to make in such reports recommendations as to the measures that should be taken by the Union or any State for the effective implementation of those safeguards and other measures for the protection, welfare and socio-economic development of the Scheduled Tribes; and

(f) to discharge such other functions in relation to the protection, welfare and development and advancement of the Scheduled Tribes as the President may, subject to the provisions of any law made by Parliament, by rule, specify.

National Scheduled Tribes Finance and Development Corporation (NSTFDC) It was set up in 2001 under the Ministry of Tribal Affairs, Government of India with head office in New Delhi.

The corporation is managed by a Board of Directors with representatives from Central Government, State Channelizing Agencies (SCA), National Bank for Agricultural and Rural Development (NABARD), Industrial Development Bank of India (IDBI), Tribal Cooperative Marketing Development Federation of India Ltd. (TRIFED) and three eminent persons representing Scheduled Tribes.

The main objects of the Corporation is to work for socio-economic and educational upliftment of Scheduled Tribes (STs), to provide better self- employment avenues so that they can become economically independent and self-reliant. The Corporation undertakes a wide range of activities for socio--economic and educational upliftment of the STs by devising and implementing financial assistance schemes exclusively for the tribal. These schemes are for providing loans to the poor STs at concessional rates of interest and on soft terms and conditions. For helping tribal students to pursue higher education, loans are offered which are subsidized by the Ministry of Human Resources Development. The Corporation also provides grants for conducting training and skill development programs for tribal youth so that they can enhance their employability /productivity or can take-up entrepreneurial activity.

The Right to Fair Compensation and Transparency in Land Acquisition, Rehabilitation and Resettlement Act, 2013

An Act to ensure, in consultation with institution of local self-government and Gram Sabhas established under the Constitute, a humane, participative, informed and transparent process for land acquisition for industrialisation, development of essential infrastructural facilities and urbanisation with the least disturbance to the owners of the land and other affected families and provide just and fair compensation to the affected families whose land has been acquired or proposed to be acquired or are affected by such acquisition and make adequate provisions for such affected persons for their rehabilitation and resettlement and for ensuring that the cumulative outcome of compulsory acquisition should be that affected persons become partners in development leading to an improvement in their post acquisition social and economic status and for matters connected therewith or incidental thereto.

Review of Laws Impacting Tribal Communities:

After a thorough review of various laws pertaining to the adivasi groups, Meena Radhakrishnna (2016) has summarized the impact of these laws as follows:

- The Fifth Schedule and PESA are proving to be significant hurdles in corporate loot in the mineral rich tribal areas.
- PESA stipulates a strict requirement of not just consultation prior to land acquisition for development projects but also in the formulation of relief and rehabilitation packages.
- Forest Rights Act has potential to safeguard adivasi land alienation. It is not working effectively because of intense opposition by commercial interests as well as the forest department which is ironically a party to its implementation.
- Right to Fair Compensation and Transparency in Land Acquisition, Rehabilitation, and Resettlement Act,2013. This Act is meant to nullify the draconian Land Acquisition Act,1894, amended in 1984.
- The Mines and Minerals (Development and Regulation) Amendment Act(MMDRAA),2015.It is the fallout of the landmark Samatha Judgment by The Supreme Court.

National Scheduled Tribe Finance and Development Corporation

With a view to pay a focused attention and accelerate the pace of economic development of Scheduled Tribes, the erstwhile National Scheduled Castes and Scheduled Tribes Financial Development Corporation (NSTFDC) was set up in April, 2001 under the Ministry of Tribal Affairs. The NSTFDC has been granted license under Section 25 of the Companies Act (A Company not for profit). The Authorized Share Capital of the NSTFDC is `500.00 crore and paid up capital is `230.50 crore as on date. In order to achieve the mandate set for the NSTFDC, (for undertaking selfemployment ventures / activities) financial assistance is extended by NSTFDC to the Scheduled Tribes, who are having annual family income upto double the poverty line. NSTFDC also provides financial assistance as grant for skill and entrepreneurial development of the target group. The financial assistance is channelized through Government owned agencies nominated by the respective Ministries / State Governments and UNION TERRITORIES Administrations. NSTFDC also provides financial assistance for procurement and marketing / minor forest produce so as to avoid the distress sale of produce / products by the Scheduled Tribes.

Eligibility criteria for the beneficiary

The beneficiary (ies) should belong to ST community and annual family income of the beneficiary (ies) should not exceed double the poverty line (DPL) income limit (presently DPL is `39,500/- per annum for the rural areas and `54,500/- per annum for the urban areas). In the case of Self Help Groups (SHGs), all the members of the SHG should belong to the ST community having annual family income upto Double the Poverty Line (DPL). Similarly for Cooperative Society, loan is extended to the eligible STs through co-operative Society having minimum 80 per cent or more STs as member of the said cooperative society. NSTFDC is implementing following programmes for the economic development of STs.

Term loan is provided for income generating activities. Marketing Support Assistance is provided for financial support for meeting the working capital requirement of the Central / State Government owned agencies and national level federations for undertaking procurement and / or marketing of minor forest produce /

agricultural produce collected / grown by the STs and / or related product / services. Marketing Support Assistance extended to the beneficiaries through the SCAs, the interest is at par with rates of interest for long term loan and the assistance is extended to the Central / State / UT owned organizations, national level federations directly involved in procurement, the interest rate is 7 per cent per annum. Assistance by way of grant is also given.

Tribal Cooperative Marketing Development Federation of India Ltd. (TRIFED)

O.W.: http://www.trifed.in

The Tribal Cooperative Marketing Development Federation of India Limited (TRIFED), was set up in 1987 as a national level apex body under the Multi State Cooperative Societies Act, 1984 (MSCS Act, 1984). After the enactment of the Multi-State Cooperative Societies Act, 2002 (MSCS Act, 2002) TRIFED is deemed to be registered under the latter Act and is also listed in the Second Schedule to the Act as a National Cooperative Society.

The Byelaws of TRIFED were revised in April, 2003 in tune with the new Multi State Cooperative Societies Act, 2002 read with the Multi State Cooperative Societies Rules, 2002. Under its revised mandate TRIFED has stopped bulk procurement in Minor Forest Produce (MFP) and surplus Agricultural Produce (SAP) from Tribals. (This procurement is now done by the State-level Tribal Cooperatives Societies / Federations). TRIFED now functions as a 'Market developer' for tribal products and as 'service provider' to its member federations.

TRIFED is now engaged in the marketing development of tribals products (natural and organic products, handicrafts, ratification etc.) through its own shops (TRIBES India) and shops selling its products on consignment basis.

Xaxa Committee Recommendations:

In order to have the latest position and socio-economic status of the scheduled tribes, the Union Government in 2013 appointed a high-level committee (HLC) of five experts headed by Prof. Virginius Xaxa. It was mandated to prepare a report and suggest effective remedial measures. The committee analysed the existing tribal situation and made recommendations on the following parameters:

- Geographical and Demographic scenario
- Legal and Administrative framework
- Livelihood status
- Health
- Education
- Land Alienation, Displacement, and Enforced migration
- Legal and Constitutional issues
- Delivery of Public Goods and Services

The salient features of this analysis and recommendations are as followers:

1. Legal and Administrative Framework:

During the colonial period, tribal communities inhabited areas were divided into 'Excluded' and 'Partially Excluded' areas for purpose of administration. Such administrative arrangements have found continuation in post-independence India in the form of Sixth and Fifth Schedules of the Constitution. Despite the power vested in the Governors of 5th Schedule States, they did not exercise their constitutional power in preventing laws detrimental to tribal interests.

The committee strongly recommends that the Governor should be mandated to take the advice of the Tribes Advisory Council and examine legislations and policies particularly those pertaining to issues such as forests, land acquisition, conservation, mines and minerals, health and education. The Governor should be made responsible for the overall functioning of the TAC.

2. Livlihood and Employment Status:

- There is dire need to establish agro-based training institutions and related labour intensive industries in tribal region.
- Water for agriculture is the greatest impediment in production. Micro watershed development programme with people-centred participatory approach is a good method for poverty reduction through natural resource management in tribal regions.

  The newly acquired land under Forest Rights Act, 2006 could be utilized in eco-forestry rather than for food grain cultivation which could give more return to the ST farmers
- Credit and marketing facilities need to be extended to the STs.

- Tribals should be encouraged to use their traditional knowledge to meet their needs by recreating their forest ecosystem and forest based livelihood.

3. Education

- The purpose of education anywhere should be to provide children with an understanding of their environment and society in which they live and to endow them with the capability to earn livelihood in local society and, for those who have desire and ability in the national job market.
- Disparity in literacy levels, enrolment and dropouts and very low enrolment in higher education should be looked into with utmost seriousness
- Keeping in view the difficulties of adjusting to a new cultural environment, teachers for schools in the tribal regions should be recruited locally.
- The State Governments should develop a policy for multilingual education, so that early learning is conducted in local language.
- Inclusion of local culture, folklore and history in the curriculum can help in building confidence of tribal children and enhance the relevance of education in their lives.
- The 'indigenous knowledge' should be documented, researched and promoted.
- Residential schools should be set up specifically for the nomadic tribes.
- There is a need for regular social audits to monitor the functioning of schools.
- State Tribal Research Institutes are in very bad shape. These should be strengthened and a Central Tribal Research Institute too should be established.

4. Health

- Social determinants of health-literacy, income, water, sanitation, fuel, food security and dietary diversity, gender sensitivity, transport connectivity – play very important role in determining the health outcomes.
- The construction of drainage system, village sanitation infrastructure, personal toilets and the environmental

measures to control mosquito breeding can be included in the MGNREGA scheme and completed on priority basis in Scheduled Areas.

- Improving nutrition of children, adolescents and pregnant and lactating women is critical for the scheduled tribe population.
- Traditional healers and dais (local midwives) play an important role in the indigenous health care. Instead of alienating and rejecting them, a sensitive way of including them or getting their cooperation in health care, must be explored. Traditional herbal medicine should be protected through community ownership. The ownership and intellectual property rights of tribal community over their own herbal medicines and practices should be ensured.
- Healthcare delivery to the scheduled tribe population should be culture sensitive and in the local language.

5. Land Alienation, Displacement and Enforced Migration

- Serious effort is required by the state to minimize displacement.
- There should be right based approach to comprehensive rehabilitation for socio-economic reconstruction of 'victims of development' including for the backlog of displaced.
- The new legislation, The Right to Fair Compensation and Transparency in Land Acquisition, Rehabilitation and Resettlement Act, 2013 is progressive in the sense that it is the first to legally mandate rehabilitation of the displaced people. The definition of 'public purpose' in the new law is very wide and will only lead to greater acquisition and displacement in the Scheduled Areas. The definition of 'public purpose' should be severely limited.
- Government agencies acquiring land with the ultimate purpose to transfer it to private companies for stated public purpose, should be kept outside the ambit of the new law, as the Public-Private partnership mode of acquiring land is simply a backdoor method of alienating land in violation of the Constitutional provision to prohibit or restrict transfer of tribal land to non-tribals in Scheduled Areas.

- It is recommended that, as directed in the landmark. Samatha judgment and the PESA Act, every Gram Sabha should have the power to prevent alienation of tribal land and further that the minerals should be exploited by the tribal people themselves.
- Gram Sabha consent should be mandatory for acquisition of land by the Government for its own use as well.
- While preparing the project cost estimates, the full cost for rehabilitation should be included, and no attempt should be made to reduce costs for a favorable cost-benefit ratio.
- The rehabilitation package and process should take into account, the cultural displacement and loss of customs and traditions. For tribal people, their strength is their community and therefore, it is imperative that they be settled and rehabilitated as a community, if they so desire.
- The role of the Governor is crucial for protecting land, community assets, culture, and traditional institutions of tribal people and to ensure that they are treated fairly. This also raises the issue of suitability of persons who occupy the important position of Governor and other offices in the Scheduled Areas.

6. Legal and Constitutional Issues

- The past twenty years have been dramatic in terms of the changes in the economy, and in the effect that economic policy has had on tribal communities. This has also been the period when laws, notably the provisions of PESA, 1996 and FRA, 2006, have been enacted which recognize autonomy and rights of tribal communities.

  The implementation of these laws is, however, sputtering and reluctant.
- The implementation of the community forest rights has hardly taken off especially for recognition of various community forest rights and rights of PVTGs and pastoralist communities.
- The democratic structure in forests with the Gram Sabhas as laid down in FRA faces great resistance from the current forest regime. The changed paradigm has not yet permeated administration.

- The import of PESA has not been internalized into administrative practice and government officials. There have been recorded cases of Gram Sabha consent being fraudulently obtained or forged.
- The encounter of the tribal with criminal law has been one of the disturbing aspects in the past decade. Large number of tribals, men and women, are in jails for what are termed 'naxal offences'
- Denotified tribes have been asking that steps be taken to remove stigma and prejudice from their lives. More specifically the Habitual Offenders Act, should be repealed.
- The persistence of bonded labour, and the trafficking, in large measure, of women from tribal areas needs a concerted effort to end it. The state has to take primary responsibility to identify, release and rehabilitate bonded labour, wherever they are found.

SOCIAL CHANGE AND CONTEMPORARY TRIBAL SOCIETIES

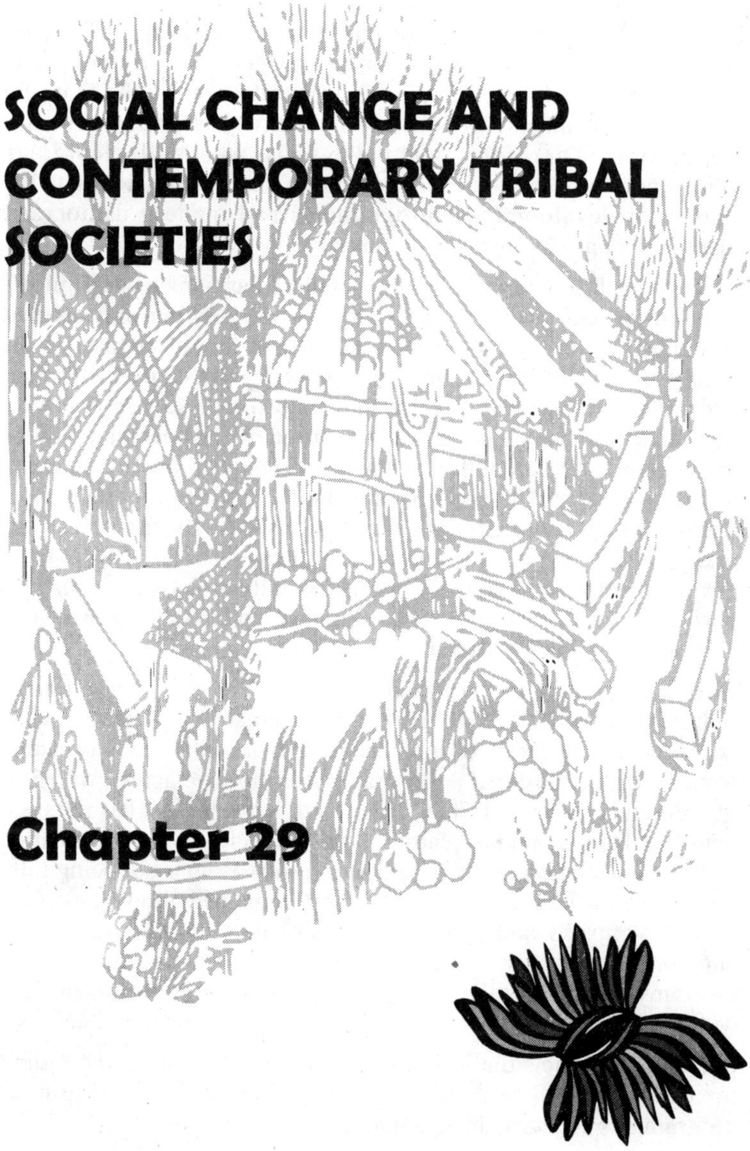

Chapter 29

Like any other society, tribal societies too undergo change. The pace of change definitely increased after independence when special welfare and development measures were taken up by the State for the socio-economic development of the backward segments of Indian population. Therefore, when we look at social change in contemporary tribal societies we largely analyse and evaluate the impact of developmental programmes and modern democratic institutions on our tribal populations.

A range of differences in the geographical locations (accessibility), population, cultural variations, levels of economy and context situations of the tribals have contributed to the differences in the impact of developmental measures, modern democratic institutions and other policies pursued by the State for these communities. Further, social change has also been caused by the opening up of the tribal areas as a result of the economic and political forces. Therefore, it is not an easy task to describe or quantify the change brought about due to all such factors. By and large the response of tribals has been mixed and uneven. If we examine changes as a result of the developmental process we come across situations which may be positive as well as negative with differences in their degree from one tribe to another and within the same tribe.

Chaudhary (1990) in the introduction to Tribal Transformation in India (5 Vols.), while highlighting their unmatched plurality, points out some salient facets of the change which are (i) Transformation from a marginalised and peripheral existence to an acute awareness of their civic rights, (ii) Their progress or development has not been upto expectations mainly due to the deficiencies in the formulation and implementation of the programmes, such as their not being fully responsive to the local felt needs; their implementation by persons lacking sympathy and insight into the tribal culture; the process of elite formation; and their being pushed into a macro capitalist market economy, (iii) The elite class has emerged through the present democratic institutions and have cornered developmental benefits.

In his opinion the situation demands serious thinking and building up of processes and conditionalities in the development programmes to meet these situations.

The Peoples of India Project (Anthropological Survey of India), completed in 1994, studied 635 tribal communities - tribes, their groups and segments including territorial units. It has come out with some quantitative data regarding tribal participation in the mainstream and their responses to developmental effort. The following changes are largely traceable to the development efforts. An elite stratum of entrepreneurs, businessmen (156 tribes), teachers (380), administrators (156), Engineers/doctors (150) and defence personnel (178) has been created; There has been a rise in the political leadership with the number of tribes playing leadership role at various levels being - Village Panchayat (362), Regional (185) and National (45); Response to education has been favourable in case of both boys and girls and incidence of dropout is less in the tribal communities. Educational level has increased from 8.53% in 1961 to 16.35% (excluding Assam) in 1981; The tribes avail of health and medical facilities and 531 tribes (83.5%) have expressed favourable attitude towards these facilities. There has been a decline in death and rise in birth rate; Many tribal communities are aware of and participate in self employment schemes initiated by the government. Their number being agriculture (438); animal husbandry (302); piggery (160); basketry (151); poultry (164); fishery (98), small scale industry (67), etc. the electronic media cover the tribal areas well-radio (91%) and T.V. (27%).

H.M. mathur citing Furer-Haimendorf says that development has succeeded in creating positive and desirable changes in several tribes. Their social economy level should be slowly rising and so is their participation in national life. However, certain groups create a drag on the process.

The general trends described above are discerned if a macro level view of tribal change is taken. But many micro level studies, more often than not, give a different impression and throw up many important issues and policy questions related to our tribal policies and programmes, such as: (1) What are the potentialities of current development strategy to deliver goods. (2) What are the alternatives and whether directions of development are quite desirable and the sections which gain through these measures are the real needy ones. (3) How the impoverishment and powerlessness of the common tribals is traceable to national policies like forest policy, construction of large projects, heavy mining and industrialisation and the direction of agricultural policies. How this can be prevented and eliminated. The situation has been labelled as 'internal colonisation'. (4) The investment in tribal areas specially through TSP have been going up but analysts find that investment on infrastructure has consumed most of these resources and they question how these investments benefit the ordinary tribals.

The above situation together with remedial action has been reflected by Dr. Bhupender Singh in his Sixth Plan Mid-Term Appraisal (1983). He concludes that : the shift in the planning strategy in favour of family oriented programmes initiated in the VI Plan has to make further strides. Till mid Sixth Plan the funds flowing into this programme were meagre. But a beginning has been made and they are liable to make their impact felt.

Though, targets achieved in family oriented programmes have exceeded the proposed numbers but a precise idea of the capacity of families to cross the poverty line is not available. The situation needs to be closely monitored and evaluated. The much needed planned coordination between family based programmes with infrastructural and human resource development need a finely balanced planning. The unified administrative structure concommitant to resource mobilisation and project plans has to be created and made responsive and accessible to the common tribal. The regional imbalances reflected in the export of national resources from tribal areas should be remedied so that these resources benefit the tribals.

Case Studies

HUNTER GATHERERS

Gadgil & Guha (1992) have adduced evidence that this group of tribal began loosing control over their means of subsistence from the early part of colonial rule. This has forced them to take to other survival strategies, as well as disorganisation and impoverishment. Jenu Kuruba with their vast traditional knowledge of forests now help the Forest Department in rearing elephants and collection of forest produce earning a mere pittance while creating large earnings for the Forest Department Hill Pandaram (Kerala) live as trespassers, in mortal fear of Forest Department servingits officers. The Chenchu have taken to crime in certain areas. Baviskar (1995) has traced criminality among the Bhil and the Bhilala of Jhabua district in Madhya Pradesh to the growing control of the State over the forest resources and degradation of cultivable lands. G.P. Reddy's study (Satyanarayana, 1990) highlights the failure of Chenchu resettlement scheme. The deficiencies were that little time was allowed for their reorientation into agriculture and poor management of agriculture operations by project officers, insenstivity of the officers to the social organisations and individualistic way of life of the Chenchu, creation of large agricultural colony which did not suit the small-group way of life of the Chenchu, and creation of Chenchu settlements amidst ryots who were afraid of them and actively discouraged Chenchu resettlements.

Artisans

Gadgil & Guha (1992) have pointed out how certain artisan activities such as ironsmithy totally died out and Agarias and Asurs had to take to poor agriculture or wage earning. Further, the availability of raw materials for other crafts like basketry and the high price charged for bamboo by the forest department has contributed to the impoverishment of the tribals. Chaudhary (1990), discussing the situation among 49 tribal communities having first level involvement in handicrafts concludes : (a) though many tribal crafts have emerged as very popular, government scheme for their promotion are not quite beneficial to the tribal craftsman themselves; (b) poor marketing of the original craft-ware has led to imitation objects coming into the market causing loss to the genuine artisans.

Another study of the **Dhokda** crafts among the Dhurva of Madhya Pradesh also points out similar drawbacks, particularly the deficiencies in the government schemes related to training, supply of tool-kits and marketing.

Shifting Cultivators

Shifting cultivators have also suffered as a result of government forest policy and the deficiencies in the alternative economic development programmes. They have, however, been resisting the government policies in a more concerted manner (Gadgil & Guha 1992). These resistance movements have mostly brought reprisals and sometimes relief, for example the success of Hill Madia move against pine plantation. Even though it has been realised often that the shifting cultivation should be controlled and substituted by a whole package of alternative pattern of cultivation and forestry, achievement of such a programme have been quite limited. Three case studies in Tripura give the impression of a partial success. **Jhum** continues to be popular though settled cultivation was gaining ground. Alternative packages viz., animal husbandry, plantation and horticulture have achieved some success. Plantation has been taken up by a section who have become substantial land owners as a result of tenancy reforms. A class of landless agricultural workers unknown earlier in the tribal areas have emerged as a result of the taking over of Jhum lands by the forest department. These people now are wage earners in the plantations.

Settled Agriculturists

Thakur's study in Dumka which related to adoption of improved agricultural techniques by tribals points out that though tribals have been made aware of various techniques they have adopted only some, for instance, line sowing and manure pits which did not involve extra expenditure. Use of chemical fertilisers has not been successful and caused even losses because of lack of irrigation. In fact dry farming research suitable for tribal areas is still wanting. The extension agents have also shown a lack of genuine interest and enthusiasm.

Mahapatra's study of Mayurbhanj also highlights a similar situation. He has specifically pointed out that creation of change needs sustained efforts. Introduction of technological changes should also be synchronised with agricultural ritual cycle and the role of tribal priests. Another study among the Santhal in Bihar pointed out that out of eight Santhal sub-groups, the Murmu (priest), the Mardi and the Tudu who are most influential and landed have gained the most through the planning process, depriving the other groups.

Moderndemocractic Institutions

The People of India study, discussing the Gond, points out that the statutory panchayats are the elected bodies. These, however, have their activities limited to planning and implementation of welfare and developmental activities at village level. 'Apparently there is no clash between the traditional Gond leadership and the statutory panchayats as yet and the village leaders who have emerged here are powerful men active in village politics and close to power structure.... and, nowadays most of the traditional panchayats have restricted their activities to deciding marital disputes.

Prasad's study of role of tribal leadership in rural Bihar fostered by the panchayat raj found that this emerging leadership was not much different from the traditional leadership in their background (education, sex, occupation, etc.) but they were inadequately trained for their role. They are quite representative but qualitatively weak. Significantly, they show a lack of any collective effort to help the masses and are oriented more towards self aggrandisement and fulfillment of their private needs. He underlines the similarities between this emerging tribal leadership and the mainstream Neta (leader) culture.

The state of the old traditional institutions in the tribal areas and their relationship with the formal statutory institutions has been critically examined in the 29th Report of the Commissioner for Scheduled Castes and Scheduled Tribes. The report points out that : (1) The traditional self governing institutions, a living facet of tribal life, have now no role in administration, development process, etc. and they get no benefits of new ideas and are isolated. Usually these institutions come into play when certain vital matters reach a crisis situation. (2) The formal institutions given to tribals in the name of self governing system could not become their own. These are largely ineffective and routinised in functioning. In fact they have become a cause of social discord due to the politics of votes and the emergence of unhealthy leadership. (3) The dichotomy of the situation i.e. social matters going to traditional institutions and others to statutory bodies has left Vie simple, common tribal confused and disillusioned.

The VII Plan discusses the desirability of recognising the traditional institutions which command widespread respect and are deep rooted. The VIII Plan while discussing measures needed to ensure tribal participation in development process recommends that traditional tribal institutions should be blended with the new system to ensure better participation of tribals. The case studies mentioned earlier also point out to such a need. However, in spite of this realisation no concrete steps, say inclusion of some traditional panchayat heads, etc. in the statutory bodies, without elections, have so far been tried. On the other hand moves are afoot in some states like M.P. and Manipur to invest more power in elected bodies by adapting the VI Schedule of the Constitution. Dr. B. D. Sharma (29th Report) goes to highlight quite a different model - the Raisabhas of Adilabad in A.P. : a confluence of the New and the Old - where a village community comes together as a group to deal with all outsiders including the government departments.

ROLE OF ANTHROPOLOGY IN TRIBAL DEVELOPMENT

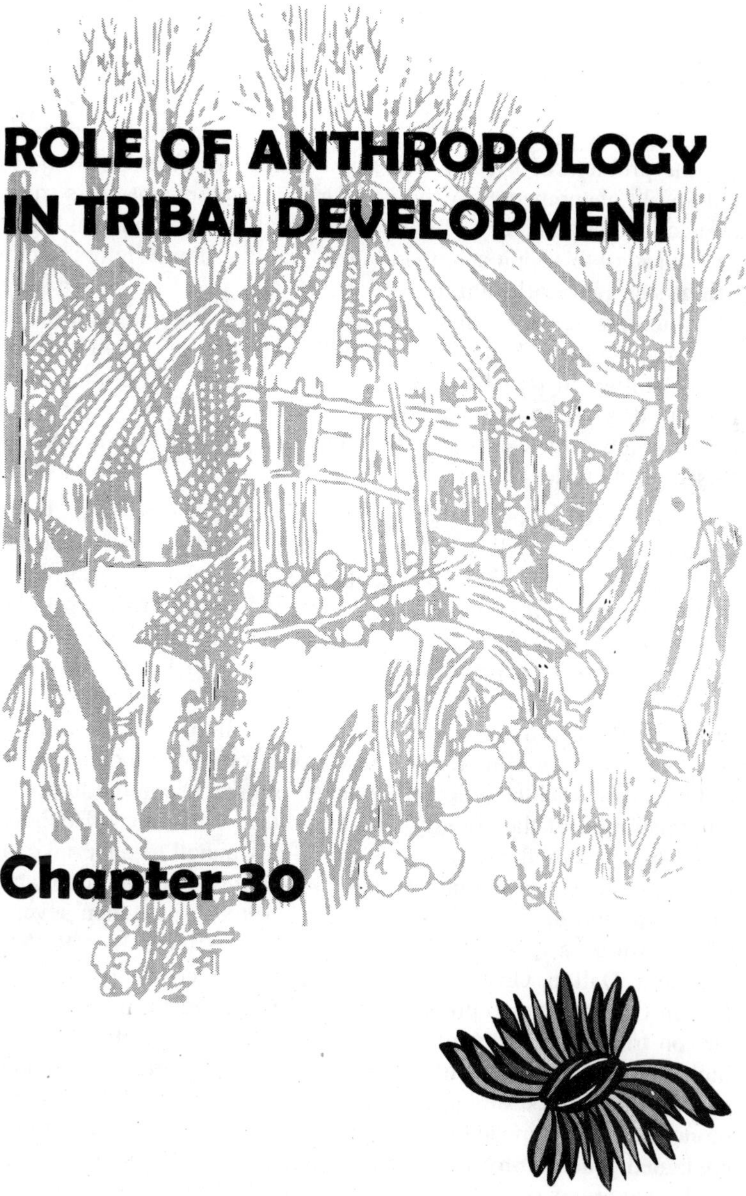

Chapter 30

Next to Africa, India has the largest concentration of tribal population, but the problem of tribal welfare or tribal development in India is not an old phenomenon. A 'policy' for the development of its tribal population was adopted in India for the first time after independence. The object of this approach was to 'level up' the administrators, social scientists, especially anthropologists, social workers and a host of voluntary agencies in the formulation and implementation of this massive plan. The involvement of anthropologists and use of anthropology in tribal welfare and development programmes in not sudden. It took decades to appreciate the knowledge of anthropology for use in practical purposes. Let us briefly review this important development.

Most of the tribal population spread in different regions of India remained isolated till 1750 or so, when administrative officers, missionaries, social workers and others started taking keen interest in them for one reason or the other. They tried to 'help' (tribal people) in their own respective ways. Their objectives and orientations were different and hence they visualised varied approaches to the tribal problems. "The importance of knowledge of anthropology for efficient administration was, perhaps, first realised as early as 1807 when the Court of Directors of East India Company made a formal decision that 'such knowledge Would be of great use in the future of administration of the country'. To this effect, Dr. Francis Buchnon was appointed by the Governor General-in-Council to undertake an ethnographic survey to enquire into the conditions of the inhabitants of Bengal and their religion" (Vidyarthi, 1968). Since then several anthropologically oriented administrative officers like Risley, Thurston, Dalton, Grigson, Gurdon and others were deputed by the British Government to prepare handbooks, gazetteers, monographs, etc. on tribes and castes of India. Thus, quite a lot of ethnographic literature was produced within a short time. Its scientific value should not be questioned severely because it was the result of some pioneering efforts made by the earliest ethnographers. These writings contained general information about land and people and were more in the nature of general description. However, the first problem-oriented work came out only in 1931 when J.H. Hutton put forward his views regarding the evil effects of contact on the tribal people. He suggested "self-governing tribal areas with free power of self-determination." S.C. Roy made similar reports regarding the tribes of Bihar. Now a 'ful-fledged' anthropologist D.N. Majumdar did field work among the Hos. He also came out with his findings, published in 1937, that the Hos had undergone much degeneration since they were studied' by Dalton in 1879. He also studied Korwas and came out with shocking conclusions regarding their plight.

However, Verrier Elwin's monumental monograph on Baigas of Central Provinces may be regarded as the first work in which anthropological view about the future of the tribes found vocal, bold and explicit expression. He lamented that Baigas were made a victim of "over hasty and unregulated process of uplift and civilization". As a remedial measure, he suggested the creation of a sort of National Park' in which Baigas and the like could be accommodated. He also suggested that "administration was to be so adjusted as to allow the tribesmen to live their life with utmost possible happiness and freedom and where missionaries of any sort were not to be allowed to break the tribal life". This work was followed by another entitled "Loss of Nerve" (1941) which contained a stronger tone in favour of isolationism'. Since Elwin's personality carried a lot of weight, he was regarded as the major spokesman of the majority of anthropologists of his time and thus anthropologists were labelled as 'isolationists', 'revivalists', 'no-changers', 'status-quoists' by the social workers aligned with the Indian National Congress Party. Besides Elwin, D.N. Majumdar, S.C. Dube, N.K. Bose, L.P. Vidyarthi and others contributed quite considerably to the writings on tribes and tribal development.

The social workers and politicians led by A.V. Thakkar, popularly known as "Thakkar Bapa" had different views the views of social worker. They exploited the situation and branded the entire community of anthropologists as 'isolationists' despite the fact that majority of anthropologists, while considering the ill effects of unregulated invasion of non-tribal people on the tribal areas, were not prepared to go to the extent of accepting the views of Elwin in go to. They just wanted that tribals should not be exploited and degenerated in the name of 'progress', 'civilization' and 'development'. But the damage had been done and allegations, half truths and insinuations were hurled at anthropology and anthropologists. While delivering R.R. Kale Memorial Lectures in 1941, Thakkar Bapa accused anthropologists of being selfish and that is why they wanted to "keep these people confined to and isolated in their inaccessible hills and jungles, something like keeping them in a glass ease of a museum for the curiosity of purely academic persons". To him, 'separatism' fend 'isolationism' seemed to be dangerous theories as they stuck at the root of national solidarity. He pleaded total assimilation of tribals and taking the posture of a typical social worker simplified the tribal problems into: (1) poverty, (2) illiteracy, (3) lack of communication, (4) ill health, (5) defects in administration, and (6) lack of leadership.

After Independence

"All these controversies that took place in the thirties and forties of the present century had a very devastating effect on the growth of applied anthropology in India. When India became independent in 1947, and the attention of the Government towards tribal welfare activities increased, the claims of anthropologists and experts on tribal problems were not taken into consideration at all. Their stand regarding tribal problems continued to be condemned at governmental level and they were not needed for anthropological research and advice by the Government" (Vidyarthi, ibid). This situation gave rise to a trend that was not at all beneficial for the tribal people. The social workers and politicians who were out to 'civilize' them at any cost acquired the role of experts on tribal problems. They found their own colleagues and partymen at the helm of governmental affairs and thus, there was nobody to prevent them from doing anything they liked. In this way, social workers assumed the roles of both semi-officials and scientists. They held administrative posts for tribal welfare schemes and represented the government on national and international conferences on tribal problems. The anthropologists stood condemned and ignored. They were not needed anywhere except in museum and survey work.

This state of affairs continued till about 1960 but anthropologists were not sitting idle licking their wounds. Silently, they were developing newer insights, perceptions and concepts. They came out with very useful and pragmatic policies and programmes of tribal development in the changed socio-political climate. Even Elwin who took an extreme position also modified his views and began to emphasise on the need for 'careful planning' and 'planned acculturation'. But the old sharp differences of opinion on prohibition, medium of instruction, etc., were not resolved.

After seeing the disastrous results of wrong approaches and non-performance of non-anthropologists, the government realised that it had done unjustice to the real experts, the anthropologists. It gave impetus to the feeling that social workers, administrators and anthropologists should work in close harmony with each other. This trend started reflecting in the composition of newly constituted tribal research institutes, tribes advisory councils and various committees of Planning Commission. Although, anthropologists accepted this olive branch, but it hardly means that they are ready to accept "to civilise the savage approach" of social workers and administrators. Any approach devoid of values is not acceptable to anthropologists working on tribal problems and spirit of parentalism cannot be allowed to dominate over the right of self-determination.

Anthropology Grappling with New Trends in Tribal Development

Before dealing with the changed role of anthropology in tribal development, it will be quite appropriate to quote Kroeber (1956) who put forward beautifully the role of anthropology as compared with roles of other disciplines in understanding humanity and implementing programmes for its betterment:

> "It is evident that anthropology, however specific it may often be in dealing with the data-aims, is ultimately a co-ordinating science somewhat as a legitimate holding corporation coordinates constituent companies. We anthropologist does, or prices, credit and banking as well as economist, or heredity with the fullness of the genetic biologist. But we face what these more intensive scholars only glance at intermittently and tangentially, if at all: to try to understand some measure how Chinese civilization and economies and human heredity, and some dozens of other highly developed special bodies of knowledge, do indeed interrelate in being all parts of man flowing out of man, centered in, him, products of him".

If anthropology, as an integrated science of man, deals 'holistically' both with the biological and cultural aspects of man, its applied or practical branch is equally comprehensive and strives to meet the need of mankind by planning for an allround development of human society.

Commenting on the role of anthropology in identifying the problems and suggesting remedial measures for the human society especially simple societies, George Foster puts forward three most important merits of anthropology:

(i) Anthropology as a point of view;

(ii) As a storehouse or treasure of factual informations;

(iii) It's distinct research methodology.

The holistic approach, belief in cultural relativism and a strong humanitarian tradition put anthropology on a different pedestal. By virtue of its vast experience of field work for more than 150 years among the simple societies, anthropologists have accumulated a vast treasure of factual information. The comparative method or cross-cultural comparison has added an important dimension to such studies. Among the tools of data collection utilised by the anthropologists 'participant observation' is a unique way of getting the most reliable information described by many as 'insiders view'. Thus, anthropology equipped with these distinct features and looking at 'development' through a different angle, may play a unique role in tribal development.

There is difference in the way an administrator looks at the tribal and the way the tribal looks at the world. Though, anthropologists lacks practical experience of administration and are sometimes unable to translate their concepts into simple language for the benefit of administrators, yet by virtue of their training in anthropology, they understand the important' of qualitative data in any programme for development which others sadly lack. Development means "growth" plus "change". It involves both the material and the human factors. The school of thought which subscribes almost wholly to what has come to be known as "growthmanship" is not acceptable to anthropologist, as opined by Vidyarthi (1981). They believe that a given number of material inputs, when assembled in certain proportions, yield the desired output measurable in quantified indicators such as rate of growth, national income, per capita income etc. They seem to be under the impression that growth, as assessed in terms of such gross indicators, is a value in itself. The non-material factors constitute for them but a context; social service a mere infrastructures; and social change, a by-product of such growth. To an anthropologist such a mechanical concept of growth is not acceptable, and he has consistently emphasised that socio-cultural factors are an integral part of the dynamics of growth and that social change is not simply a non-functional or a dysfunctional side effect of development planning (ibid).

In this context the concept of development has to be defined and operated in terms of the cultural background of the community concerned. While striving for the development of a group or an area, due emphasis has to be given to their traditional values and historical experiences. However, a practitioner of anthropology enjoys certain advantages over others who deal with the tribals. His residence for a period of time among them is paralleled only by missionaries or a few social workers. Administrators hardly even find time to spend more than occasional moments among the people for whose welfare or development they are responsible. "Whereas missionaries and social workers think it their task to teach, to change, the anthropologist is there only to learn. This double advantage of the anthropologist-long residence in an area and a concerted effort to learn and understand—qualifies him as the only 'outsider' able to give concrete and thorough recommendations for action" (Edward Jay, 1968). But at the same time, the anthropologist does not claim to prescribe panacea for all evils. He tries to understand the 'insider's view' of the problems and provides concrete and pragmatic recommendations to the government.

Another point which puts an anthropologist on a different pedestal is that he is not obsessed with 'end' only. For him means are as important as end because he understands it pretty well that wrong and coercive means prove counter-productive in any scheme of tribal development. Various failures in the governmental tribal development schemes bear testimony to this fact. Four decades of tribal development have not produced any satisfactory results. Now most of impartial analysts believe that this failure is due to unrealistic planning, apathetic bureaucracy, neglect of local and felt needs of the people, ignoring their cultural values and non-material indicators.

This state of affairs is also due to the fact that administrators have failed to appreciate that anthropologists are the only ones who can guide and advise most effectively in matters concerning tribal people. With their specialized knowledge, deep perception, sympathetic attitude and rigorous field-oriented approach, anthropologists are in a unique position in this respect. It is high time that administrators as 'generalists' and anthropologists as 'specialists' come together to collaborate in a team spirit , to make, tribal development programmes a 'pleasant' success. In this way anthropology can be used to best advantage of the whole society in general and the tribal people in particular.

ROLE OF NGOs AMONG TRIBAL COMMUNITIES

Chapter 31

When we talk of the role of non-tribal agencies in tribal welfare, we start with the work of Christian missionaries and stop at enumerating the names of the present day voluntary social organizations. In this way we tend to forget the role of thousands of rishis, sanyasis and ascetics who were probably the first people from the civilized world to live amidst the tribals for any considerable period of time and first to do something for their upliftment. Saints and seers very often went to forests to enjoy the pleasures of nature and practice austerity for the attainment of salvation. They were quite numerous and some of them lived in the caves of the Himalayas or the Vindhays till their death. They were kind and gentle to the animals and we may be pretty sure that they were equally kind and gentle to the ancestors of the tribal people of today amongst whom they lived. It is because of this that the Gonds of Central India, the tribes of Arunachal Pradesh or Ladakh or any other part of the Himalayas remember those saints and seers with great affection. There are folk songs and folktales about them. "These saints specially gave them medicines and attended to them whenever they suffered. We have, therefore, the traditions of Sabri and Eklavya of the medieval age" (Narayanjee, 1968). Dhebar Commission's Report (1960-61) also supports this assertion and adds that though at that time there was no idea of catering to their physical and material needs and no programmes of social welfare, but these sanyasis and others carried with them an atmosphere of peace and love which even now is one of the greatest gifts that we can give to people anywhere.

CHRISTIANITY as an Agency of Welfare

It were the Christian missionaries of the western countries who first brought to the tribal people of India, their welfare programmes. K. N. Sahay (1968) very aptly remarks that of the various agencies responsible for changing the cultural canvas of Indian tribals as well as other such downtrodden communities, Christian missionaries would perhaps claim to be the oldest, having further set an example of high spirited social service and reforms which was later followed by many others. They were pioneers in the educational programmes and they opened the first hospitals in the tribal areas Also, they were among the first to inspire the tribal people with the idea of progress and to awaken them to a sense of their rights.

Whenever and wherever the Christian missionaries have gone for evangelization, it has been supported by various welfare schemes for the converts such as opening of schools, dispensaries, hospitals, orphanages, vocational centres and other measures for eradicating miseries and providing material comforts to these people. Central Indian tribes and the tribes of north-eastern region have been centres of activities of these missionaries. Apart from providing educational and health facilities throughout the length and breadth of tribal India, various missionary organizations did pioneering work in the field of economic programmes. For example, the credit goes to the Catholic missionaries of Chotanagpur region for starting the cooperative credit societies in the region. Various missionary institutions dealing with agricultural programmes taught the tribals modern means of agriculture. Through a series of vocational training centres, the tribals were trained to earn more through subsidiary occupations.

Briefly speaking, Christianity has been responsible for introducing a number of welfare measures among the so far neglected and exploited tribal communities of India, and thus improving their social and economic conditions. As Sahay (ibid) puts it, such welfare activities of the Christian missionaries, popularly known as 'the work of mercy', are considered an inseparable part of the evangelization and they must be carried together though this approach of the missionaries has attracted criticisms from different sections of the non-Christian mass.

M.N. srinivas (1962), while dwelling upon the problem of Indian unity, touches this issue by saying that "the idea that it is the paramount duty of the believers in the one true religion to convert outsiders to their faith, seems natural to the proselytising religions but it appears as intellectual and moral aggression to Hindus. This is specially so when the people who are converted are desperately poor and illiterate. The opening of schools, hospitals and other welfare agencies by missionaries in areas where Harijans and the tribals live, appears to the Hindus as only baits in the trap of conversion. The linking up of humanitarianism with proselytization has made the former suspect. Even very liberal, westernized Hindus feel this way".

The insistence on proselytizing has, unfortunately, vitiated the value of their work in the eyes of many. As Dhebar Commission's Report puts it, at many places the effect of their teaching has been to break up families and divide villages. One may see a village, which at one time worked and lived as a single unit, now split into a Christian hamlet and a non-Christian hamlet. There are villages where no fewer than five different Missions have been carrying on propaganda, opening separate schools and teaching different forms of Christianity. Also, the attitude of some missionaries has been completely negative and destructive. To them everything which is not Christian is "heathen" and some of the finest aspects of tribal life have been abandoned in the process. The tribals have been taught to despise their past and as a result a strong inferiority complex has been created. To be fair, however, it is not only they, who have been guilty of causing confusion and deterioration of tribal culture. Some social workers and other non-official agencies as well as narrow-minded government officials have also tended to make the tribals despise their past and look down on their own culture.

However, despite some weaknesses, Christianity has been a powerful agency of tribal welfare in India. It is a pleasure to see some of their schools, hospitals and vocational training centres being run in isolated and geographically hostile areas. From the point of view of simplicity, economy and efficiency, the other social agencies have a lot to learn from them. It is a tribute to their devotion and self-sacrifice in the remotest hills and forests that when we wish to speak of an ideal social worker, we say that he has missionary spirit.

Social Workers and Other Voluntary Institutions

India has an old tradition of selfless social work and voluntary social organizations are not a new phenomenon. As far back as 1871, Bhil Seva Mandal was formed in Gujarat and an ashram at Miraknedi in Panchmahal district was established to work among the Bhil and Rani Parej. A. V. Thakkar, popularly known as Thakkar Bapa, was the moving spirit behind this organization. Later on, he emerged as the greatest worker in tribal welfare in modern times. Before India attained independence, he had established twenty one such institutions in various parts of the country. There was a magic in his personality. He could create workers, attract workers and hold on to the workers. The history of three decades of dogged endeavour on the part of this singularity quiet and dedicated yet principled personality is a romance of social work in India. In 1948, he alongwith Dr. Rajendra Prashad, our first President, founded the Bhartiya Adimajati Sevak Sangh. Its objective is "the development of the tribal communities in India socially, economically, culturally and educationally, with a view to enable them to take their legitimate place in the national life of the country as equal citizens". This apex institution has been mostly concerned with the coordination of activities of various affiliated and recognized institutions. As the Dhebar Commission's Report puts it, it has played no small part in helping government shape its tribal welfare policy at the stage of preparation of the Constitution and therefore the plans and development. This apex institution has today behind it as affiliated or recognized institutions over hundred bodies throughout the country. These institutions have been directing their energies towards the economic progress and educational development of the tribes. Such pioneering commendable work as Forest Labourers Cooperatives in Gujarat and Maharashtra is a tribute to the dedication of this organization.

The other voluntary agencies meriting special mention are the Servants of India Society and the Ramakrishna Mission. In recent years, they have bean working for the promotion of welfare of the tribals at the state and national levels. Their activities relate to education, medical relief, cooperation and occasionally to local self government. The Ramakrishna Mission has most of its branches in Assam, Bihar and West Bengal. Its institutions are maintaining successfully their traditions of service with special emphasis on character building and are free from all taints of proselytisation.

Some other important non-official agencies, which include tribal welfare in their programmes are : Sarva Seva Sangh, Gandhi Smarak Nidhi, Kasturba Smarak Nidhi, Adimajati Seva Mandal, Ashok Ashram, the Tata Institute of Social Sciences, Bhartiya Lok Kala Mandir, etc.

Most of the non-official agencies have been working mainly in the fields of education and public health but gradually, they are extending their work to include tribal development blocks, cooperation, forest, trade and industry, cottage and village industries, cooperative farming, animal husbandry, panchayat work, cultural activities, prohibition and legal assistance, etc.

To enable them to expand their activities amongst the tribal population, the Central Government has been giving grants-in-aid to such organizations as are of all-India character; the State government give grants-in-aid to the organizations functioning in their respective states.

The importance of enlisting the support of non-official organizations in promoting welfare of the tribal communities has generally been recognized. As members of advisory committees in states, their representatives are consulted in the formulation and implementation of tribal development programmes.

The Shilu Ao Committee has noticed a tendency on the part of voluntary agencies to restrict their sphere of operations to the more developed tribal areas. This has resulted, in some cases, in an overlapping of activities by a number of voluntary organizations operating in the same area. Further, the voluntary organizations should be encouraged to build up cadres of trained and devoted workers who will take up service in the cause of tribal welfare as a career. The Bhartiya Adimajati Sevak Sangh is now receiving financial assistance from the Centre for building up a dependable cadre of life workers for selfless service among the tribal communities on the lines of the Servants of India Society and Servants of the People Society.

It is necessary in any democratic framework that a measure of the constructive activity on the national level should be done under non-official auspices. These activities satisfy the urge of the normal human being to be of some use to the community in his spare time and give the benefit of his special abilities to those who are in need of them. Further, "the best administrative machinery of even a highly responsible and responsive democratic government, by its very nature, is bound to be impersonal in character and a non-official organization can more easily provide the personal touch" (Dhebar Commission). Through this personal touch these organizations can harness the latent energies of the masses into useful channels for their development.

EPILOGUE

People are resisting the takeover of their sources of Livlihood and Common resources

They made us many Promises
More than I can remember
But they fulfilled just one
They promised to take our land
And they took it

There has been a systematic failure in giving tribals a stake in the modern economic processes, introducing into their living spaces

BIBLIOGRAPHY

Adam, L. 1949 Primitive Art. Hermondsworth : Pelican.

Aiyappan, A 1937 Social and Physical Anthropology of Nayadis of Malahar. Madras: Government Press.

1945 Iraoas and Culture Change. Madra : Government press.

1965 "Some Patterns of Tribal Leadership". Economic Weekly, Vol. 17,No. 2 .

Alamehiba, A.M. 1961 Woromung: An Ao Naga Village. Census of India, 1961, Vol. L, Monograph No.1, New Delhi: Office of.the Registrar General of India.

Anand, V.K 1968 Nagaland in Transition, New Delhi: Associated Publishing House.

Anderson, J.D. 1913 The Peoples of India, Cambridge.

Archer, W.G. 1947 "Ritual Friendship in Santhal Society", Man In India, Vo. 27, No.1.

Atal, Yogesh 1968 The Changing Frontiers of Caste. New Delhi: National Publishing House.

Atkinson, Edwin 'I', 1973 The Himalayan Gazeteer. Delhi: Cosmos Publications .

.Aurora, G.S. 1972 Tribe-Caste-Class Encounters. Hyderabad: Administrative Staff College of India.

Bagchi, P.C. 1920 Pre-AryanandPre-Dravidian, in India. Calcutta.

Bage, S.K. 1965 "Anthropologist and Tribal Administration", Journal of Social Research, Vol. 8, No. 1.

Bailey,F.G. 1957 *Caste and the Economic Frontier.* Bombay: Oxford University Press.'

1960 *Tribe, Caste and Nation: A Study of Political Activity and Political Change in Highland Orissa.* Manchester : Manchester University Press.

1961 "Tribe and Caste in India", *Contributions to Indian Sociology,* No.5.

Bardhan,A.B. 1977 *Ansuljhi Janjati Samasya* (Hindi). Delhi: Communists Party of India.

Barkataki, S. 1969 *Tribes of Assam-India: The Land and People* (Compiled). New Delhi: National Book Trust.

Banerjee, A.C. 1950 *The Constitution of the Indian Republic.* Calcutta: A. Mukherhee & Co. Ltd.

Benerji, M. 1964 *Primitive Man in India.* Ambala.

Belshaw, C.S. 1965 *Traditional Exchange and Modern Markets.* New Jersey & New Delhi: Prentice Hall.

1972 "Development: The Contribution of Anthropology", *International Social Science Journal,* Vol. 24.

Benedict, Ruth 1934 *Patterns of Culture. Boston:* Hughton.

Benfield, E.C. 1958 *The Moral Basis of Backward Society.* New York : Free Press.

Berreman, Gerald D. 1962 *Behind Many Masks.* Ithaca: Cornell University Press.

Beteille, Andre (Ed) & T.N. Madan 1975 *Encounter and Experience: Personal Accounts of field*

Work. Delhi: Vikas Publishing House.

Bhagwati, Jagdish 1966 *The Economics of Under-developed Countries*. New York: McGraw Hill.

Bhargava, B.S. 1949 *The Ctiminal Tribes*. Lucknow : Ethnographic and folk Culture Society.

Bhartiya Adimjati Sevak Sangh 1957 *Tribes of India*. Delhi.

Bhowmik, KL. 1971 *Tribal India,' A profile in Indian Ethnology*. Calcutta: World Press.

Bhatt, G.S. 1963 Bharat Mein Samajshastra, Prajati Evam Sanskriti (Hindi). Sahitya Sadan, Dehradun.

Biswas, P.C. 1956 *Santhals and Santhal Parganas*. Delhi.

Boas, Franz 1963 *The Mind of Primitive Man*. New York, Free Press.

Boddley, John H. 1982 *Victims of Progress*. California: The Benjamin Cummings Publishing Company.

Bose, J.K 1935 "The Gana N okma Ceremony of the Garo of Assam", *Man in India*, Vol. 15, No.4.

Bose, N.K 1941 "The Hindu Method of Tribal Abroption", *Science and Culture*, Vol. 7

1967a *Culture and Society in India*. Bombay: Asia Publication House.

1967b *Problems of National Integration*. Simla Indian Institute of Advanced Study.

1971 *Tribal Life in India*. New Delhi: National Book Trust.

Bose, S.C. 1960 "Nomadism in High Valleys of Uttarakhand and Kumaon",

		Geographical Review of India, Vol. 22.
Briggs,. G.N.	1920	*The Chamar,* Calcutta: Calcutta Association Press.
Burn, R.	1902	*Census of India,* Vol. 16. Allahabad: Government Press.
Cantile, Keith	1934	*Notes on Khasi Law.* Akerdeen: Henry Munroe Ltd.
Cameron, WB.	1966	*Modern Social Movements.* New York: Random House.
Carstairs, Morris	1957	*Twice Born.* London : The Hogarth Press.
Chakrabrati, M. & D. Mukherjee	1971	*Indian Tribes.* Calcutta : Saraswati Library.
Chattopadhya KP.	1953	"Tribal Education", *Man in India,* Vol. 33, No. 1.
Chaturvedi, S.C.	1964	*Andaman Island.* Delhi: National Book Trust.
Chauhan, B.R.	1970	*Towns in the Tribal Setting.* Delhi: National Publishing House.
Childe, V.G.	1946	*What Happened in History?* New York, Penguin.
Crooke, W.	1896	*The Tribes and Castes of the North-Western Provinces of Agra and Oudh,* Vol. 2. Calcutta: Superintendent, Government Press.
Culshaw, W.J.	1945	"The Santhal Rebellion", *Man In India,* Vol. 25, No.4.
	1949	*Tribal Heritage: A Study of the Santhals.* London: Lutterworth Press.
Dalton, E.T.	1872	*Descriptive Ethnology of Bengal.* Calcutta: Government of Bengal.
Danielou, Alain	1964	*Hindu Polytheism...* New York: Pantheon Books.
Das,A.K & S.K Banerjee	1962	*The Lepchas of Darjeeling District ...* Calcutta: Tribal

		Welfare Department, Government of West Bengal.
Das A.K. & M.K. Raha	1967	*The Rabhas of West Bengal.* Calcutta: Government of West Bengal.
Das, R.K	1971	*"The Problems of Tribal Identity in Manipur"*, The Eastern Anthropologist, Vol. 24, No.2,
Das,T.	1931	*The Wild Kharia of Manbhum.* Calcutta.
Das, T.C.	1945	*The Purums : An Old Kuki Tribe of Manipur.* Anthropological Papers No.7. Calcutta : University of Calcutta.
Dave, P.C.	1960	*The Graeias,* Delhi: Bhartiya Adimjati Sevak Sangh
Dee, Brown	1973	*Bury My Heart at Wounded Knee.* New York: Bantom Books.
Devy, GN, Geoffre Davis (ed) *et.al.*	2013	*Knowing Differently: The Challenge of the Indigenous,* Routledge India, New Delhi
Dhan, R.O.	1367	*These Are My Tribesmen: The Oraon :* Ranchi: Lutherian Church Press.
Diamond, A.S.	1935	*Primitive Law.* London.
Doshi, J.K.	1974	*Social Structure and Social Change in a Bhil Village.* New Delhi: New Heights.
Dovring, F.	1965	"Bondage, Tenure and Progress", *Comparative Studies in Society and History,* Vol. 7.
Dube, Leela	1969	*Matriliny in Islam.* Delhi: National Publishing House.
Dube, S.C.	1947	*Field Songs of Chhattisgarh.* Lucknow: Universal Press.
	1951	*The Kamar.* Luchnow: The Universal Publishers.
	1958	*India's Changing Villages.* London: Routledge and Kegan Paul.

(Ed.) 1977 *Tribal Heritage of India* Delhi. Vikas Publishing House.

Dutta, Kalikinkar 1940 *The Santhal Insurrection. Calcutta :* Calcutta University.

Dutta, Parul Nabendu 1956 *The Santhat : A Study in Culture Change.* Delhi: Manager of Publications, Government of India.

Dutta, Majumdar 1959 *The Tangsae.* Shillong: North East Frontier Agency.

Ehrenfels, U.R. 1952 *Kadar of Cochin.* Madras: Universiry of Madras.

Ellis, R.H. 1924 *A Short Account of the Laccadiv Island & Minicoy.* Madras.

Elwin, Verrier 1939 *The Baiga.* Londou: John Murray.

1942 *The Agaria.* London: Oxford Universiry Frees.

1943 *Muria Murder and Suicide.* London: Oxford Universiry Press.

1944 *Eolkrales of Mahakoshal.* London. Oxford Universiry Press.

1947 *The Muria and Their Ghotul.* Bombay: Oxford Universiry Press.

1948 "Notes on the Juang". *Man in India.* Vol. 28, Nos. 1-2.

1949 *The Myths of Middle India.* London. Bombay, Oxford Universiry Prees.

1950 *Bonda Highlanders.* Bombay. Oxford University Press.

1954 *Tribal Myths of Orissa.* London: Oxford Universiry Press.

1955 *The Religion of An Indian Tribes (Saoras).* London: Oxford Universiry Press.

	1958	*Myths of the North-East Frontier of India.* Shillong : North East Frontier Agency.
	1959	*India's North East Frontier in the Nineteenth Century.* London: Oxford Universiry Press.
	1960a	*A Philosophy for NEFA.* Shillong : Government of Assam.
	1960b	*The Tribal World of Verrier Elwin.* Bombay: Oxford Uni.versiry Press.
	1961	*Nagaland.* Shillong : Research Department, Advisor's Secretariat.
	1968	*The Kingdom of the Young.* London: Oxford University Press.
	1969	The Nagas in the Nineteenth Century. Bombay: Oxford Universiry Press.
Enthoven, R.E.	1920	*Tribes and Castes of Bombay* (3 Vols.). Bombay: Government Central Press.
Evans-Prichard, E.E.	1937	*Witchcraft, Oracles and Magic Among the Azande.* Oxford: Clarendon Press.
	1940	*The Nuer.* Oxford: Clarendon Press.
	1956	*Social Anthropology.* London: Lowe and Brydone Ltd.
Firth, Raymond,	1951	*Elements of Social Organisation.* Watts and Co.
	1955	"Some Principles of Social Organisation", Calcutta *Journal of the Royal Anthropological Institute,* No, 85.
Frode, C. Daryll	1950	*Habitat, Economy and Society,* London: Methuen & Co.

Fuchs, Stephen 1960 *The Gond and Bhumia of Eastern Mandla.* Bombay: New Literature Publishing Co.

1965 *Rebellious Prophets.* Bombay: Asia Publishing House.

1973 *The Aboriginal Tribes of India.* New Delhi: The Macmillan Company.

Furer-Heimendorf, Christoph von 1939 *The Naked Nagas.* London : Routledgy and Kegan Paul.

1943 *The Chenchu:* London: Macmillan.

1945 *The Reddis of Bison Hills:* A Study in Acculturation. London: Macmillan.

1948 *Rajgonds of Adilahad* : A Peasant Culture of Deccan. London : Macmillan.

1955 *Himalayan Barbary.* London: John Murray.

1962 *The Apatanis and Their Neighbourhood.* London: Routledge and Kegan Paul.

1969 *The Konyak Nagas : An Indian Frontier Tribe.* New York: Holt, Reinhart and Winston.

1976 *Return to the Naked Nagas.* New Delhi: Vikas Publishing House.

Gans, Herbert 1962 *The Urban Villagers.* New York : Macmillan.

Ghosh, Biswait (ed.) 2020 *Social Movements: Concepts, Experiences and Concerns*, Sage Publications, New Delhi.

Ghurye, G.S. 1943 *The Aborigines-so-called-and Their Future.* Poona : Gokhle Institute of Politics and Economics.

1950 *Caste and Class in India.* Bombay: Popular Book Depot.

	1957	*The Mahadev Kolis.* Bombay: Popular Book Depot.
	1963	*The Scheduled Tribes.* Bombay: Popular Prakashan.
Gluckman, Max	1965	*Politics, Law and Ritual in Tribal Societies.* London: Basil Blackwell,
Gorer, Geofrey	1938	*Himalayan Village:* An Account of the Lephas of Sikkim. London: Michael joseph,
Government of India	1959	*Adivasi.* Delhi: Publication Division.
Government of Madhya *Pradesh*	1964	*The Tribes of Madhya Pradesh* Bhopal.
	1967	*A Study of Tribal People and Trible Areas of Madhya Pradesh.* Bhopal.
Government of Rajasthan	1956	*Tribal Rehabilitation in Rajasthan,* Jaipur.
Griffith, Keith & A.R. Khan	1978	"Poverty in theThird World: Ugly Facts and Fancy Models", *World Development,* March, 1978.
Griffith, W.G.	1944	"Folklore of the Kols",. *Man In India,* Vol. 24, No.2.
	1946	*The Kol Tribes of Central India.* Calcutta : Royal Asiatic Society of Bengal.
Grigson, W.V.	1938	*The Maria Gonda of Bastar.* Oxford.
Grierson, G.A.	1916	*The Linguistic Survey of India,* Calcutta : Government of India.
Guha, B.S.	1938	*The Racial Elements of India.* Bombay: Popular Prakashan.
Gurdon, P.R.T.	1914	*The Khasie.* London: Macmillan & Co.
Harris, Marvin	1971	*Culture, Man and Nature : Introduction to General Anthropology,* New York : Thomas-Cromwell.

Hasan, Amir

1971 *A Bunch of Wild Flouiers and Other Essays.* Lucknow : Ethnographic and Folk Culture Society.

1972 *The Kols of Patha.* Allahabad : Kitab Mahal.

Hasnain, Nadeem

1975 'The Kolta: A Study in the Ethnography of the Poor." *The Eastern Anthropologist,* Vol. 28, No.4.

1982 *Bonded for Ever.* Dehi : Harnam Publications.

1988 Shias and Shia Islam in India: A study in Society and Culture. Delhi

1988 Readings in Indian Anthropology. Delhi Harnam Publications.

1991 Tribal India. Delhi, Palaka Prakashan.

1997 General Anthropology. Delhi, Jawahar Publisher and Distributor.

1998 Indian Anthropology. Delhi, Palaka Prakashan.

2003 Introducing Social-Cultural Anthropology. Delhi, Jawahar Publisher and Distributor.

2004 Indian Society and Culture: Continuity and Change. Lucknow, Bharat Book Centre.

2005 OBCs in the Process of Change. Delhi, Serial Publication.

2010 Anthropology in India.

2013 Contested Identities in the Globalised World.

2016 Indian Society and Social Issues.

2019 Indian Society: Themes and Social Issues, McGraw Hill Education, New Delhi.

2020 Handbook of Sociology, Surjit Publications, Delhi

2021 Sociology of Marginalised Communities and Weaker Sections of India, SAGE India, New Delhi.

Hastings, James (Ed.) 1908-26 *Encyclopedia of Religion and Ethics. (13* Vols.) New York : Scribers.

Hatch, W.J. 1928 *The Land Pirates of India,* London: Seeley Service and Company Ltd.

Henry, Jules 1964 *Jungle People.* New York : Random House.

Herkovits, M.J. 1950 *Man and His Works, New York : Knopf.*

1952 *Economic Anthropology.* New York: Knopf.

Hivale, S. *1946* *The Pardians.* Bombay: Oxford Universiry Press.

Hockings, Paul *1965* *Culture Change Among the Badaga : A Community in South India.* Berkley: California Universiry Press.

Hodson, T.C. *1908* *The Meithis.* London: David Natt.

1921 "The Garo and khasi Marriage Systems Contrasted", *Man in India,* Vol. 1, No.2.

1922 *The Primitive Culture of India.* Calcutta. The Royal Asiatic Society.

Hoebel, E.A. 1954 The Law of the Primitive man: *A Case* Study in Comparative Legal Dynamics. Harvard: Harvard Univerairy Press.

Hutton, J.H. 1921a *The Angami Nagas.,* London: Macmillan.

1921b *The Sema Nagas,* London: Macmillan.

	1951	*Caste in India.* Bombay: Oxford Universiry Press.
Hu, C.T.	1956	"Marriage by Exchange Among the Tharus-with a Geneological Case Study" *The Eastern Anthropologist,* Vol. 10, No.2
I.L.O.	1953	*Indigenous Peoples.* Geneva.
Indian Conference of Social Work	1964	*Souvenir on welfare of Tribes and Denotified Communities.* Bhopal.
Iyer, L.K. Anantha Krishnal	1935	*The Mysore Tribes and Castes,* Vol. 1. Mysore : The Mysore University.
Jay, Edward	1970	*A Tribal Village of Middle India.* Calcutta: Anthro-pological Survey of India.
Jones, Steve	1978	"Tribal Underdevelopment in India", *Development and Change,* Vol. 9, No. 1.
Joshi, M.M.	1967	*Bastar : India'a Sleeping Giant.* New Delhi: Peoples' Publishing House.
Kaberry, Phillis M.	1939	*Aboriginal Woman: Sacred and Profane.* London: George Routledge and Sons Ltd.
Kar, P .C.	1920	*British Annexation of Garo Hills.* Calcutta.
Karsten, R.	1935	*The Origins of Religion.* London: Trubner and Co.
Kapadia, KM.	1961	*Marriage and Family in India.* Bombay.
Karwe, lrawati	1953	*Kinship Ogranisation in India.* Poona : Deccan College.
	1961	Hindu Society: An Interpretation. Poona: Sangam.
Kluckhonn, C.	1950	*Mirror for Man.* London: George G. Harrap & Co. Ltd.
Koppers Wilhelm	1954	"Primitive ManandHis World Picture", *The Eastern Anthropologist,* Vol. 8, No.3.

Krader, L. 1959 "The Ecology of Nomadic Pastoralism", *International Social Sciences Journal,* Vol. 11, No. 14.

Kutty, A.R. 1972 *Marriage and Kinship in an Island Society.* Delhi: National Publishing House.

Lal, A.K. 1977 *Politics of Poverty: A Study of Bonded Labour.* New Delhi: Chetna.

Lathan, R.G. 1959 *Ethnography of India.* London: Macmillan.

Leach E.R. 1954a *The Political Systems of Highland Burma.* London: G Bell & Sons.

1954b "Aesthetics" in E.E. Evans Pritchard's 'The Intitutions of Primitive Society'. London: Basil Blackwell.

Leuva, K.K. 1963 *The Asur : A Study of Primitive Iron Smelters.* Delhi: Bhartiya Adimjati Sevak Sangh.

Levi-Btrarrsa, C. 1966 *The Savage Mind.* London: Weidenfeld and Nicholson.

Lewis, I.M. 1968 "Tribal Society" in David L. Sirs (Ed.) *International Encyclopedia of the Social Sciences.* Vol. 16. London : Macmillan.

Linton, R (Ed.) *1945* *The Science of Man in World Crises.* Columbia University Press.

Lowie, R.H. *1921* *Primitive Society.* London: Roudedge & Kegan Paul Ltd.

1924 *Primitive Religion.* New York.

Luiz, A.A.D. *1962* *Tribes of Kerala.* New Delhi: Bharatiya Adimjati Sevak Sangh.

Mahapatra, L.K. *1970* *Transformation of Tribal Society in India.* Delhi: Delhi University National Lecture.

Maine, H. 1861 *Ancient Law.* London.

Majumdar, D.N. 1944a *The Fortunes of Primitive Tribes.* Lucknow: Universal Publishers.

1944b *Races and Cultures of India.* Lucknow: Universal Publishers.

1950 *The Affairs of a Tribe : A Study in Tribal Dynamics.* Lucknow : Universal Publishers.

1962 *The Himalayan Polyandry.* Bombay: Asia Publishing House.

Majumdar, D.N. & T.N. Madan 1967 *An Introduction to Social Anthropology.* Bombay: Asia Publishing House.

Malinowski, B. 1948 *Magic, Science and Religion.* Boston and Glenco.

1949 *Crime and Coustom in Savage Society.* London: Routledge & Kagan Paul Ltd.

Mamoria, C.B. 1957 *Tribal Demography in India.* Allahabad Kitab Mahal.

Man, RS. 1973 "Jarwas of Andaman-An Analysis of *Hostility",Man in India,* Vol. 53, No.2.

Mandelbaum, David G. 1970 *Society in india.* California: University of California Press .

Mankekar. D.R. 1967 *On the Slippery Slopes in Nagaland.* Bombay. Manakatala.

Marret, R.R. 1914 *The Threshold of Religion.* New York.

Marriot, Mckim (Ed.) 1976 *Development Administration in Tribal Areas.* Jaipur : The H.C.M. State Institute of Public Adminstration.

(Ed.) 1977 *Anthropology in the Development Process*: Bombay: Vikas Publishing House.

Mathur, KS. 1964 *Caste and Ritual in a Malwa Village.* Bombay: Asia Publishing House.

Mathur, K.S. & B C. Agarwal (Ed) 1974 *Tribe, Caste and Peasantry.* Lucknow: Ethnographic & Folk Culture Society.

Mayer, A.C. 1952 *Land and Society in Malabar.* London: Oxford University Press.

Mclaughlin, Barry (Ed.) 1969 *Studies in Social Movements.* New York, Free Press.

Mead, Margaret 1929 *Coming of Age in Samoa.* London: Jonathan Cape.

1930 *Growing up in the New Guinea.* New York: William Marrow.

1955 *Cultural Patterns and Technological Change.* UNESCO : Mentor Books.

Metcalfe, Thomas R. 1965 *The Aftermath of Revolt in India 1832-1870,* Princeton : Princeton University Press.

Mills, J.P. 1922 *The Lhota Naga.* London: Macmillan.

1926 *The Ao Naga.* London: Macmillan.

1936 *The Rengma Naga.* London: Macmillan.

Misra, B.B. 1959 *The Central Administration of the East India Company* 1773 –1834. Bombay: Oxford University Press.

Misra U,S & P.K.Tewari 1975 *Bhartiya Adivasi* (Hindi). Lucknow: Uttar Pradesh Hindi Grantha Academy.

Mohanty, Manoranjan (Ed.) 2011 Weapon of the Oppressed: An inventory of Report's Rights in India, Councel for Social Development & Danish Books, Delhi.

Morgan, L.H. 1877 *Ancient Society,* New York.

Mukherjee, B & B.C. Roy chowdhary and D. Ghosh. 1973 *The Chero of the Palamau.* Calcutta : Anthropological Survey of India

Mukherjee, D.P. 1958 *Diverities.* New Delhi: People's Publishing House.

Mardock, G.P. *et al* 1950 *Outline of Cultural Materials.* New Haven: Human Relations Area Files Inc.

Murthy, B.S. 1969 Depressed and Oppressed Forever in Agong. Delhi: S Chand & Co.

Nadel, S.F. 1953 *Anthropology and Modern Life.* Canberra: Australian National University.

Naik, T.B. 1956 *The Bhils.* Delhi: Bhartiya Adimjati Sevak Sangh.

Nair, Kusum 1961 *Blossoms in the Dust: The Human Element in India Development.* London: Gerald Duckworth and Co. Ltd.

Nakane, Chie 1967 *Garo and Khasi.* The Hague: Mouton.

Nash, Manning 1966 *Primitive and Peasant Economic Systems.* San Fransicso : Chandler.

Nath, Y.U.S. 1960 *Bhils of Ratnamal.* Baroda: the M.S University of Baroda.

Oakley, E.S. 1905 *Holy Himalayas.* Edinburgh; Oliphant Anderson & Ferrier.

Oaten, Farley 1909 *Travel and Travellers in India 1400* - 1700. London: Kegal Paul.

Office of the Commission For Scheduled Castes and Scheduled Tribes 1968 *Handbook on Scheduled Castes and Scheduled Tribes. New* Delhi.

O'Malley, L.S.S. 1935 *Popular Hinduism.* Cambridge: Cambridge University Press.

Orans, Martin 1965 *The Santhals : A tribe in Search of a Greate Tradition,* Detroit: Wayne State University Press.

Oraon, Karitk 1964 "Tribes and Tribalism of India" *Journal of Social Research,* Vol. 17, Nos. 1-2.

Pandey, B.M. 1968 "Development Schemes as Factors of Change in Triba' Areas" *Journal of Social Research,* Vol. 11, No.2.

Pant, S.D. 1935 *The Social Economy of the Himalayas.* London: George Allen & Unwin Ltd.

Pangtey, KS. 1969 *Lonely Furrows of the Borderland:* Lucknow : Universal Publishers.

Parmar, Y.S. 1975 *Polyandry in the Himalayas.* Delhi: Vikas Publishing House

Parry, N.E. 1932 *The Lakhers.* London; Macmillan.

Patel, M.L. 1974 *Changing Land Problems of Tribal India.* Bhopal: Progress Publishers.

Playfair, A. 1909 *The Garos.* London: Nutt.

Prabhu, P.N. 1954 *Hindu Social Organisation,* Bombay: Popular Book Depot.

Prasad, Saileshwar 1974 *Where the Three Tribes Meet.* Allahabad: Indian International Publication.

Publication Division 1973 *The Tribal People of India.* New Delhi: Government of India.

Radcliff-Brown, A.R. 1948 *The Andaman Islanders,* Glencoe: Illinois Free Press.

1952 Structure and Function in Primitive *Society.* London: Cohen and West.

Radeliff-Brown, A.R. & Daryll Forde 1950 *African Systems of Kinship and Marriage.* London: Oxford University Press.

Radin, Paul 1953 *The World of Primitive Man.* New York. Grove Press.

Radhakrishna, Meena (ed.) 2016 *First Citizens: Studies on Adivasi's, Tribals and Indigenous Poeple of India,* Oxford University Press, New Delhi.

Raghaviah, V. 1956 *Tribes of India.* Delhi: Bhartiya Adimjati Sevak Sangh.

1976 *Tribal Revolts.* Nellore Andhra Rashtriya Adimjati Sevak Sangh.

Rao, Prasad 1971 "Sahukar and Tribal Society, *Tribe,* Vel 28, No. 3-4.

Read, Herbert 1946 *Art and Society,* London: Faber and Faber.

Redfield, Rebert 1941 *The Folk Culture of Yucatan.* Chicago: University of Chicago Press.

1953 *The Primitive World and Its Transfermotion.* Ithaca: The Cornell University Press.

1955 *The Little Community.* Chicago: University of Chicago Press.

1956 *Peasant Society and Culture: Anthorpological Approach to Civilzation.* Chicago : University of Chicago press.

Risley, H.H. 1915 *The People of India.* New Delhi: Oriental Books Reprint Corporation.

Rivers, W.H.R. 1906 *The Todas.* London: Macmillan.

Robertson, Alexander 1938 *The Mahar Folk: A Study of Untouchables in Maharasthra.* Calcutta : Y.M.C.A. Publishing House.

Rose, H.A. 1914 *Tribes and Castes of Punjab and North-West Frontier Provinces,* Vol. III. Lahore : Civil and Military Gazettee Press.

Roy Burman, B.K.	1966	*"Some dimentions of transformation of tribal societies in India"*, *Journal of Social Research,* Vol. 11, No. 1.
Roy Burman, B.K. & S.P.Thukral	1970	*"Demographic and Socio-economic Profiles of the Hill Areas of North-Eastern India. Census of India,* 1961. New Delhi: Office of the Registrar General of India.
Roy, David	1938	"The Place of the Khasis in the World". *Man in India,* Vol. 18.
Roy, Mrinal	1967	"Changing Pattern of Leadership in an Oraon Village" in L.P. Vidyarthi (ed.) *Leadership in India.* Bombay: Asia Publishing House.
Roy, S.C.	1912	*The Mundas and Their Country, Ranchi:* City Bar Library.
	1915	*The Oraons of Chotanagpur.* Ranchi : City Bar Library.
	1925	*The Birhor,* Ranchi : Man in India Office.
	1935	*The Hill Bhuiyas of Orissa.* Ranchi : Man in India Office.
Roy, S.C. & R.C. Roy	1937	*The Kharia:* Ranchi :Man in India Office.
Rusell. R.V. and R. B. Hiralal	1916	*The Tribes and Castes of the Central Provinces of India,* Vol. III. London: Macmillan.
Rustomji, N.K.	1955	"Tribal Administration in the North East Frontier Agency" in *The Adivasis.* Delhi: Publication Division, Govt of, India.
Sachidanand, S.	1954	"Birsa : An Adivasi Fighter for Freedom", *Vanyajati* Vol. 4.
	1964	*Cultural Change in Tribal Bihar.* Calcutta (Kolkata) : Book land.

	1965	Profiles of Tribal Cultures in Bihar. Calcutta (Kolkata): Firma K.L. Mukhopadhyay.
	1967	"Socio-economic Aspects of Tribal Education" *in Tribal Education in India.* New Delhi: N.C.E.R.T.
	1968	*The Tribal Vllage in Bihar: A Study in Unity and Extension.* New Delhi: Munshi Ram Manohar Lal.
	1976	*The Harijan Elite,* Delhi: Thompson Press.
Sahay, B.N.	1969	*Pragmatism in Development: Application of Anthropology.* New Delhi: Book Hive.
Sahlins, Marashall D.	1968	*Tribesmen.* New York: Prentice Hall.
Sarkar, S.S.	1974	*The Aboriginal Races of India.* Calcutta.
Save, KJ.	1945	*The Warlis,* Bombay.
Saxena, R.N.	1962	*Social Economy of a Polyandrous People.* London : Asia Publishing House.
Schneider, D. and K Gough	1961	*Matrilineal Kinship.* Berkley and Los Angeles: University of California Press.
Schneider, Harold K.	1975	"Economic Development and Anthropology", Annual Review of Anthropology.
Shah, P.G.	1964	*Tribal Lfe of Gujarat.* Bombay: Gujarat Research Society.
Shah, Ghansyham,	1990	Social Movements in India, Delhi: Sage.
Shakespeare, J.	1912	*The Lushai-Kuki Clans.* London: Macmillan.
Sharma, B.D.	1977	"Planning for Educational Development In Tribal Areas."

(Occassional Papers on Tribal Development), Ministry of Home Affairs, New Delhi.

1978 "Tribal Development Administration" in S.K Sharma (ed) *Dynamics of Development* : An Inrernational Prespective. Delhi: Concept.

Shaw, William 1929 *Notes on the Thadow Kukis.* Calcutta : Government of Assam.

Shukla, B .. K. 1959 *The Daflas of the Subansiri Region.* Shillong: North Eastern Frontier of India.

Siddiqu, M.KA. 1971 *Hinduitan Ke Adivasi* (Urdu). Calcutta : Anthropological Survey of India.

Singh, Bhupender 1977 "Tribal Development at Cross-roads: A Critique and a Plea", *Man in India,* Vol. 57, No.3.

Singh,Inderjit 1944 *The Gondwana and the Gonds.* Lucknow : Universal Publishers.

Singh, K Suresh (ed.) 1966 *Dust storm and the Hanging Mist.* Calcutta : Firma KL. Mukhopadhya.

1972 *Tribal Stitution in India* Simla: Indian Institute of Advanced Study.

Singh, Yogendra 1973 *Modernisation of Indian Tradition.* Delhi: Thompson Press.

Sinha, D.P. 1968 *Culture Change in an Inter-Tribal Market.* London: Asia Publication House.

Sinha, Kamleswar 1970 *Meghalaya : Triumph of the Tribal Genius.* New Delhi: Indian School Supply Depot.

Sinha, Raghuvir 1962 *The Akas.* Shillong: Research Department, Advisor's Secretariat.

Sinha, Surjit	1957	"Tribal Culture of Peninsular India", *Man in India,* Vol. 37, No.3.
	1965	"Tribe-Caste and Tribe-Peasant Continua in Central India". *Man in India,* Vol. 45, No. 1.
	1968	*"Tribal Solidarity and Messianic Movements*", Contributions of Indian Sociology. New Series, No. 11.
Sinha, S.C. & Jyotisen and S. Panchabi	1969	"The Concept of diku among the tribes of Chotanagpur", *Man in India,* Vol. 49, No.2.
Smith, W.C.	1925	*The Ao Naga Tribe of Assam.* London: Macmillan.
Sparkman, John J.	1961	"Economic, Social and Political Inplications of Community Development", *Community Development Review,* Vol. 6.
Spicer, Edward H.	1952	*Human Problems in Technological Change:* A Case Book. New York: Russell Sage Foundation,
Srinivas, M.N.	1953	*Religion and Society among the Coorgs of South India.* Oxford ; The Clarendon Press.
Srivasatava, S.K	1958	*The Tharus : A Study in Cultural Dynamics.* Agra: Agra University Press.
Srivasatava, V.K (ed)	2021	*India's Tribe :Unfolding Realities,.* Sage Publications, New Delhi.
Steiner, Franz	1967	*Taboo.* Harmondsworth : Penguin.Steiner, Franz 1967
Sunder, Nandini	2016	*The Scheduled Tribes and their India:* Politics, Identities and Work, Oxford University Press, New Delhi
Thaper, Romesh (ed.)	1977	*Tribe, Caste and Religion.* New Delhi: Macmillan.

Thurnwald, R. 1933 "Nomads", *Encylopedia of Social Sciences.*

Thurstan, E. & Rangachari 1909 *Castes and Tribes in Southern India,* Vol. 2. Madras: Government Press.

Thusu, KN. 1965 *The Dhurwas of Bastar.* Calcutta: Anthropological Survey of India.

Tylor, E.B. 1913 *Primitive Culture.* London.

U.N.O. 1979 *Rural Development Administration in India:* Some Emerging Policy Issues. Bangkok.

Venkat Rao, A 1976 *A Century of Tribal Politics.* New Delhi: S Chand.

Vidyarthi, L.P. 1963 *The Maler: A Case Study in Nature-Man-Spirit Complex of a Hill Tribe in Bihar.* Calcutta: Book land.

1904 *Cultural Contours of Tribal Bihar.* Calcutta: Punthi Pustak.

1968 *Applied Anthropology in India.* Alllahabad : Kitab Mahal.

1969 *Cultural Configuration of Ranchi:* Calcutta : Bookland.

(ed.) 1981 *Tribal Development and Its Administration.* New Delhi: Concept Publishers.

Vidyarthi, L.P. & B.K Rai 1977 *Tribal Culture of India.* New Delhi: Concept Publishers.

Virottam, B. 1969 *The Nagabansis and Cheros.* New Delhi: Munshi Ram Manohar Lal.

Watt, George 1887 "The Aboriginal Tribes of Manipur", *Journal of the Royal Anthropological Institute,* Vol. 16.

Westermark, E. 1926 *A Short History of Marriage.* London: Macmillan.

Wilke, Arthur S., Fran French & Raj P. Mohan 1979 "Tribal India" Unintentional Acculturation". *Bulletin of the International Committee on Urgent Anthropological and Ethnological Research,* No. 21.

Wilkinson, Paul 1971 *Social Movements,* London: Pall Mall.

Wilson Godfrey & Monica Wilson 1945 *The Analysis of Social Change.* Cambridge: Cambridge University Press.

Wiser, William A. 1936 *The Hindu Jajmani System.* Lucknow: Lucknow Publishing House.

Wolf, Eric 1966 *Peasants.* New York : Prentice Hall.

Xaxa, Virginous 2008 *State, Society and Tribes: Issues in Post-Colonial India,* Pearson India Educational Services, Chennai.

2014 *Report of the High Level Committee on Socio-economic, Health and Educational Status of Tribal Communities,* Ministry of Tribal Affairs, New Delhi.

Zaltman, G. & R, Duncan 1977 *Strategies of Planned Change.* New York: John Wiley.

Reports and Proceedings

Report of the Study Team on Tribal Development Programmes, Planning Commission, 1969.

Shilu Ao Committee Report, 1969.

Report of the Steering Group on Development of Backward Classes and Social Welfare for the Fifth Five Year Plan, Planning Commission.

Report of the Task Force on Development of Tribal Areas, New Delhi. Planning Commission.

Report of the Scheduled Areas and Scheduled Tribes Commission headed by U.N.Dhebar, 1960–61. Government of India.

Report of the Special Working Group on Cooperation for Backward Classes, 1962-Ministry of Home Affairs, Government of India.

Tribal Development in the Fifth Plan: Some Basic Policy Papers. Vol. 1,1975. (Reportofthe Task Force on Developmentof Tribal Areas he added by L.P. Vidyarthi. Ministry of Home Affairs, Government of India.)

Reports of the Commissioner for Scheduled Castes and Scheduled Tribes, Government of India.

Report of Group on Administrative Arrangement and Personel Policies in Tribal Areas. Ministry of Home Affairs, Government of India.

Five Year Plans

Report of Kolta Enquiry Committee, Lucknow: Government of Uttar Pradesh.

Reports of the National Commission for Scheduled Castes and Scheduled Tribes.

Reports of the National Commission for Scheduled Tribes.

Annual Reports of the Ministry of Tribal Affairs.

ANNEXURES

ANNEXURES

I

General Characteristics of Scheduled Tribes

Origin of the Term "Scheduled Tribe"

THE need to specify tribes and tribal communities as "Scheduled Tribes" arose only after the Constitution of India came into force on January 26, 1950. In the Government of India Act, 1935, a reference was made to the "Backward Tribes" and the Thirteenth Schedule to the Government of India (Provincial Legislative Assemblies) Order, 1936, specified certain tribes as backward in the then provinces of Assam, Bihar, Orissa, Central Provinces and Berar, Madras and Bombay. However, the first serious attempt to list "Primitive Tribes" in the country was made during the Census of 1931.

Specification of Scheduled Tribes

ARTICLE 342 of the Constitution provides that the President may with respect of any State or Union Territory specify the tribe or tribal communities or parts or groups within tribes or tribal communities which shall be deemed to be Scheduled Tribes in relation to the State or Union Territory. In pursuance of this provision the President made an order in 1950, called the Constitution (Scheduled Tribes) Order, 1950 in relation to the then Part 'A' and Part 'B' States,. In the following years a similar order was issued in respect of the Part 'C' States.

Revision of List of Scheduled Tribes

Under the Constitution, the Presidential Orders, specifying the Scheduled Tribes, once issued can be varied only by a Law of Parliament. The need for varying the orders first arose when Andhra State was formed in 1953 and again on the creation of the new State of Himachal Pradesh a year later; The implementation of the recommendations of the Backward Classes Commission necessitated a further revision of these orders in 1956. These orders were revised once again on the creation of the now states of Maharashtra and Gujarat by the Bombay Reorganization Act, 1960. Separate orders were made also for the Andaman and Nicobar Islands in 1959 and for Dadra and Nagar Haveli in 1962. The re-organization of Punjab in 1966 resulted in the transfer of lists of Scheduled Tribes from Punjab to Himachal Pradesh. More recently five tribes in Uttar Pradesh and an equal "number of tribal communities in Goa, Daman and Diu have been declared as Scheduled Tribes under the Constitution (Scheduled Tribes) (Uttar Pradesh) order 1967 and the Constitution (Goa, Daman and Diu) Scheduled Tribes Orders, 1968 respectively.

The Advisory Committee (1965)

THE Constitution has not expressly enunciated the principles or policy which should govern the classification of Tribes and Scheduled Tribes. However, it will be evident from a perusal of the special 'provisions relating to Scheduled Castes and Scheduled Tribes in the Constitution that the classification proceeds on the recognition of their all round backwardness which in the case of Scheduled Tribes is mainly due to their habitation in inaccessible areas thus cutting them from the mainstream of development and the consequent need for special measures for their advancement and welfare. Primitiveness and backwardness were the tests applied for specifying a tribe as a Scheduled Tribe in the lists prepared on the Scheduled Tribes in 1950 and 1956. These lists, however, came in for criticism on a number of occasions in Parliament as well as outside on the ground that they lacked consistency and contained several anomalies. Accordingly, in June 1956, an Advisory Committee was set up for advising the Government on the revision of lists of Scheduled Castes and Scheduled Tribes. The Committee, which submitted its report in August 1965, suggested revised lists of Scheduled Castes and Scheduled Tribes.

II

Tribal Languages

Abar Adi, Agaria, Aimol, Aka/ Hrusso,Anal,Andamanese*, Angami, Ao, Asuri, Banjari/Labhani, Beriya*, Bhili, Bhumji, Birjia/Brijia, Binjhia, Bodo Boro, Chang-Naga, Chiru, Chote, Dafla, Deori, Dimaea, Gadaba, Garo, Gondi, Hakkipikki*, Halam, Hengna*, Hmar, Ho, Jatapu*, Juang, Knbui, Kachn Naga, Kanauri, Kharia, Khasi, Kisan, Koch, Koda, Kora, Kolami, Kom, Konda, Konyak, Korku, Korwa, Kota, Koya, Kui, Kuki (unspecified), Kuruk / Oraon, Lakhar, Lalung, Lambadi, Lamkang, Lepeha, Lhota (Naga), Lushai / Mizo, Makware, Mao, Maram, Maring, Mikir, Mcithei (Manipuri), Miri, Mishmi, Mru, Munda (mundari), Naga (unspecified), Nicobarese, Noct, Onge*, Paite, Paraja, Parji, Pawai, Phom, Pochury, Purum, Rabha, Ralte, Rangkhol, Rengma, Santali, Savara (Snora), Serna (Naga), Shompen*, Simta (Naga), Singpho, Tangkhul, Tangsa, Thado, Toda, Tripuri, Uchai*, Vaiphei, Vagdi, Wancho, Yimchungre, Zemi Naga.

* These mother tongues though considered unclassifiable are presumed to be tribal.

III

Modalities for Deciding Claims for Inclusion in, Exclusion from and Other Modifications in the Orders Specifying Scheduled Castes and Scheduled Tribes Lists

MODALITIES for deciding claims for inclusion in, exclusion from and other modifications in the Orders specifying Scheduled Castes and Scheduled Tribes have been notified. Such proposals are required to be processed as indicated below:-

(a) Cases favoured by both the State Governments and the Registrar General of India (RGI) in their most recent reports would be referred to the National Commission for Scheduled Castes and Scheduled Tribes for their opinion. They would be forwarded to the Commission individually or in batches, as may be practicable, along with the comments of the State Governments and the RGI as well as any relevant material / information furnished by them or by representations.

(b) Some issues concern not one but several States e.g. the status of SC/ST migrants. These would also be referred to the National Commission if the RGI and majority of concerned States have supported modification.

(c) It may be suggested to the Commission that, while examining the above cases, they should associate, through panels or other means, expert individuals, organizations and institutions in the fields of anthropology, ethnography and other social sciences, in addition to the State Governments, RGI and the Anthropological Survey of India, on regional basis. They may also consider holding public hearings in areas relevant to the claims under examination. These guidelines cannot be binding on the Commission, but may be suggested in the interest of fuller examination of the cases. The Commission would also be requested to give priority to cases in which the Courts have given directives regarding decision within a stipulated time period. (In such cases, extension of time would be sought from the courts where necessary, citing these modalities for the determination of claims). Such cases would be separately processed and sent for earlier decision.

(d) Amending legislation would be proposed to the Cabinet in all cases in which the National Commission, RGI as well as the State Governments have favoured modification. Those cases with which the State Governments and the RGI are in agreement, but which the Commission have not supported, would be rejected at the level of Minister for Social Justice and Empowerment.

(e) Claims for inclusion, exclusion or other modifications that neither the RGI nor the concerned State Governments have supported would not be referred to the National Commission. These would be rejected at the level of the Minister for Social Justice and Empowerment.

(f) In case of claims recommended by the concerned State Governments / Union Territory Administrations, but not agreed to by the Registrar General of India, the concerned State Government / Union Territory Administration would be asked to review and further justify their recommendations in the light of the comments of the RGI. On receipt of the further clarification from the State Government/Union Territory Administration, the proposal would be referred to the RGI for comments. In such cases, where the RGI does not agree to the point of view of the State Government/Union Territory Administration on a second reference, the Government of India may consider rejection of the said proposal.

(g) Claims in respect of which the comments of either the RGI or the State Government or of both are awaited would remain under consideration until their views are received. Thereafter, they would be dealt with in accordance with the modalities at (a) to (f) above.

(h) Claims recommended suo-moto by the National Commission would be referred to RGI and the State Governments. Depending on their responses, they would be disposed of in accordance with the modalities at (d) to (f) as may be applicable.

Note:- The Note for the 'Cabinet Committee on Scheduled Castes, Scheduled Tribes and Minorities' moved by Ministry of Social Justice & Empowerment, vide their Note No. 12016/36/96 -SCD (RL Cell) dated 17.12.1998 and Note dated 17.01.2002

IV

Scheduled Castes and Scheduled Tribes Population

(Highest & Lowsest)

Scheduled Castes :	166,635,700	16.2%
Scheduled Tribes :	84.326,240	8.2%

Scheduled Castes

State with highest proportion of Scheduled Castes	Punjab (28.9 %)
State with lowest proportion of Scheduled Castes	Mizoram (0.03 %)
UT with highest proportion of Scheduled Castes	Chandigarh (17.5%)
UT with lowest proportion of Scheduled Castes	D & N Haveli (1.9%)
District with highest proportion of Scheduled Castes	Koch-Bihar (50.1%)
District with lowest proportion of Scheduled Castes	Law ngtlai Mizoram (0.01 %)

Scheduled Tribes

State with highest proportion of Scheduled Tribes	Mizoram (94.5 %)
State with lowest proportion of Scheduled Tribes	Goa (0.04 %)
UT with highest proportion of Scheduled Tribes	Lakshadweep (94.5 %)
UT with lowest proportion of Scheduled Tribes	A 8 N Islands (8.3 %)
District with highest proportion of Scheduled Tribes	Sarchhip, Mizoram(98.1%)
District with lowest proportion of Scheduled Tribes	Hathras, Uttar Pradesh (0.01%)

V

Ranking of States / Union Territories by Scheduled Tribes Concentration

Rank in 1981	State/Union Territory	Percentage of Scheduled Tribe Rank
	State	
1	Mizoram	1
2	Meghalaya	2
3	Nagaland	3
4	Arunachal Pradesh	4
5	Tripura	5
6	Manipur	6
7	Odisha	7
8	Madhya Pradesh	8
9	Sikkim	9
10	Gujarat	10
11	Assam	11
12	Rajasthan	12
13	Maharashtra	13
14	Bihar	14
15	Andhra Pradesh	15
16	West Bengal	16
17	Karnataka	17
18	Himachal Pradesh	18
19	J&K	19
20	Tamil Nadu	20
21	Kerala	21
22	Uttar Pradesh	22

	Union Territory	
1	Lakshadweep	1
2	Dadra & Nagar Haveli	2
3	Goa, Daman & Diu	3
4	A & N Islands	4

VI

Scheduled Tribes

Some Important Facts and Figures at a Glance

(1) Scheduled Tribes are notified in 30 States/UTs. The number of ethnic groups notified as STs is 750. During 2011 census about ten crore persons, comprising 8.60 percent of the total population of the country, were enumerated as belonging to Scheduled Tribes.

(2) About 55 percent of the Scheduled Tribes population are concentrated in the eastern and central tribal belt including West Bengal, Bihar-Jharkhand, Madhya Pradesh-Chattisgarh, Odisha and part of Telengana; about 28% are in the western tribal belt consisting of Gujarat, Maharashtra, Rajasthan, Dadra and Nagar Haveli and Goa, Daman and Diu. Only about 6 % of the Scheduled Tribes population are found in the south consisting of parts of Andhra Pradesh, Karnataka, Kerala and Tamil Nadu, about 10 are in the north east India, 0.83 are in Himachal Pradesh and 0.10 are in Lakshadweep and Minicoy Islands and Andaman and Nicobar Islands.

(3) There are four states, Meghalaya (85.94), Nagaland (89.15) Arunachal Pradesh (64.22), Mizoram (94.46) and two Union Territories namely Dadra and Nagar Haveli (62.24) and Lakshadweep (94.51) where 60 or more of the population belong to Scheduled Tribes categories. There are also five states where more than 20 of the population are tribals. These are Chattisgarh (31.76), Manipur (34.20), Odisha (22.43). Sikkim (20.60), Tripura (31.05), Jharkhand (26.30).

(4) There are 24 districts outside the states with tribal majority population, where 50 or more of the population belong to the Scheduled Tribes.

(5) There are 650 Blocks where they are in majority.

(6) 93,846 villages in the country have been listed as tribal villages.

(7) It is estimated that more than 75 of the tribal population live in areas where they are in majority.

(8) Areas inhabited by the tribals constitute a significant part of the backward areas of the country.

(9) It is estimated that the predominant tribal areas comprise of about 20% of the total geographical area of the country.

(10) If the clusters of villages, blocks, districts and states having 50 or more of their population as tribals are plotted on the map, it is found that there is almost a contagious tribal belt starting from Thane district in Maharashtra to Tengnaoupal district in Manipur, with lateral extensions in the sub-Himalayan region in the north and towards the coast in the south.

(11) Some of the tribes in the north-east and the sub-Himalayan region have their agnates beyond the borders of India.

(12) It is estimated that whereas the tribal areas constitute about 20% of the total geographical area of the country, about 70 of the mineral resources, bulk of the forests and water and hydel power resources, are located in these areas.

(13) During 1961 only 2.61 of tribal population were enumerated in urban areas. In 1971 the percentage went upto 3.52. Later, a large number of towns and industrial establishments have come up among the tribal areas. But even then the percentage of urban population among the tribes was only 7%.

(14) The percentage of literacy among the Scheduled Tribes, according to 1991 census, is 29.60; in 1971 it was 11.30. It rose sharply to 47.10% in 2001 and 56.91% in 2011. Inter-state variations in the percentage of literacy was however quite considerable, ranging from 17% in Andhra Pradesh to 75% in Mizoram.

(15) There are few tribal communities in India today who depend entirely on forestry and food gathering. The Birhor, Chenchu, etc. who are considered to be gatherers, do not live mainly on the objects gathered by them. They either barter the same with the cultivators or sell the same to the traders for outside market.

(16) Shifting cultivation is estimated to cover 20 million acre area and is practised by 3.55 lakh families. However, settled agriculture is the predominant source of livelihood among the overwhelming majority of the tribals. But even in areas where they live with the non-tribals the lands cultivated by them are comparatively infertile and less productive.

(18) Household industry as the main source of livelihood is found only among small tribes with scattered population like the Mahali

(basket makers) of West Bengal and Bihar and the I Agaria (iron smelters) of Madhya Pradesh.

(19) The number of tribal communities living under extremely underdeveloped stage and hence identified as 'primitive tribes' for special treatment are 76 in number an their population is merely 1.5 million only.

(20) Tribal Sub-Plan Area:

(i)	No. of ITDP	181
(ii)	Population covered	536.49 lakh
(iii)	Scheduled Tribe Population	325.82 Lakh
(iv)	Percentage of ST Population to total ST Population in TSP States	63.81
(v)	No. of Districts Fully covered	22
(vi)	No. of District Partly covered	97
(vii)	No. of Blocks Fully covered	633
(viii)	No. of Blocks Partly covered	233

(21) The Tribal Sub-Plan (TSP) is in operation in 18 states and 2 Union Territories namely, Andhra Pradesh, Assam, Bihar, Gujarat, Himachal Pradesh, Jammu & Kashmir, Karnataka, Kerala, Madhya Pradesh, Maharashtra, Manipur, Orissa, Rajasthan, Tamil Nadu, Sikkim, Tripura, Uttar Pradesh, West Bengal, Andaman & Nicobar Island, Goa. Daman & Diu.

VII

Sex Ratio of Scheduled Tribe Population in India 1961 - 2011

(In %)

Census Year	Sex Ratio of Scheduled Tribes		
	Total	Rural	Urban
1961	987	990	895
1971	982	985	896
1981	983	988	912
1991	972	976	920
2001	978	981	944
2011	990	991	980

VIII

Select Major & Minor Tribes and Their Distribution

Major Tribes

1. The Gond, about 17 million, in Madhya Pradesh, Maharashtra, Andhra Pradesh, Gujarat and Orissa.
2. The Bhil, about 7 million, in Madhya Pradesh, Maharashtra, Rajasthan and Gujarat.
3. The Santhal, about 4.5 million, in Bihar, Orissa and West Bengal.
4. The Oraon, about 2.5 million, in Bihar, Orissa, West Bengal and Madhya Pradesh.
5. The Mina, about 2.5 million, in Rajasthan and Madhya Pradesh
6. The Munda, about 2.5 million, in Bihar, Madhya Pradesh, Orissa and West Bengal.
7. The Khond, about 1.5 million, in Bihar, Orissa, Madhya Pradesh, West Bengal and Maharashtra.
8. The Ho, about 1 million, in Bihar, Orissa and West Bengal.
9. The Naga, about 1 million, in Nagaland and other north eastern states.

Minor Tribes

1. Shompen, 220
2. Jarwa, 442
3. Onge, 118
4. Sentenalese, 80
5. Great Andamanese, 61

All Inhabiting Various Islands of Andaman & Nicobar

IX

List of the Particularly Vulnerable Tribal Groups (PVTGs)

(Earlier Called as Primitive Tribal Groups)

State / UT wise

Name of the State /UT	Name of PTGs
1. Andhra Pradesh	1. Bodo Gadaba 2. Bondo Poroja 3. Chenchu 4. Dongria Khond 5. Gutob Gadaba 6. Khond Poroja 7. Kolam 8. Kondareddis 9. Konda Savaras 10. Kutia Khond 11. Parengi Poroja 12. Thoti
2. Bihar (including Jharkhand)	13. Asurs 14. Birhor 15. Birjia 16. Hill Kharia 17. Korwas 18. Mai Paharia 19. Parhaiyas 20. Sauria Paharia 21. Savar

3. Gujarat	22. Kathodi 23. Kotwalia 24. Padhar 25. Siddi 26. Kolgha
4. Karnataka	27. Jenu Kuruba 28. Koraga
5. Kerala	29. Cholanaikayan (a section of Kattunaickans) 30. Kadar 31. Kattunayakan 32. Kurumbas 33. Kcraga
6. Madhya Pradesh (including Chhattisgarh)	34. Abujh Marias 35. Baigas 36. Bharias 37. Hill Korbas 38. Kamars 39. Saharias 40. Birhor
7. Maharashtra	41. Katkaria (Kathodia) 42. Kolam 43. Maria Gond
8. Manipur	44. Marram Nagas
9. Orissa	45. Birhor 46. Bondo 47. Didayi 48. Dongria-Khond 49. Juangs 50. Kharias

	51. KutiaKondh 52. Lanjia Sauras 53. Lodhas 54. Mankidias 55. Paudi Bhuyans 56. Soura 57. Chuktia Bhunjia
10. Rajasthan	58. Seharias
11. Tamil Nadu	59. Kattu Nayakans 60. Kotas 61. Kurumbas 62. Irulas 63. Paniyans 64. Todas
12. Tripura	65. Reangs
13. Uttar Pradesh (including Uttarakhand)	66. Buxas 67. Raj is
14. West Bengal	68. Birhor 69. Lodhas 70. Totos
15. Andaman & Nicobar Islands	71. Great Andamanese 72. Jarawas 73. Onges 74. Sentinelese 75. Shompens

X

Tribal Areas (Sixth Schedule Areas)

TRIBAL areas generally mean areas having preponderance of tribal population. However, the Constitution of India refers tribal areas within the States of Assam, Meghalaya, Tripura & Mizoram, as those areas specified in Parts I, II, IIA & III of the table appended to paragraph 20 of the Sixth Schedule. In other words, areas where provisions of Sixth Schedule are applicable are known as Tribal Areas. In relation to these areas Autonomous District Councils, each having not more than thirty members have been set up. These councils serve as an instrument of self-management and have powers of legislation and administration of justice apart from executive, developmental and financial responsibilities. State-wise details of Tribal Areas are as under: -

Part I

1. The North Cachar Hills District
2. The Karbi-Anglong District

Part II

1. Khasi Hills District
2. Jaintia Hills District
3. The Garo Hills District

Part IIA

Tripura Tribal Areas District

Part III 3

1. The Chakma District
2. The Mara District
3. The Lai District

1. Substituted by the Government of Assam Notification No. TAD/R/115/74/47, dated 14.10.1976 for 'The Mikir Hills District"

2. Substituted by the Government of Meghalaya Notification No. DCA 31/72/11, dated the 14th June, 1973, Gazette of Meghalaya, Pt, VA, dated 23.6.1973, p. 200.
3. The words 'The Mizo District" omitted by the Government of Union Territories (Amendment) Act, 1971, s. 13 (w.e.f. 29.4.1972).
4. Inserted by the Mizoram District Councils (Miscellaneous Provisions) Order, 1972 published in the Mizoram Gazette, 1972, dated the 5th May, 1972, Vol. I, Pt. II, p. 17 (w.e.f. 29.4.1972).
5. Substituted by the Sixth Schedule to the Constitution (Amendment) Act, 1988 (67 of 1988), S.2 for serial number 2 & 3 and the entries relating thereto.
6. Inserted by the Constitution (49th Amendment) Act, 1984 s. 4 (w.e.f. 1.4.1985)

XI

Administration of Scheduled Areas and Tribal Areas

IN THE chapter on objectives and strategy, we have dealt with the question of translation of Constitutional provisions into reality for the scheduled tribe population. The present chapter is devoted to amplification of some of the provisions of the Fifth Schedule particularly with reference to their operation so far. In the second section of this chapter, we deal with administration of tribal areas. The distinction between Scheduled Areas and tribal areas needs to be understood. Scheduled Areas are those defined by a notification of the President under the Fifth Schedule. Attempts have been made to make the Schedule Area's and TSP areas co-terminus; by and large they are. However, the term "tribal areas' does not have exact connotation, but may be understood to include TSP areas, pockets of tribal concentration etc. The observations in the latter section of this chapter are meant to apply to tribal areas.

2. The Fifth Schedule of the Constitution imposes a special responsibility on the State for peace and good Government of the tribal areas. The executive powers of the Union extends to giving directions to thc State as to the administration of such areas. The regulation making powers conferred by the Fifth Schedule on the Governor is a unique device designed to help imparting flexibility to the Union and State laws applicable to the Scheduled Areas. Purposefully used, the provisions of the Fifth Schedule can be of great help in reinforcing the effectiveness of the TSP mechanism in the tribal areas.

3. So far, however, the provisions of the Fifth Schedule have not been utilized co the full extent by the States. Though sub-para 2 of paragraph 5 of the Fifth Schedule visualizes making regulations for the peace and good Government of Scheduled Areas specifically for:

(a) prohibiting or restricting transfer of land by or among members of scheduled tribes;

(b) regulating allotment of land to members of such tribes; and

(c) regulating carrying on the business of money-lending;

There are quite a few States which have not formulated regulations on a number of these items or, having formulated, adequate law to check money lending in the Scheduled Areas. So far as land alienation law is concerned, the State of Kerala having passed the Kerala Scheduled Tribes (Restriction of Transfer of Land and Restoration of Alienated Land) Act, 1975 have not yet enforced the Act in the Scheduled Areas. The State of Andhra Pradesh have issued an executive order detracting considerably, from applicability of the Andhra Pradesh (Scheduled Areas) Land Transfer Regulation; 1959, by stipulating that lands of tribals in possession of non-tribals who own less than 5 acres irrigated land or 10 acres unirrigated land need not be restored to tribals.

4. Anti-exploitative measures contribute substantially to the success of tribal sub-Plan strategy. The anti-exploitative measures can be legislated deriving sanction from the provisions of the Fifth Schedule, which have a wide amplitude. The measures have to be implemented earnestly to be able to provide adequate support to the development measures under the TSP. The Dhebar Commission (1961) had observed in paragraph 5.20 of its Report that the provision of paragraph 5 of the Fifth Schedule should be implemented 'within a given period'. There is even now a case for reiterating this view. We hope that all the State Governments will institute necessary action in any case before the end of the first year of the Seventh Plan to enact where necessary, and implement the relevant measures.

5. Mention has already been made of the fact that the Government of a State has been empowered to make regulation for peace and good government of the Scheduled Areas. Regulations have been framed as indicated earlier in the context of conditions prevalent in these areas. Nevertheless, tribal resurgence has been asserting itself against exploitation in land, labour, forest and excise etc. They have also not been happy with induction of foreign funds, infiltration into tribal areas and proselytisation. Other modes of exploitation have been dealt with in a separate chapter. Here, we urge that (a) entry into tribal areas of outsiders, particularly foreigners, should be

regulated; (b) foreign funds and foreign agencies should not be allowed to operate in Scheduled Areas, and for the purpose, the Foreign Exchange (Regulation) Act, 1978 may be modified.

GOVERNOR'S REPORT

6. Para 3 of the Fifth Schedule of the Constitution requires the Governor of each State having Scheduled Areas to make a report to the President regarding administration of such areas in the State. The prevalent feeling is that these reports have more or less fallen into routine grooves and mostly tend to be a modified version of the annual reports of the Tribal Development departments. The Union Government has not yet formally prescribed the items or aspects which should go into the annual reports of the Governors. There is no doubt that a rigid format will be undesirable and the Governors having vast powers under the Fifth Schedule for the administration of the Scheduled Areas can be relied upon to report and keep the President informed of important problems of Scheduled Areas. Even so, the Ministry of Home Affairs should examine the manner in which Governor's report to the President can reflect the correct state of affairs in tribal areas of a State and the extent to which guidelines should be formulated.

Tribes Advisory Councils

7. Para 4 of the Fifth Schedule of the Constitution enjoins establishment of a Tribes Advisory Council in each State having Scheduled Areas. Such Councils can be established in States having Scheduled Tribes though not Scheduled Area, if the President so directs. There has been a growing feeling that the frequency of meetings of the Tribes Advisory Council leaves much to be desired. The rules for the working of Tribes Advisory Councils in various States prescribe that the Council would meet 4 times a year in case of Kerala, Tripura, Utter Pradesh and Rajasthan and twice a year in case of Andhra Pradesh, Bihar, Himachal Pradesh, Maharashtra, Orissa and West Bengal. The number of times that the Council may meet in a year has not been specified in the States of Madhya Pradesh, Tamil Nadu and Gujarat. Thus, there is no uniformity in the prescription as to the number of meetings to be held by the Tribes Advisory Council. It appears desirable to prescribe uniformly for all the concerned States that the Council should meet at least once in each half year and twice in a year, while

leaving the provisions regarding larger number of meetings in certain States unchanged.

8. Of great practical consideration is the actual number of meetings of the Tribes Advisory Council held in the States. As Tribes Advisory Council is an important instrument fashioned to take an over-view of the efficacy these substantially contribute, by way of constructive criticism and suggestions, to the toning up of the administration, tile Governor of the State may have to playa bigger role in ensuring timely and purposive meetings of these Councils. In view of the clear position in paragraph 3 of the 5th Schedule that the executive power of the Union shall extend to giving of directions to the States as to the administration of the Scheduled Areas in the States and in view of the fact that association and participation of tribal representatives at the highest level in the States is an important prerequisite and aid to ensure success of tribal programmes, we would suggest the Union Government might give specific directions to the States to activise the Tribes Advisory Council to an adequate degree.

Administration of Tribal Areas

9. The tribal sub-Plan has been in operation since 1974-75 for varying periods in the tribal areas of the country. Special provisions on administration and control of tribal areas have been incorporated in the Fifth Schedule of the Constitution in pursuance of Article 244(1) of the Constitution. These provisions apply to administration of the Scheduled Areas and Scheduled Tribes in States other than the States of Assam and Meghalaya. Wide powers are conferred on the Governors of the States to make regulations for peace and good Government of the Scheduled Areas under this Schedule.

10. The administrative units which cover the Scheduled Areas tribal areas in the country are the following:-

    (1) ITDP/ITDPAs comprising tribal majority areas in the States cover 22 whole Districts, 633 whole blocks, besides 97 part . Districts and 280 part blocks. They take care of most of the geographical areas of tribal concentration. While Orissa and Andhra Pradesh have opted for an agency model registered under the Societies Registration Act and named these units as ITDAs, other

States have preferred to keep them as Government organisations. There are at present 181 ITDAs /ITDPs spread all over the country.

(2) Where tribals live inter-mixed with general population, constituting at least 50 per cent of the ectal population in a pocket, a special approach for development of such pockets known as "modified area development approach" has been adopted. There were 245 projects for such MADA pockets during the final year of the Sixth Plan. These projects are in charge of part-time or whole-time special officers.

(3) For the most backward section of the scheduled tribes termed as 'primitive tribes' projects have been formulated. These projects numbering 72 comprise specific entities as the smallest units of tribal area administration by posting of special staff for the purpose.

11. Apart from the above, some States have resorted to the device of autonomous regional Tribal Development Authorities. In Bihar, the States Government has established three Tribal Development Authorities for North Chhotanagpur, South Chhotanagpur and Santhal Pargana regions by Statute. In all the three cases, the Chief-Minister is the Chairman. A Regional Development Commissioner assisted by a secretariat and supervisory powers over all concerned sectors of development touching the tribal population and with separate secretariat and Directorate level officers attached to him functions as the secretary of authorities. The idea of a separate Regional Authority for Tribal Development has been tried recently (1980) by Madhya Pradesh and five regional authorities for tribal areas of Baster, East Zone, Central Zone, North-Zone and South-West Zone have been set up. But in this case the authorities have been established by administrative order with divisional Commissioner as the President of the authorities and with a Minister of the State functioning as President of the Advisory and Review Committee for these authorities. In the latter, the local MLAs and MPs, Janpad President and Division Commissioner who is the President of the authority are members. Both in Bihar and Madhya Pradesh, the purpose of institution of such special authorities is to ensure speedy execution of schemes of development for scheduled tribes by higher administrative and financial delegation to the authorities

and through coordination of the sectoral programmes at a sufficiently high level.

12. The ITDPs were intended to develop and translate into reality the concept of co-ordinated work at that level by field level consultation amongst planning and executioning officers of different sectoral programmes. With this end in view, a sufficiently senior officer was suggested to be posted as the Project Administrator to such units, while the District Collector functioned as the Chairman of the Project Level/ Project Implementation Committees. While there is no doubt that posting of wholetime project officers / project administrators has imparted keenness to implementation of tribal development programmes to a degree, it can be observed that the integration originally visualised at the ITDP level has not been fully realised. The main reasons appear to be the following :-

(1) In quite a few States, the project officers / the project administrators have not been given the co-ordinating role, either by themselves or on behalf of the Collector, for the programmes undertaken within the project area. While declaration of intention of Government to this effect is not lacking in many States, in practice these officers have not grown beyond the statue of another staff officer of the Collector, on account of lack of' clear cut mechanism for day-to-day co-ordination.

(2) Specific administrative and financial delegations to project administrators do not generally cover work and programme of other development departments and are generally confined to work and programme of the tribal welfare / tribal development department. In fact, in some States they handle programmes related to the special Central assistance only while in an odd-State or so they have been reduced to supernumerary state. Thus, their status has been highly down-graded from that of comprehensive coordinators visualised in the TSP set-up.

(3) In some States like Orissa and Andhra Pradesh the project administrators have been authorised to make entries in the annual performance records (CRs) of the Block Development Officers. But this does not apply to all the States and relationship between the Block and the ITDP continues to be somewhat undefined and ambiguous.

(4) The relationship between the autonomous Tribal Development authorities and the ITDPs needs to be specifically spelt out with the project officers being taken in as full-fledged members of such authorities.

(5) Programmes of economic development for the rural areas like the IRD have special agencies, namely, the DRDA for implementation and there is no direct link-up between the DRDA and the ITDP except that the Project Officer of the ITDP is a member of the DRDA. The same applies to the programmes like DPAP, NREP and RLEGP. In the perspective of the situation in which these special programmes developed, a 'district view' or a 'block view' rather than an "ITDP view" has been taken. There is need for clear inter-linkage between the rural development agencies and ITDP.

Measures for Co-ordination at Project Level

13. Coordination of programmes at the ITDP level is essential if an integrated approach to development of scheduled tribes is to be adopted. We appreciate that in the historical context of the growth of the developmental administration in the districts in the country, if may not be convenient or easy to put the ITDP project administrator in sole controlling charge of all items of development administration within his jurisdiction. Such a step may lead, vis-a-vis departmental supervisors, dilution of responsibility and control and may generate unnecessary cross correspondence. But we have no doubt that an ITDP Officer can conveniently be both the nodal officer for tribal development of the area and the controlling officer for tribal development of the area. This should be quite practicable particularly in ITDPs which comprise of whole sub-Division/Blocks. In such cases, the Project Officer/ Project Administrator could function as the controlling officer and supervision officer of all developmental agencies and programmes in the project areas. The feeling that the project officer is only another staff officer of the Collector would not hold good in such cases provided a clear-cut line of command is defined by the State Governments. Such an arrangement may not pose any difficulty in 22 full districts and 633 full blocks which are covered under ITDPs. In rest of the ITDP areas where part districts / Blocks are covered 1 view has to be taken in each case.

14. In case of schemes like IRDP, DRAP, RLEGP and NREP in other areas the Project Officer could be declared as the

intermediate level supervisory officer in respect of the tribal project area under the district collector, with powers to report on the performance of the officers implementing these programmes.

15. Over a period of time, it has been felt by the State Administrations that it may not be possible to vest the Project Administrator (PA) who are normally in Class I of the State Service with powers of control over the other district level officers many of whom are also generally in Class I of the State or all India Services. Apart from mere protocol or rank, the other important objective has been not to entrust control to an officer who does not oversee the whole of a district level officer's work. To strike a balance mid-way respecting both the existing structure of the district administration and the urgent requirements of tribal development, we would suggest as follows:-

    The PAs belonging to the superior services of the State all India cadres may make annual entries in the performance records of all Class II Officers of all developmental services and cadres of the State Governments working in the project areas. The PAs may at their discretion inspect both the offices and the field work of such Class II officers working within their jurisdiction.

16. As the above observations would show, while we would suggest the ITDP to be an agency for implementation of programmes we would like to make it a sufficiently strong agency for intervention in several important sectors. To this end it would be desirable to strengthen the ITDPs by providing them with a few Assistant Project Administrators who would be in charge of specific sectors of development arid would assist the Project Administrator. The number of officers to assist the PA in this manner would depend upon the size and population covered in an ITDP and scheme required to be taken up in the area.

17. Apart from the above suggestions, in order to make the ITDP an effective agency for intervention in developmental administration in tribal areas, the Project administrator / officer may in suitable cases head the subdivision / Block level Development Committees in the tribal sub-Plan areas and where the SDOs / Collectors are the Chairman of such Committees at any level, the Project administrator / officer

should invariably be made a member of such committees. In this connection recommendations on these lines under "Participation and involvement of Tribals in Tribal Area Administration" may also be seen.

District/Region/State Level

18. The Collector is the Chairman of ITDP level project formulation/implementation committee which has both officials and non-officials as its' members. In the States of Gujarat and Maharashtra where the district level Panchayati Raj administration is functioning satisfactorily, the Executive Officer in-charge of the Zila Parishadas also been fully kept in the picture. There is no gain-saying that unifying authority of the Collector should be fully brought into play to make the tribal area administration more effective and meaningful.

19. Between the ITDP / District on the one hand the Tribal Development Department at the State level on the other, there are two important functionaries namely (1) the Divisional Commissioners and (2) the Tribal Development Commissioners in different States. There are Additional or Joint Commissioners below the Tribal Development Commissioners in State like Maharashtra and Rajasthan not attached to the office of the Divisional Commissioners but in-charge of independent territorial and functional jurisdictions. In certain other States there are separate Directors for tribal development besides the office of the, Tribal Development Commissioner, with specific responsibilities entrusted to the Director(s) at the State level, but with no field functionaries under him. The Position is not very clear and exercise of supervision and control has not been found to be very satisfactory whether relating to formulation of plans and schemes or relating to day-to-day administration. The time has now come, to put this matter on a sound basis with an intelligible string of command flowing from top to bottom and an equally intelligible and decipherable picture of accountability. To fulfil such a requirement we would recommend as follows :-

(1) In the Tribal Development Department at the State level a post of Commissioner for Tribal Development should be instituted in all the States. This functionary should co-ordinate all plan and non-plan programmes in the sphere of tribal development. He shall equally be responsible for pursuing and reviewing implementation of the protective

and anti-exploitative measures designed to improve the lot of the tribals.

(2) There may be one or more Directors under the Tribal Development Commissioner for looking to general welfare schemes, specific area planning, project formulation and implementation of protective and anti-exploitative measures.

(3) At the Divisional Commissioner's level officers of the rank of Additional Directors / Joint Directors could be posted in full charge of all the items which the Commissioner handles at the State level. These officers should work under the supervision and guidance of the Divisional Commissioners as the Commissioner of division, like the Collector of the District is the node where all activities, development and regulatory, are co-ordinated and synthesised.

(4) The Project Administrator of the ITDP should have the authority to supervise the work of the sub-Division Block/Taluk level Tribal Welfare Officers posted within his jurisdiction besides exercising authority as recommended in para 5.3.

(5) At the district level, the District Tribal Development Officer by whatever designation he is called, may be strengthened to discharge his duties effectively in presenting a complete picture of tribal area programmes, both developmental and protective, to be District Collector and act in accordance with the policy guidelines in the matter from the State Government. These officers should not act merely as the stipend/ scholarship distribution officers which is the case in some States at present.

20. We do not recommend disturbing changes in the existing organisational pattern all at a time. But we would strongly urge that a clear chain of command and accountability in decision making, implementation and supervision be attempted so as to streamline the administration in the tribal areas as effectively as possible. In our view, it would be more advisable, to strengthen the tribal area administration at the appropriate level as indicated above including the ITDP level and ensure suitable participation and involvement of the traditional tribal institutions and their functionaries as suggested elsewhere, rather than

multiply intermediate agencies of the nature of autonomous Regional Development authority.

State Level Committees

21. Some States have Cabinet sub-Committees presided over by the Chief Minister to review and take policy decision or formulation and implementation of tribal development programmes. Some States have committees functioning under the Chief Minister' comprised of other Ministers and concerned State-level officers. Some other states have committees comprised of other Ministers, Tribal Development and officials, States like Bihar, Orissa, Madhya Pradesh and Andhra Pradesh have committees functioning under Chief Secretaries or Development Commissioners. The basic requirement is that the committees should function effectively and regularly with a view to integration and coordination of tribal development programmes. So long as such committees fulfil this objective, they should be allowed to continue. Where they are dormant, the underlying cause of inactivity should be extirpated, if necessary by performing a thorough overhaul. Social scientists, academicians and thinkers of repute might be associated with these bodies with advantage.

Role of Project Administrators of ITDPs in Protective Sphere

22. Providing service under one roof is an important concept under public administration in general, though it is emphasised more in the context of business administration. In tribal area administration, this has found favour already with a few State Governments who have invested the project Administrators of the ITDPs with powers under several protective legislations, besides their developmental role. A specific mention may be made of the State of Andhra Pradesh where the PAs are wielding appellate authority under the land alienation and moneylending legislations in force in the State. Apart from the desirability of the "one-door" approach so far as the tribals are concerned, equally welcome would be the likely performance of the institution of the Project Administrator as a more competent and effective functionary in tribal area administration if they are kept in picture to deal with the exploitative forces operating in the tribal sphere. Being specifically entrusted with the tribal sector it is also expected

that the PAs will feel more actively involved in implementation of the protective measures and hence may be alive to give a boost to their implementation. We would, therefore, recommend that the PAs who are generally senior officers of the State and All India Services may be invested with appellate powers of the Collector under legislations relating to land alienation, money and such other legislation as may be necessary. Adequate supporting staff to deal with this item of work should be provided to them.

EffectiveSupervision over MADA Pockets and Primitive Tribe Projects

23. Project-level committees have not been formed for pockets of tribal concentration under modified area development approach in most of the States, though the Ministry of Home Affairs had requested the State Governments to this effect. The functioning of these committees has not been regular wherever they exist. The Special Officers-in-charge of these projects are inadequately supervised in most of the States, there being no direct hierarchy of supervision over them. This situation applied equally well to the primitive tribe projects. In the interest of effective supervision, it will be desirable to place the MADA pockets and primitive tribes projects under the supervision of the Project Administrator of the nearby ITDPs, as far as possible. Except where Project level committees have been constituted separately for the MADA pockets and the primitive tribe projects, and the concerned State Governments intend to continue these separate PLCs., the Project-level Committees for the ITDP may also function MUTATIS MUTANDIS as the PLC for these projects. This will have the further advantage of doing away with a plethora of committees and meetings.

Personnel Policy

24. The Maheshwar Prasad Group on Administration in the Tribal Areas recommended several measures to be taken in the sphere of selection of officers, creation of special cadres, institution of it system of special leave and other service benefits, besides special allowance, for personnel posted to the tribal areas. The Seventh Finance Commission awarded an amount of Rs. 30.71 crores for payment as compensatory allowance to such staff working in 13 States. The Eighth Finance Commission

has awarded Rs. 30 crores for payment of compensatory allowance to State employees posted in tribal areas and Rs. 37.82 crores for construction of residential accommodation in tribal areas. While the States have, in ' general, accepted the recommendations of the Maheshwar Prasad Group, implementation of the suggestions have been hesitant and tardy. It will be desirable for the States to re-examine the recommendations in the context of their situation for fast implementation of the recommendations. In particular, we would suggest that programmes of training and re-orientation of personnel belonging to all cadres of services connected with tribal area development may form a part of the curriculam in all entry-training programmes for all Gazetted Officers. Orientation and refresher training programmes for both Gazetted and non-Gazetted officers should be provided to Revenue, Forest, Community and Rural Development, Agriculture, Animal Husbandry, Village and Small Industries, including Sericulture Department field officers. The Tribal Research Institutes and special institutes for training Government personnel may be strengthened to cope up with the training, refresher and orientation-training, requirement.

25. We find that tribal areas continue to face the prospect of scarcity of personnel and unfilled vacancies. The situation does not seem to have improved markedly notwithstanding the measures taken by State Governments so far, as the Report of another Working Group set up by the, Planning Commission on Manpower Requirement and shortages in Hill/ Tribal Areas would show. Prima Facie this would imply that the existing measures of compensation and incentives have not been adequate to persuade government servants' to join duty in tribal areas. The Maheshwar Prasad Group had recommended that in such an event a separate cadre of some selected and scarce services should be build for tribal areas or where a separate cadre is not foreseen to be viable, sub-cadres of the State cadres should be though of. Positions in such cadre or sub-cadre could be filled up either on the basis of allurement by incentives or through recruitment specifically made to fill up the posts therein. We have no reports to show what action has been taken in the matter, but vacancies in tribal areas continue to exist. We would urge adoption of the recommendation made by the Maheshwar Prasad Group particularly in respect of health and medical cadres. In the

recruitment of field-based functionaries whose cadres are generally regional or district-based, preference should be given to tribal and local persons. They should be put through intensive training programmes .

26. Development of weaker sections of the population should be a full subject in all entry or training management programmes of a State. In case of officers in the forest service and other services in States having sizeable tribal area, tribal development should be a full subject, covering one or two papers.

Fifth Schedule [Article 244(1)]

Provision as to the Administration and Control of Scheduled Areas and Scheduled Tribes

Part A

GENERAL

1. **Interpretation.**—In this Schedule, unless the context otherwise requires, the expression "State" does not include the [States of Assam 3 [,4 [Meghalaya, Tripura and Mizoram.]]]

2. **Executive power of a State in Scheduled Areas.**—Subject to the provisions of this Schedule, the executive power of a State extends to the Scheduled Areas therein.

3. **Report by the Governor to the President regarding the administration of Scheduled Areas** — The Governor of each State having Scheduled Areas therein shall annually, or whenever so required by the President, make a report to the President regarding the administration of the Scheduled Areas in that State and the executive power of the Union shall extend to the giving of directions to the State as to the administration of the said areas.

Part B

Administration and Control of Scheduled Areas and Scheduled Tribes

4. **Tribes Advisory Council** —

   (1) There shall be established in each State having Scheduled Areas therein and, if the President so directs, also in any State having Scheduled Tribes but not Scheduled Areas therein, a Tribes Advisory Council consisting of not more than twenty members of whom, as nearly as may be, three-fourths shall be the representatives of the Scheduled Tribes in the Legislative Assembly of the State:

Provided that if the number of representatives of the Scheduled Tribes in the Legislative Assembly of the State is less than the number of seats in the Tribes Advisory Council to be filled by such representatives, the remaining seats shall be filled by other members of those tribes;

(2) It shall be the duty of the Tribes Advisory Council to advise on such matters pertaining to the welfare and advancement of the Scheduled Tribes in the State as may be referred to them by the Governor;

(3) The Governor may make rules prescribing or regulating, as the case may be;

(a) the number of members of the Council, the mode of their appointment and the appointment of the Chairman of the Council and of the officers and servants thereof;

(b) the conduct of its meetings and its procedure in general; and

(c) all other incidental matters.

5. Law applicable to Scheduled Areas—

(1) Notwithstanding anything in this Constitution, the Governor may by public notification direct that any particular Act of Parliament or of the Legislature of the State shall not apply to a Scheduled Area or any part thereof in the State or shall apply to a Scheduled Area or any part thereof in the State subject to such exceptions and modifications as he may specify in the notification and any direction given under this sub-paragraph may be given so as to have retrospective effect;

(2) The Governor may make regulations for the peace and good government of any area in a State which is for the time being a Scheduled Area;

In particular and without prejudice to the generality of the foregoing power, such regulations may-prohibit or restrict the transfer of land by or among members of the Scheduled Tribes in such area;

(b) regulate the allotment of land to members of the Scheduled Tribes in such area;

(c) regulate the carrying on of business as money-tender by persons who lend money to members of the Scheduled Tribes in such area;

(3) In making any such regulation as is referred to in sub-paragraph (2) of this paragraph, the Governor may repeal or amend any Act of Parliament or of the Legislature of the State or any existing law which is for the time being applicable to the area in question.

(4) All regulations made under this paragraph shall be submitted forthwith to the President and, until assented to by him, shall have no effect.

(5) No regulation shall be made under this paragraph unless the Governor making the regulation has, in the case where there is a Tribes Advisory Council for the State, consulted such Council.

PART C
SCHEDULED AREAS

6. Scheduled Areas—

(1) In this Constitution, the expression "Scheduled Areas" means such areas as the President may by order declare to be Scheduled Areas.

(2) The President may at any time by order —

(a) direct that the whole or any specified part of a Scheduled Area shall cease to be a Scheduled Area or a part of such an area;

(a) increase the area of any Scheduled Area in a State after consultation with the Governor of that State;

(b) alter, but only by way of rectification of boundaries, any Scheduled Area;

(c) on any alteration of the boundaries of a State or on the admission into the union or the establishment of a new State, declare any territory not previously included in any State to be, or to form part of, a Scheduled Area;

(d) rescind, in relation to any State or States, any order or orders made under this paragraph, and in consultation with the Governor of the State concerned, make fresh orders redefining the areas which are to be Scheduled Areas and any such order may contain such incidental and consequential provisions as appear to the President to be necessary and proper, but save as aforesaid, the order made under sub-paragraph (1) of this paragraph shall not be varied by any subsequent order.

PART D

AMENDMENT OF THE SCHEDULED

7. Amendment of the Schedule. —

(1) Parliament may from time to time by law amend by way of addition, variation or repeal any of the provisions of this Schedule and, when the Schedule is so amended, any reference to this Schedule in this Constitution shall be construed as a reference to such Schedule as so amended.

(2) No such law as is mentioned in sub-paragraph (1) of this paragraph shall be deemed to be an amendment of this Constitution for the purposes of article 368.

XII

The Land Acquisition Act, 1894 (as amended up to 1998) — A Review

The Land Acquisition Act of 1894 was primarily enacted to ensure that in matters related to land, the role of the Collector was decisive and his award was to be accepted as final except when altered by a decree in a regular suit by the Court. This Act also dispensed with assessors who helped in valuation of land along with the judge in case of reference. The acquisition process was made elaborate and the Collector more powerful.

The Process of Land Acquisition

The Land Acquisition Act is used to acquire land which is privately owned. The Act describes the circumstances and purposes for which the Central and state governments acquire land. According to this Act, the process of acquiring land may be categorized into four stages.

Stage I

A Preliminary notification is issued by the government stating that particular land is needed or may be needed for '1 public purpose or for a company (Section-4). The notice which is a public notice is required to be published in three ways.

1. If the Central Government intends to acquire the land then the notice must be published in the Gazette of India and if the state intends to acquire the land then it must be published in the gazette of that state.
2. The notice must be published in at least two newspapers, one of which must be in a regional language.
3. The Collector is required to post the gist of the notice at convenient public places and other conspicuous places in the village or town in which the land is located. This notification is essentially to enable the government to survey the land in

order to establish its suitability for the said purpose. Any officer authorised by the government may carry out this process.

It is imperative to note that any person interested 2 who has an objection to the said intention, may under Section 4(1) file his/her objection, in writing, within 30 days to the Collector who is required to give the objector an opportunity of being heard and to record the reasons for the collector's decision in this regard. The report of the Collector is filed to the 'appropriate government" whose decision is final.

Stage II

The government is required to make a formal declaration of the intended acquisition. The publication of this declaration is to be done in the same manner as the intention notification, i.e., in the official gazette, in two newspapers and posting notices in public places in the village/town where the land in question is located (Section 6).

The declaration must state inter alia the district, the approximate area and the public purpose for which the land is needed. Also if a plan of the said purpose has been prepared then the place where the plan can be inspected should be stated. In case the land is being acquired for a company then the details of the company should be stated.

Thereafter, the Collector is to take the order from the Government for acquisition and the land is to be marked out, measured and planned (Section 7, 8).

Stage III

This stage involves :

a) giving a public notice at convenient places and individual notices to the persons interested in the land to be acquired to file claims for compensation. (Section 9).

b) inquiry into the measurements, value and claims leading to an award by the Collector. In case of disagreement the person interested can make reference to the court.

Stage IV

This is the final stage of the proceedings relating to the acquisition of land. At this stage the Collector takes possession of the land (Section 16) and compensation made to the affected parties (Section 31 to 34). Thus, the possession of land can be taken taking only after the Collector makes the award. With the Collector possession of the land, rights .to it are vested completely with the government, free of all encumbrances.

Land Acquisition (Amendment) Act, 1984

The Act was drastically amended in 1984 by the Central Government. Among other things the Act set a time limit for the completion of all proceedings, from the intention notification for acquisition of land to the issue of (declaration of intended acquisition under Section 6. Under this section it is stipulated that no declaration shall be made after a period of three years for land covered under Section 4(1) in case of Land Acquisition (Amendment and Validation) Ordinance, 1967 but before the commencement of Land Acquisition (Amendment) Act, 1981. Also, no declaration shall be made after a period of one year for land covered under section 4(1) after the commencement of Land Acquisition (Amendment) Act, 1984.

The amended Act also sets the time limit of two years within which the Collector must make his award (Section 11 A). As regards compensation, the amended Act fixed a price of 12 percent p.a. interest for the period commencing from the date of the intention notification and ending with the date of the Collector's award and also a payment of solatium at the rate of 30 percent of the market value of the acquired land (i.e. compensation for loss because of suffering or injured feelings). The amended Act also provided for an opportunity to those who are' dissatisfied with the Collector's award to apply to him for a re-determination of the compensation payable on the basis of an order for higher compensation from the Reference Court. Though, the above mentioned changes by the amended Act may prove beneficial for the people for a more expedited compensation, the amendments have provisions which have made the State more powerful in terms of the discretionary powers that are now vested with the State under Section 17. Under the urgency clause for acquisition the State can dispense with Section 5-A under which the person interested can file objections to proposed acquisition.

Land Acquisition Amendment Bill, 1998

The recently proposed Land Acquisition Amendment Bill of 1998 further strengthens the Collector's position. Despite some provisions such as bringing the R&R (Resettlement and Rehabilitation) on the statute book, a more transparent approach and curtailing the time period for officials to act faster, there are critical gaps which require serious consideration. The attempt here is not to go into details but to present the trends that would emerge with the existing laws being modified by the above mentioned Amendment Bill. It is stipulated that the proposals must be complete in all respects before it is brought before the Collector. This will certainly prohibit the proposals, which are often rushed through mostly due to extraneous considerations. As regards the time limits, on the one hand the time between initial declaration and public purpose declaration has been reduced from three years to six months, on the other hand the time for filing objections to any intended acquisition process has been reduced to twenty one days. This will certainly pose hardships to the affected persons who are often illiterate and marginalised. The Collector's role has been made far more powerful in deciding cases including appeals on objections. Another example is Section-12, which has been freshly introduced, and it takes away the Court's power regarding compensation, making it over to the Collector. The reference and revision concerning appeals on acquisition can only be done in the High Court. It is well known that litigation costs one very high and it would almost be impossible for the common man to afford costs relating to legal intervention in High Courts. This certainly makes it more difficult for the common man to get a fair value for his land. Presently, it is under the 'market value', which does not take into account several benefits that are associated with ownership of land, thus making the compensation unjust.

Going by the current trends, the present amendments are far from being ideal. In the wake of liberalisation, acquisition of land is going to be easier for multinationals through Government Corporations and this will further marginalise the underprivileged.

Public Purpose

The issue of 'public purpose' is perhaps, the most contentious and probably the most debatable issue that has beset the Court as well as the intelligentsia. The following section will try as far as possible to develop a trend, if any, of the views of the court, that has emerged on the question of public purpose, public good and public interest as far as the Land Acquisition Act is concerned. Specifically, this study will try to list out the guidelines and the criteria that are used in arriving at a conclusion as to which purpose is of public interest or otherwise. There are various other Acts such as the Indian Forest Act, 1927, Wildlife Protection Act, 1972 under which the acquisition of land for the purposes of the Act is also deemed to be for 'public purpose'.

(Courtesy: The Other Media,)

XIII

National Forest Policy Resolution 1988

I. PREAMBLE

In resolution No. 13/52-F, dated the 12th May 1952 Government of India in the erstwhile Ministry of Food and Agriculture enunicated a Forest Policy to be followed in the management of State Forests in the country. However, over the year, forests in the country have suffered serious depletion. This is attributable to relentless pressures arising from ever-increasing demand for fuelwood, fodder and timber, inadequacy of protection measures; diversion of forest lands to non-forest uses without ensuring compensatory afforestation and essential environmental safeguards; and the tendency to look upon forests as revenue earning resource. The need to review the situation and to evolve, for the future a new strategy of forest conservation has become imperative. Conservation includes preservation, maintenance, sustainable utilisation, restoration and enhancement of the natural environment. It has thus become necessary to review and revise the National Forest Policy.

2. BASIC OBJECTIVES

The basic objectives that should govern the National Forest Policy are the following:-

- Maintenance of environmental stability through preservation and, where necessary, restoration of the ecological balance that has been adversely disturbed by serious depletion of the forests of the country.
- Conserving the natural heritage of the country by preserving the remaining natural forests with the vast variety of flora and fauna, which represent the remarkable biological diversity and genetic resources of the country .
- Checking soil erosion and denudation in the catchment areas of rivers, lakes, reservoirs floods and droughts and for the retardation of siltation of reservoirs.

- Checking the extension of sand-dunes in the desert areas of Rajasthan and along the coastal tracts.
- Increasing substantially the forest/tree cover in the country through massive afforestation and social forestry programmes, especially on all denuded, degraded and unproductive lands.
- Meeting the requirements of fuel wood, fodder, minor forest produce and small timber of the rural and tribal populations.
- Increasing the productivity of forests to meet essential national needs.
- Encouraging efficient utilisation of forest produce and maximising substitution of wood.
- Creating a massive people's movement with the involvement of women, for achieving these objectives and to minimise pressure on existing forests.

The principal aim of Forest Policy must be to ensure environmental stability and maintenance of ecological balance including atmospheric equilibrium which are vital for sustenance of all life forms, human an, animal and plant. The derivation of direct economic benefit must be subordinated to this principal aim.

3. ESSENTIALS OF FOREST MANAGEMENT

Existing forests and forest land should be fully protected and their productivity improved. Forest and vegetal cover should be increased rapidly on hill slopes, in catchment areas of rivers , lakes and reservoirs and ocean shores and on semi-arid, arid and desert tracts.

Diversion of good and productive agricultural lands to forestry should be discouraged in view of the need for increased food production.

For the conservation of total biological diversity, the network of national parks, sanctuaries, biosphere reserves and other protected areas should be strengthened and extended adequately.

Provision of sufficient fodder, fuel and pasture, specially in areas adjoining forest, is necessary in order to prevent depletion of forests beyond the sustainable limit. Since fuelwood continues to be the predominant source of energy in rural areas, the programmes of afforestation should be intensified with special emphasis on augmenting fuelwood production to meet the requirement of the rural people.

Minor forest produce provides sustainance to tribal population and to other communities residing in and around the forests. Such produce should be protected, improved and their production should be enhanced with due regard to generation of employment and income.

4. STRATEGY

Area Under Forests

The national goal should be to have a minimum of one-third of the total land area of the country under forest or tree cover. In the hills and in mountainous regions, the aim should be to maintain two-third of the area under such cover in order to prevent erosion and land degradation and to ensure the stability of the fragile eco-system.

Afforestation, Social Forestry and Farm Forestry

A massive need-based and timebound programme of afforestation and tree planting, with particular emphasis on fuelwood and fodder development, on all degraded and denuded land in the country, whether forest or non-forest land, is a national imperative.

It is necessary to encourage the planting of trees alongside of roads, railway lines, rivers and streams and canals, and on other unutilised lands under State/Corporate, institutional or private ownership. Green belts should be raised in urban/industrial areas as well as in arid tracts. Such a programme will help to check erosion and desertification as well as improve the micro-climate.

Village and community lands, including those on foreshores and I environs of tanks, not required for other productive uses, should be taken up for the development of tree crops and fodder resources. Technical ' assistance and other inputs necessary for initiating such programmes should be provided by the Government. The revenues generated through such programmes should belong to the panchayats where the lands are vested in them; in all other cases, such revenues should be shared with the local communities in order to provide an incentive to them. The vesting, in individuals, particularly from the weaker sections (such as landless labour, small and marginal farmers, scheduled castes, tribals, women) of certain ownership rights over trees, could be considered, subject to appropriate regulations; beneficiaries would be entitled to usufruct and would in turn be responsible for their security and maintenance.

Land laws should be so modified wherever necessary so as to facilitate and motivate individuals and institutions to undertake tree-farming and grow fodder plants, grasses and legumes on their own land. Wherever possible, degraded lands should be made available for this purpose either on lease or on the basis of a tree-patta scheme. Such leasing of the land should be subject to the land grant rules and land ceiling laws. Steps necessary to encourage them to do so must be taken. Appropriate regulations should govern the felling of tree on private holding.

Management of State Forests

Schemes and projects which interfere with forests that clothe steep slopes, catchments of rivers, lakes and reservoirs, geologically unstable terrain and such other ecologically sensitive areas should be severely restricted. Tropical rain/moist forests, particularly in areas like Arunachal Pradesh, Kerala, Andaman & Nicobar Islands, should be totally safeguarded.

No forest should be permitted to be worked without the Government having approved the management plan, which should be in a prescribed format and in keeping with the National Forest Policy. The Central Government should issue necessary guidelines to the State Government in this regard and monitor compliance.

In order to meet the growing needs for essential goods and services which the forests provide, it is necessary to enhance forest cover and productivity of the forests through the application of scientific and technical inputs. Production forestry programmes, while aiming at enhancing the forest cover in the country and meeting national needs, should also be oriented to narrowing, by the turn of the century, the increasing gap between demand and supply of fuelwood. No such programme, however, should entail clear-felling of adequately stocked natural forests. Nor should exotic species be introduced through public or private sources, unless long-term scientific trials undertaken by specialists in ecology, forestry and agriculture have established that they are suitable and have no adverse impact on native vegetation and environment.

Rights and Concessions

The rights and concessions, including grazing, should always remain related to the carrying capacity of forests. The capacity itself should be optimised by increased investment, silvicultural research and development of the area. Stall-feeding of cattle should be encouraged. The requirement of the community, which cannot be met by the right and concessions so determined, should be met by development of social forestry outside the reserved forests.

The holders of customary rights and concessions in forest areas should be motivated to identify themselves with protection and development of forests from which they derive benefits. The rights and communities living within and around forest areas, specially the tribals.

The life of tribals and other poor living within and near forests revolves around forests. The rights and concessions enjoyed by them should be fully protected. Their domestic requirements of fuelwood, fodder, minor forest produce and construction timber should be the first charge on forest produce. These and substitute materials should be made available through conveniently located depots at reasonable prices.

Similar consideration should be given to scheduled castes and other poor living near forests. However, the area, which such consideration should cover, would be determined by the carrying capacity of the forests.

Wood is in short supply. The long-term solution for meeting the existing gap lies in increasing the productivity of forests, but to relieve the existing pressure on forests for the demands of railway sleepers, construction industry (particularly in the public sector), furniture and panelling, mine-pit props, paper and paper board etc. substitution of wood needs to taken recourse to. Similarly, on the front of domestic energy, fuelwood needs be substituted as far as practicable with alternate sources like bio-gas, LPG and solar energy. Fuel-efficient "Chulhas" as a measure of conservation of fuelwood need to be popularised in rural areas.

Diversion of Forest Lands for Non-forest Purposes

Forest land or land with tree cover should not be treated merely as a resource readily available to be utilised for various projects and programmes, but as a national asset which requires to be properly safeguarded for providing sustained benefits to the entire community. Diversion of forest land for any non-forest purpose should be subject to the most careful examinations by specialists from the standpoint of social and environmental costs .and benefits. Construction of dams and reservoirs, mining and industrial development an expansion of agriculture should by consistent with the needs for conservation of trees and forests. Projects which involve such diversion should at least provide in their investment budget, funds for re-generation/ compensatory afforestation.

Beneficiaries who are allowed mining and quarrying forest land and in land covered by trees should be required to repair and revegetate the area in accordance with established forestry practices. No mining lease should be granted to any party, private or public, without a proper mine management plan appraised from the environmental angle and enforced by adequate machinery.

Wildlife Conservation

Forest Management should take special care of the needs of wildlife conservation, and forest management plans should include prescriptions for this purpose. It is specially essential to provide for "corridors" linking the protected areas in order to maintain genetic continuity between artificially separated sub-sections of migrant wild-life.

Tribal People and Forests

Having regard ,to the symbiotic relationship between the tribal people and forests, a primary task of all agencies responsible for forest management, including the forest development Corporations should be associate the tribal people closely in the protection, re-generation and development of forests as well and provide gainful employment to people living in and around the forest, with special attention to the following:-

- One of the major causes for degradation of forest is illegal cutting and removal by contractors and their labour. In order to put an end to this practice, contractors should be replaced by institutions such as tribal co-operatives, government corporations, etc., as early as possible.
- Protection, regeneration and optimum collection of minor forest produce along with institutional arrangement for the marketing of such produce;
- Development of forest villages on par with revenue villages; Family-oriented schemes for .improving the status of the tribal beneficiaries; and
- Undertaking integrated area development programmes to meet the need of the tribal economy in and around the forest areas, including the provision of alternative sources of domestic energy on a subsidised basis, to reduce pressure on the existing forest areas.

Shifting Cultivation

Shifting cultivation is affecting the environment and productivity of land adversely. Alternative avenues of income, suitably harmonised with the right land-use practices, should be devised to discourage shifting cultivation. Efforts should be made to contain such cultivation within the area already affected, by propagating improved agricultural practices. Area already damaged by such cultivation should be rehabilitated through social forestry and energy plantations.

Damage to Forests from Encroachments, Fires and Grazing

Encroachment on forest lands has been on the increase. This trend has to be arrested and effective action taken to prevent its continuance. There should be no regularisation of existing encroachments.

The incidence of forests fires in the country is high. Standing trees and fodder are destroyed on a large scale and natural regeneration annihilated by such fires. Special precautions should be taken during the fire season. Improved and modern management practices should be adopted to deal with forest fires.

Grazing in forest areas should be regulated with the involvement of the community; Special conservation areas, young plantations and regeneration areas should be fully protected. Grazing and browsing in forest areas need to be controlled. Adequate grazing fees should be levied to discourage people in forest areas from maintaining large herds of non-essential livestock.

Forest Based Industries

The main considerations governing the establishment of forest-based industries and supply of raw material to them should be as follows:-

- As far as possible, a forest-based industry should raise the raw material needed for meeting its own requirements, 'preferably by establishment of a direct relationship between the factory and the individuals who can grow the raw material by supporting the individuals with inputs including credit, constant technical advice and finally harvesting and transport services.
- No forest-based enterprise, except that at the village or cottage level, should be permitted in the future unless it has been first cleared after a careful scrutiny with regard to assured availability of raw material. In any case, the fuel, fodder and timber requirements of the local population should not be sacrificed for this purpose.
- Forest-based industries must not only provide employment to local people on priority but also involve them fully in raising trees and raw material.
- Natural forests serve as a gene pool resource and help to maintain ecological balance. Such forests will not, therefore, be made available to industries for undertaking plantation and

for any other activities, Farmers, particularly small and marginal farmers, would be encouraged to grow on marginal/degraded lands available with them wood species required for industries. These may also be grown along with fuel and fodder species on community lands not required for pasture purposes, and by Forest department/corporations on degraded forests, not earmarked for natural regeneration.

- The practice of supply of forest produce to industry at concessional prices should cease. Industry should be encouraged to use alternative raw materials. Import of wood and wood products should be liberalised.

The above considerations will however, be subject to the current policy relating to land ceiling and land laws.

Forest Extension

Forest conservation programme cannot succeed without the willing support and co-operation of the people. It is essential, therefore, to inculcate in the People, a direct interest in forests, their development and conservation, and to make them conscious of the value of trees, wildlife and nature in general. This can be achieved through the involvement of educational institutions, right from the primary stage. Farmers and interested people should be provided opportunities through institutions like Krishi Vigyan Kendras, Trainers Training Centres to learn agrisilvicultural and silvicultural techniques to ensure optimum use of their land and water resources. Short-term extension courses and lectures should be organised in order to educate farmers. For this purpose, it is essential that suitable programmes are propagated through mass media, audio-visual aids and the extension machinery.

Forestry Education

Forestry should be recognised both as a scientific discipline as well as a profession. Agriculture universities and institutions dedicated to the development of forestry education should formulate curricula and courses for imparting academic education and promoting post-graduate research and professional excellence, keeping in view the manpower needs of the country. Academic and professional qualifications in forestry should be kept in view for recruitment to the Indian Forest Service and the State Forest Service. Specialised and orientation courses for developing better management skills by inservice training need to be encouraged, taking into account the latest development in forestry and related disciplines.

Forestry Research

With the increasing recognition of the importance of forests of environmental health, energy and employment, emphasis must be laid on scientific forestry research, necessitating adequate strengthening of the research base as well as new priorities for action. Some broad priority areas of research and development needing special attention are:-

(i) Increasing the productivity of wood and other forest produce per unit of area per unit time by the application of modern scientific and technological methods.

(ii) Revegetation of barren/marginal/waste/mined lands and watershed areas.

(iii) Effective conservation and management of existing forest resources (mainly natural forest eco-systems).

(iv) Research related to social forestry for rural/tribal development.

(v) Development of substitutes to replace wood and wood products.

(vi) Research related to wildlife and management of national parks and sanctuaries.

Personnel Management

Government policies in personnel management for professional foresters and forest scientists should aim at enhancing their professional competence and status and attracting and retaining qualified and motivated personnel, keeping in view particularly the ardous nature of duties they have to perform, often in remote and inhospitable places.

Forest Survey and Data Base

Inadequacy of data regarding forest resources is a matter of concern because this creates a false sense of complacency. Priority needs to be accorded to completing the survey of forest resources in the country on scientific lines and to updating information. For this purpose, periodical collection, collation and publication of reliable data on relevant aspects of forest management needs to be improved with recourse to modern technology and equipment.

Legal Support and Infra-structure Development

Appropriate legislation should be undertaken, supported by adequate infrastructure, at the Centre and State levels in order to implement the policy effectively.

Financial Support for Forestry

The objectives of this revised Policy cannot be achieved without the investment of financial and other resources on a substantial scale. Such investment is indeed fully justified considering the contribution of forests in maintaining essential ecological processes and life-support systems and in preserving genetic diversity. Forests should not be looked upon as a source of revenue. Forests are a renewable natural resource. They are a national asset to be protected and enhanced for the well-being of the people and the Nation.

XIV

The Scheduled Tribes and Other Traditional Forest Dwellers (Recognition of Forest Rights) Act, 2006

Background

FOR many tribal people and other forest communities, forests are the source of livelihood, identity, customs and traditions. The forest dwelling scheduled tribes and other traditional forest dwellers inhabiting forests for generations were in occupation of the forest land for centuries. However, their rights on their ancestral lands and their habitats had not been adequately recognized despite them being integral to the very survival and sustainability of the forest eco-system. The traditional rights and interests of forest dwelling scheduled tribes and other traditional forest dwellers on forest lands were left unrecognized and unrecorded through faulty reservation process during consolidation of State forests, in the past.

THE forest dwelling tribal people and the forests are inseparable, a factor that also ensures conservation of ecological resources stemming from the very ethos of tribal life. The conservation processes for creating wilderness and forest areas for production forestry somehow ignored the bonafide interests of the tribal community from the point of view of legislative framework in the regions where tribal communities primarily inhabited. The simplicity of tribes and their general ignorance of modern regulatory frameworks precluded them from asserting their genuine claims to resources in areas where they belonged and depended upon. The modern conservation approaches also advocated exclusion rather than integration. It was much later that forest management regimes initiated action to recognize the occupation and other rights of the forest dwellers and integrated them in designs of management. Insecurity of tenure and fear of eviction from the lands where they had lived and thrived for generations were perhaps the biggest reasons why tribal communities felt emotionally as well as physically alienated from forests and forest lands. This historical injustice needed correction and, therefore, the Government enacted the Scheduled Tribes and Other Traditional Forest Dwellers (Recognition of Forest Rights) Act, 2006, which is commonly known as Forest Rights Act (FRA). The Act came into operation with the notification of Rules on 01-01-2008 for carrying out the provisions of the Act.

The Act also goes beyond the "recognition" of forests rights and also empowers the forest rights holders, Gram Sabhas and local level institutions with the right to protect, re-generate, conserve and manage any community forest resource. This marks a decisive step forward in resource governance itself. Hailed rightly as a milestone in the history of tribal peoples' and forest dwellers' movements, the Act endeavors to facilitate their political empowerment to govern the forests for sustainable use and conservation. Precisely for these reasons, it becomes important to take firm proactive steps to make the necessary paradigm shift, particularly by the State Governments.

Salient Features of the Forest Rights Act

THE Salient features of the Act are given as under:

(1) Section 3 of the Act lists the rights which shall be the forest rights of the forest dwelling Scheduled Tribes and Other Traditional Forest Dwellers. These forest rights are:

(a) right to hold and live in the forest land under the individual or common occupation for habitation or for self-cultivation for livelihood by a member of members of a forest dwelling Scheduled Tribe or other traditional forest dweller;

(b) community rights such as nistar, by whatever name called, including those used in erstwhile Princely States, Zamindari or such intermediary regimes;

(c) right of ownership, access to collect, use, and dispose of minor forest produce which has been traditionally collected within or outside village boundaries;

(d) other community rights of uses or entitlements such as fish and other products of water bodies, grazing (both settled or transhumant) and traditional seasonal resource access of nomadic or pastoralist communities;

(e) rights including community tenures of habitat and habitation for primitive tribal groups and pre-agricultural communities;

(f) rights in or over disputed lands under any nomenclature in any State where claims are disputed;

(g) rights for conversion of Pattas or leases or grants issued by any local authority or any State Government on forest lands to titles;

(h) rights of settlement and conversion of all forest villages, old habitation, unsurveyed villages and other villages in forests, whether recorded, notified or not into revenue villages;

(i) right to protect, re-generate or conserve or manage any community forest resource which they have been traditionally protecting and conserving for sustainable use;

(j) rights which are recognized under any State law or laws of any Autonomous District Council or Autonomous Regional Council or which are accepted as rights of tribals under any traditional or customary law of the concerned tribes of any State;

(k) right of access to biodiversity and community right to intellectual property and traditional knowledge related to biodiversity and cultural diversity;

(l) any other traditional right customarily enjoyed by the forest dwelling Scheduled Tribes or other traditional forest dwellers, as the case may be which are not mentioned in clause (a) to (k) but excluding the traditional right of hunting or trapping or extracting a part of the body of any species of wild animal;

(m) right to in situ rehabilitation including alternative land in cases where the Scheduled Tribes and other Traditional forest dwellers have been illegally evicted or displaced from forest land of any description without receiving their legal entitlement to rehabilitation prior to the 13th day of December, 2005.

(2) Section 3(2) of the Act provides for diversion of forest land for certain facilities managed by the Government notwithstanding anything contained in the Forest Conservation Act, 1980 and which involved felling of trees not exceeding seventy five trees per hectare and the forest land to be diverted for the purpose is less than one hectare and the clearance of such development project is recommended by the Gram Sabha.

(3) Section 4(1) of the Act recognizes and vests forest rights in forest dwelling Scheduled Tribes and Other Traditional Forest Dwellers notwithstanding anything contained in any other law for the time being in force.

(4) Section 4(2) of the Act provides for modification or resettlement of forest rights in critical wildlife habitats of National Parks and Sanctuaries for the purpose of creating inviolate areas for wildlife conservation subject fulfillment of conditions such as process of recognition of rights is complete in all the areas under consideration, no other reasonable option exists, it has been established that the activities or the impact of the present right holders will cause irreversible damage and threaten the existence of wildlife and their habitat, free and informed consent of the concerned Gram Sabhas has been obtained, resettlement or alternative package has been prepared and communicated that provides a secure livelihood for the affected individuals and communities and fulfils the requirements of such affected families and communities given in the relevant laws and policy of the Central Government, and the resettlement should take place only after the facilities and land allocation at the resettlement location are complete. It is also provided that critical wildlife habitats from which right holders are relocated shall not be subsequently diverted for other users.

(5) Section 4(3) of the Act subjects the recognition and vesting of the forest rights to the condition that the forest dwelling Scheduled Tribes or Other Traditional Forest Dwellers had occupied the forest land before the 13th day of December, 2005. Section.4(4) stipulates that the rights conferred under this Act shall be heritable but not alienable or transferable and shall be registered jointly in the name of both the spouses in case of married persons.

(6) A very important and crucial safeguard has been provided to the forest right holders vide Section 4(5) which mandates that no forest dwelling Scheduled Tribes and Other Traditional Forest Dwellers shall be evicted or removed from the forest land under his occupation till recognition and verification procedure is complete.

(7) The right to hold and live in the forest land under the individual or common occupation for habitation and for

self-cultivation for livelihood by a member or members of a forest dwelling Scheduled Tribes or Other Traditional Forest Dwellers shall be restricted to area under actual occupation and shall in no case exceed an area of four hectares as per Section 4(6) of the Act. Section 4(7) of the Act provides that forest rights shall be conferred free from all encumbrances and procedural requirements.

(8) The forest rights recognized and vested under this Act includes the right of land to forest dwelling Scheduled Tribes and Other Traditional Forest Dwellers who can establish that they were displaced from their dwelling and cultivation without land compensation due to State development interventions and where the land has not been used for the purpose for which it was acquired within five years of the said acquisition as per Section 4(8) of the Act.

(9) Section 5 of the Act empowers the holders of forest rights, the Gram Sabha and the village level institutions to (a) protect the wildlife, forest and bio-divesity (b) ensure that adjoining catchment area, water sources and other ecological sensitive areas are adequately protected (c) ensure that the habitat of forest dwelling Scheduled Tribes and other traditional forest dwellers is preserved from any form of destructive practices affecting their cultural and natural heritage and (d) ensure that the decisions taken in the Gram Sabha to regulate access to community forest resources and stop any activity which adversely affects the wild animals, forest and the bio-diversity are complied with.

(10) Section 6 (Chapter IV) of the Act deals with the authorities and procedures to vest forest rights in forest dwelling Scheduled Tribes and other traditional forest dwellers. There is a three tier structure of authorities to vest forest rights. The Gram Sabha is the initiating authority for determining the nature and extent of individual or community forest rights or both that may be given to the forest dwelling Scheduled Tribes and other traditional forest dwellers. The Sub Divisional Level Committee (SDLC) examines the resolution passed by the Gram Sabha and forwards it to the District Level Committee (DLC) for the final decision. Any person

aggrieved by the resolution of the Gram Sabha may prefer a petition to the Sub-Divisional Level Committee and any person aggrieved by the decision of the Sub-Divisional Level Committee may prefer a petition to the District Level Committee. The decision of the District Level Committee on the record of forest rights is final and binding. There is a State Level Monitoring Committee (SLMC) to monitor the process of recognition and vesting of forest rights and to submit to the nodal agency such returns and reports as may be called by that agency.

(11) Section 7 of the Act has a provision for punishment of any authority or officer for contravention of any provision of this Act or any rule made thereunder.

(12) The Ministry of Tribal Affairs, Government of India is the nodal agency for the implementation of this Act as per Section 11 of the Act.

(13) Section 12 empowers the Central Government to issue directions to the authorities referred to in Chapter IV of the Act.

(14) As per Section 13 of the Act, the provisions of this Act shall be in addition to and not in derogation of the provisions of any other law for the time being in force.

Status of Implementation of the Act

AS ON 30-11-2016, the total number of claims filed under FRA is 42,43,668 out of which 36,88,859 claims have been disposed off and 17,30,729 titles have been issued. Odisha has the distinction of issuing highest number of titles which is 4,05,509 (3,99,996 individual titles and 5,513 community titles). Madhya Pradesh has the distinction of having highest forest area over which titles have been issued under this Act. The total forest area over which title has been issued in Madhya Pradesh is 21,10,991.87 acres. Statement showing percentage of titles distributed over number of claims (State-wise) under the Act as on 30.11.2016 is given in **Annexure-7**.

Initiatives taken by the Ministry during the year

THE Ministry of Tribal Affairs has integrated all the thematic aspects of project execution in respect of legal and procedural challenges in implementation of FRA. The Ministry has also been continuously attempting to provide clarifications and directions to resolve these challenges. This year the focus has been on dissemination and outreach of these efforts to the remotest areas. Moreover, the Ministry has also been attempting to strengthen the monitoring of the implementation procedure, analyzing the intervention areas and extending support to over lapses. Following actions have been taken in this direction:

- ❖ The Ministry maintains a regular monitoring of the progress in the distribution of title deeds across all States. A regular update is sought from all States in the form of Monthly Progress Report (MRR) which is also published on the website of the Ministry every month. The MPR also helps identifying the high / low performing States and the need for interventions.
- ❖ The Ministry had conducted an analysis of the performance of all States based on MPRs collected for a spectrum of past 3 years. The results in terms of pendency rate, rate of rejection and proportional collection of claims were eye opening. Through this analysis, nine States have been identified as low performing States and this Ministry has written to the Principal Secretaries of these States seeking justification of their current status. The letter has also sought to undertake review of rejected claims to ensure that no wrongful rejections are made.
- ❖ A joint review meeting under the chairmanship of Secretary, Ministry of Tribal Affairs and Additional Secretary, Ministry of Home Affairs was undertaken on 26-05-2016 through video conferencing with the Principal Secretaries / Secretaries of States of the 29 worst affected LWE districts on status of FRA Implementation.
- ❖ Again a video conference was held by the Additional Secretary (LWE) on 23-08-2016 with the Representatives of the LWE affected States along with the Ministry of Tribal Affairs to review the progress of distribution of title deeds under Forest Rights Act, 2006 across 35 most LWE affected areas which sought to achieve a separate reporting over progress in distribution of title deeds in LWE areas, reasons of rejection of claims, suo-moto review of rejected claims and guidelines for better use of distributed lands in these areas.
- ❖ Ministry of Tribal Affairs has written to the Chief Secretaries of the State Governments where the Rate of

Rejection of FRA claims is very high. FRA provides a reasonable opportunity to the claimant for presenting his case in case of Rejection. Considering the accessibility of legal services to the tribal, this is a suo-moto action and the State Governments have been directed to mandatorily review the Rejected claims since 1st April 2014 if the same has not undergone reconsideration through means of re-appeal in either of decisive body. Review of the claims rejected prior to the said date is subject to the discretion of the State Government.

❖ A workshop was organized on 26-08-2016 under the chairmanship of Joint Secretary, MoTA for operationalization of MIS system developed to monitor the progress of implementation of FRA. State Nodal Officers and Technical persons from the States attended the workshop.

❖ The Hon'ble Prime Minister inaugurated the first National Tribal Carnival on 25th October 2016 which was followed by thematic seminars in different domain including Forest Rights Act. The seminar was chaired by the Hon'ble Minister of Tribal Affairs; other dignitaries included Ministers from States, Member of Parliament, Members of State Legislature, Joint Secretary, MoTA, DIG, MoEFCC and experts from academia. There was a panel discussion followed by questions by the communities and civil society. A Tribal Diary depicting the cultural diversity of major tribal communities in India was also released by the Hon'ble Minister of Tribal Affairs.

❖ Section 5 of FRA recognizes that the forest dwellers are integral to the very survival and sustainability of the forest ecosystem. Under the FR Rule 4(1)(e), the Gram Sabha is required to constitute Committees for the protection of wildlife, forest and biodiversity which shall prepare a conservation and management plan for community forest resources in order to sustainably and equitably manage community forest resources. MoTA, in consultation with MoEFCC, has developed Guidelines to provide an enabling framework within which the Gram Sabha, through the Committee under Rule 4(1)(e) can meet its responsibilities under the provisions of the Act to protect, regenerate conserve and manage the community forest resource.

- In order to achieve effective results in implementation of the Forest Rights Act, 2006, the Ministry is running a project titled 'Strengthening the National Capacity in Tribal Areas' in association with United Nations Development Program (UNDP). Under the project, several consultations and workshops are held and literature is being produced for dissemination of information. In the current year following documents were generated and circulated.

XV

Codification of Customs and Customary Laws of Tribal Communities

The tribals in India present a variety of socio-cultural practices and customs. Many of the tribals are already exposed to non-tribal communities for a very long period and this may have influenced the original rigidity of customs of the tribals. In general, the tribal communities are largely covered by their own traditions in social conduct. The tribal customs in regard to marriage, divorce, inheritance, administration of justice in the community, particularly in regard to trial of minor offence etc. continue to guide the tribal communities' behaviour. Study of the customary laws of the tribal communities is, therefore, useful for our understanding of tribal societies and necessary for better administration for these areas and people. It is with this aim in view that codification of customary tribal laws was first mooted as early as in 1982. Attempts were made through some State Governments, Tribal Research Institutes and the Anthropological Survey of India. It may, however, be noted that the ASI or the TRIs are not equipped for studies relevant to legal needs. The studies are mainly based on ethnographical interest and cannot serve the purpose of law. This limitation was recognised by the Working Group of the 7th Five Year Plan which made the following recommendations:

> "Penetration into the heart of a custom or tradition is essential to determine its binding charter on the tribal community. Any wrong judgement on the part of the officer-in-charge of such compilation may lead to serious consequences. In this background, to dub such compilations as "customary law" and publish them under the auspices of a State Government or Government of India may be risky, particularly when recognised tribal institutions are no longer extant in many cases from whom a confirmation as to the

accuracy of such "customary laws" could be obtained. Such compilations may perhaps, should be captioned as "Some Traditional Tribal Customs" rather than as "customary laws". This may leave the way open for further improving such compilations, if need be".

It also listed the customs that-would be of particular interest to the State i.e. ownership of property and inheritance, family and kinship, traditional tribal village offices and other institutions and succession to such offices.

2. The progress made so far indicates that from the States of Andhra Pradesh, Gujarat, Kerala, Maharashtra, Rajasthan, Uttar Pradesh, Tripura and Himachal Pradesh information on a few aspects of tribal customs of 41 communities have been collected. The Anthropological Survey of India has covered 55 tribal communities in their survey of tribal customs. The ASI is contemplating a publication based on their studies.
3. The Law Research Centre, Northern Region in the Guwahati High Court has taken up a scheme to codify/compile the customs and customary laws of tribals in Five North-Eastern States. The Ministry of Welfare has requested six major tribal States, namely Andhra Pradesh, Bihar, Gujarat, Madhya Pradesh, Orissa and Rajasthan to entrust this work to the Tribal Research Institutes. Progress in this work is yet to pick up.
4. The approach of the Working Group for the 7th Five Year Plan should be retained during the 8th Plan. However, if the basic objectives of better understanding for better administration is to be achieved, then the plecemea compilation attempts made so far needs to be modified. The Working Group made the following recommendations for the 8th Plan :-
   (i) Complete compilation of the main customs, namely ownership of .property and inheritance, family and kinship, traditional tribal offices and other institutions of a particular tribe should be done instead of covering some customs with wider coverage of tribes. This would give an integrated picture of the entire tribe.
   (ii) Compilation could be taken up as a fully funded Central Scheme drawn up by the States having Tribal Research Institutes, to take up the task through the Tribal Research Institutes within a specific time schedule.
   (iii) The compilation could also be done through a legal cell in the Law Departments of the Tribal Sub-Plan States,

on the lines of the Law Research Centre in the Guwahati High Court.

(iv) The Anthropological Survey of India should be in overall charge of these compilations and devise suitable mechanism for monitoring and reviewing of the progress in consultation with the Tribal Research Institutes and the Law Departments of the States.

(Source: Report of the Working Group on Development and Welfare of Scheduled Tribes During Eighth Five Year Plan, 1989)

XVI

Chronological Records of Tribal Revolts

Year	Revolt
1778	Revolt of the Pahariya Sirdars of Chhotanagpur against the British Government
1784 - 1785	Koli disturbances (Maharashtra)
1789	Revolt in Tamar of Chhotanagpur
1794 - 1795	- do-
1795 - 1800	Chuari Movement in Bihar
1798	Panchet estate sale revolt
1801	Tamar revolt in Bihar
1803	Kova uprising in the Rampa area of the East Godavari Agency, Andhra Pradesh
1807 - 1808	Chhotanagpur Tribal Revolts
1809 - 1828	Bhil revolt in Gujarat
1811, 1817, 1820	Bihar Agrarian Tribal Revolts
1818	The Koli revolt (Maharashtra)
1825	Singphos attached and set fire to the British magazine at Sadiya
1827	Mishmis murdered explorer Wilcox
1828	Revolt of Assam tribes against the British under Gomdhar Konwar who was defeated by Lt. Rutherford
1828	Singhphos's Chief attacked Sadiya with 3000 tribal warriors
1829	Revolt of Khasis of Assam
1828	Singhphos's Chief attacked Sadiya with 3000 tribal warriors
1829	Revolt of Khasis of Assam

1829	Teerut Singh (Assam) massacred the British Generals and their Indian Sepoys
1831 - 1832	The Great Kol insurrection
1820, 1832, 1867	Munda revolts in Bihar
1832 - 1833	Kherwar rising under the leadership of Bhagirath in Bihar
1835	Deflas of NEFA (Assam) raided British Plains' subjects and British took to reprisals to avenge
1835	Raja of Jaintia Hills (Assam) was deposed by the British owing to his anti-British activities, and given a pension
1836	Mishmis (Assam) killed botanist Griffith suspecting his intentions
1838	Naik revolt in Gujarat
1839 - 1843	Khampti (Assam) rising
1839	Khamptis attacked and killed the British Agent, Adam White and 80 other officers and soldiers.
1842	Captain Blunt's troops attacked by Bastar Gonds. Blunt had to withdraw
1842	Lushais (Assam) raided the British territory of Arakan, Sylhet and defeated the British forces
1843	Singhpo Chief Nirang Phidu attacked the British garrison and killed several soldiers
1844	Lushais attacked Manipuri villages. Reprisal by the British followed. Lushai leader Lal Sukla arrested and transported for life
1846	Bhil revolt under Kuwar Jivo Vasavo in Gujarat
1849	Kadma Singpho attacked British villages in Assam and was captured
1850	Revolt of Chakra Bisoi, the Kondh tribal leader in orissa
1855	The revolt of the Santhals in Bihar

1855	Eden's punitive expedition against Mishmis to avenge their killing of two missionaries
1858	Naikda's revolt against the British in Gujarat
1857 - 58	Bhil revolt (Gujarat) under the leadership of Bhagoji Naik and Kajar Singh
1857	Revolt of Mariram Dewan and Saring Raja of Assam, their arrest by the British Govt.
1860	Lushai Chief raided British Tripura and killed 186 British subjects
1860 - 1862	Revolt of Syntengs of Jaintia Hills
1861	The Phulaguri uprising of tribal peasants
1861	The Juang revolt in Orissa
1862	Revolt of Syntengs of Jaintia Hills
1862	Andhra Agency Koya tribal revolt against Muttadars (Petty tribal Zamindars) and their supporters, the British
1869 - 1879	Dhanbad Santhal unrest (Bihar) against Raja of Tundi subsequently settled by Colonel Dalton.
1872 - 1873	Daflas quelled by British military expedition
1879	Naga revolt
1879	Andhra Agency Koya revolt against Muttadars and the British
1880	Koya revolt under Tammandora's's leadership in Malkangiri, Orissa
1883	Sentinel islanders attack Humphery (Andamans)
1889	Sardari (Munda leaders') agitation against the British Government
1891	Manipur revolt led 'by Tikendraji Singh against the British
1892	Eastern Lushais' rising against the British
1895	Birsa Munda's arrest
1911	Bastar tribal uprising
1913, 1914, 1920, 1921	Tana Bhagat rebellions in Bihar

1922	Rampa rebellion of Koyas under Alluri Sree Rama Raju against the British
1932	Rani Guidallo's Naga non-Christian revolt (Assam)
1941	Gond and Kolam revolt against the British Government in Adilabad district of Andhra Pradesh, led by Bhimu
1942	Lakshmana Naik's Koraput revolt in Orissa.
1942–1945	Revolts against Japanese occupation army by the Tribes of Andaman group of islands
1956 – 1958	Warli revolt (Maharashtra)
1963 – 1971	Naga revolt
1966 –1971	Mizo revolt

XVII

Commissions, Committees, Etc. on Tribal Development

S. No.	Name of the Committee	Chairman	Set up by	Constituted on	Report Submitted
1	2	3	4	5	6
1.	Backward Classes Commission	Kaka Kalekar	President of India	29-1-1953	30-3-1955
2.	Scheduled Areas and Scheduled Tribes Commission	U.N. Dhebar	— Do —	28-4-1960	October 1961
3.	Backward Classes Commission	B.P. Mandal	— Do —	1-1-1979	December 1980
4.	Commissioner for Scheduled Castes and Scheduled Tribes*		— Do —	1950	Annually
(ii)	***Constituted by the Parliament***				
1.	Parliamentary Committee on* the Welfare of Scheduled Castes and Scheduled Tribes	Member of Parliament (Sh. A.C. Das)	Parliament	18-12-1968	Till the end of April, 1983, 159 reports on various subjects submitted

2.	Joint Committee on the Scheduled Castes and Scheduled Tribes Order, (Amendment) Bill, 1967	A.K. Chanda	— Do —	26-3-1968	15-11-1969
(iii)	***Related to Specific aspects of Tribal Development including specification of Scheduled Tribes***				
1.	Advisory Committee on the Revision of the Lists of Scheduled Castes and Scheduled Tribes	B.N. Lokur	Department of Social Secutiry	1-6-1965	27-7-1965
2.	Committee on Social Multipurpose Tribal Blocks	Verrier Elwin	Ministry of	1-5-1959	30-3-1960
3.	Special Working Group on Cooperation for Backward Classes	M.P. Bhargava	—Do—	15-6-1961	Sept. 1962
4.	Committee on Tribal Economy in Forest Areas	Hari Singh	Department of Social Security	7-5-1965	March 1967
5.	Study Group on Tribal Labour and Employment	L.P. Vidyarthi	Min. of Labour	24-12-1966	28-8-1969
6.	Working Group on Administrative Arrangements and Personnel Policies in Tribal Areas	Maheshwar	Ministry of Home Affairs	17-10-1978	
7.	Working Group on Monitoring & Evaluation on Tribal Development	Dr. Bhupinder Singh	— Do—	July 1978	July, 1979

8.	The Commission for Scheduled Castes and Scheduled Tribes †		— Do—	21-7-1978	Annually
9.	Committee on Forests and in India	B.K. Roy Burman	— Do—	9-4-1980	6-9-1982
10.	Study Team on Working on the	K.S.. Bawa	Ministry of Agriculture	3-12-1971	24-9-1973
11.	Study Group on Relief Indebtedness Land Alienation and Restoration in Tribal Development Areas	P.S. Appu	— Do—	Dec. 1971	Oct. 1972
12.	Committee on Orientation Forest Education in India	K.M. Tiwari	Ministry of Home	5-12-1982	Dec. 1983
13.	Committee on Forest Programme for Alleviation of Poverty	C.L. Bhatia	— Do —	12-3-1982	Oct. 1984
14.	Largesized Multi-purpose Societies (LAMPS) cadre Management	B.Bandopadyaya	— Do —	30-10-1980	Sept. 1984

contd .....

(iv) In Pursuance of Planning and Development efforts

1.	Study Team on Social Welfare and Welfare of Backward Classes	Renuka Roy	Committee on Plan Projects	5-1-1958	9-7-1959
2.	Study Group on the Welfare of the Weakly Sections of the Village Community	J.P. Narain	Ministry of C.D. and Cooperation	8-12-1960	12-10-1961
3.	Study Group on Tribal Development Programmes	T. Shilu AO	Planning Commission	26-10-1966	19-9-1969
4.	Task Force on Development of Tribal Areas	L.P. Vidyarthi	— Do —	5-4-1972	
5.	Working Group on Tribal Development during Medium Term Plan, 1978-83	L.P. Vidyarthi	Ministry of Home Affairs	3-2-1978	July, 1978
6.	National Committee Development of Backward Classes	B. Sivaraman	Planning Commission	30-11-1978	June 1981 (The Committee submitted a separate report on development of Tribal Areas)
7.	High Power Panel on Minorities Scheduled Castes and Scheduled Tribes	Dr. Gopal Singh	Ministry of Home Affairs	May 1980	1983

contd ...

8.	Working Group on Tribal Development during Seventh Plan	S. Narayanaswamy	— Do —	4-10-1983	Dec 1984
9.	Xaxa Committee	Prof. Virginous	Govt. of India		2013

* The Committee consists of 30 members : 20 from Lok Sabha and 10 from Rajya Sabha. The tenure is for one year. This is now a Standing Committee of Parliament.

** The Special Officer (Commissioner for Scheduled Castes and Scheduled Tribes) appointed by the President under Article 338 of the Constitution has been submitting annual reports since 1950.The tenure of the incumbent is generally of five years.

† The term of office of the Chairman and the Members of the Commission is ordinarily for three years.

XVIII

Tribes Shop

Tribals constitute 8.14% of the total population of the country, numbering 84.51 million (2001 Census) and cover about 15% of the country's area. The fact that tribal people need special attention can be observed from their low social, economic and participatory indicators Whether, it is maternal and child mortality, size of agricultural holdings or access to drinking water and electricity tribal communities lag far behind the general population. 52% of Tribal population is Below Poverty Line and what is staggering is that 54% tribals have no access to economic assets such as communication and transport.

These indicators underline the importance of the need of livelihood generating activities based on locally available resources so that gainful employment opportunities could be created at the doorstep of tribal people. Recognizing this need for initiating such livelihood generating activities in a sustained and focused manner, the Ministry of Welfare (now Ministry of Tribal Affairs) established an organization to take up marketing development activities for Non Timber forest produce (NTFP) on which a tribal spends most of his time and derives a major portion of his/her income, In 1987, the Tribal Co-operative Marketing Development Federation of India Limited (TRIFED) was set up with an aim to serve the interest of the tribal community and work for their socio-economic development by conducting its affairs in a professional, democratic and autonomous manner for undertaking marketing of tribal products.

Further to achieve the aim of accelerating the economic development of tribal people by providing wider exposure to their art and crafts, TRIBES INDIA, the exclusive shops of tribal artifacts were set up all over India by TRIFED. They showcase and market the art and craft items produced by the tribal people and thus demonstrate the magical mystique of tribal India espousing tribal cause.

XIX

Integrated Tribal Development Projects/ Agencies (ITDPs / ITDAs)

The ITDPs are generally contiguous areas of the size of a Tehsil or Block or more in which the ST population is 50% or more of the total. On account of demographic reasons, however ITDPs in Assam, Karnataka, Tamil Nadu, West Bengal may be smaller or not contiguous. Andhra Pradesh and Orissa have opted for an Agency model under the Registration of Societies Act and the ITDPs there are known as ITD Agencies (ITDAs). So far 194 ITDPs/ITDAs have been delineated in the country in the states of Andhra Pradesh, Assam, Bihar, Gujarat, Himachal Pradesh, Karnataka, Kerala, Madhya Pradesh, Maharashtra, Manipur, Orissa, Rajasthan, Sikkim, Tamil Nadu, Tripura, Uttar Pradesh, West Bengal and Union Territories of Andaman & Nicobar Island and Daman &. Diu. In Jammu and Kashmir though no ITDP has been delineated yet the areas having ST Population in the State are treated as covered under the TSP strategy. In eight states having scheduled areas the ITDPs/ITDAs are generally co terminus with TSP areas. The ITDPs/ITDAs are headed by Project Officer though they may be designated Project Administrators or Project Directors.

Modified Area Development Approach (MADA) pockets

These are identified pockets of concentration of ST population containing 50% or more ST population within a total population of minimum of 10,000. The total number of MADAs identified so far in the various TSP States is 259. Generally, MADA pockets do not have separate administrative structures to implement development programmes. The line Departments of the State Govt. are expected to implement development programmes in MADA pockets under the overall control of the District authorities.

Clusters

These are identified pockets of tribal concentration containing 50% or more ST population within a total population of about 5,000 or more. As in the case of MADA pockets, there are no separate administrative structures for Clusters. So far 82 Clusters have been identified in various T.S.P. states.

Primitive Tribal Groups (PTGs)

Primitive tribal groups are tribal communities among the STs who live in near isolation in inaccessible habitats. They are characterised by a low rate of growth of population, pre-agricultural level of technology and extremely low levels of literacy. So far 75 PTGs have been identified.

XX

PESA, 1996

The PROVISION OF THE PANCHAYATS (Extension to the Scheduled Areas), Act, 1996 No.40 of 1996

(24th December, 1996)

An Act to provide for the extension of the provisions of Part IX of the Constitution relating to the Panchayats to the Scheduled Areas.

Be it enacted by Parliament in the Forty-seventh Year of the Republic of India as follows:-

Short title

1. This Act may be called the Provisions of the Panchayats (Extension to the Scheduled Areas) Act, 1996

Definition

2. In this Act, unless the context otherwise requires, "Scheduled Areas" means the Scheduled Areas as referred to in Clause (1) of Article 244 of the Constitution.

Extension of part IX of The Constitution

3. The provision of Part IX of the Constitution relating to Panchayats are hereby extended to the Scheduled Areas subject to such exceptions and modifications as are provided in section 4.

Exceptions and modifications to part IX of The Constitution

4. Notwithstanding anything contained under Part IX of the Constitution, the Legislature of a State shall not make any law under that Part which is inconsistent with any of the following features, namely:-

(a) a State legislation on the Panchayats that may be made shall be in consonance with the customary law, social and religious practices and traditional management practices of community resources.

(b) a village shall ordinarily consist of a habitation or a group of habitations or a hamlet or a group of hamlets comprising a community and managing its affairs in accordance with traditions and customs;

(c) every village shall have a Gram Sabha consisting of persons whose names are included in the electoral rolls for the Panchayat at the village level;

(d) every Gram Sabha shall be competent to safeguard and preserve the traditions and customs of the people, their cultural identity, community resources and the customary mode of dispute resolution;

(e) every Gram Sabha shall -

i. approve of the plans, programmes and projects for social and economic development before such plans, programmes and projects are taken up for implementation by the Panchayat at the village level;

ii. be responsible for the identification or selection of persons as beneficiaries under the poverty alleviation and other programmes;

(f) every Panchayat at the village level shall be required to obtain from the Gram Sabha a certification of utilisation of funds by that Panchayat for the plans, programmes and projects referred to in clause(e);

(g) the reservation of seats in the Scheduled Areas at every Panchayat shall be in proportion to the population of the communities in that Panchayat for whom reservation is sought to be given under Part IX of the Constitution.

Provided that the reservation for the Scheduled Tribes shall not be less than one-half of the total number of seats;

Provided further that all seats of Chairpersons of Panchayats at all levels shall be reserved for the Scheduled Tribes;

(h) the State Government may nominate persons belonging to such Scheduled Tribes as have no representation in the Panchayat at the intermediate level or the Panchayat at the disctrict level:—

Provided that such nomination shall not exceed one-tenth of the total members to be elected in that Panchayat;

(i) the Gram Sabha or the Panchayats at the appropriate level shall be consulted before making the acquisition of land in the Scheduled Areas for development projects and before re-setling or rehabilitating persons affected by such projects in the Scheduled Areas; the actual planning and implementation of the projects in the Scheduled Areas shall be coordinated at the State level;

(j) planning and management of minor water bodies in the Scheduled Areas shall be entrusted to Panchayats at the appropriate level;

(k) the recommendations of the Gram Sabha or the Panchayats at the appropriate level shall be made mandatory prior to grant of prospecting licence or mining lease for the minor minerals in the Scheduled Areas;

(l) the prior recommendation of the Gram Sabha or the Panchayats at the appropriate level shall be made mandatory for the grant of concession for the exploitation of minor minerals by auction;

(m) while endowing Panchayats in the Scheduled Areas with such powers and authority as may be necessary to enable them to function as institution of self-government, a State Legislature shall ensure that the Panchayats at the appropriate level and the Gram Sabha are endowed specifically with-

(i) the power to enforce prohibition or to regulate or restrict the sale and consumption of any intoxicant;

(ii) the ownership of minor forest produce;

(iii) the power to prevent alienation of land in the Scheduled Areas and to take appropriate action to restore any unlawfully alienated land of a Scheduled Tribe;

(iv) the power to manage village markets by whatever name called;

(v) the power to exercise control over money lending to the Scheduled Tribes;

(vi) the power to exercise control over institutions and functionaries in all social sectors;

(vii) the power to control over local plans and resources for such plans including tribal sub-plans;

(n) the State Legislations that may endow Panchayats with powers and authority as may be necessary to enable them to function as institutions of self-government shall contain safeguards to ensure that Panchayats at the higher level do not assume the powers and authority of any Panchayat at the lower level or of the Gram Sabha;

(o) the State Legislature shall endeavour to follow the pattern of the Sixth Schedule to the Constitution while designing the administrative arrangements in the Panchayats at district levels in the Scheduled Areas.

Continuance of existing laws on panchayats:

5. Notwithstanding anything in Part IX of the Constitution with exceptions and modifications made by this Act, any provision of any law relating to Panchayats in force in the Scheduled Areas, immediately before the date on which this Act receives the assent of the President, which is inconsistent with the provisions of Part IX with such exceptions and modifications shall continue to be in force until amended or repealed by a competent Legislature or other competent authority or until the expiration of one year from the date on which this Act receives the assent of the President;

Provided that all the Panchayats existing immediately before such date shall continue till the expiration of their duration unless sooner dissolved by a resolution passed to that effect by the Legislative Assembly of that State or, in the case of a State having Legislative Council, by each House of the Legislature of that State.

NOTES

NOTES